ALSO BY SARAH SCHLESINGER

The Low-Cholesterol Oat Plan
(with Barbara Earnest)

The Low-Cholesterol Olive Oil Cookbook
(with Barbara Earnest)

The Pointe Book
(with Janice Barringer)

The Garden Variety Cookbook

5 0 0
FAT-FREE
RECIPES

500 FAT-FREE RECIPES

A COMPLETE GUIDE TO REDUCING THE FAT IN YOUR DIET

500 Recipes from Soup to Dessert Containing
One Gram of Fat or Less

SARAH SCHLESINGER

Villard Books
New York • 1994

Copyright © 1994 by Sarah Schlesinger
All rights reserved under International and Pan-American Copyright
Conventions. Published in the United States by Villard Books, a
division of Random House, Inc., New York, and simultaneously in
Canada by Random House of Canada Limited, Toronto.
Villard Books is a registered trademark of Random House, Inc.

Library of Congress Cataloging-in-Publication Data
Schlesinger, Sarah.
500 fat-free recipes: a complete guide to reducing the fat in your diet:
500 recipes from soup to dessert containing one gram of fat or less/
Sarah Schlesinger.—1st ed.
p.   cm.
Includes index.
ISBN 0-679-41589-0
1. Low-fat diet—Recipes. I. Title. II. Title:
Five hundred fat-free recipes.
RM237.7.S35   1994   93-15429
641.5'638—dc20

Manufactured in the United States of America on acid-free paper

9   8

Book Design by Chris Welch

To Sam, whose good heart is the source and center of my happiness.

To Dr. Robert Press and Dr. Barbara A. Cochran, for their caring concern and their many gifts of kindness to people I treasure.

FOREWORD

::

Each of my four cookbooks has been directly inspired by my husband's fight against heart disease and our resulting interest in the health implications of diet and nutrition. In September 1991, after we learned that Sam's arterial blockages had returned nine years after bypass surgery, we discovered Dr. Dean Ornish's book *Dr. Ornish's Program for Reversing Heart Disease Without Drugs or Surgery* (Random House, 1990). Since that time we have followed Dr. Ornish's reversal and prevention diet with great success. Since the diet requires a dramatic reduction in fat and cholesterol consumption, we embarked on a new and daunting cooking adventure.

Within the first week of trying to make a fat-free diet work in the midst of two very busy schedules, we felt totally thwarted. Although we had been eating conservatively for some time, this latest adjustment proved the most difficult to make.

Since we quickly discovered that it remains almost impossible to eat a fat-free meal in a restaurant in America today, we realized that the emphasis on consuming a fat-free diet would have to center on preparing food at home.

I soon found myself spending frantic, seemingly endless hours searching through hundreds of cookbooks looking for recipes that met our new fat-free criteria. I found that such recipes were almost nonexistent. As I began developing my own recipes, I concluded that a comprehensive collection of fat-free recipes would be a vital and welcome tool for anyone who is trying to reduce his or her fat consumption for any reason.

As we have explored the world of fat-free cooking, we have found that there are limitless ways to enjoy good food without added fat. So whether you are trying to reverse heart disease, change the nature of your diet to preserve good health, or simply take off a few pounds, you'll find that the recipes in this book can help you reach your goal.

Special thanks to Robert Cornfield, Diane Reverand, Cynthia Gossage, and all the enthusiastic cooks and tasters who shared in the process of creating this book.

CONTENTS

::

500
FAT-FREE
RECIPES

INTRODUCTION

::

500 Fat-Free Recipes is a collection of five hundred delicious ways to cut the fat from your diet. Each recipe contains only 1 gram of fat or less per serving and offers a simple, quick, convenient, and delicious strategy for cooking without added fat or fat-laden ingredients. This book provides a one-stop resource for creating nonfat dishes at home ranging from soup to dessert.

The recipes, which contain only the minimal amount of fat naturally found in foods, are also low in cholesterol and sodium and high in nutrients and fiber. Instead of depending on fat for flavor, they imaginatively highlight, maximize, and combine natural flavors.

500 Fat-Free Recipes can help you to reduce fat intake, one of the most important steps to better health. These recipes are not only ideal for individuals on a highly fat-restricted diet, but also for anyone wishing to cut his or her total fat intake to any degree. In fact, these recipes can allow you to indulge your occasional cravings for higher-fat foods because the absence of fat in these dishes will help to limit your daily fat calories.

• THE TRUTH ABOUT FAT •

While Americans often seem obsessed with eating, we pay surprisingly little attention to which foods we consume in terms of their effect on our bodies. In contemporary American life we too often choose the foods we eat based on convenience and taste rather than on their nutritional content. It becomes more and more apparent that this lack of nutritional focus is a dangerous choice. According to the Surgeon General of the United States, diet plays a role in the diseases that cause 70 percent of the deaths in this country.

Nowhere is our failure to acknowledge this potentially fatal connection between the food we eat and our health more full of risk than in the area of fat consumption.

The average American eats 135 pounds of fat a year. As a result we are often overfed but undernourished because so many of the food calories we consume are in the form of fats. This excess fat intake is our number one nutrition hazard.

In recent years studies have revealed that those societies around the world that consume diets high in fat have high rates of heart disease and cancer, while those that partake of low-fat diets have significantly lower rates of these diseases. For instance, in a long-term study the Chinese Academy of Preventive Medicine discovered that the average Chinese consumes 30 percent more calories but 60 percent less fat than the average American. The average Chinese weighs less and has a lower heart disease rate and lower cancer rate than the average American.

In addition to contributing to heart disease and cancer, high consumption of fats has also been linked to diabetes, stroke, and obesity as well as other health problems including acne, skin rashes, allergies, bloating, constipation, dizziness and vertigo, indigestion, and hormonal imbalances leading to menstrual cramps and premenstrual distress. Eating excess fat can lead to impaired blood circulation, which leads to fatigue and can affect normal immune functions, creating increased vulnerability to illness.

In view of the growing evidence that our health is seriously compromised by the consumption of too much fat, it is important that we learn to control the amount of fat in our diets. In order to do this we have to become conscious of our current rate of fat consumption and learn the best techniques for reducing our fat intake.

Before launching into a program of fat control, it is helpful to understand exactly what fat is and how it functions in our bodies.

Fat is found in all living things. Fat, protein, carbohydrate, vitamins, minerals, and water are the nutritional building blocks of our food supply. Fat is our most concentrated form of food energy since each gram of fat provides us with 9 calories, while protein and carbohydrate provide only 4 calories per gram. A tablespoon of fat contains 120 calories. Most of the reserved energy in the human body is stored in the form of fat. In addition to providing energy, fat helps the body absorb the fat-soluble vitamins A, D, E, and K.

Like other foods, fats can be broken down into basic chemical units. The main components of fat are called fatty acids. There are three types of fatty acids found in all fats: saturated fat, polyunsaturated fat, and monounsaturated fat. While all fats consist of varying amounts of these three types of fatty acids, a fat is named after the type of fatty acid that it contains in the largest quantity. Fats in which saturated fatty acid predominates are called saturated fats and are usually solid at room temperature (e.g., meat fat, butter, cheese). Fats in which polyunsaturated fatty acid predominates are called polyunsaturated fats and are usually liquid at room temperature (e.g., corn, safflower, and sesame oils). Fats in which monounsaturated fatty acid predominates are called monounsaturated fats and are usually semisolid at room temperature (e.g., olive oil, canola oil, and peanut oil). Any fat is still *100 percent fat* regardless of its type.

As Americans have learned more in the past fifteen years about how different fatty acids can affect our overall body chemistry, we have begun cutting back on the cholesterol and saturated fat in our diets. As a result, many food manufacturers have switched from using saturated fats to partially hydrogenated vegetable oils made from soybean and corn oils.

However, a number of studies, including an Agriculture Department study released in October 1992, have revealed that these oils, which are found in margarine, vegetable shortening, and many manufactured food products, may also cause heart disease. The suggestion that there are dangers in consuming fats high in polyunsaturated fat as well as saturated fat has caused many consumers to shift to consuming more fats high in monounsaturates.

The next step is to think in terms of trimming as many sources of all types of fat and cholesterol from our diets as possible. In other words, the safest course of action related to fat is to eat less of it.

The first step in cutting back on fat is to determine how many of the calories we eat each day should be fat calories. In order to ascertain your own level of fat consumption, you first need to determine how many calories you eat in a normal day. Next you have to decide what percentage of your calories will come from fat.

While major health organizations such as the American Heart Association and the *Government's Dietary Guidelines* are currently suggesting that the average American's diet should include no more than 30 percent of total calories in the form of fat, many medical experts and nutritionists feel that this figure is still not low enough. Increasingly, they suggest that a diet including no more than 20 percent, 15 percent, or even 10 percent of total calories in the form of fat is preferable.

Marion Nestle, the chairwoman of the Department of Nutrition at New York University, was quoted in the "Eating Well" column of *The New York Times* on July 31, 1991, as saying that "I don't think there is any question that the 30 percent is a compromise. It was picked out of the hat. No one ever thought it was optimal. It was never based on comparative or experimental data. There is a fair amount of evidence that it should be less than 20 percent."

Both Dr. Dean Ornish, author of *Dr. Dean Ornish's Program for Reversing Heart Disease* (Random House, 1990) and the Pritikin diet and health program advance the view that the optimal amount of fat in the daily diet should not exceed 10 percent. Each of these programs has demonstrated that a diet with all added fat removed can actually help unclog blocked arteries as part of a total program of diet, exercise, and stress management without the intervention of drugs or invasive techniques.

Once you determine what percentage of your daily caloric intake will be in the form of fat, you can figure out how many grams of fat you can consume each day by doing a simple equation. Multiply the percentage of fat by the total number of calories you will consume and then divide the resulting number by 9 (the number of grams in each fat calorie). For example, if you are eating 1,500 calories a day and want to consume only 15 percent of those calories as fat calories, multiply 1,500 by .15. The resulting figure is 225 calories. Then divide 225 by 9 and the figure you get is 25. Therefore, you can eat 25 grams of fat a day if you want to hold your fat consumption level to 15 percent of total calories.

To give you an idea of how far this "fat budget" will take you in today's high-fat world, 1 tablespoon of vegetable oil contains 14 grams of fat, 1 beef hot dog contains 17 grams, an 8-ounce bag of potato chips contains 88 grams of fat, and a hamburger, french fries, and a milk shake contain a total of 64 grams.

As you learn to control your fat intake, you will need to work on balancing high-fat meals with low-fat meals and high-fat recipes with low-fat recipes. You need to become thoroughly acquainted with the fat content of everything you eat. Even if you eat only the lowest-fat foods, you can use up half your daily fat limit by adding the wrong salad dressing to your spartan salad.

When you begin to slash the fat from your diet, it is natural to be concerned about the other end of the spectrum. Is it safe to eat only a minimal amount of added fat? The answer is yes. Most of us are currently consuming eight times as much fat as the 14 grams a day our bodies need. These 14 grams can supply the essential fatty acids required to synthesize a number of important substances.

All natural foods contain some fat; it is present in every whole food we eat. The body makes all the fat you need from these foods and also manufactures fat from excess proteins and carbohydrates. Consequently, your body will be receiving fat whether you supply it in the form of added fat calories or not. For example, a cup of pinto beans naturally contains 0.9 gram of fat, 1/2 cup of corn contains 1.1 grams of fat, 1 cup of oatmeal contains 2.4 grams of fat, and 1 cup of whole wheat flour contains 2 grams of fat.

The two essential forms of fatty acid that the body can't make are linoleic and linolenic acid. The latest research says you need 0.1 percent of total calories in the form of these acids, the amount you consume in a slice of whole wheat bread. Other good sources are corn, wheat flour, wheat bran, oatmeal, brown rice, and beans.

Calcium intake, which is also a major health concern, does not have to be adversely impacted by a fat-free diet. In fact, the presence of fat in the diet can interfere with calcium absorption. The amount of calcium present in fat-laden dairy products is still present in those that are nonfat. Calcium is also present in plant foods including broccoli, spinach, kale, collard greens, dried fruits, dried beans, and peas. Calcium intake is of particular concern to women at risk for osteoporosis, who should consume at least 1,000 milligrams of calcium a day.

If you give up meat as part of your fat-reduction diet, be aware of the need to replace iron and some B vitamins with food choices such as dark green leafy vegetables, dried beans, dried peas, whole-grain and enriched cereals, and dried fruits. People needing extra iron include women with excessive menstrual bleeding, and pregnant or lactating women.

The concern over fat in the diet is not limited to adults. Many of the medical problems caused by fat have their roots in childhood eating habits. Parents need to become more sensitive to the amount of fat their children are consuming.

Prior to age two, fat intake should not be restricted due to growth demands, but the National Heart, Lung, and Blood Institute recommends that children over two should follow the same dietary guidelines related to fat as adults. Children should eat a diet consisting of a wide variety of foods and enough calories to support growth and development. Fat intake should be no more than 30 percent of total calories with saturated fat no more than 10 percent of total calories and cholesterol intake less than 300 milligrams a day. Check with your pediatrician for information about the right percentage of fat calories in your children's diets.

• ABOUT 500 *FAT-FREE RECIPES* •

500 Fat-Free Recipes has been designed to guide you through the process of learning to cook at home without fat. The 1 gram or less of fat found in each recipe is derived from natural foods. Unlike the recipes usually found in "low-fat" cookbooks, these recipes include no oil, butter, margarine, or shortening of any kind. All dairy ingredients included are available on the market in nonfat form. Natural ingredients that are high in fat such as avocados, seeds, and nuts are also avoided.

If you wish to cut your fat consumption back to 10 percent of total calories, these recipes will allow you to do that easily and deliciously. You will no longer have to go through stacks of cookbooks searching for a way to create great-tasting fat-free meals.

On the other hand, you may wish to use these recipes as part of a diet that includes meat, fish, poultry, and tofu (which is rather high in fat). In that case, you can still lower your overall fat consumption considerably. While meat, fish, poultry, and tofu are not among the ingredients used in this book, you can use any of the five hundred nonfat recipes in combination with these foods. It is also possible to add small quantities of meat, fish, or chicken to many of the recipes to adapt them for family members who may be on different diet plans.

Eating a high-fat diet is learned behavior, and like all learned behaviors changing it requires a period of adjustment. While fat is not a flavor, it carries flavor elements and gives a creamy texture to foods. When deleting the added fat from recipes, it is important to pay added attention to highlighting the natural flavors of foods by using a variety of ingredients such as herbs and spices that enhance character and flavor. After a few months of reducing the amount of added fat in your diet, you will be amazed at how much more aware of subtle tastes you become and how unnecessary and unappealing the taste of fat can seem.

• YOUR TOTAL DIET PICTURE •

In addition to considering your fat intake, you should also keep in mind the recommendations of the American Heart Association, the American Cancer Institute, and the United States Department of Agriculture that your daily food intake include 20 to 35 grams of fiber; five to nine servings of fruits and vegetables, particularly those high in antioxidants—vitamins C, E, and beta carotene (e.g., *broccoli, carrots, strawberries, and cantaloupe*);

and no more than 2,400 to 3,000 milligrams of sodium. (In fact, many health experts are encouraging a lower sodium intake of about 1,800 milligrams a day.)

Be sure to couple your dietary program with a physically active life-style to reap the benefits that exercise can contribute to your overall health.

As you plan your total diet, there are a number of nutrition information sources that you can call toll-free for assistance. These include:

National Center for Nutrition and Dietetics Consumer Nutrition Hotline
(800) 366-1655
Hours: M–F 9 A.M. to 4 P.M.

Nutrition Information Service at the University of Alabama at Birmingham
(800) 231-DIET
Hours: M–F 9 A.M. to 4 P.M.

American Institute for Cancer Research Nutrition Hotline
(800) 843-8114
Hours: M–F 9 A.M. to 5 P.M.

▪ SHOPPING FOR NONFAT FOODS ▪

When shopping for the commercially prepared nonfat foods used in the recipes in this book, be sure to read labels with great care. The Food and Drug Administration allows a product with less than half a gram of fat per serving to call itself fat-free. This figure might be listed as "O" or as "less than 1 gram." Also be wary of the actual size of the "serving."

Remember that fat is probably present in most unpackaged, unlabeled commercially prepared foods and that you will be unable to determine fat content on such items.

Nonfat foods are found in the special diet sections of some supermarkets, but are now most frequently being shelved with the higher-fat varieties in each product category.

The foods generally used as ingredients in this book can be readily found in supermarkets, but if they are not currently being stocked by the supermarkets in your area, check specialty foods shops such as health food outlets. You may have to shop in several supermarkets to find the fullest range of fat-free ingredients. Stores are adding fat-free products somewhat cautiously as they assess consumer interest. Consequently it is a good idea to tell your store manager that you are pleased with his or her stocking a particular nonfat product.

The number of commercially produced nonfat foods in all categories —from cheeses to dressings to snacks such as crackers, potato chips, pretzels, and corn chips—continues to grow rapidly. As you learn about them from advertisements and other sources, you can do a service for yourself and other fat-watching consumers by asking your supermarket manager to stock them. You should also consider writing to manufacturers or calling their toll-free numbers to applaud the creation of nonfat products and request items like fat-free soups that have been slower to appear on the market.

Often in packaging nonfat foods manufacturers tend to increase the sodium counts. If you are paying particular attention to your salt intake, be sure to check the sodium content on the label.

▪ COOKING WITHOUT FAT ▪

Many other liquids can be used to replace the fat in cooking, which you will discover in the recipes in this book. Water, defatted chicken stock, vegetable stock, wine, or sherry can be used to sauté ingredients. Nonfat dairy products such as nonfat yogurt, nonfat cottage cheese, and nonfat sour cream can be substituted for higher-fat products. Fruit purées can be substituted for fat in baking.

Having the right nonstick cookware is important when you are not using fat in cooking. For pan-sautéing, a pan with a T-Fal finish is adequate. Wear-Ever's Silverstone and top-of-the-line Supra, which are heavy commercial-gauge aluminum pans, are good all-purpose nonstick choices. Buy these with nonstick interiors and removable handles so they can be popped into the oven or under the broiler. A Calphalon griddle made of heavy-gauge anodized aluminum works well for cooking pancakes. Before investing in an expensive set of nonstick cookware, buy the smallest, least expensive sauté pan or saucepan to test its nonstick qualities.

A plastic gravy strainer or fat separator cup with a long spout can be used to remove fat from soups, stocks, and sauces.

Steaming

Steaming foods is one of the simplest ways to avoid cooking with fat. To steam foods, you will need a heavy saucepan with a snugly fitting lid and a steamer insert. This insert is a folding stainless steel basket, which should be available wherever kitchenware is sold. There are now a number of saucepan-basket combinations on the market that are designed to be steamers.

When steaming foods, fill the saucepan with approximately an inch of water, add the prepared food in the steamer basket, cover with the lid, and steam on medium heat. Most vegetables that have been cut in serving-size pieces will steam in about five minutes. Denser foods such as small new potatoes, winter squash, and large green beans will take ten or fifteen minutes. When cooking these longer-steaming foods, be sure to check the saucepan to see if more water may be needed. Foods cooked lightly by steaming instead of boiling keep more of their water-soluble vitamin content intact.

When steaming, try using wine in place of water, or adding lemon juice or flavored vinegars to the water. Steaming liquids can be seasoned with garlic, onions, leeks, whole peppercorns, bay leaves, fresh and dried herbs such as rosemary, basil, oregano, thyme, and dill.

Microwaving

Microwaving is another way of preserving the vitamin content and flavor of foods while cutting down on the need for fat, since microwaves cook foods quickly, many in their own natural moisture content. For recipe ideas and cooking techniques, see For the Microwave, beginning on page 373.

Pressure Cooking

Pressure cookers cook with superheated steam under high pressure and can cut preparation time of many foods from 50 to 70 percent. The moist steam cuts down on fat needed in cooking, and vitamins and minerals are retained because pressure-cooked food cooks quickly and is insulated from oxygen. Unlike old-fashioned pressure cookers, the newest models have valves that are fully automatic, quiet, and self-regulating. The valve automatically releases excess air when pressure is too high.

Pan-Sautéing/Steam Frying

You can sauté foods in spite of the fact that you are not using fat by using small amounts of other liquids such as nonfat, low-sodium chicken broth, vegetable broth, fruit or vegetable juice, vinegar, lemon juice, water, or wine. Use a nonstick pan with a treated finish. To sauté, place a pan over a medium-high flame. Add liquid. Bring to a sizzle. Add food and stir quickly, making sure all the ingredients are cooked evenly. To "brown" food, allow all the liquid to cook down until the food begins to brown. Deglaze the pan by adding a small amount of liquid after the food is sufficiently cooked.

Baking

When baking, you can cut fat calories by avoiding the need to oil baking pans. Either buy high-quality nonstick bakeware or line pans with baking pan liners. These may be in the form of reusable parchment paper, which is available in rolls and in precut round and square shapes of varying sizes at most kitchen supply stores. Another good choice is the Magic Baking Sheet made by Von Snedaker. This sturdy, reusable product wipes clean and is truly "nonstick." It is available in a variety of sizes and shapes and can be found in cooking supply stores or ordered from Von Snedaker at 12021 Wilshire Boulevard, Suite 231, Los Angeles, CA, 90025. It is microwave safe. When using muffin tins, use paper liners. If you find that you must oil a baking pan, use a nonstick vegetable cooking spray and spray surface as lightly as possible. You could also fill an inexpensive plastic spray bottle with either olive oil or canola oil to use for this purpose.

While baked goods prepared without fat will never duplicate the taste and texture of those prepared with fat, fat-free baking can produce an array of treats to satisfy your sweet tooth. Many of the recipes in this book replace the fat or shortening used in baking with banana purée, applesauce, or prune purée. This adds the nutrients and fiber in the fruit as well as reducing fat. Remember to wrap baked goods made without fat in plastic wrap and refrigerate them since they will tend to become stale more quickly.

Be sure to test baked foods for doneness as they are cooking rather than relying entirely on suggested baking times since your oven temperature may not be identical to those in which the recipes were tested.

Grilling

When grilling foods, try using commercial fat-free Italian dressing, lemon juice, or one of the dressings in this book as a marinade to avoid fat calories.

Ingredients

Here's a guide to shopping for the ingredients used in *500 Fat-Free Recipes:*

Angel Food Cake Mix—Angel food cakes, which are free of fat and cholesterol, are a dessert staple on a fat-free diet. If you don't have time to make Angel Food Cake from scratch from the recipe on page 347, there are a number of angel food cake mixes on the market to choose from.

Apple Juice Concentrate—Apple juice concentrate can be used to sweeten some dishes. It can be found frozen in the freezer section of your supermarket or packaged in a box in the canned and bottled juice section.

Applesauce—Buy natural applesauce without added sugar. Applesauce can be substituted for butter and margarine in many recipes to reduce fat, calories, and cholesterol. Applesauce provides moisture and stability when used as a fat alternative in baked goods. It performs best when it is used in recipes containing other wet ingredients such as skim milk or fresh fruit. Replace ½ cup butter with ½ cup natural applesauce.

Arrowroot—Arrowroot is a delicate thickener for sauces. It has a neutral flavor and does not mask or alter natural flavors. It reaches its maximum thickening power before boiling and results in very clear sauces. Two teaspoons arrowroot can replace 1 tablespoon cornstarch or 1½ teaspoons can replace 1 tablespoon flour. Combine arrowroot with 2 tablespoons cold water before adding to sauce. Then add gradually to thicken. Arrowroot can be found on the spice rack in most supermarkets.

Artichoke Hearts—Canned artichoke hearts are baby artichokes with tender leaves and a bottom in which the bristly choke is undeveloped and therefore edible. Buy only artichoke hearts packed in water. They can be stored unopened on a cool, dry pantry shelf for a year. Drain the water before using. Once opened, store canned artichokes in the refrigerator for up to four days.

Bagels—Look for "water" bagels and avoid those made with egg. Check labels on packaged bagels for fat content.

Baking Powder—Baking powder is a combination of an acid, an alkali, and a starch that keeps the other ingredients stable and dry. The powder reacts with liquid by foaming and the resulting bubbles can aerate and raise dough. Buy double-acting baking powder. Don't expose baking powder to steam, humid air, wet spoons, or moisture. Store it in a tightly sealed container for no more than six months. To test the strength of baking powder, place 1 teaspoon powder into ⅓ cup hot water. If the mixture fails to fizz and bubble, the baking powder is no longer potent.

Baking Soda—This plain white powder is an alkali, one of the ingredients in baking powder. It is also called bicarbonate of soda. When kept dry and well covered, it can be stored for as long as three months.

Bamboo Shoots—Bamboo shoots are the edible portion of young bamboo plants. Once you have opened canned bamboo shoots, cover them with water and refrigerate. If you drain the shoots regularly and re-cover them with water, they will keep for one month.

Barley—This is a hearty grain with a chewy texture and nutty taste. It looks like rice and puffs up when cooked. The soluble fiber in barley is believed to be just as effective as oats in lowering cholesterol. Barley is commercially hulled to shorten the cooking time. Pearled barley is the most common variety.

Beans—Beans are a vital part of a fat-free diet because they are high in fiber and low in fat. They are rich in protein and vitamins and contain no cholesterol. Some studies have shown that beans can lower cholesterol levels. When eaten in the same day as any whole-grain food, they also provide a high-quality form of protein, which is very important for anyone not eating meat, fish, or poultry. Beans are an inexpensive food and as consumer demand for them increases, companies are selling higher-quality canned beans and dried beans that require less soaking.

Keep the following beans and legumes on hand in dried and/or canned form: kidney, black, pinto, Great Northern, cannelini, lima, and navy beans, and lentils, split peas, and black-eyed peas.

Since beans and other high-fiber foods can cause intestinal gas, products are now appearing on the market such as Beano (made by AkPharma Inc. in Pleasantville, NJ). A few drops of Beano added to a dish of beans can help break down the sugars that cause excess gas. Changing the water frequently while soaking dried beans can also make them easier to digest.

You can store cooked beans in the refrigerator for one week. They can be frozen in individual serving containers and quickly microwaved as needed. Slightly undercook beans you are planning to freeze.

Dried Beans—When cooking with dried beans, 1 cup (8 ounces) is equal to 2 to 2½ cups cooked beans.

STOVETOP METHOD: To cook beans using the conventional stovetop method, first wash and pick over beans, discarding cracked or shriveled ones. To cut down on cooking time, presoak them for 2 hours or overnight in a large bowl and cover with several inches of water. (The beans will expand to about twice their size.) A quicker presoak method is to bring the beans to a boil, cover tightly, remove from heat, and let sit for 1 hour. If you can't presoak, add 30 minutes to the cooking time. Lentils, black-eyed peas, and split peas do not need to be soaked before cooking. To cook, discard the soaking water. Place 3 parts fresh water and 1 part beans in a large, heavy pan. You can add garlic cloves, as well as onion, celery, and carrot chunks or a chile pepper or bay leaf. (Remove bay leaf before serving.) Partially cover the pan. Cook black beans, limas, and small white beans for $1\frac{1}{2}$ hours; black-eyed peas, lentils, and split peas for 1 hour; and Great Northern, kidney, and pinto beans for 2 hours. Test for doneness by tasting. Beans should be cooked until they are soft. Avoid adding tomatoes or salt until the end of the cooking process because these ingredients can prevent your beans from softening.

MICROWAVE METHOD: The microwave makes cooking dried beans more convenient. Microwaved beans retain their taste and texture after cooking. They can be prepared in one simple step without presoaking. Combine the washed and picked-over beans with water ($1\frac{1}{4}$ cups dried beans to 2 to 3 quarts water) in a large bowl. Seal airtight with a double layer of unvented plastic wrap and microwave for $1\frac{3}{4}$ hours on HIGH. (Some very dry beans can take 2 hours).

PRESSURE-COOKER METHOD: Except for lentils and split peas, which can block the pressure valve, beans cook nicely in a pressure cooker. Presoaking is unnecessary. Bring the washed beans to boil in three times their volume of water. Only fill cooker half full. Cover and bring to 15 pounds of pressure. Cook beans for 15 to 30 minutes; cool immediately. Smaller beans take less time; larger beans will need to cook for the longer period.

Canned Beans—Read labels on canned beans carefully. Most beans contain some natural fat, which will be indicated on the label. However, avoid those that have meats like bacon or pork added. Look for low-sodium products and/or drain them and rinse well before adding to a recipe. Rinsing can reduce the sodium in canned beans by half. When buying canned vegetarian baked beans in tomato sauce, look for those that are packed in low-sodium sauce.

Bean Sprouts—Sprouts are the infant plants that grow out of beans in a moist, warm environment. Look for moist and crisp-looking sprouts with a fresh scent. The shorter the tendrils, the younger and tenderer the sprout. Fresh sprouts will keep for seven to ten days in a plastic bag in the refrigerator. They should be kept moist but don't allow a lot of free water to build up on the inside of the bag. Canned bean sprouts are also available.

Beer—Beer and/or nonalcoholic beer are used as flavorings in some recipes.

Bread—Buy French, Italian, whole wheat, and rye breads that are made without fat. Major bread manufacturers are now producing fat-free breads.

Buckwheat—Actually the pyramid-shaped seed of a fruit, buckwheat has a rich and earthy flavor. It can be used in cereals, pilafs, or salads and also ground into flour for use in pancakes and baked goods.

Bulgur—Bulgur is made from whole wheat kernels. The wheat kernels are parboiled, dried, and partially debranned, then cracked into coarse fragments to make bulgur.

Butter Substitutes—Natural nonfat, low-calorie, low-sodium, instant butter-flavored granule substitutes contain no cholesterol. They can be turned into a liquid by adding water or may be sprinkled in dry form directly on hot, moist foods. In liquid form, they can be used with baked potatoes and pancakes and in sauces and soups. They are available in $1/2$-ounce packets and in jars. One-half teaspoon of these granules equals the taste of 2 teaspoons butter; 8 teaspoons mixed with $1/2$ cup hot water equals $1/2$ cup or 8 tablespoons liquid butter.

Catsup—Shop for low-sodium catsup.

Cheeses—There are many fat-free cheese products on the market. Be sure to check the labels for their cholesterol content as well as fat content since some of these products are also cholesterol free. Parmesan cheese, mozzarella cheese, cheddar cheese, Swiss cheese, American cheese, cream cheese, ricotta cheese, and cottage cheese are all available in fat-free form. Most of these cheeses are made from skim milk. Both fat-free cheese slices and grated products can also be found.

Chicken—While poultry is not used often in the recipes, chicken breasts and other chicken parts are used to produce broth, which is then defatted. The skin and fat should be removed before using chicken parts to prepare broth.

Chicken Broth—Look for fat-free, low-sodium canned chicken broth. If you cannot find fat-free chicken broth, remove lid and refrigerate in a glass or plastic container overnight (or place in freezer for 30 minutes) until fat congeals and rises to the top. Skim fat off before using. A recipe for making nonfat chicken broth can be found on page 83. Make a large quantity of chicken broth and freeze in cubes for easy access. Homemade broth will have the maximum flavor and quality if it is reduced by one third.

Cocoa—Cocoa is dry, powdered, unsweetened chocolate from which cocoa butter (i.e., fat) has been removed. Cocoa can replace unsweetened chocolate in many recipes. Look for cocoa with 1 gram or less of fat per serving.

Cookies—Commercially made fat-free cookies can be used for crumb crusts. More and more varieties of fat-free cookies are appearing on supermarket shelves. You can choose among fudge cookies, oatmeal cookies, or fruit-flavored cookies such as apple, date, apricot, and raspberry. Select a cookie for your crumb crusts that will best complement the filling you are using.

Corn Chips—You can either create your own fat-free corn chips by cutting fat-free corn tortillas into smaller sections and baking them (see recipe, page 75) or by buying commercially prepared fat-free, baked corn chips.

Cornmeal—Cornmeal is ground yellow or white corn kernels. Yellow cornmeal has more vitamin A. Cornmeal can be used to make polenta, an Italian pudding or mush that can be eaten hot or cold with cheese, sauce, and other ingredients sprinkled over it. It can be served in place of potatoes or as a main dish with a salad.

Cornstarch—This silky white powder is a thickener for sauces, puddings, and pie fillings. Look for an expiration date on the box.

Couscous—A precooked cracked wheat product that is an alternative to rice, couscous is made from white durum wheat from which the bran and germ has been removed. Once cooked it has a very light, airy quality and a silky texture. Couscous can be found with other grains such as rice or in the imported food aisle.

Crackers—A variety of nonfat crackers can be found in most supermarkets.

Cranberry Juice Concentrate—Cranberry juice concentrate can be used to sweeten some dishes. It can be found frozen in the freezer section of your supermarket or packaged in a box or bottled in the canned and bottled juice section.

Cream of Tartar—When the sediment that collects in wine casks is refined, it turns into the tiny white crystals called cream of tartar. Cream of tartar helps to produce a creamy texture in sugary recipes. Cream of tartar comes in a can or jar with a snug lid. It can be kept on a cool, dry shelf for up to a year.

Curry Powder—Curry powder is a blend of different herbs and spices that vary according to the country of origin. Varieties can differ in intensity of flavor, so use carefully. Curry flavor becomes stronger in a dish that is refrigerated and then reheated.

Dijon Mustard—Dijon is a strong French mustard that is easy to find in supermarkets. Avoid varieties with added oil or eggs. Store in the refrigerator.

Dressings—There are now many fat-free commercially made salad dressings on the market. In addition to being used on salads, these dressings can be used as marinades for grilling and on garlic bread. Some fat-free dressings are packaged in dried form to be mixed as needed at home. There are also nonfat dressing recipes included in this book. (See Dressings, Sauces, and Relishes beginning on page 271.)

Flours:

Unbleached All-Purpose Flour—Unbleached flour has no chemicals added to whiten or to age the flour artificially. Unbleached flour has a creamy off-white color. All-purpose flour is a mixture of hard, high-gluten wheat and soft wheat suitable for both bread and dessert making.

Cake Flour—Cake flour is made from soft wheat. Since it is a lower-protein flour, it can help your baked goods turn out light and fine textured.

Whole Wheat Flour—Whole wheat flour contains all the parts of the kernel—the bran, the germ, and the endosperm. Whole wheat flour should have a sharp, fresh scent.

Eggs and Egg Substitute—Egg whites contain all the protein in an egg and no fat or cholesterol. You can substitute 2 egg whites for 1 whole egg. When buying commercial egg substitutes, be sure to check the labels for fat content. Buy brands with 1 gram fat or less per serving. Eight ounces (1 cup) of a commercial egg substitute replaces 4 whole eggs and 8 egg whites. Two ounces (¼ cup) egg substitute is equivalent to 1 medium egg. You can also combine 1 egg white with ¼ cup egg substitute if you are making scrambled eggs.

English Muffins—Check package labels to be sure you are buying nonfat English muffins.

Extracts—Extracts have an intense flavor that is produced by dissolving the essential oils of foods in alcohol. There are also imitation extracts made from chemicals that taste similar to their natural counterparts. Shop for natural extracts including vanilla, almond, maple, chocolate, and rum. Amaretto (almond-flavored) liqueur is occasionally used in the recipes.

Fruit:

Fresh Fruit—Fresh fruits used in the recipes include apples, bananas, blackberries, blueberries, cantaloupe, cherries, cranberries, red and green grapes, grapefruits, honeydew melons, kiwis, mangoes, navel oranges, nectarines, papayas, peaches, pears, pineapple, plums, raspberries, strawberries, and tangerines.

Canned Fruit—Buy fruit packed in juice or water. Canned fruits used in the recipes include pineapples (crushed and chunk), mandarin oranges, pears, peaches, and apricots.

Dried Fruit—Keep raisins, dried apricots, peaches, pears, dates, pineapple slices, and prunes on hand. Dried fruit can be plumped in your microwave by combining ½ cup mixed, dried fruit with 2 tablespoons orange juice and microwaving for 2 minutes on HIGH until juice is absorbed. Let stand 5 minutes.

Frozen Fruit—Use frozen fruit when fresh fruit is not in season. Frozen fruits used in the recipes include blackberries, blueberries, cranberries, peaches, and strawberries. Frozen fruit should be packed with no sugar added.

Fruit Juice—Shop for natural juices without added sugar or syrup. Juices used in the recipes include grapefruit, orange, cranberry, apple, pineapple, white grape, and red grape as well as pear and apricot nectar.

Garlic—Buy fresh garlic, chopped garlic packed without oil, and minced dried garlic. When buying fresh garlic, look for bulbs with large cloves. Store garlic in a cool, dry place. Roast fresh garlic in its skin to bring the flavor out before adding to a dish instead of sautéing. Before adding minced garlic to a dish, try microwaving it with a bit of lemon juice for 30 seconds. To microwave a whole head of garlic, trim the top of the head and place in a 1-cup measure with 3 tablespoons nonfat chicken broth. Cover with vented plastic wrap. Microwave on HIGH for 10 minutes. Let stand 5 minutes. Use as a spread on nonfat French bread.

Gelatin—Gelatin is a dry, powdered protein made from animal by-products. Buy unflavored gelatin.

Gingerroot—Fresh gingerroot, which adds a distinctive, spicy flavor to many dishes, can be found in the produce department of many supermarkets. To use, peel the tan skin and thinly slice the root. You can freeze leftover gingerroot wrapped in plastic freezer wrap until ready to use.

Graham Crackers—Graham crackers, reduced to crumbs in your blender, can be used as pie shells. Look for fat-free varieties.

Herbs—While fresh herbs are always preferable to dried herbs in terms of flavor, they are not always easy to obtain. Therefore, with the exception of parsley, which is widely available, I have suggested using dried herbs in the recipes. However, any time you have access to fresh herbs, you should certainly use them. Use three parts fresh herbs for one part dried. Keep dried herbs tightly covered in an airtight container. Don't expose them to extremely high heat or intense light. They are best if used within six months to a year, so it is wise to date containers at the time you purchase or store them. To maximize the flavor of dried herbs, soak them for several minutes in a liquid you will be using in the recipe, such as stock, lemon juice, or vinegar. Crush dried herbs before using by rubbing them between your fingers. The recipes in this book frequently call for basil leaves, rosemary leaves, thyme leaves, dill leaves, tarragon leaves, bay leaves, chives, cilantro, mint, marjoram, oregano, paprika, sage, and tarragon.

Herb Teas—Herb teas in a wide variety of flavors can be found on supermarket shelves in the coffee and tea aisle.

Honey—Honey is sweeter than granulated sugar and easier to digest. Its flavor and sweetness vary, depending on what kind of nectar bees were eating when they made the honey. You can store liquid honey in its jar for up to a year in a cool, dry, dark place. Be sure the cap is tightly closed. Thin honey that starts to crystallize by placing it in a pan of hot water.

Horseradish—Prepared horseradish is mixed with vinegar and packed in jars. You can store it in the refrigerator for three to four months, but it will lose pungency as it ages. Fresh horseradish is a woody-looking root with a fiery flavor. It can be stored in the refrigerator for three weeks.

Jams and Jellies—Buy all-fruit jams, jellies, and marmalades that are sugar-free and made with fruit and fruit juices.

Lemon Juice and Lime Juice—Lemon and lime juices are most flavorful when they are freshly squeezed. Store fresh lemons and limes in the refrigerator, or if using within a few days, at room temperature.

Lemon Peel—Either grate the peel of fresh lemons or buy grated lemon peel in the spice section of your supermarket.

Maple Syrup—Pure maple syrup is more expensive than pancake syrups made by mixing artificial maple flavoring with corn syrup. However, the taste of pure maple syrup is well worth the difference in price. Once opened, the syrup should be refrigerated. It will last a year in the refrigerator. Cold pure maple syrup does not pour easily, so you should leave it at room temperature for an hour before serving.

Mayonnaise Dressings—A number of fat-free mayonnaise products are available in which the fat has been replaced with starch and emulsifiers. While these dressings may not have the flavor of regular mayonnaise when tasted plain, they work well when combined with seasonings and other ingredients. Be aware of the rather high sodium content of these products.

Meringue Powder—Dried meringues can be prepared according to package directions and used in place of egg whites. Meringue powder is available wherever baking supplies are sold.

Milk—Buy fresh skim milk, nonfat buttermilk, and instant nonfat dry milk.

Evaporated Skim Milk—Evaporated skim milk is a product that can add the richness of cream to soups, sauces, and desserts with almost none of the fat. This is heat-sterilized, concentrated skim milk with half the water removed. As a result, the consistency of evaporated skimmed milk more resembles whole milk. Evaporated skimmed milk can be whipped to a consistency similar to that of whipped cream. (See recipe, page 371.) It contains twice the calories of regular skim milk, but has 738 milligrams of calcium per cup. Once a can of evaporated skim milk has been opened, the contents should be refrigerated, tightly sealed, and used within five days.

Molasses—Molasses consists of the plant juices pressed from sugar cane that are then purified and concentrated by boiling. After opening, you can store molasses for another twelve months on the shelf.

Mushrooms—Buy young, pale, button mushrooms. Brush them and wipe them with a damp cloth. If you need to wash them, be sure to dry them thoroughly. When serving them raw, sprinkle with lemon juice or white wine to keep them light in color.

Shiitake Mushrooms—Also called dry forest mushrooms, shiitake mushrooms can be found in the produce departments of many supermarkets. They are parasol shaped, colored brownish-black, and have a light garlic aroma. They contain B vitamins and minerals. To reconstitute the dry mushrooms, soak them in enough water to cover for about 30 minutes, or until they are soft. Drain. Squeeze out excess water. Remove and discard stems.

Oats—Shop for old-fashioned rolled oats or quick oats. Avoid instant oat products.

Orange Juice Concentrate—Orange juice concentrate can be used to sweeten some dishes. It can be found in the freezer section of your supermarket.

Orange Peel—Either grate the peel of fresh oranges or buy grated orange peel in the spice section of your supermarket.

Orzo—Orzo is a tiny pasta that resembles elongated rice or barley.

Parsley—While other fresh herbs can be hard to find, parsley is widely available and should always be used in its fresh form if possible. It will chop finely if it is thoroughly dried with a dish towel before chopping.

Pasta—A cup of cooked macaroni or spaghetti (about 2 ounces dry) has barely a trace of fat or cholesterol. Most of the 210 calories in a cup of cooked pasta comes from complex carbohydrates. Stored in a cool, dry place, dried pasta keeps indefinitely. Be sure to store fresh pasta in the refrigerator until ready to cook. It should be used within two or three days of purchase or according to the date on the package. It can also be stored in the freezer and thawed before cooking. Dried and fresh pasta are both made from flour and water or flour and eggs. If you are watching your cholesterol, you want to avoid pasta made with whole eggs. However, there are now a number of fresh and dried pastas made with flour and egg whites. Durum wheat, the hardest, or semolina, the coarsest grind of durum, makes the most flavorful and resilient pasta. Pasta made from softer flours tends to turn soggy quickly. For main dish recipes allow 2 ounces of pasta per person.

Dried whole-grain and/or white pasta in the form of spaghetti, eggless noodles, macaroni, lasagne, spirals, angel hair, bowties, cavatelli, conchiglie, fettucine, fusilli, linguine, penne, rigatoni, rotelle, vermicelli, and ziti are used in the recipes.

COOKING TIPS: Pasta taste and texture can be improved by cooking only until it becomes "al dente" or firm, but edible. Since you will be cooking the pasta without adding fat to the water, you should prevent it from sticking to the pot by cooking it in a large volume of rapidly boiling water. You should use at least 4 quarts per pound of dry pasta. Leave the pot uncovered. When placing longer pasta in the pot to cook, hold it at one end and dip the other end into the water, curling it around the pan and into the water as it softens. To avoid excess sodium, the water in pasta recipes is not salted. Fresh pasta cooks much more quickly than dried pasta. Test fresh pasta as soon as the water returns to a boil by cutting a piece in half. If it's not done, you will see a thin line of white in the center. Turn cooked pasta into a large colander and shake several times to get the water out. Don't rinse unless you need to cool the pasta off quickly.

Peppers:

Bell Peppers—Sweet, thick-fleshed bell peppers come in several colors. The flavor of red peppers is slightly sweeter than the familiar green-pepper taste. Yellow peppers are even sweeter and more mellow.

Fresh Chile Peppers—Jalapeño peppers, frequently used in these recipes, are usually found green, but are sometimes red when ripe. They are small and blunt tipped and range from hot to fiery. They will contribute less heat to a recipe if the seeds are removed. Be sure to wear protective gloves when handling pepper seeds or be careful to wash your hands immediately after handling them. Roasting the peppers will also lessen the heat and concentrate the flavors.

Canned Chile Peppers—Canned green chiles are used in the recipes. They can found in the international foods section of your supermarket with other ingredients used in Mexican cooking.

Dried Chile Peppers—Whole jalapeños and other varieties of chile peppers can also be found in dried form. Store the peppers by hanging them up or tossing them in a basket. If kept cool and dry, they can be stored for a year.

Pepper Sauce—Tobasco-type sauces are very hot purées of red chiles, vinegar, and numerous seasonings. They are bright red when fresh. They will last up to a year at room temperature. When a pepper sauce turns brown, throw it out.

Pickles—Although pickles are high in sodium, small quantities of dill pickles and pickle relish are used in the recipes to add flavor.

Pita Bread—Buy whole wheat nonfat pita breads (also called pocket breads). Store in the refrigerator wrapped in tightly closed plastic bags.

Popcorn—Buy popcorn and pop it yourself in the microwave or in an air popper to avoid added salt and fat. Sprinkle with herbs, spices, or nonfat Parmesan cheese.

Potato Chips—Nonfat baked potato chips both with and without salt in regular and barbecue flavors are now on the market.

Pretzels—A number of nonfat, baked pretzels and pretzel chips are now on the market both with and without salt.

Prunes—Prunes have become an important part of fat-free eating due to the discovery that they can replace fat in baking. Prunes are very high in pectin, which forms a protective coating around the air in baked goods giving the foods the volume and lift usually provided by fat. Pectin can also enhance and trap flavor. Prunes are high in sorbitol, a humectant that attracts and binds moisture. Butter and shortening keep food moist because they cannot evaporate. So prune purée in baking serves the same purpose as shortening, keeping baked goods moist. For prune purée, you can either make your own from whole prunes, buy commercially prepared baby-food puréed prunes, or buy prune butter, which is located in either the jam and jelly or baking section of your supermarket. To make your own purée from whole prunes, place 1 cup prunes and ¼ cup water in a food processor or blender and purée.

Pudding Mix—Most pudding mixes are fat-free. Check the labels to be sure, and always make them with skim milk.

Pumpkin purée—Pumpkin purée is available in cans. If you want to purée your own pumpkin, you can either steam, boil, or microwave fresh pumpkin cut in 1½-inch cubes and purée cooked cubes in a blender. To steam fresh pumpkin, boil ¾ to 1 inch water in a steamer and place pumpkin cubes in a steamer basket or colander and cover. Steam for 15 minutes or until tender. To boil, add pumpkin cubes to a large pot full of rapidly boiling water. Pumpkin should cook in 8–12 minutes. To microwave, place pumpkin cubes in a covered dish and microwave on HIGH for 8 minutes.

Quinoa—A nutty, light-brown grain originally from Peru, quinoa is high in protein and fiber and has a more sturdy texture and flavor than rice. It makes an excellent substitute for rice.

Rice:

   Arborio Rice—This is a short-grained Italian rice.

   Basmati Rice—The word *basmati* means "queen of fragrance," and this Indian rice has a nutlike aroma.

   Brown Rice—Brown rice is processed to remove the tough outer hull but not the bran. It is sometimes parboiled, a process that hardens the grains, ensuring that they remain separated when cooked. It is available in both long-grained and short-grained varieties. The long-grained kind tends to result in a less gummy cooked rice. Brown rice has a superior nutritional profile when compared to white rice because it is still covered with bran. However, it has a higher natural fat content than white rice. One cup uncooked brown rice equals 4 cups cooked.

   To cook brown rice, use a saucepan with a snug lid. The proportion of liquid to rice is two to one. Bring liquid to a boil. Rinse rice. Add to boiling liquid. Stir once, cover, and bring to a boil again. Reduce heat and simmer, covered, for 30 minutes. Remove from heat. Leave cover on the pan for another 15 minutes to allow rice to steam.

   White Rice—Regular white rice has been milled to remove the hull, germ, and most of the bran. It is available in both long and short grain. One cup uncooked white rice equals 3 cups cooked.

   To cook white rice, rinse under cold water and drain. Bring to boil twice as much water as grain you are using. Stir in the rice and return the mixture to a boil. Lower the heat to simmer, cover tightly, and cook until all the liquid is absorbed and the grain is tender. Don't uncover or stir until time is up.

Wild Rice—Actually the seed of aquatic grass that grows in marshes, wild rice takes longer to cook than cultivated rice. It is dark greenish-brown in color and has a distinctive, nutty flavor. It is rich in fiber, vitamins, and minerals. To make wild rice, bring 2 cups nonfat chicken broth or water to a boil in a medium saucepan. Reduce heat, cover, and simmer for 1 hour or until rice is tender and kernels are slightly open. Drain rice. Cooked wild rice can also be frozen.

Rice Bran—This is a bran product similar to oat bran in its cholesterol-lowering properties. If not available at your grocery store, rice bran can be found at health food stores. Like oat bran, it can be eaten as a hot cereal, and also used in baking.

Salsa—Salsas, which are relishes made from chopped vegetables, can be found in the condiments aisle or with the international foods in your supermarket. Some fresh-vegetable salsas are also kept in the refrigerator case alongside fresh tortillas.

Sour Cream—Shop for nonfat sour cream.

Soy Sauce—Light soy sauce contains from 33 to 46 percent less sodium than regular soy sauce, with little or no difference in flavor resulting from the sodium reduction.

Sparkling Water—Sparkling mineral water can be found in all super-markets.

Spices—Keep dried spices tightly covered in an airtight container. Don't expose them to extremely high heat or intense light. Dried spices are best if used within six months to a year, so it is wise to date containers at the time you purchase or store them. During the summer months, store ground cayenne pepper, paprika, chili powder, and crushed red pepper in the refrigerator. Spices used in the recipes include black and white pepper, chili powder, cloves, ground cayenne pepper, crushed red pepper, allspice, caraway seeds, celery seeds, dry mustard, mustard seeds, poppy seeds, ground and stick cinnamon, ground coriander, ground cumin, ground ginger, nutmeg, paprika, saffron, and turmeric.

Sugar—Table sugar is sucrose, a highly refined product made from sugar beets or sugar cane. It is so refined that it is nearly 100 percent pure and almost indestructible. Powdered or confectioners' sugar (in a range of textures from coarse to superfine) and brown sugar are variations on granulated sugar and share its very long shelf life. Brown sugar contains granulated sugar coated with refined, colored, molasses-flavored syrup. Light brown sugar has less molasses flavor and dark brown sugar has more. Store granulated sugar in an airtight container at room temperature. Confectioners' sugar and brown sugar should be stored in an airtight plastic bag inside a glass jar.

Sugar Substitutes—If you choose to buy sugar substitutes, be aware of their particular chemical compositions and any resulting health implications.

Tomato Products—When buying canned tomatoes, tomato purée, and tomato paste, look for low-sodium products. Italian plum tomatoes are the best substitute for fresh tomatoes. Do not keep unopened canned tomato products for more than six months. Store them on a cool, dry shelf. After opening, canned tomato products should be stored in clean, covered glass containers. They tend to take on a metallic flavor if left in their cans. You can keep them in the refrigerator for a week. Leftover tomato paste and tomato sauce can be frozen for up to two months in airtight containers. Drop leftover tomato paste by the tablespoon on a sheet of wax paper and freeze. When frozen, place in a plastic freezer bag and store in freezer until needed.

Sun-Dried Tomatoes—Buy dry-packed sun-dried tomatoes if possible. If you can only find them packed in oil, rinse them in boiling water before using.

Tortillas—Tortillas are available made from flour or corn. Corn tortillas usually do not contain oil or shortening. Tortillas can be warmed in the microwave by wrapping them in a damp paper towel and microwaving for 1 minute on HIGH. You will find a recipe for nonfat flour tortillas on page 317.

Vegetables:

Fresh Vegetables—Fresh vegetables used in the recipes include asparagus, beets, broccoli, brussels sprouts, cabbage (white and green), carrot, cauliflower, celery, corn, cucumber, eggplant, green beans, lettuce (romaine, red leaf, green leaf), lima beans, mushrooms, okra, onion (white onion, yellow onion, red onion, scallions, leeks), parsnips, potatoes (new potatoes, red-skinned potatoes, Idaho potatoes, white potatoes), pumpkin, radish, green peas, snow peas, spinach, summer squash (yellow summer squash, zucchini, pattypan), sweet potatoes, Swiss chard, tomatoes, turnip, winter squash (acorn, Hubbard, butternut), watercress, and wax beans.

Canned Vegetables—Buy canned vegetables with no added salt. Canned vegetables used frequently in the recipes include beets, corn, pumpkin, and tomatoes.

Frozen Vegetables—Use frozen vegetables when vegetables needed for the recipes are not in season. Look for frozen vegetables with no added salt or fat. Frozen vegetables used frequently in the recipes include corn, green peas, lima beans, and spinach.

Vegetable Broth—Commercially packaged nonfat vegetable broth is very difficult to find. Check canned and dried products for fat contents. Recipes for making vegetable broth are included in the Soup chapter. Make it in large quantities and freeze in cubes for easy access.

Vegetable Juices—Mixed vegetable juice and tomato juice are used in the recipes. Look for low-sodium juices.

Vegetable Spray—Buy nonstick vegetable spray with the lowest fat count possible in case you need it to spray baking pans or other utensil surfaces while cooking. You can also buy an inexpensive plastic spray bottle and fill it with olive oil or canola oil.

Vinegars:

Vinegars are very sour liquids fermented from a distilled alcohol, often wine or apple cider. Vinegar tightly capped keeps up to one year at room temperature, or until sediment appears at the bottom of the bottle.

Wine Vinegar—Buy red and white wine vinegars.

Balsamic Vinegar—Balsamic vinegar adds an elegant, complex sweet and sour taste to food. It is aged in Italy in wooden casks for about four years with the skins from grapes used to make red wine, which gives it a winelike sweetness. The longer it is aged, the more mellow it becomes. When replacing regular vinegar with balsamic, you can use a lot less because the balsamic is so flavorful.

Other Vinegars—Buy apple cider vinegar, rice wine vinegar, as well as herb- and fruit-flavored vinegars to add diversity to dressings and other recipes.

Water Chestnuts—The canned variety of water chestnut, which is round and woody and about the size of a cherry tomato, can be refrigerated, covered in liquid, for one week after opening.

Wine—Dry white wine, red wine, and sherry are used as flavoring in some of the recipes. Nonalcoholic wines or grape juice can be substituted if desired.

Wonton Wrappers—Wonton wrappers can be used not only for wontons and dumplings but are a quick and easy way to prepare dishes often made with fresh pasta dough like ravioli and tortellini. They can also be baked and used as a substitute for crackers. Some are made with fat, so watch the package labels. They can be found in the produce or frozen food sections of supermarkets and in oriental groceries.

Yeast—Dry yeast is granulated and comes in small foil envelopes or jars.

If packed in foil envelopes, it keeps for months at room temperature up to the expiration date. If in a jar, close the cap tightly after opening and store in the refrigerator until the expiration date. Some recipes call for fast-acting dry yeast, which is also packed in foil envelopes or jars and marked "fast-acting." Fast-acting yeast reduces rising time.

Yogurt:

Yogurt is one of the most healthful foods you can eat. Eight ounces will provide you with 25 percent of the RDA for protein and 300 to 400 milligrams of calcium. It's a good source of riboflavin, phosphorus, and potassium. But only nonfat plain yogurt, which has substantially fewer calories per ounce than regular or low-fat yogurt and less than 1 gram of fat per serving.

Yogurt Cheese—Yogurt cheese is made by draining the liquid from nonfat yogurt. Instructions are given with recipes that use yogurt cheese throughout the book.

Frozen Yogurt—Buy nonfat frozen yogurt.

Seasoning Guide

Since cooking without fat has an impact on the flavor of food, it is important to become aware of seasonings as an alternative. As a bonus, herbs and spices are nutritious. For example, paprika is high in vitamin A and parsley is high in vitamin C.

It's a good idea to create some herb and spice mixtures of your own. The following mixes can be used to accent vegetable dishes, soups, and salads. To prepare them, combine in a plastic bag and crush with a rolling pin, or place in a blender. Spoon into a small tightly covered jar or shaker. Store in a cool, dark place for up to a year.

- Combine 1 tablespoon ground nutmeg, 1 tablespoon ground ginger, 1 tablespoon ground cloves, and 2 teaspoons ground white pepper.
- Combine 2 tablespoons dried parsley, 1 tablespoon dried tarragon, 1 teaspoon dried chives, 1 teaspoon dried basil, and 3 tablespoons dried chervil.
- Combine ¼ teaspoon celery seed, ½ teaspoon ground white pepper, 1¼ teaspoons thyme leaves, 2½ teaspoons dry mustard, 2½ teaspoons paprika, 2½ teaspoons garlic powder, 5 teaspoons onion powder.
- Combine 1 tablespoon dill weed, 1 tablespoon basil, ¼ teaspoon dried grated lemon peel, 1 teaspoon celery seed, 2 tablespoons onion powder, pinch of black pepper, 1 teaspoon oregano leaves.

- Combine 4 teaspoons ground savory, 1 tablespoon dry mustard, 2½ teaspoons onion powder, 1¾ teaspoons curry powder, 1¼ teaspoons ground white pepper, 1¼ teaspoons ground cumin, ½ teaspoon garlic powder.
- Combine 1 teaspoon ground cinnamon, 1 teaspoon ground nutmeg, 1½ teaspoons dried sage leaves, ½ teaspoon dried thyme leaves, 1 tablespoon onion powder, 2 tablespoons dried oregano, 2 tablespoons mild curry powder, 1 tablespoon ground ginger, 5 crushed whole cloves, and ¼ teaspoon chili powder.
- To make your own curry powder, combine ½ tablespoon ground cardamom, pinch of cayenne, ½ tablespoon cloves, 6 tablespoons coriander, 1½ tablespoons cumin seed, and 1½ teaspoons turmeric.

Here are some herb and spice combinations to try on vegetable dishes:

Asparagus: ginger, basil, minced onion, mustard seed, tarragon
Beets: allspice, bay leaves, caraway seeds, cloves, dill, ginger, mustard seed, savory, tarragon
Broccoli: nutmeg, minced onion, marjoram, basil
Brussels Sprouts: basil, savory, minced onion, caraway, dill, mustard seed, nutmeg, tarragon
Cabbage: nutmeg, minced onion, caraway, allspice, clove
Carrots: ginger, nutmeg, minced onion, dill, allspice, bay leaves, fennel, ginger, mace, marjoram, mint, thyme
Cauliflower: dry mustard, basil, paprika, minced onion, caraway seed, dill, mace, tarragon
Corn: dry mustard, minced onion, basil, thyme, nutmeg
Cucumber: basil, dill, mint, tarragon
Eggplant: marjoram, oregano
Green Beans: dill, savory, curry powder, minced onion, oregano, sage, basil, marjoram, tarragon, thyme, mint, mustard seed
Lima Beans: marjoram, oregano, sage, savory, tarragon, thyme
Mushrooms: oregano, basil, thyme, curry powder
Onions: caraway seed, mustard seed, nutmeg, oregano, sage, thyme
Peas: basil, dill, marjoram, mint, oregano, allspice, poppy seed, rosemary, sage
Potatoes: caraway, nutmeg, dry mustard, minced onion
Spinach: minced onion, minced garlic, nutmeg, savory, thyme, basil, mace, marjoram, oregano
Sweet Potatoes: cinnamon, cloves, ginger, allspice, nutmeg, cardamom

Tomatoes: dill, minced onion, basil, bay leaves, celery seed, oregano, sage,
   tarragon, thyme
Winter Squash: cinnamon, nutmeg, basil, tarragon
Zucchini: oregano, minced garlic, tarragon, basil, dill

To flavor soup and stock, try making these small herb bouquets: Place 8 sprigs fresh parsley flat on a 5-inch square of doubled, clean, dry cheese-cloth. Place bay leaf on top, and spoon thyme over it. Fold up sides and tie securely with white cotton thread. These bundles can be frozen. No defrosting is needed before using.

When you want to suggest a meaty flavor in foods, try adding sage, thyme, fennel, rosemary, garlic, onions, or vinegar.

When you want a "salty" flavor, try celery seed, sesame seed, garlic, parsley, light soy sauce, fresh lemon juice, and hot spices such as chili powder and cayenne pepper.

When you want to sweeten foods, try vanilla extract, almond extract, allspice, cardamom, nutmeg, mace, mint, cloves, ginger, and cinnamon.

Experiment with new seasonings to vary the taste of the fat-free dishes you serve. Here's a quick inventory of some you might want to explore.

Mexican: chili powder, cumin, cilantro, oregano
Oriental: ginger, rice vinegar, fennel, curry powder, cilantro, hot mustard
   powder, horseradish, garlic, cayenne
Indian: curry powder, cumin, coriander, turmeric, garlic, saffron, mint, cinnamon
Scandinavian: caraway, cardamom, lemon, garlic, dill, paprika, black pepper,
   vinegar
French: tarragon, nutmeg, chervil, wine
French Country: garlic, basil, rosemary, sage, thyme, white pepper, vinegar
Italian: oregano, basil, fennel, rosemary, onion, garlic, parsley, red pepper flakes,
   wine, wine vinegar

Nonfat Snacks

Among the best nonfat snacks are air-popped popcorn, fresh fruit, pretzels (check the label to be sure they are made without fat), rice cakes (in many flavors including caramel corn!), baked corn chips, baked potato chips, fat-free cereals, fat-free bagels, fat-free bread sticks, fat-free fig and apple bars, and fat-free animal crackers. Keep a watchful eye on the cracker and cookie area of your supermarket for new fat-free snack products.

Other fat-free snacks include fruit sherbets, frozen fruit bars, fat-free and cholesterol-free frozen yogurt, nonfat yogurt, skim milk, honey, all-fruit jelly and jam, angel food cake, cocoa made with skim milk and nonfat chocolate syrup or powder, dried fruits, fruit juice, instant puddings made with skim milk, hard candy, jelly beans, licorice, gumdrops, and fruit-flavored gelatin.

Experiment with making milk shakes using skim milk and nonfat frozen dessert products. There are some milk-shake machines on the market that use skim milk to create a nonfat drink with the richness of whole milk.

When indulging in commercially prepared fat-free baked goods and snacks, remember that they may have high sugar, sodium, and calorie counts in spite of lack of fat. Be particularly aware of the serving size when checking labels on these products.

You will find many recipes for snack foods and drinks throughout this book.

Preparing Frozen Meals

Don't fall into the trap of trading nutrition for convenience. Consider making your own frozen dinners in advance instead of relying on commercially prepared frozen meals. A small amount of effort invested in advance will save a lot of time later on without sacrificing good nutrition. Get in the habit of freezing seasonal treats and you'll have a treasure trove of great seasonings, side dishes, and extras to last all year long. Double recipes when making sauces, soups, stews, and baked pasta dishes so that you can package and freeze the extra batch.

To get ready to freeze, you will need some freezer bags, heavy foil, freezer paper, and plastic wrap designed for freezer use, wire twisters, plastic freezer containers, strong tape, labels, and a marking pencil to label your meals with information about foods, portion size, and date frozen. Your frozen dishes will take the same time to cook in the oven or microwave as those that are commercially prepared.

Cool hot food before freezing it. Package food airtight to avoid freezer burn and protect taste, extracting as much air as possible before sealing.

• EATING OUT •

Controlling your fat intake is simple if you eat at home. But most of us are not able to cook and eat at home all the time. Our life-style, which often includes two-income families, commuting, and extra hours at work, leaves an inadequate amount of time for planning, cooking, and eating all meals at home. Unfortunately, one of the hardest aspects of cutting down on fat consumption is the difficulty involved in eating out on a reduced-fat diet. Although the manufacturers of prepared foods have heard the consumer's voice demanding new fat-free products, the American restaurant industry has responded with astounding slowness to this issue.

Planning ahead is essential if you expect to find fat-free restaurant foods. Call or visit the restaurant where you are planning to dine ahead of time and ask if they can accommodate your special diet requests. If you are choosing a particular restaurant in the interest of being able to join friends who do not have your diet concerns, make sure that there are some foods on the menu that you will be able to order. Often this involves ordering a group of side dishes such as plain baked potatoes and applesauce or appetizers rather than entrées.

Good choices for fat-free dieters are Chinese restaurants, since their kitchen staffs seem uniquely willing to adjust to a request for a fat-free meal. Since most Chinese meals are made to order, you can often design a dish to suit your needs even if it does not appear on the menu. For instance, if there is a listing for sautéed string beans with pork in garlic sauce, you could ask that the string beans be steamed instead of sautéed, that the pork be eliminated, and that the garlic sauce be prepared without oil. Another possibility is to ask for the string beans to be sautéed in water, chicken broth, juice, or wine instead of oil. There are often steamed dishes on the menu ranging from steamed vegetable dumplings to an entrée of steamed mixed vegetables. You can request that the chef mix you a small quantity of oil-free sauce to be served on the side. We have gotten in the habit of carrying along a small plastic container of light soy sauce, minced garlic, rice vinegar, and minced ginger mixed at home in case the kitchen can't supply the oil-free sauce. In that case, you can order a steamed dish, sauce it yourself, and be sure that you are eating fat-free.

Other ethnic restaurants can be good choices, but you need to communicate with the kitchen in advance and not make assumptions. For example, Italian restaurants should be able to provide a salad and spaghetti or linguine with steamed vegetables, but sauce may be a problem if sauces have been prepared in advance since most sauces are made with olive oil. You could ask that your pasta and vegetables be tossed with fresh tomatoes or you could bring your own sauce along. You might also want to bring a small container of fat-free Parmesan cheese. You could order a salad dressed with lemon juice or balsamic vinegar, and have fresh fruit for dessert. A Mexican restaurant may be able to provide steamed corn tortillas, a fat-free bean dish, salsa, and toppings such as chopped lettuce and tomato.

Other carry-along possibilities include small plastic containers of fat-free salad dressings, fat-free mayonnaise, and butter substitutes.

Inquire whether appetizer and salad selections that happen to be fat-free can be ordered as entrées as well.

When ordering dishes in restaurants that involve dressings or sauces, even if you are assured they are fat-free, be sure to ask for them on the side. That way in case there has been a misunderstanding and the sauce or dressing does appear to contain some oil, you won't have ruined your whole meal.

When you have to eat breakfast out, you can order dry cold cereals such as Grape-Nuts or Nutri-Grain that are fat-free. Learn which varieties of commercially prepared cereals fit that description and ask for them by name since your server will probably not know. Ask for skim milk with your cereal. If skim milk is not available, you can moisten your cereal with fruit juice instead. Fresh fruit can be ordered with your cereal or separately. Bagels, toasted English muffins, and whole-grain toast are fairly safe choices. Remember to ask for them unbuttered and ask for jam or jelly to spread on them. Even if the restaurant has egg-substitute or egg-white omelets, they may be cooked in fat. You can ask for hard-boiled eggs and only eat the whites if you are avoiding cholesterol. Pancakes and waffles are probably made with eggs, so it's best to avoid them.

The safest source of lunch in the outside world is a salad bar. You can choose greens, beans, plain pasta and rice, chopped egg whites, beets, sprouts, mushrooms, raw broccoli, onions, carrot, celery, cauliflower, raw zucchini and summer squash, as well as any other available raw vegetable choices. Avoid croutons and marinated selections on the salad bar. Take along fat-free dressing in case it's not one of the dressing choices. Look for a restaurant that serves a pita pocket overstuffed with raw vegetable salad. Be wary of soups since most of them are made with fat at some point in the cooking process. Mexican, Chinese, and vegetarian restaurants should offer fat-free possibilities.

Remember that you have the right to ask your waiter or waitress questions about how food is prepared and to place your order in a way that solves your dietary needs. You also have the right to return food if it is not served as requested.

When traveling on airlines, ask for the food options when you make your reservations. While specific options vary from airline to airline, you can inquire about which option comes closest to meeting your fat-free diet. Possibilities include fruit plates and strict vegetarian plates. Airlines also vary as to when an order for a special meal has to be placed. Be sure to call again to confirm your order and inform the flight attendant that you have ordered a special meal when you board the plane. Since it is unlikely that you will find an entire meal that meets your needs, you may want to take some fat-free snacks on board with you.

When traveling by plane, train, bus, or car, you may want to carry along special supplies including fresh fruit, all-fruit jams, dried fruit, apple butter, fresh cut-up vegetables, tomato or vegetable juice, mineral water, seasonings, and fat-free dressings. For long car trips you might also want to take dry cereal and instant nonfat dry milk, whole-grain pita, mustard, canned beans, and fat-free soups as well as an electric nonstick pot in case you end up needing to prepare your own food in an area where you can't find anything fat-free.

When traveling in a foreign country, learn the necessary phrases to express your needs. For instance, you can say "All my food must be fat-free" around the world in one of the following languages:

Spanish: Es necessario que mi comida no tenga grasa.
German: Mein Essen darf kein Fett enthalten.
French: Tout doit être préparé sans gras.
Italian: Niente douvebbe essere fritto.

When you're invited to dine at a friend's home or have to attend a family holiday celebration, make your dietary needs clear in advance. Help your host or hostess understand what they can do to accommodate you in this regard. If you fail to mention a fat-free diet in advance, you may find few things you can eat on the table. Once you reach a gathering, feel secure about politely turning down food that is not on your diet and don't feel that you need to offer excuses or apologies. If you suspect that you may be getting into a situation that will offer you few fat-free choices, eat at home before attending the event.

▪ USING THE RECIPES ▪

Brand Names

Certain brand names are mentioned to provide examples of food items on the market that are acceptable choices. Also look for other products of similar composition with different trade names that may be equally acceptable.

Nutritional Content Analysis

The recipes in this book have been nutritionally analyzed using Nutritionist III software. The primary sources of the Nutritionist III data base are USDA Handbooks #81-#8-16.

A nutritional analysis is given for each recipe on a per-serving basis. This analysis includes: calories; fat (in grams); cholesterol (in milligrams); protein (in grams); carbohydrates (in grams); dietary fiber (in grams); and sodium (in milligrams). Whole numbers in the analyses are rounded off to the nearest digit.

When the ingredient listing gives more than one choice, the first ingredient listed is the one analyzed. Optional ingredients are not included in the analyses.

Recipes that call for chicken stock are analyzed based on defatted homemade stock.

Due to inevitable variations in the ingredients you may select, nutritional analyses should be considered approximate.

Be aware of the fact that some recipes are considerably higher in sodium than others because certain fat-free products such as fat-free mayonnaise and fat-free cheeses have very high sodium contents. If you are particularly concerned about controlling sodium intake, be sure to check the sodium counts on individual recipes.

BREAKFASTS, LUNCHES, AND SNACKS

BREAKFAST

Pumpkin Patch Pancakes · Ginger-Molasses Pancakes · Berry-Bran Pancakes · Honey-Apple Waffles · Pear-Cinnamon Muffins · Apple-Oat Muffins · Cranberry Muffins · Corn Bread Muffins · Baked French Toast · Quick Fruit Toast · Fruit Toast Deluxe · Ricotta-Apricot Toastwich · Cinnamon-Raisin Bagels · A.M. Frozen Fruit Pops · Baked Potato Pancakes with Applesauce

LUNCHES

Egg Salad Sandwich Supreme · Red Pepper Mini-Pizza · Cottage Cheese–Fruit Salad · Pineapple-Cheese Open-Faced Sandwiches · Eggplant Sandwiches · Summertime Tomato Sandwich · Baked Bean Melts · Super Quick Bean Sandwich · Vegetable-Cheese Bagel · Vegetable-Tortilla Wraps · Black Bean Sandwich Deluxe · Veggie-Pita Melts · Pinto Bean Burritos · Apple-Pear Tortilla Roll-Ups · Whole-Grain Veggie Sandwiches · Chili-Bean Hero · Stuffed Pitas · White-Bean Sandwich

S N A C K S

Acapulco Dip • Parsley-Ricotta Dip • Eggplant Dip • Pico de Gallo Dip • Curry Dip • Veggie Dip • Black Bean Dip • Artichoke Dip • Broccoli-Tomato Dip • Fiesta Dip • Lima Bean Spread • Red Pepper Dip • Spinach Dip • Mango Dip • Ginger-Mustard Dip • Garlic-Dill Pita Chips • Parmesan Crisps • Oven-Baked Corn Chips • Bagel Chips • Wonton Chips • Cauliflower Bites • Melon Bites • Ricotta-Yogurt Celery Sticks • Pineapple Bites • Skinny Skins

BREAKFASTS

::

✳ Pumpkin Patch Pancakes ✳

YIELD: 4 servings (2 pancakes each) • *PREPARATION TIME: 20 minutes* •
COOKING TIME: 20 minutes

Pumpkin, brown sugar, ginger, and nutmeg are combined in these spicy
pancakes. Top with Honeyed Cranberries (page 209).

1 cup unbleached all-purpose flour	*¹/₄ teaspoon ground ginger*
2 teaspoons baking powder	*1 cup skim milk*
2 tablespoons brown sugar, firmly packed	*¹/₂ cup canned pumpkin puree*
	1 tablespoon apple butter
¹/₄ teaspoon ground nutmeg	*2 egg whites, at room temperature*

1. Sift flour, sugar, baking powder, nutmeg, and ginger into a large bowl.
2. Stir in milk, pumpkin, and apple butter.
3. In a separate bowl, beat egg whites with an electric mixer on high until stiff peaks form.
4. Gently fold egg whites into pancake batter.
5. Spoon ¹/₃ cup batter for each pancake on a nonstick griddle or skillet, or a skillet or griddle lightly sprayed with vegetable cooking spray.
6. Turn pancakes when tops are covered with bubbles and edges are lightly browned.
7. Cook on the second side for 2 minutes or until browned.

Calories Per Serving: 190	Carbohydrates: 38 g
Fat: .6 g	Dietary Fiber: .6 g
Cholesterol: 1 mg	Sodium: 63 mg
Protein: 7.4 g	

❋ Ginger-Molasses Pancakes ❋

YIELD: 4 servings (2 pancakes each) • *PREPARATION TIME: 20 minutes* •
COOKING TIME: 20 minutes

These pancakes have the flavor of gingerbread. Try serving them topped
with Chunky Spiced Applesauce (page 206).

1 cup unbleached all-purpose flour	*½ cup skim milk*
1½ teaspoons baking powder	*1 tablespoon apple butter*
½ teaspoon ground cinnamon	*3 tablespoons molasses*
½ teaspoon ground ginger	*2 egg whites, at room temperature*
Pinch of ground cloves	

1. Sift flour, baking powder, cinnamon, ginger, and cloves into a large bowl.
2. Stir in milk, apple butter, and molasses.
3. In a separate bowl, beat egg whites with an electric mixer on high until stiff.
4. Gently fold egg whites into pancake batter.
5. Spoon ¼ cup batter for each pancake on a nonstick griddle or skillet, or a griddle or skillet lightly sprayed with vegetable cooking spray.
6. Turn pancakes when tops are covered with bubbles and edges are lightly browned.
7. Cook on the second side for 2 minutes or until browned.

Calories Per Serving: 183	Carbohydrates: 38 g
Fat: .4 g	Dietary Fiber: .2 g
Cholesterol: .5 mg	Sodium: 170 mg
Protein: 6 g	

❋ Berry-Bran Pancakes ❋

YIELD: 5 servings (2 pancakes each) • *PREPARATION TIME: 20 minutes* •
COOKING TIME: 15 minutes

These pancakes are made with rice bran, which has cholesterol-lowering
properties similar to those of oat bran. Serve topped with Strawberries in
Orange Flavor (page 217).

1 cup unbleached all-purpose flour
3/4 cup rice bran
1 tablespoon sugar
1 teaspoon baking powder
1/2 teaspoon baking soda

1 1/4 cups nonfat buttermilk
3 egg whites, lightly beaten
2 cups chopped fresh or frozen
   strawberries

1. Sift flour, bran, sugar, baking powder, and baking soda into a large bowl.
2. Combine buttermilk and egg whites.
3. Add buttermilk mixture to flour mixture, stirring until smooth.
4. Spoon 1/4 cup batter for each pancake on a nonstick skillet or griddle, or a skillet or griddle lightly sprayed with vegetable cooking spray.
5. Turn pancakes when tops are covered with bubbles and edges are lightly browned.
6. Cook on the second side for 2 minutes or until browned.
7. Serve topped with strawberries.

Calories Per Serving: 245
Fat: .9 g
Cholesterol: 1.25 mg
Protein: 13 g

Carbohydrates: 47 g
Dietary Fiber: 9.5 g
Sodium: 253 mg

✳ *Honey-Apple Waffles* ✳

YIELD: 6 servings (1 waffle each) • *PREPARATION TIME: 25 minutes* •
COOKING TIME: 20 minutes

These waffles are a best bet for breakfast when topped with Blueberry Topping (page 293).

1 1/2 cups unbleached all-purpose
   flour
1/2 cup whole wheat flour
2 teaspoons baking powder
1 1/2 teaspoons baking soda
1/2 teaspoon ground cinnamon

1/4 teaspoon salt (optional)
1 1/3 cups nonfat buttermilk
1 1/3 cups apple juice
1 tablespoon honey
4 egg whites, at room temperature

1. Sift all-purpose flour, whole wheat flour, baking powder, baking soda, cinnamon, and salt, if using, into a large bowl.

Honey-Apple Waffles *(cont'd)*

2. Stir in the buttermilk, apple juice, and honey.
3. Beat egg whites in a separate bowl with an electric mixer on high until stiff peaks form.
4. Gently fold the egg whites into the waffle batter.
5. Heat a nonstick waffle iron, or a waffle iron lightly sprayed with vegetable cooking spray until hot. Pour waffle batter onto iron and cook until waffles are lightly browned and steam has stopped rising.

Calories Per Serving: 221	Carbohydrates: 44 g
Fat: .6 g	Dietary Fiber: 2 g
Cholesterol: 1.2 mg	Sodium: 420 mg
Protein: 8.9 g	

✳ *Pear-Cinnamon Muffins* ✳

YIELD: 12 small or 6 large muffins (2 small muffins or 1 large muffin each) •
PREPARATION TIME: 20 minutes • *COOKING TIME: 18 minutes*

Chopped pear and cinnamon are featured players in these delicious muffins. Spread warm muffins with nonfat ricotta cheese or all-fruit jam. Serve with Mulled Apple Warmer (page 335).

1½ cups unbleached all-purpose flour	*1 teaspoon ground cinnamon*
	¼ teaspoon salt (optional)
¾ cup sugar	*⅔ cup plain nonfat yogurt*
2 teaspoons baking powder	*⅔ cup skim milk*
1 teaspoon baking soda	*⅓ cup chopped pear*

1. Preheat oven to 400 degrees.
2. Sift flour, sugar, baking powder, baking soda, cinnamon, and salt, if using, into a mixing bowl.
3. Stir in yogurt, milk, and chopped pear until dry ingredients are just moistened.
4. Transfer batter to nonstick or paper-lined muffin cups, or to muffin cups lightly sprayed with vegetable cooking spray. Bake for 18 minutes or until muffin tops are lightly browned and a wooden toothpick inserted into the middle of a muffin comes out clean.

Variation

- Substitute blueberries for the pear.

Calories Per Serving: 117	Carbohydrates: 26 g
Fat: .2 g	Dietary Fiber: .5 g
Cholesterol: .4 mg	Sodium: 140 mg
Protein: 2.8 g	

✳ *Apple-Oat Muffins* ✳

YIELD: 12 small or 6 large muffins (2 small muffins or 1 large muffin each) •
PREPARATION TIME: 20 minutes • *COOKING TIME: 30 minutes*

These apple-oat muffins are flavored with cinnamon and maple syrup.
Serve with Spicy Cranberry Warmer (page 335).

¹/₂ cup pitted prunes	*¹/₄ teaspoon salt (optional)*
2 tablespoons water	*1¹/₂ teaspoons ground cinnamon*
1²/₃ cups unbleached all-purpose	*¹/₂ cup skim milk*
flour	*¹/₄ cup maple syrup*
¹/₂ cup old-fashioned rolled oats	*2 egg whites, lightly beaten*
¹/₂ cup brown sugar, firmly packed	*1 cup chopped apple*
1 tablespoon baking powder	

1. Preheat oven to 375 degrees.
2. Place prunes and water in a food processor or blender and purée.
3. Combine flour, oats, brown sugar, baking powder, salt, if using, and cinnamon in a bowl.
4. In a separate bowl, beat together the prune purée, milk, maple syrup, egg whites, and apples.
5. Stir the wet ingredients into the dry ingredients until the dry ingredients are just moistened.
6. Transfer batter to nonstick or paper-lined muffin cups, or to muffin cups lightly sprayed with vegetable cooking spray. Bake for 30 minutes or until muffin tops are lightly browned and a wooden toothpick inserted into the middle of a muffin comes out clean.

Note: You can substitute ¹/₃ cup commercially prepared puréed prune

Apple-Oat Muffins *(cont'd)*
baby food or prune butter (found in jam and jelly or baking section of
your supermarket) for the prune purée.

Calories Per Serving: 154   Carbohydrates: 34 g
Fat: .4 g   Dietary Fiber: 1 g
Cholesterol: .2 mg   Sodium: 57 mg
Protein: 3 g

✳ *Cranberry Muffins* ✳

YIELD: 12 small muffins or 6 large muffins (2 small muffins or 1 large muffin each)
• *PREPARATION TIME: 20 minutes* • *COOKING TIME: 35 minutes*

Fresh or frozen whole cranberries and oats are the featured ingredients in
these wholesome muffins. Puréed prunes are substituted for fat in this
recipe. Serve with Apple-Carrot Pick-Me-Ups (page 331).

½ cup pitted prunes   *1 teaspoon baking soda*
2 tablespoons water   *¼ teaspoon salt (optional)*
1⅓ cups unbleached all-purpose   *½ cup skim milk*
* flour*   *1 teaspoon vanilla extract*
1 cup old-fashioned rolled oats   *2 egg whites, lightly beaten*
¾ cup sugar   *½ cup whole cranberries, fresh or*
1 teaspoon baking powder   * frozen*

1. Preheat oven to 375 degrees.
2. Place prunes and water in a food processor or blender and purée.
3. Combine flour, oats, sugar, baking powder, baking soda, and salt, if
   using, in a bowl.
4. In a separate bowl, mix together the prune purée, milk, vanilla, egg
   whites, and cranberries.
5. Stir the wet ingredients into the dry ingredients until the dry ingredients are just moistened.
6. Transfer batter to nonstick or paper-lined muffin cups, or to muffin
   cups lightly sprayed with vegetable cooking spray. Bake for 18
   minutes or until muffin tops are lightly browned and a wooden toothpick inserted into the middle of a muffin comes out clean.

Note: You can substitute ⅓ cup commercially prepared puréed prune baby food or prune butter (found in jam and jelly or baking section of your supermarket) for the prune purée.

Calories Per Serving: 149   Carbohydrates: 33 g
Fat: .6 g   Dietary Fiber: 1.3 g
Cholesterol: .2 mg   Sodium: 112 mg
Protein: 3.7 g

✳ *Corn Bread Muffins* ✳

YIELD: 8 muffins (1 muffin each) ▪ *PREPARATION TIME: 20 minutes* ▪
COOKING TIME: 12 minutes

These muffins are a great way to start the day and are also a delicious addition to the breadbasket at the dinner table. Serve with Tomato Zingers (page 329).

½ cup unbleached all-purpose flour   *1 egg white*
1 teaspoon baking powder   *1 cup skim milk*
1 tablespoon sugar   *¼ cup applesauce*
½ cup cornmeal

1. Preheat oven to 350 degrees. Use nonstick muffin tins, or muffin tins sprayed lightly with vegetable cooking spray, and place tins in oven to warm for 5 minutes before filling.
2. Combine flour, baking powder, sugar, and cornmeal in a mixing bowl.
3. In a separate bowl, combine egg white, milk, and applesauce.
4. Add wet ingredients to dry ingredients and stir until dry ingredients are just moistened.
5. Spoon batter into warmed muffin tins. Each tin should be about ⅔ full. Bake for 12 minutes or until muffins are lightly browned and a wooden toothpick inserted in the center of a muffin comes out clean.

Calories Per Serving: 78   Carbohydrates: 15 g
Fat: .4 g   Dietary Fiber: 1.5 g
Cholesterol: .5 mg   Sodium: 26 mg
Protein: 2.9 g

❋ *Baked French Toast* ❋

YIELD: 4 servings ▪ *PREPARATION TIME: 10 minutes* ▪
COOKING TIME: 11 minutes

French toast is actually an American breakfast dish of sliced bread dipped in beaten eggs and milk and then cooked. Top this fat-free low–cholesterol version with puréed fresh or frozen fruit, or pure fruit jam blended with nonfat plain yogurt. Serve with Grapefruit Warmers (page 334).

½ cup skim milk
4 egg whites
½ teaspoon vanilla extract

Pinch of ground nutmeg
4 ½-inch-thick slices nonfat whole-
grain or French bread

1. Preheat oven to 450 degrees.
2. Combine milk, egg whites, vanilla, and nutmeg in a shallow bowl.
3. Dip the bread in the milk mixture, coating both sides.
4. Spray a baking sheet with vegetable cooking spray or line with a nonstick baking liner. Arrange bread on baking sheet in a single layer.
5. Bake for 6 minutes or until French toast is lightly browned. Turn bread over and bake for 5 more minutes or until lightly browned.

Variations
▪ Coat the bread with the milk-egg mixture and cook in a nonstick skillet over medium heat, turning once, until both sides are lightly browned.
▪ Top with fresh fruit and yogurt.
▪ Mix 6 juice-packed canned peaches with 1 teaspoon firmly packed brown sugar, ¾ cup plain nonfat yogurt, and 2 tablespoons maple syrup. Spoon over French toast.

Calories Per Serving: 79
Fat: .05 g
Cholesterol: .5 mg
Protein: 6 g

Carbohydrates: 13 g
Dietary Fiber: 0 g
Sodium: 161 mg

❋ *Quick Fruit Toast* ❋

YIELD: 1 serving ▪ *PREPARATION TIME: 10 minutes*

This easy fruit and toast combination is a fast, nutritious morning starter.
Serve with Apple Shakes (page 323).

2 ½-inch-thick slices nonfat whole-grain bread or 1 nonfat whole-grain bagel, split and toasted	2 tablespoons honey 1 banana, peeled and sliced 2 tablespoons plain nonfat yogurt

1. Spread toast or toasted bagel halves with honey.
2. Top with sliced bananas and yogurt.

Variations

▪ Substitute rye bread for whole-grain bread, nonfat cottage cheese for honey, fresh navel orange slices for bananas, and all-fruit raspberry jam for yogurt.
▪ Spread bread with 2 tablespoons honey and 2 tablespoons nonfat cream cheese. Top with dried apricots instead of bananas. Delete the yogurt.

Calories Per Serving: 294	Carbohydrates: 71 g
Fat: .6 g	Dietary Fiber: 2 g
Cholesterol: .5 mg	Sodium: 31 mg
Protein: 3 g	

❋ *Fruit Toast Deluxe* ❋

YIELD: 4 servings ▪ *PREPARATION TIME: 20 minutes*

Try this slightly more elaborate fruit toast on a more leisurely morning.
Serve with Honey–Vanilla Refreshers (page 331).

4 ½-inch-thick slices nonfat whole-grain bread, lightly toasted 1 cup sliced fresh or thawed, frozen strawberries 2 kiwis, peeled and sliced 1 banana, sliced	½ cup fresh or thawed, frozen raspberries 1 cup nonfat cottage cheese 1 teaspoon grated orange rind 1 teaspoon orange juice

Fruit Toast Deluxe *(cont'd)*

1. Preheat oven to 350 degrees.
2. Arrange toast on a baking sheet.
3. Combine strawberries, kiwis, bananas, and raspberries. Spoon fruit onto toast slices.
4. Bake for 10 minutes until fruit is warmed through.
5. Combine cottage cheese, orange rind, and orange juice and spoon over fruit toast.

Calories Per Serving: 159	Carbohydrates: 30 g
Fat: .5 g	Dietary Fiber: 3.4 g
Cholesterol: 3 mg	Sodium: 342 mg
Protein: 11g	

✳ Ricotta-Apricot Toastwich ✳

Yield: 4 servings (2 toast triangles each) • *Preparation Time: 20 minutes* • *Cooking Time: 5 minutes*

Here nonfat ricotta cheese and cottage cheese are broiled with apricots, ginger, and all-fruit orange marmalade on slices of whole-grain toast. Serve with Nectarine-Honey Refreshers (page 325).

4 ½-inch-thick slices nonfat whole-grain bread
¼ cup nonfat ricotta cheese
⅓ cup nonfat cottage cheese
½ cup juice-packed canned apricots, drained and crushed

1 tablespoon all-fruit orange marmalade
Pinch of ground ginger

1. Toast bread and cut each slice into 2 triangles. Preheat broiler.
2. Combine ricotta cheese, cottage cheese, apricots, marmalade, and ginger.
3. Spread ricotta mixture on toast triangles.
4. Broil until ricotta mixture is bubbly.

Calories Per Serving: 84	Carbohydrates: 16 g
Fat: .05 g	Dietary Fiber: .5 g
Cholesterol: 1.2 mg	Sodium: 184 mg
Protein: 5.4 g	

✳ *Cinnamon-Raisin Bagels* ✳

Yield: 4 servings ▪ *Preparation Time: 15 minutes*

Honey, brown sugar, cinnamon, and raisins are mixed with nonfat cottage cheese and spread on toasted nonfat bagels.

1/2 cup nonfat cottage cheese
4 tablespoons plain nonfat yogurt
1 tablespoon honey
1 teaspoon brown sugar, firmly
*   packed*

Pinch of ground cinnamon
1/2 cup raisins
4 nonfat bagels

1. Place cottage cheese in a blender or food processor and process until very smooth.
2. Combine smooth cottage cheese with yogurt, honey, brown sugar, cinnamon, and raisins.
3. Split bagels in half and toast.
4. Spread cottage cheese mixture on toasted bagel halves.

Calories Per Serving: 269
Fat: .1 g
Cholesterol: 3 mg
Protein: 15 g

Carbohydrates: 52 g
Dietary Fiber: .9 g
Sodium: 378 mg

✳ *A.M. Frozen Fruit Pops* ✳

Yield: 2 servings ▪ *Preparation Time: 10 minutes*

Put these in the freezer on your way to bed and they'll be ready to grab on your way out the door in the morning.

1/2 cup chopped fresh or frozen
*   strawberries, or canned juice-*
*   packed peaches*

1 cup plain nonfat yogurt
1 small banana, chopped

1. Combine yogurt, banana, and strawberries.
2. Transfer yogurt-fruit mixture to 2 paper or plastic cups. Insert a small plastic spoon in each cup and freeze overnight.

A.M. Frozen Fruit Pops *(cont'd)*

Calories Per Serving: 127
Fat: .6 g
Cholesterol: 2 mg
Protein: 7 g

Carbohydrates: 24 g
Dietary Fiber: 1.8 g
Sodium: 88 mg

❋ *Baked Potato Pancakes with Applesauce* ❋

YIELD: 4 servings (2 pancakes each) ▪ *PREPARATION TIME: 25 minutes plus 15 minutes chilling time* ▪ *COOKING TIME: 22 minutes*

Although fried potato pancakes are off-limits in fat-free eating, you can enjoy these baked pancakes instead. Try serving with Uncooked Tomato Relish (page 300) instead of applesauce.

1¹/₂ pounds Idaho potatoes, peeled and coarsely grated
¹/₄ teaspoon black pepper
2 tablespoons chopped onion

2 tablespoons unbleached all-purpose flour
2 cups unsweetened applesauce

1. Preheat oven to 500 degrees.
2. Rinse grated potatoes in cold water and press moisture out of them using paper towels.
3. Combine pepper, onion, and flour.
4. Place potatoes and seasoning mixture in bowl. Mix well. Chill for 15 minutes.
5. Lightly spray 2 baking sheets with vegetable cooking spray or line with baking-sheet liners. Divide potato mixture into 8 portions. Form each portion into a mound in your hands. Place 4 mounds on each cookie sheet and press each mound into the shape of a 5-inch pancake, approximately ¹/₄ inch thick.
6. Bake for 10 minutes. Press pancakes down with a spoon or spatula. Bake for 5 minutes more. Turn pancakes gently. Bake until second side is crisp, about 7 minutes.
7. Serve with applesauce.

Calories Per Serving: 240
Fat: .4 g
Cholesterol: 0 mg
Protein: 3 g

Carbohydrates: 58 g
Dietary Fiber: 5 g
Sodium: 11 mg

LUNCHES

::

✳ *Egg Salad Sandwich Supreme* ✳

YIELD: 4 servings • *PREPARATION TIME: 15 minutes* •
COOKING TIME: 20 minutes to boil the eggs

Egg whites are dressed up with mustard, celery, onion, and green pepper
in this sandwich. You'll never miss the yolks! Serve with Potato-Tomato
Soup with Bell Peppers and Chiles (page 103).

8 large eggs	*3 tablespoons nonfat yogurt*
1/2 cup chopped celery	*1/4 teaspoon black pepper*
1/3 cup chopped scallion	*1 teaspoon Dijon mustard*
1/3 cup chopped green bell pepper	*8 slices nonfat rye bread*
1 tablespoon nonfat mayonnaise	*Romaine lettuce leaves*

1. Place eggs in a saucepan and cover them with cold water. Over medium heat bring the water to a boil. Immediately reduce heat and let
   water simmer for 15 minutes.
2. Plunge hard-cooked eggs into cold water. When they have cooled,
   shell them and discard the yolks, reserving the whites.
3. Chop the egg whites.
4. Combine the chopped egg whites, celery, scallion, green pepper, mayonnaise, yogurt, black pepper, and Dijon mustard in a bowl.
5. Spread four slices rye bread with the egg salad mixture. Top with
   romaine lettuce leaves and the remaining four slices rye bread.

Calories Per Serving: 151	Carbohydrates: 25 g
Fat: .1 g	Dietary Fiber: .6 g
Cholesterol: 0 mg	Sodium: 387 mg
Protein: 12 g	

✳ *Red Pepper Mini-Pizza* ✳

YIELD: 4 servings ▪ *PREPARATION TIME: 15 minutes* ▪
COOKING TIME: 8 minutes

You can substitute other vegetables of your choice such as sliced blanched zucchini, sliced carrots, chopped spinach, sliced yellow summer squash, red onion and chopped green, yellow, purple, or orange peppers on these easy pizzas. Served with a tossed salad and Tomato-Herb Dressing (page 203).

4 unsliced nonfat whole wheat pita
   breads, about 4 inches in diameter
1 cup low-sodium tomato sauce
$^{1}/_{2}$ cup finely chopped red bell pepper
$^{1}/_{2}$ cup zucchini, shredded
$^{1}/_{2}$ cup finely chopped onion

$^{1}/_{2}$ cup finely chopped fresh
   mushrooms
$^{1}/_{2}$ cup shredded nonfat mozzarella
   cheese
2 tablespoons grated nonfat
   Parmesan cheese (optional)

1. Preheat oven to 400 degrees.
2. Separate each pita pocket into 2 round halves. Place pita halves, smooth side down, on a nonstick baking sheet, or on a baking pan lined with a baking-pan liner, and bake for 5 minutes or until crisp. Lower heat to 350 degrees.
3. Spread tomato sauce on tops of pita breads.
4. Top each pita bread with red pepper, zucchini, onion, and mushrooms.
5. Sprinkle mozzarella cheese over mini-pizzas. Sprinkle with Parmesan cheese, if using.
6. Bake until hot for 10 minutes or until cheese has melted.

Variation
▪ Substitute nonfat cottage cheese for nonfat mozzarella.

Calories Per Serving: 167
Fat: .7 g
Cholesterol: 5 mg
Protein: 12 g

Carbohydrates: 26 g
Dietary Fiber: 1.6 g
Sodium: 464 mg

✳ *Cottage Cheese–Fruit Salad* ✳

YIELD: 8 servings ▪ *PREPARATION TIME: 20 minutes*

A medley of fruit is mixed with cottage cheese and scallions. Serve with Red Pepper–Plum Tomato Soup with Dill (page 105).

2 tablespoons chopped scallions	*2¹/₂ cups halved fresh or thawed,*
2 cups nonfat cottage cheese	*frozen strawberries*
2 bananas	*1 kiwi, sliced*
1 teaspoon lemon juice	*1 cup seedless grapes*
2 cups fresh or juice-packed canned	
pineapple chunks	

1. Combine scallions and cottage cheese.
2. Peel and slice bananas. Sprinkle with lemon juice.
3. Toss together bananas, pineapple, strawberries, kiwi, and grapes.
4. Serve fruit in bowl or individual cups topped with the cottage cheese mixture.

Calories Per Serving: 93	Carbohydrates: 20 g
Fat: .45 g	Dietary Fiber: 2.6 g
Cholesterol: 1.5 mg	Sodium: 127 mg
Protein: 5 g	

✳ *Pineapple-Cheese Open-Faced Sandwiches* ✳

YIELD: 4 servings ▪ *PREPARATION TIME: 15 minutes*

Spread a great-tasting mixture of whipped cottage cheese, pineapple, and raisins on whole-grain bread. Serve with Strawberry-Spinach Salad (page 242).

1 cup nonfat cottage cheese	*¹/₂ cup juice-packed canned*
1 teaspoon lemon juice	*pineapple, drained*
¹/₂ cup raisins	*4 slices nonfat whole-grain bread*

1. Place cottage cheese and lemon juice in a blender or food processor and process until smooth.
2. Combine smooth cottage cheese with raisins and pineapple.
3. Spread cottage cheese mixture on 4 slices of whole-grain bread.

Pineapple-Cheese Open-Faced Sandwiches (cont'd)

Calories Per Serving: 154
Fat: .1 g
Cholesterol: 3 mg
Protein: 10 g

Carbohydrates: 31 g
Dietary Fiber: 1 g
Sodium: 342 mg

✳ *Eggplant Sandwiches* ✳

YIELD: *4 servings* ▪ PREPARATION TIME: *15 minutes* ▪
COOKING TIME: *35 minutes*

Eggplant simmered in tomato sauce and baked on crusty French bread
makes a hearty meal. Serve with Potato-Leek Soup (page 106).

*¹/₄ cup water, nonfat chicken broth,
    or vegetable broth*
1 onion, diced
2 cloves garlic, minced
1 teaspoon dried oregano leaves
1 teaspoon dried basil leaves
1 medium eggplant, diced
*3 cups chopped fresh or low-sodium
    canned tomatoes*

1 zucchini, diced
1 red bell pepper, seeded and diced
¹/₄ teaspoon black pepper
4 crusty nonfat French rolls, split
*¹/₂ cup nonfat grated Parmesan
    cheese (optional)*

1. Heat water or both in a large saucepan over medium heat. Add onion
   and garlic. Cook and stir until onion is soft. Add more liquid during
   this process if necessary.
2. Add oregano, basil, eggplant, and tomatoes. Cook over medium-low
   heat for 15 minutes.
3. Preheat oven to 350 degrees.
4. Add zucchini, red bell pepper, and black pepper to saucepan. Simmer
   for 10 minutes.
5. Cover a baking pan with aluminum foil or a baking-pan liner. Place
   halved rolls on sheet and toast lightly.
6. Remove 4 roll halves, leaving the other 4 halves on the baking sheet.
   Top the 4 halves on the baking sheet with the eggplant mixture. If
   desired, top with nonfat Parmesan cheese. Bake for 6 minutes.
7. Top with other roll halves and serve.

Calories Per Serving: 161
Fat: .6 g

Carbohydrates: 35 g
Dietary Fiber: 4 g

Cholesterol: 0 mg   Sodium: 193 mg
Protein: 6.6 g

✳ *Summertime Tomato Sandwich* ✳

YIELD: 6 servings • *PREPARATION TIME: 20 minutes plus 3 hours*
yogurt draining time

This simple sandwich is a special treat when tomatoes are at their peak in
late summer.

¹/₂ cup plain nonfat yogurt	*¹/₂ teaspoon dried chives*
¹/₂ cup nonfat cream cheese, softened	*¹/₂ teaspoon dried basil leaves*
1 clove garlic, minced	*1 loaf French bread*
¹/₂ teaspoon dried thyme leaves	*3 ripe tomatoes, sliced*
¹/₂ teaspoon dried cilantro leaves	*1 medium onion, peeled and sliced*

1. Line a colander with a coffee filter or several layers of clean, dry cheese-
   cloth. Place the yogurt in the colander in the sink and allow liquid to
   drain for 3 hours.
2. Combine drained yogurt, cream cheese, garlic, thyme, cilantro,
   chives, and basil.
3. Cut the bread in half lengthwise and spread with yogurt-cheese mixture.
4. Place the tomato slices and onion slices on top of the yogurt.
5. Top with the remaining half of the bread and cut into 6 servings.

Calories Per Serving: 128   Carbohydrates: 22 g
Fat: .3 g   Dietary Fiber: 1 g
Cholesterol: 3.6 mg   Sodium: 285 mg
Protein: 8 g

✳ *Baked Bean Melts* ✳

YIELD: 6 servings • *PREPARATION TIME: 15 minutes plus bean cooking time* •
COOKING TIME: 45 minutes

Beans, onion, green bell pepper, brown sugar, molasses, and Dijon mustard are topped with tomato slices and nonfat cheese in these terrific
sandwiches. Serve with Rainbow Fruit Bowl (page 219).

Baked Bean Melts *(cont'd)*

2 cups home-cooked or canned navy
    beans, or canned vegetarian baked
    beans in tomato sauce
¹/₃ cup chopped onion
¹/₃ cup chopped green bell pepper
1 tablespoon brown sugar, freshly
    packed

1 tablespoon molasses
2 teaspoons Dijon mustard
¹/₄ teaspoon ground white pepper
6 slices whole wheat bread
6 slices tomato
6 slices nonfat cheese

1. Preheat oven to 400 degrees.
2. Combine beans, onion, green pepper, brown sugar, molasses, mustard, and white pepper in an oven-proof casserole.
3. Bake for 40 minutes, stirring twice.
4. Remove casserole from oven. Turn on broiler. Place bread slices on a foil-covered baking pan.
5. Spread the bean mixture on the bread slices. Top with a slice of tomato and a slice of cheese.
6. Place under the broiler until the cheese has melted.

Calories Per Serving: 175
Cholesterol: 0 mg
Protein: 12 g

Carbohydrates: 31 g
Dietary Fiber: .4 g
Sodium: 298 mg

✳ *Super Quick Bean Sandwich* ✳

YIELD: 4 servings ▪ *PREPARATION TIME: 10 minutes* ▪
COOKING TIME: 5 to 8 minutes

Here's an extra-quick version of an open-faced bean sandwich. Serve with Carrot Soup (page 93).

1 cup canned vegetarian baked beans
4 slices nonfat whole-grain bread or
    2 nonfat whole-grain bagels, split
    in half

2 tablespoons nonfat cottage cheese
¹/₄ teaspoon ground paprika

1. Mash the beans slightly and spread on the bread or bagel half. Preheat broiler.
2. Top each open-faced sandwich with ¹/₂ tablespoon cottage cheese. Sprinkle with paprika.

3. Place the bean sandwiches under the broiler until they are warm and slightly brown.

Variation

- Delete the cottage cheese. Sprinkle the beans with minced garlic, chili powder, and chopped scallions.

Calories Per Serving: 89
Fat: .5 g
Cholesterol: .4 mg
Protein: 3 g

Carbohydrates: 17 g
Dietary Fiber: .4 g
Sodium: 257 mg

✳ *Vegetable-Cheese Bagel* ✳

YIELD: *6 servings* • PREPARATION TIME: *25 minutes* •
COOKING TIME: *10 minutes*

This super sandwich is made on a whole-grain or rye bagel. Serve with Black Bean–Vegetable Soup (page 100).

1½ cups nonfat cottage cheese
¼ cup chopped radishes
2 tablespoons chopped red bell pepper
½ cup chopped celery
¼ cup chopped green bell pepper

2 tablespoons chopped fresh parsley
1 clove garlic, minced
½ cup minced scallions
¼ teaspoon black pepper
6 nonfat bagels, split and lightly toasted

1. Preheat broiler.
2. Mash the cottage cheese and combine with radishes, red pepper, celery, green pepper, parsley, garlic, scallions, and black pepper.
3. Spread vegetable-cheese mixture on bagels and broil for 8 to 10 minutes, watching to be sure they don't burn.

Calories Per Serving: 195
Fat: .06 g
Cholesterol: 3 mg
Protein: 15 g

Carbohydrates: 33 g
Dietary Fiber: .4 g
Sodium: 380 mg

✳ *Vegetable-Tortilla Wraps* ✳

YIELD: *4 servings* ▪
PREPARATION TIME: *20 minutes plus 1½ hours chilling time*

You can fill these easy-to-assemble tortillas with a wide variety of shredded raw vegetables. Here they're made with carrots, zucchini, scallions, and red bell pepper. Serve with Sweet Potato–Carrot Soup (page 111).

3 tablespoons shredded carrot
3 tablespoons shredded zucchini
1 tablespoon finely chopped scallion
2 tablespoons finely chopped red bell pepper
1 tablespoon fresh chopped parsley

¼ teaspoon dried basil leaves
½ garlic clove, minced
3 tablespoons nonfat cream cheese
5 tablespoons nonfat cottage cheese
4 nonfat flour or corn tortillas

1. Combine carrot, zucchini, scallions, red pepper, parsley, basil, garlic, cream cheese, and cottage cheese.
2. Cover and chill for 1½ hours.
3. Place a quarter of the vegetable-cheese mixture in the center of each tortilla. Fold the two side flaps of each tortilla inward and roll up from the bottom.

Calories Per Serving: 79
Fat: .04 g
Cholesterol: 2.8 mg
Protein: 5.6 g

Carbohydrates: 15.9 g
Dietary Fiber: .3 g
Sodium: 176 mg

✳ *Black Bean Sandwich Deluxe* ✳

YIELD: *4 servings* ▪ PREPARATION TIME: *10 minutes plus bean cooking time*

This black bean spread is served on a nonfat whole-grain French roll with romaine lettuce, red pepper rings, and fresh tomato and onion slices. Serve with a salad topped with Honey-Mustard Dressing (page 281).

2 cups home-cooked or canned black beans, drained and rinsed
1 tablespoon chili powder
½ teaspoon ground cumin

4 whole-grain French rolls, split in half
Romaine lettuce leaves
1 medium tomato, thinly sliced

1 red bell pepper, seeded and thinly sliced in rings   *1 onion, thinly sliced*

1. Place the beans, chili powder, and cumin in a food processor or blender and purée.
2. Spread the bean purée on 4 of the roll halves.
3. Top with the romaine lettuce, red pepper rings, tomato and onion slices, and remaining roll halves.

Calories Per Serving: 292   Carbohydrates: 55 g
Fat: .9 g   Dietary Fiber: 5.4 g
Cholesterol: 0 mg   Sodium: 302 mg
Protein: 15 g

✳ *Veggie-Pita Melts* ✳

YIELD: 4 servings • *PREPARATION TIME: 20 minutes* •
COOKING TIME: 8 minutes

Here pita breads are spread with Dijon mustard, topped with sautéed vegetables, and baked with shredded nonfat mozzarella cheese and sliced tomatoes. Serve with Split Pea Soup with Carrots (page 101).

¼ cup water, chicken broth, or vegetable broth
½ cup julienned carrots
½ cup julienned yellow squash
½ cup sliced mushrooms
½ cup julienned onions
½ cup julienned green bell pepper
½ teaspoon black pepper
3 tablespoons Dijon mustard
4 nonfat pita breads
8 slices fresh tomato
¼ cup shredded nonfat mozzarella cheese

1. Preheat oven to 375 degrees.
2. Heat water or broth in a skillet over medium heat. Add carrots, squash, mushrooms, onions, and green pepper. Cook and stir over medium heat until tender. Add more liquid during this process if necessary.
3. Drain mixed vegetables and season with black pepper.
4. Spread mustard on unsplit pitas.
5. Top with mixed vegetables, tomato slices, and mozzarella.
6. Place pitas on baking sheet and bake for 8 minutes or until cheese melts.

Veggie-Pita Melts *(cont'd)*
  Calories Per Serving: 178
  Fat: 1 g
  Cholesterol: 5 mg
  Protein: 13 g

  Carbohydrates: 26 g
  Dietary Fiber: 2 g
  Sodium: 608 mg

✳ *Pinto Bean Burritos* ✳

YIELD: *4 servings* ▪ PREPARATION TIME: *15 minutes plus bean cooking time* ▪
COOKING TIME: *10 minutes*

Pinto beans accented with chili powder and cumin are combined here with chiles, tomatoes, scallions, and crisp lettuce in a tortilla wrapping. Serve with Raspberry-Pear Toss (page 215).

*2 cups home-cooked or canned pinto
  beans, drained and rinsed
1 teaspoon ground chili powder
1 teaspoon ground cumin
1/2 cup canned, chopped green chiles*

*4 nonfat flour or corn tortillas
1 cup chopped tomato
1/2 cup chopped scallions
1 cup shredded romaine lettuce
1 cup nonfat plain yogurt*

1. Heat beans, chili powder, cumin, and chiles in a small saucepan until warmed through.
2. Heat tortillas in an unoiled heated skillet for 1 minute on each side, or by following microwave instructions on tortilla package.
3. Place warm tortillas on individual serving plates. Top each tortilla with bean mixture. Sprinkle each with a quarter of the chopped tomatoes, scallions, romaine lettuce, and yogurt.
4. Fold tortilla in half and serve.

  Calories Per Serving: 220
  Fat: 1 g
  Cholesterol: 1 mg
  Protein: 12.9 g

  Carbohydrates: 43 g
  Dietary Fiber: 7 g
  Sodium: 214 mg

✳ *Apple-Pear Tortilla Roll-Ups* ✳

YIELD: *4 servings* ▪ PREPARATION TIME: *15 minutes*

Apples, pears, and raisins make an unexpected filling for a tortilla. Serve with Buttermilk-Zucchini-Apple Soup (page 107).

½ cup finely chopped apple
½ cup finely chopped pear
¼ cup shredded nonfat mozzarella
  cheese
¼ cup applesauce

2 tablespoons raisins
2 teaspoons lemon juice
Pinch of ground cinnamon
4 nonfat flour tortillas

1. Combine apple, pear, cheese, applesauce, raisins, lemon juice, and cinnamon.
2. Spread the bottom section of each tortilla with one quarter of the apple-pear mixture. Fold the bottom flap over the filling, the two side flaps inward, and then roll up each tortilla.

Calories Per Serving: 113
Fat: .2 g
Cholesterol: 2.5 mg
Protein: 5 g

Carbohydrates: 24 g
Dietary Fiber: 1.3 g
Sodium: 149 mg

✳ *Whole-Grain Veggie Sandwiches* ✳

YIELD: *4 servings* • PREPARATION TIME: *25 minutes*

Carrots, green pepper, celery, spinach, and tomato are included in the stuffing for this hearty sandwich. Serve with Cranberry Poached Peaches (page 213).

¾ cup nonfat cottage cheese
¾ cup plain nonfat yogurt
¼ cup grated carrot
¼ cup grated green bell pepper
¼ cup grated celery
1 teaspoon minced scallion

2 tablespoons Dijon mustard
1 teaspoon prepared horseradish
4 whole-grain French rolls
Fresh spinach leaves
4 thick slices fresh tomato

1. Place cottage cheese and yogurt in a blender or food processor and process until smooth.
2. Combine cottage cheese–yogurt mixture, carrot, green pepper, celery, and scallion.
3. Combine mustard with horseradish. Cut rolls in half lengthwise. Spread mustard-horseradish mixture on bottom of rolls.
4. Place spinach leaves on top of mustard. Place tomatoes on top of spinach leaves.

Whole-Grain Veggie Sandwiches *(cont'd)*

5. Spread cheese-yogurt mixture on top halves of rolls. Place bottom halves of rolls on tops.

Calories Per Serving: 223	Carbohydrates: 37 g
Fat: .4 g	Dietary Fiber: 1 g
Cholesterol: 3 mg	Sodium: 472 mg
Protein: 16 g	

✳ *Chili-Bean Hero* ✳

YIELD: 4 servings • PREPARATION TIME: 15 minutes plus bean cooking time and 2 hours chilling time

One of the hardest things about being on a fat-free diet is finding a good carry-along sandwich filling. This Mexican-flavored bean spread is a perfect solution. Enjoy it on long, crusty nonfat rolls. Also take along a slice of Carrot Cake (page 345).

2 cups home-cooked or canned pinto beans, black beans, or Great Northern beans, drained and rinsed	1 teaspoon Dijon mustard
	2 teaspoons cider vinegar
	2 tablespoons chopped fresh parsley
	Pinch of cayenne pepper
1 clove garlic, minced	4 long, crusty, nonfat French or Italian rolls
2 tablespoons diced, canned, green chiles or green bell pepper	
	1 large tomato, chopped and drained
2 tablespoons chopped onion	1 cup chopped romaine lettuce

1. Combine beans, garlic, chiles or green pepper, onion, mustard, vinegar, parsley, and cayenne pepper in a blender or food processor. Process until smooth.
2. Refrigerate for 2 hours.
3. Cut rolls in half lengthwise and spread bean mixture on one half of bread. Top with chopped tomato and lettuce, and other half of roll.

Calories Per Serving: 279	Carbohydrates: 52 g
Fat: .7 g	Dietary Fiber: 7 g
Cholesterol: 0 mg	Sodium: 346 mg
Protein: 15 g	

✳ *Stuffed Pitas* ✳

YIELD: 4 servings ▪ *PREPARATION TIME: 15 minutes plus vegetable cooking time*

Here a medley of raw and steamed vegetables is seasoned with cumin and stuffed in whole-grain pitas.

1 cup diced zucchini, steamed
¹/₂ cup chopped broccoli florets,
* steamed*
¹/₂ cup sliced mushrooms
1 tomato, chopped
1 green bell pepper, chopped

¹/₂ cooked cup fresh, canned, or
* frozen corn kernels*
1 teaspoon ground cumin
1 cup grated nonfat shredded cheese
* (optional)*
4 whole-grain pita breads

1. Combine zucchini, broccoli, mushrooms, tomato, green pepper, corn, cumin, and cheese.
2. Stuff vegetable mixture into the 4 pita bread pockets.

Calories Per Serving: 144
Fat: 1 g
Cholesterol: 0 mg
Protein: 5.9 g

Carbohydrates: 29 g
Dietary Fiber: .9 g
Sodium: 224 mg

✳ *White-Bean Sandwich* ✳

YIELD: 4 servings ▪ *PREPARATION TIME: 10 minutes plus 35 minutes garlic roasting time and bean cooking time*

This white-bean spread tastes best if it can be made with fresh basil leaves. Keep this dish in mind when you see fresh basil at your supermarket. When fresh basil isn't available, you can substitute a combination of fresh parsley and dried basil. Serve with Tomato-Jalapeño Salad (page 244).

4 cloves garlic
2 cups cooked or canned cannellini
* beans, drained and rinsed*
¹/₂ cup fresh basil leaves or ¹/₃ cup
* fresh parsley leaves mixed with*
* 1 teaspoon dried basil leaves*

2 tablespoons red wine vinegar
8 slices whole-grain bread
¹/₂ cup chopped red bell pepper
Romaine lettuce leaves
¹/₂ cup thinly sliced cucumber

White-Bean Sandwich *(cont'd)*

1. Preheat oven to 350 degrees.
2. Place garlic cloves in a small baking pan. Roast for 35 minutes or until garlic is very soft. Squeeze garlic cloves at one end to press out softened garlic.
3. Combine roasted garlic with beans, basil or parsley-basil mixture, and vinegar in a blender or food processor and process until smooth.
4. Spread 4 slices of whole-grain bread with the white bean mixture.
5. Sprinkle red peppers over bean mixture on bread. Top with romaine leaves and cucumber slices. Top with second piece of bread.

Calories Per Serving: 162	Carbohydrates: 31 g
Fat: .6 g	Dietary Fiber: 6.5 g
Cholesterol: 0 mg	Sodium: 18 mg
Protein: 8.7 g	

SNACKS

::

✳ *Acapulco Dip* ✳

YIELD: 6 servings (5 tablespoons each) • *PREPARATION TIME: 15 minutes*

This dip is a blend of nonfat cottage cheese, nonfat cheddar cheese, onion, chili powder, and cumin. Serve with Skinny Skins (page 79).

1 cup nonfat cottage cheese
¼ cup nonfat grated cheddar cheese
¼ cup chopped onion
¼ cup plain nonfat yogurt
¼ cup low-sodium catsup

1 tablespoon chopped fresh parsley
1 teaspoon chili powder
1 clove garlic, chopped
Pinch of ground cumin

1. Combine cottage cheese, cheddar cheese, onion, yogurt, catsup, parsley, chili powder, garlic, and cumin in a bowl.
2. Transfer to a food processor or blender. Process until smooth.

Calories Per Serving: 43
Fat: .1 g
Cholesterol: 2 mg
Protein: 6 g

Carbohydrates: 5 g
Dietary Fiber: .3 g
Sodium: 251 mg

✳ *Parsley-Ricotta Dip* ✳

YIELD: 6 servings (¼ cup each) • *PREPARATION TIME: 10 minutes*

Nonfat ricotta cheese is the basic ingredient in this vegetable dip. Serve with Garlic-Dill Pita Chips (page 74).

1½ cups chopped fresh parsley
1 teaspoon dried dill leaves
1 cup nonfat ricotta cheese

¼ cup nonfat plain yogurt
1 tablespoon lemon juice

Parsley-Ricotta Dip *(cont'd)*

1. Place parsley, dill, ricotta cheese, yogurt, and lemon juice in a blender or food processor.
2. Process until smooth.

Calories Per Serving: 15
Fat: .07 g
Cholesterol: .5 mg
Protein: 1.6 g

Carbohydrates: 2.3 g
Dietary Fiber: .7 g
Sodium: 14 mg

❈ *Eggplant Dip* ❈

YIELD: *8 servings (¹/₃ cup each)* • PREPARATION TIME: *15 minutes* •
COOKING TIME: *20 minutes*

Broiled eggplant is chopped and mixed with lemon juice, onion, parsley, garlic, and black pepper in this dip. Serve with slices of Whole Wheat Baguette (page 310).

1 pound eggplant
¹/₃ cup lemon juice
¹/₄ cup minced onion

1 tablespoon chopped fresh parsley
1 teaspoon minced garlic
¹/₄ teaspoon black pepper

1. Prick eggplant with a fork. Broil eggplant for 20 minutes, turning several times.
2. Peel eggplant and chop pulp.
3. Mix eggplant with lemon juice, onion, parsley, garlic, and black pepper.

Variation
- Delete lemon juice and substitute 2 teaspoons cider vinegar. Add ¹/₂ cup nonfat cottage cheese. Delete garlic and add ¹/₄ teaspoon ground cumin in Step 3.
- Use half lemon juice and half lime juice. Add 1 jalapeño pepper, seeded and minced, 1 teaspoon ground cumin, ¹/₄ teaspoon ground cinnamon, and 1 teaspoon ground coriander.

Calories Per Serving: 18
Fat: .1 g
Cholesterol: 0 mg
Protein: .5 g

Carbohydrates: 4 g
Dietary Fiber: 1 g
Sodium: 2 mg

✳ *Pico de Gallo Dip* ✳

YIELD: 6 servings (¹/₄ cup each) • *PREPARATION TIME: 20 minutes*

Serve with Oven-Baked Corn Chips (page 75) and vegetable sticks. Do not make more than three hours ahead of serving time.

2 cups finely chopped fresh or canned
  low-sodium tomatoes, drained
¹/₄ cup minced scallions
2 fresh jalapeño peppers (leave seeds
  in if you want a very hot sauce,
  remove for a milder sauce)

1 clove garlic, minced
1 tablespoon ground coriander
1 teaspoon dried oregano leaves
3 tablespoons lime juice
¹/₂ cup low-sodium tomato juice

Combine the tomatoes, scallions, jalapeños, garlic, coriander, oregano, lime juice, and tomato juice in a serving bowl. Refrigerate if not serving immediately.

Variations

- Substitute white distilled vinegar for lime juice, and green bell peppers for jalapeños.
- Combine 1 cup Pico de Gallo Dip with 1 cup nonfat sour cream.

Calories Per Serving: 24
Fat: .3 g
Cholesterol: 0 mg
Protein: 1 g

Carbohydrates: 5 g
Dietary Fiber: .8 g
Sodium: 54 mg

✳ *Curry Dip* ✳

YIELD: 6 servings (3 tablespoons each) • *PREPARATION TIME: 10 minutes plus
1 hour chilling time*

Curry powder, cumin, and lemon juice flavor this yogurt dip. Serve with fresh vegetables.

1 cup plain nonfat yogurt
1 teaspoon curry powder
¹/₂ teaspoon lemon juice

¹/₂ teaspoon ground cumin
¹/₄ teaspoon black pepper

Curry Dip *(cont'd)*

1. Combine yogurt, curry powder, lemon juice, ground cumin, and black pepper. Chill for 1 hour.

Calories Per Serving: 23
Fat: .2 g
Cholesterol: .7 mg
Protein: 2 g

Carbohydrates: 3 g
Dietary Fiber: 0 g
Sodium: 29 mg

✳ *Veggie Dip* ✳

YIELD: 6 servings (¼ cup each) • *PREPARATION TIME: 15 minutes*

Fresh vegetables and cottage cheese are combined with lemon juice, scallions, and dill. Serve with Parmesan Crisps (page 74).

1½ cups nonfat cottage cheese
1 tablespoon lemon juice
2 tablespoons grated carrot
2 tablespoons grated green bell pepper

2 tablespoons grated radish
1 tablespoon minced scallions
1 tablespoon chopped fresh parsley
½ teaspoon dried dill leaves

1. Combine cottage cheese and lemon juice in a blender or food processor and process until smooth.
2. Transfer to a bowl. Stir in carrot, green pepper, radish, scallions, chopped parsley, and dried dill.

Calories Per Serving: 42
Fat: 0 g
Cholesterol: 3 mg
Protein: 8 g

Carbohydrates: 3 g
Dietary Fiber: 4 g
Sodium: 251 mg

✳ *Black Bean Dip* ✳

YIELD: 8 servings (¼ cup each) • *PREPARATION TIME: 10 minutes plus bean cooking time*

Serve this dip on a bed of lettuce leaves surrounded by carrot, zucchini, celery, and cucumber sticks.

2 cups home-cooked or canned black   ¹/₂ teaspoon ground cumin
    beans, drained and rinsed   2 tablespoons red onion, chopped
1 tablespoon chili powder   1 clove garlic, minced

1. Place the beans, chili powder, cumin, red onion, and garlic in a food
   processor or blender and purée.

Variation
- Substitute 1 tablespoon orange juice and 2 tablespoons balsamic vinegar for the chili powder and cumin.

Calories Per Serving: 60   Carbohydrates: 10 g
Fat: . 4g   Dietary Fiber: 2 g
Cholesterol: 0 mg   Sodium: 10 mg
Protein: 3 g

✳ *Artichoke Dip* ✳

YIELD: *6 servings (¹/₄ cup each)* ▪ PREPARATION TIME: *20 minutes plus 1 hour
chilling time*

In this dip artichokes are combined with garlic, parsley, lemon juice, red
bell pepper, and nonfat Parmesan cheese. Serve with Bagel Chips (page
76).

1¹/₂ cups water-packed artichoke   1 tablespoon nonfat Parmesan cheese
    hearts, drained and chopped   1 tablespoon chopped fresh parsley
2 tablespoons chopped red bell   1 tablespoon lemon juice
    pepper   1 clove garlic, chopped
1 tablespoon nonfat mayonnaise   ¹/₂ teaspoon dried basil leaves
1 tablespoon water   ¹/₂ teaspoon dried oregano leaves

1. Combine artichoke hearts, red pepper, mayonnaise, water, Parmesan
   cheese, parsley, lemon juice, garlic, basil, and oregano in bowl.
2. Transfer to a blender or food processor and process until smooth.
   Refrigerate for at least 1 hour before serving.

Calories Per Serving: 41   Carbohydrates: 9 g
Fat: 0 g   Dietary Fiber: . 6 g
Cholesterol: 0 mg   Sodium: 48 mg
Protein: 1 g

✳ *Broccoli-Tomato Dip* ✳

YIELD: 8 servings (¹/₄ cup each) ▪ *PREPARATION TIME: 15 minutes plus broccoli steaming time and 1 hour chilling time*

Use this dip as a substitute for guacamole since a single avocado can weigh in at a walloping 30 grams of fat. Serve with raw vegetable sticks and Hot Tomato Cocktail (page 337).

1¹/₂ cups broccoli stalks, peeled and steamed	*1 clove garlic, minced*
	1 small tomato, diced
1¹/₂ tablespoons lemon juice	*¹/₄ cup chopped onions*
¹/₂ teaspoon ground cumin	*1 green chile pepper, chopped*

1. Place broccoli stalks, lemon juice, cumin, and garlic in a blender or food processor and process until smooth. Add tomato, chopped onions, and chile pepper.
2. Chill for 1 hour.

Calories Per Serving: 11	Carbohydrates: 2 g
Fat: .1 g	Dietary Fiber: .7 g
Cholesterol: 0 mg	Sodium: 6 mg
Protein: .7 g	

✳ *Fiesta Dip* ✳

YIELD: 8 servings (¹/₄ cup each) ▪ *PREPARATION TIME: 15 minutes plus bean cooking time*

This dip is made with kidney beans, tomato juice, onions, and garlic. Serve with nonfat crackers, vegetable sticks, and Broccoli-Tomato Dip (above).

2 cups home-cooked or canned red kidney beans, drained and rinsed	*1 clove garlic, halved*
	¹/₂ teaspoon ground cumin
¹/₄ cup low-sodium tomato juice	*Pinch of teaspoon cayenne pepper*
¹/₂ cup chopped onion	

1. Place beans, tomato juice, onion, garlic, cumin, and cayenne in a food processor or blender and purée.

Calories Per Serving: 63
Fat: .3 g
Cholesterol: 0 mg
Protein: 3 g

Carbohydrates: 11 g
Dietary Fiber: 3 g
Sodium: 4 mg

✳ *Lima Bean Spread* ✳

YIELD: 8 servings (¹/₃ cup each) ▪ *PREPARATION TIME: 20 minutes plus bean cooking time and 4 hours refrigerating time*

Here lima beans are combined with lemon juice, garlic, red onion, cilantro, parsley, cumin, and cayenne. Serve with slices of crusty nonfat bread and Garden Cocktails (page 332).

3 cups cooked fresh or frozen lima
    beans
¹/₂ cup lemon juice
1 tablespoon minced garlic
2 tablespoons minced red onion

1 teaspoon dried cilantro leaves
2 tablespoons fresh minced parsley
¹/₂ teaspoon ground cumin
¹/₂ teaspoon cayenne pepper
¹/₄ teaspoon black pepper

1. Place lima beans in a blender or food processor and purée until smooth.
2. Place puréed beans in a bowl and blend in lemon juice, garlic, red onion, cilantro, parsley, cumin, cayenne, and black pepper.
3. Cover and chill for 4 hours before serving.

Calories Per Serving: 85
Fat: .3 g
Cholesterol: 0 mg
Protein: 4 g

Carbohydrates: 17 g
Dietary Fiber: 4.7 g
Sodium: 12 mg

✳ *Red Pepper Dip* ✳

YIELD: 8 servings (¹/₄ cup each) ▪ *PREPARATION TIME: 15 minutes plus 8 hours yogurt draining time*

This is an ideal dip for raw vegetables and also works as a spread for crackers. You can thicken drained yogurt by draining it for a longer period of time than that suggested here. The yogurt in this recipe is drained for eight hours.

Red Pepper Dip *(cont'd)*

> 3 cups plain nonfat yogurt
> 1 red bell pepper, seeded and finely
>   chopped
> 1 clove garlic, minced

> 2 scallions, chopped
> 1/2 teaspoon dried thyme leaves
> 1/4 teaspoon black pepper
> 1 tablespoon white wine vinegar

1. Line a colander with a coffee filter or several layers of clean, dry cheese-cloth. Place yogurt in a colander set inside a deep bowl. Cover with plastic wrap and refrigerate for 8 hours. Discard liquid in bowl.
2. Combine drained yogurt with red pepper, garlic, scallions, thyme, black pepper, and vinegar in a blender or food processor. Process until smooth.

Variation

- Substitute basil for the thyme and balsamic vinegar for the white wine vinegar.

Calories Per Serving: 51
Fat: .2 g
Cholesterol: 1.5 mg
Protein: 5 g

Carbohydrates: 7 g
Dietary Fiber: .2 g
Sodium: 65 mg

❋ *Spinach Dip* ❋

YIELD: *8 servings (1/2 cup each)* • PREPARATION TIME: *15 minutes plus 1 hour chilling time*

This dip combines spinach and yogurt with scallions and fresh parsley. Serve with a platter of raw vegetables and chunks of Garlic Bread (page 318).

> 3 cups plain nonfat yogurt
> 1 cup finely chopped fresh or
>   thawed, frozen spinach
> 1/2 cup chopped fresh parsley

> 1/2 cup chopped scallions
> 1 teaspoon dried dill leaves
> 1 clove garlic, minced

1. Combine yogurt, spinach, fresh parsley, scallions, dill leaves, and garlic.
2. Chill for 1 hour before serving.

Calories Per Serving: 57

Carbohydrates: 8 g

Fat: .2 g

Dietary Fiber: .7 g

Cholesterol: 1.5 mg

Sodium: 89 mg

Protein: 5 g

❊ *Mango Dip* ❊

YIELD: 4 servings (¹/₄ cup each) • *PREPARATION TIME: 15 minutes plus 2 hours chilling time*

Ripe juicy mango is combined here with scallions, lime juice, chopped parsley, and chiles. Serve with Wonton Chips (page 76) and pineapple chunks.

1 cup chopped mango
2 tablespoons chopped scallions
1¹/₂ tablespoons lime juice

1 tablespoon chopped fresh parsley
2 tablespoons chopped, canned green chiles

1. Combine mango, scallions, lime juice, parsley, and chiles.
2. Chill for 2 hours.

Calories Per Serving: 37

Carbohydrates: 9 g

Fat: .2 g

Dietary Fiber: 1 g

Cholesterol: 0 mg

Sodium: 32 mg

Protein: .3 g

❊ *Ginger-Mustard Dip* ❊

YIELD: 6 servings (¹/₄ cup each) • *PREPARATION TIME: 10 minutes*

Serve this multiflavored dip with fresh carrot and red bell pepper sticks. It can be stored in the refrigerator for two days.

1¹/₂ cups plain nonfat yogurt,
drained of any liquid
1 teaspoon minced fresh gingerroot
5 teaspoons Dijon mustard

2¹/₂ teaspoons dried dill leaves
2¹/₂ teaspoons brown sugar, firmly packed

Ginger-Mustard Dip *(cont'd)*

1. Mix together the yogurt, gingerroot, mustard, dill, and brown sugar.

Calories Per Serving: 44
Fat: .2 g
Cholesterol: 1 mg
Protein: 3 g

Carbohydrates : 6 g
Dietary Fiber: 0 g
Sodium: 99 mg

✳ *Garlic-Dill Pita Chips* ✳

YIELD: 8 servings (9 chips per serving) • *PREPARATION TIME: 10 minutes* • *COOKING TIME: 8 minutes*

These crispy chips make a great accompaniment for dips and soups. Keep them stored in an airtight container. Serve with Apple-Zucchini Soup (page 91).

6 nonfat whole wheat pita breads
1 tablespoon garlic powder

1 tablespoon dried dill leaves

1. Preheat oven to 325 degrees.
2. Split each pita bread in half. Cut each half into 6 triangular pieces and arrange with their rough sides up, close together on baking sheets.
3. Combine garlic powder and dill. Sprinkle on pita chips.
4. Bake for 8 minutes, until chips are lightly browned and crispy.

Calories Per Serving: 83
Fat: .4 g
Cholesterol: 0 mg
Protein: 3 g

Carbohydrates: 16 g
Dietary Fiber: .5 g
Sodium: 162

✳ *Parmesan Crisps* ✳

YIELD: 4 servings (6 chips per serving) • *PREPARATION TIME: 10 minutes* • *COOKING TIME: 10 minutes*

These crisps are made with pita bread and nonfat Parmesan cheese. Serve with Old Country Mushroom-Barley Soup (page 100).

3 nonfat whole wheat pita breads
2 tablespoons nonfat Parmesan
  cheese

1. Preheat oven to 350 degrees.
2. Split pita breads and cut each half into quarters. Lay pitas with their rough sides up, close together, on baking sheet.
3. Sprinkle with Parmesan cheese.
4. Bake for 10 minutes or until crispy.

Calories Per Serving: 80
Fat: .4 g
Cholesterol: .2 mg
Protein: 3 g

Carbohydrates: 15 g
Dietary Fiber: 0 g
Sodium: 174 mg

✳ *Oven-Baked Corn Chips* ✳

YIELD: 6 servings (12 chips each) • *PREPARATION TIME: 10 minutes* • *COOKING TIME: 8 minutes*

These chips are made from corn tortillas. You can mist them with water and sprinkle them with garlic powder, cumin, cayenne, or the spice of your choice before baking. Serve with Red Pepper Dip (page 71).

12 corn tortillas

1. Preheat oven to 400 degrees.
2. Stack 4 tortillas and cut them into 6 pie-shaped wedges. Repeat with remaining tortillas.
3. Spread wedges on a nonstick baking sheet in one layer. Bake for 8 minutes or until crisp.
4. Cool and store in an airtight container if not using immediately.

Calories Per Serving: 100
Fat: 0 g
Cholesterol: 0 mg
Protein: 2 g

Carbohydrates: 26 g
Dietary Fiber: no data
Sodium: 56 mg

✳ *Bagel Chips* ✳

YIELD: 6 servings (6 chips each) • *PREPARATION TIME: 15 minutes* •
COOKING TIME: 15 minutes

You can make your own bagel chips at home. For flavored chips, sprinkle bagel slices with Parmesan cheese, garlic powder, herbs, or cinnamon. Serve with Great Northern Bean Soup (page 102).

6 plain nonfat bagels

1. Using a serrated knife, cut each bagel into 6 round slices.
2. Place slices on wire racks. Place racks on baking sheets.
3. Spray slices with water.
4. Bake for 15 minutes or until crispy.
5. Store in an airtight container.

Calories Per Serving: 150	Carbohydrates: 29 g
Fat: 0 g	Dietary Fiber: 1.1 g
Cholesterol: 0 mg	Sodium: 290 mg
Protein: 7 g	

✳ *Wonton Chips* ✳

YIELD: 6 servings (10 chips each) • *PREPARATION TIME: 10 minutes* •
COOKING TIME: 8 minutes

Baking wonton wrappers is a convenient way to create crispy fat-free chips. Serve with Ginger-Mustard Dip (page 73).

30 nonfat wonton wrappers
 (2-inch squares)

1. Preheat oven to 375 degrees.
2. Cut wonton wrappers in half diagonally and arrange in a single layer on baking sheets.
3. Spray lightly with water.
4. Bake for 8 minutes or until lightly browned.
5. Serve warm or cold. Store in airtight container.

Calories Per Serving: 75
Fat: 0 g
Cholesterol: 0 mg
Protein: 3 g

Carbohydrates: 14 g
Dietary Fiber: 0 g
Sodium: 145 mg

✳ *Cauliflower Bites* ✳

YIELD: 6 servings ▪ *PREPARATION TIME: 15 minutes plus overnight refrigeration time* ▪ *COOKING TIME: 3 minutes*

Serve these tangy cauliflower florets with cherry tomatoes and small steamed new potatoes garnished with minced parsley.

4 cups cauliflower florets
1/2 cup white wine vinegar
1 teaspoon dried basil leaves

1 teaspoon dried oregano leaves
1 clove garlic, minced
1/2 teaspoon mustard seeds

1. Blanch cauliflower florets in boiling water for 3 minutes. Drain.
2. Heat wine vinegar with basil, oregano, garlic, and mustard seeds in a small saucepan. As soon as vinegar comes to a boil, pour it over the cauliflower in a glass bowl.
3. Marinate overnight in the refrigerator.

Calories Per Serving: 21
Fat: .2 g
Cholesterol: 0 mg
Protein: 1 g

Carbohydrates: 4 g
Dietary Fiber: 1 g
Sodium: 10 mg

✳ *Melon Bites* ✳

YIELD: 4 servings ▪ *PREPARATION TIME: 10 minutes*

Here fresh honeydew melon is tossed with lime juice and chili powder. Serve with Black Bean Dip (page 68) and nonfat corn chips.

1/2 honeydew melon, seeded, skin removed, and cut into chunks

1/3 cup lime juice
1 1/2 teaspoons chili powder

Melon Bites *(cont'd)*

1. Place the melon chunks, lime juice, and chili powder in a bowl and toss well.
2. Serve with wooden picks.

Calories Per Serving: 53	Carbohydrates: 14 g
Fat: .3 g	Dietary Fiber: 1 g
Cholesterol: 0 mg	Sodium: 22 mg
Protein: .8 g	

✳ *Ricotta-Yogurt Celery Sticks* ✳

Yield: 8 servings (2 celery sticks each) • *Preparation Time: 10 minutes plus 8 hours standing time*

Here crisp celery sticks are stuffed with a mixture of nonfat ricotta cheese and yogurt.

1 cup nonfat ricotta cheese	*1 teaspoon grated lemon peel*
¼ cup plain nonfat yogurt	*½ teaspoon black pepper*
1 tablespoon chopped scallion	*16 stalks celery, trimmed and chilled*

1. Combine ricotta cheese and yogurt.
2. Line a colander with a coffee filter or several layers of clean, dry cheese-cloth. Place cheese-yogurt mixture in colander and set over a deep bowl. Cover with plastic wrap and refrigerate for 8 hours. Discard liquid in bowl.
3. Combine yogurt-cheese mixture with scallion, lemon peel, and pepper.
4. Stuff each celery stalk with 1 tablespoon of yogurt-cheese mixture.

Variation

- Delete scallions and lemon peel. Add 1 tablespoon grated carrot, 1 tablespoon minced green bell pepper, 1 tablespoon finely chopped cucumber, and 1 tablespoon fresh minced parsley. Serve in hollowed-out cherry tomatoes instead of celery sticks.

Calories Per Serving: 19	Carbohydrates: 3 g
Fat: .1 g	Dietary Fiber: 1 g
Cholesterol: .4 mg	Sodium: 75 mg
Protein: 1 g	

✳ *Pineapple Bites* ✳

YIELD: 4 servings ▪ *PREPARATION TIME: 5 minutes plus 24 hours marinating time*
▪ *COOKING TIME: 13 minutes*

These pineapple chunks are marinated in vinegar, sugar, cloves, and cinnamon. Serve surrounded by chunks of mango, kiwi slices, and steamed sugar snap peas.

*2 cups juice-packed canned
    pineapple chunks, drained, with
    ¹/₃ cup juice set aside
¹/₃ cup white wine vinegar*

*¹/₂ cup brown sugar, firmly packed
¹/₂ teaspoon ground cloves
1 teaspoon ground cinnamon*

1. Place reserved pineapple juice, vinegar, brown sugar, cloves, and cinnamon in a saucepan. Simmer for 10 minutes.
2. Add pineapple chunks and bring to a boil. Remove from heat.
3. Transfer to a glass bowl and marinate in refrigerator for 24 hours.
4. Drain and serve with wooden picks.

Calories Per Serving: 158
Fat: .2 g
Cholesterol: 0 mg
Protein: .6 g

Carbohydrates: 41 g
Dietary Fiber: 1 g
Sodium: 11 mg

✳ *Skinny Skins* ✳

YIELD: 6 servings (4 pieces each) ▪ *PREPARATION TIME: 15 minutes plus
potato baking time*

These crispy baked potato skins are made with natural butter substitute. Serve with mugs of Tomato Broth (page 87) and a platter of pears and apples sprinkled with lemon juice.

*6 large Idaho potatoes, baked
4 ounces natural butter substitute,
    such as Molly McButter or
    Butter-Buds, mixed with ¹/₄ cup
    hot tap water*

Black pepper

Skinny Skins *(cont'd)*

1. Cut baked potatoes in half lengthwise and scoop out the inside, leaving a ¼-inch shell. Reserve the insides of the potatoes for another use.
2. Cut each potato half in half lengthwise.
3. Coat the inside of each shell with the butter substitute mixture and sprinkle with black pepper.
4. Broil 6 inches from the heat for 5 minutes or until the skins have browned.

Variation

- After the potatoes have been under the broiler for 3 minutes, sprinkle the potatoes with grated nonfat cheese. Return to the broiler until the cheese melts.

Calories Per Serving: 148
Fat: .2 g
Cholesterol: 0 mg
Protein: 3 g

Carbohydrates: 34 g
Dietary Fiber: 3 g
Sodium: 68 mg

SOUPS

STOCKS

Basic Chicken Broth • Basic Vegetable Stock • Quick Vegetable
Stock • Roast Vegetable Stock • Tomato Broth • Mushroom Stock

HOT SOUPS

Garden Tomato Soup • Borscht • Cantonese Vegetable Soup •
Apple-Zucchini Soup • Celery Soup • Carrot Soup • Summer
Squash and Orzo Soup • Minestrone Soup • Lentil-Potato Soup •
Succotash Soup • Banana-Squash Soup • Curried Broccoli-Apple
Soup • Cauliflower Soup with Confetti Garnish • Black Bean–
Vegetable Soup • Old Country Mushroom-Barley Soup • Split Pea
Soup with Carrots • Green Pea–Spinach Soup • Great Northern Bean
Soup • Potato-Tomato Soup with Bell Peppers and Chiles • Bean
Bag Soup • Red Pepper–Plum Tomato Soup with Dill • Potato-Leek
Soup • Pinto Bean Chili Soup • Butternut-Zucchini-Apple Soup

COLD SOUPS

Gazpacho • Chilled Yellow Squash Soup • Sweet Potato–Carrot
Soup • Apple-Plum Soup • Blueberry-Orange Soup • Nectarine
Soup • Pear Soup

Soup can be a first course or a meal in itself. Always serve soup with good bread. If you have difficulty finding nonfat options for lunch on working days, try packing some homemade soup in a wide-mouth thermos. Often soup is not a good choice to order at a restaurant or to buy in prepared form at your supermarket since few soups are prepared without fat. If you are ordering soup in a restaurant, be sure to ask about its fat content, and check labels on commercially packaged soup carefully. While there are a number of low-sodium soups on the market, there has been little attention to fat reduction in this product area. Since most soups freeze well and can be easily defrosted in your microwave, make large batches and freeze in individual serving containers.

To thicken soups and give them a creamier texture, purée a cooked potato and stir into soup. You can also purée half of the soup and stir it back into the pot.

STOCKS

::

Chicken and vegetable stocks have an important role to play in fat-free cooking since they add flavor to soups and can be used as a base for many fat-free dishes and as a sautéing liquid. They can also double as a hot beverage. Longer-simmering stocks will produce a more intense flavor. Since it is rather time consuming to make most stocks, it's a good idea to make a large quantity and freeze it. One of the simplest ways to create a supply of vegetable stock is to simply keep a quart jar in the refrigerator to which you add any water remaining when you cook fresh or frozen vegetables. Try freezing stocks in ice-cube trays or muffin tins, wrapping the frozen cubes in plastic freezer wrap, and placing them in tightly sealed plastic bags for future use.

✳ *Basic Chicken Broth* ✳

YIELD: 2 quarts (8 1-cup servings) • *PREPARATION TIME: 15 minutes plus several hours standing time* • *COOKING TIME: 2 hours*

Chicken broth is often used as a substitute for fat in sautéing. It can be kept in the refrigerator for three days or frozen for up to two months.

4 pounds chicken parts, skin and surface fat removed	*2 bay leaves*
	¼ cup chopped fresh parsley
4 quarts cold water	*½ teaspoon dried basil or dill leaves*
1 medium onion, quartered	*½ teaspoon dried thyme leaves or dried tarragon leaves*
4 whole cloves	
1 carrot, cut in chunks	*½ teaspoon ground white pepper*
2 stalks celery, cut in chunks	*2 cloves garlic, minced*

1. Place chicken pieces and water in a large, heavy soup pot. Bring to a boil slowly, reduce heat, and skim off the foam that rises to the surface. Do not return to a boil or fat will be reabsorbed by the broth.

Basic Chicken Broth *(cont'd)*

2. Add onion, cloves, carrot, celery, bay leaves, parsley, basil or dill, thyme or tarragon, pepper, and garlic. Simmer, partially covered, for 2 hours or until reduced by half.
3. Strain broth through a fine sieve or a strainer lined with a double layer of clean, dampened cheesecloth. Press down on the solids gently while straining to extract as much liquid as possible. Discard solids.
4. Let broth stand at room temperature until lukewarm. Refrigerate for several hours or overnight. Skim off all fat that has risen to surface or pour through a soup strainer.

Variations
- Add 1 cup chopped fresh or low-sodium canned tomatoes, another chopped onion, and 2 additional cloves garlic, minced, in Step 2. Delete cloves and bay leaves.
- Delete basil, thyme, and bay leaves. Add ½ teaspoon curry powder and ½ teaspoon dried dill leaves.
- For a more concentrated broth, return to soup pot after straining and boil until the flavor becomes more intense.
- Bake skinned chicken parts at 350 degrees for 25 minutes before making stock. Drain fat from baking pan.

Calories Per Serving: 15
Fat: .1 g
Cholesterol: 0 mg
Protein: .5 g

Carbohydrates: 3.4 g
Dietary Fiber: .9 g
Sodium: 27.6 mg

✻ *Basic Vegetable Stock* ✻

YIELD: 1 quart (4 1-cup servings) • *PREPARATION TIME: 20 minutes* •
COOKING TIME: 1³/4 hours

This and the following vegetable stocks can be refrigerated for 2 days or frozen for 3 months. For an added flavor boost you can also add a touch of vinegar or mustard, lemon or lime.

2 carrots, cut in chunks
½ teaspoon grated fresh gingerroot
4 stalks celery, cut in chunks

1 large leek or onion, chopped
2 turnips or parsnips, cut in chunks
3 whole cloves

½ teaspoon dried sage leaves
½ teaspoon curry powder
3 cloves garlic, minced

2 cups low-sodium canned puréed
   tomatoes
2 quarts water

1. Place carrots, gingerroot, celery, leek or onion, turnips or parsnips, cloves, sage, curry powder, garlic, tomatoes, and water in a large, heavy soup pot.
2. Bring to a boil and skim surface as foam rises to the top. Reduce heat and simmer for 1½ hours or until reduced by half.
3. Allow soup to cool to room temperature. Strain the liquid, pushing down on solids gently to extract as much liquid as possible. Discard solids.

Variation
- Place unstrained soup and solids in a food processor or blender and blend until liquefied.

Calories Per Serving: 151
Fat: .7 g
Cholesterol: 0 mg
Protein: 4.3 g

Carbohydrates: 36.2 g
Dietary Fiber: 8.2 g
Sodium: 101 mg

✳ Quick Vegetable Stock ✳

YIELD: *1 quart (4 1-cup servings)* • PREPARATION TIME: *25 minutes* •
COOKING TIME: *30 minutes*

7¼ cups water
1 small onion, diced
3 cups chopped vegetables and
   vegetable trimmings (You can
   include carrots, turnip, celery,
   leftover outer leaves of cabbage,
   lettuce, broccoli, mushroom
   trimmings, imperfect spinach
   leaves, pea pods, cut-away
   portions of tomatoes, zucchini,
   and cauliflower, parsley stems,
   etc.)

½ teaspoon dried thyme leaves
½ teaspoon black pepper
¼ cup chopped fresh parsley
1 bay leaf

Quick Vegetable Stock *(cont'd)*

1. Heat ¼ cup of the water in a large, heavy soup pot over medium heat. Add onion. Cook and stir over medium heat for 5 minutes or until lightly browned. Add more water during this process if necessary.
2. Place vegetables and trimmings, the remaining 7 cups water, thyme, pepper, parsley, and bay leaf in the soup pot and bring rapidly to a boil. Skim off foam that rises to the surface.
3. Reduce heat and simmer for 25 minutes.
4. Allow soup to cool to room temperature. Strain the liquid, pushing down on solids gently to extract as much liquid as possible. Discard solids.

Variation

- Place unstrained soup and solids in a food processor or blender and blend until liquefied.

Calories Per Serving: 18
Fat: .2 g
Cholesterol: 0 mg
Protein: 1.6 g

Carbohydrates: 3.5 g
Dietary Fiber: 1.7 g
Sodium: 48 mg

✳ *Roast Vegetable Stock* ✳

YIELD: 2 quarts (8 1-cup servings) • *PREPARATION TIME: 20 minutes* •
COOKING TIME: 3 hours and 15 minutes

In this stock the vegetables are roasted before being simmered with herbs.

*½ medium butternut or acorn
   squash, cut into chunks*
2 turnips, quartered
4 large onions, coarsely chopped
5 carrots, cut in chunks
4 stalks celery, cut in chunks

3 cloves garlic
3 medium tomatoes, chopped
1 teaspoon dried thyme leaves
¼ cup chopped fresh parsley
1 teaspoon ground white pepper
4 quarts water

1. Preheat oven to 450 degrees.
2. Combine squash, turnips, onions, carrots, celery, garlic, and tomatoes in a shallow baking dish.
3. Bake for 50 minutes, stirring several times.

4. Place roasted vegetables, thyme, parsley, and white pepper in a heavy soup pot with the water. Bring to a boil, reduce heat, and simmer for 2 hours or until reduced by half.
5. Cool to room temperature. Strain the liquid, pushing down on solids gently to extract as much liquid as possible. Discard solids.

Variation
- Place unstrained soup and solids in a food processor or blender and blend until liquefied.

Calories Per Serving: 88	Carbohydrates: 20.8 g
Fat: .5 g	Dietary Fiber: 5.2 g
Cholesterol: 0 mg	Sodium: 70.5 mg
Protein: 2.8 g	

✳ *Tomato Broth* ✳

YIELD: 1¹/₂ quarts (6 1-cup servings) • *PREPARATION TIME: 15 minutes* •
COOKING TIME: 10 minutes

This is a quick broth that can be served hot or cold with a dab of fat-free sour cream. You can also use it as a soup base or a sautéing liquid.

¹/₄ cup water	*¹/₂ cup chopped celery*
1 medium onion, chopped	*3 whole cloves*
6 cups low-sodium tomato juice	*1 teaspoon dried basil leaves*
1 bay leaf	

1. Heat the water in a large saucepan or soup pot over medium heat. Add onion. Cook and stir over medium heat for 5 minutes or until lightly browned. Add more water if necessary during this process.
2. Add tomato juice, bay leaf, celery, cloves, and basil. Bring to a boil and simmer for 5 minutes.
3. Allow soup to cool to room temperature. Strain the liquid, pushing down on solids to extract as much liquid as possible. Discard solids.

Variation
- Place unstrained soup and solids in a food processor or blender and blend until liquefied.

Tomato Broth *(cont'd)*

Calories Per Serving: 53
Fat: .2 g
Cholesterol: 0 mg
Protein: 2.2 g

Carbohydrates: 12.8 g
Dietary Fiber: 3.4 g
Sodium: 34 mg

✳ *Mushroom Stock* ✳

YIELD: 1 quart (4 1-cup servings) • *PREPARATION TIME: 10 minutes* •
COOKING TIME: 20 minutes

This simple mushroom stock can be used as flavoring for a wide variety
of fat-free dishes or as a sautéing liquid.

4 cups water
4 cups chopped mushroom stems and
  pieces

1. Bring water to a boil in a large saucepan.
2. Add mushrooms, reduce heat, and simmer for 15 minutes.
3. Place in a food processor or blender and purée.

Calories Per Serving: 18
Fat: .3 g
Cholesterol: 0 mg
Protein: 1.5 g

Carbohydrates: 3.3 g
Dietary Fiber: .9 g
Sodium: 9 mg

HOT SOUPS

::

✳ Garden Tomato Soup ✳

Yield: 6 servings • Preparation Time: 25 minutes •
Cooking Time: 30 minutes

This soup is made with a bounty of vegetables including celery, zucchini, yellow summer squash, green bell pepper, carrots, mushrooms, and corn. Serve with Eggplant Sandwiches (page 54).

¼ cup water, nonfat chicken broth, vegetable stock, or wine
1 clove garlic, minced
¾ cup chopped red onion
¾ cup chopped scallions
1 cup chopped celery
3½ cups chopped fresh or canned low-sodium tomatoes, with liquid
¾ cup diced zucchini
¾ cup diced yellow summer squash or pattypan squash

½ cup chopped green bell pepper
¾ cup thinly sliced carrots
¾ cup sliced mushrooms
1⅔ cups fresh, frozen, or canned corn kernels
3 cups water
1 teaspoon dried oregano leaves
¼ teaspoon black pepper

1. Heat water in a heavy soup pot over medium heat. Add garlic, red onion, scallions, and celery. Cook and stir over medium heat until tender. Add more liquid during this process if necessary.
2. Place 1 cup of the tomatoes in a blender or food processor and purée.
3. Add puréed and chopped tomatoes, zucchini, yellow summer squash or pattypan squash, green pepper, carrots, mushrooms, corn, water, oregano leaves, and black pepper. Bring to a boil.
4. Reduce heat, cover, and simmer for 25 minutes.

Variation
- Substitute 1½ cups sliced green beans for the zucchini and yellow summer squash.

Garden Tomato Soup *(cont'd)*

Calories Per Serving: 91
Fat: .6 g
Cholesterol: 0 mg
Protein: 3.9 g

Carbohydrates: 21.2 g
Dietary Fiber: 3.8 g
Sodium: 49 mg

✳ *Borscht* ✳

YIELD: 8 servings (1 cup each) ▪ *PREPARATION TIME: 30 minutes* ▪
COOKING TIME: 50 minutes

This hearty peasant soup with sweet and sour accents can be served hot
or cold. Garnish with a dollop of nonfat yogurt or sour cream and a
sprinkling of dill. Serve with Carrot-Corn Bread (page 313).

½ cup water, nonfat chicken broth,
*   or vegetable stock*
2 cups shredded cabbage
1 cup shredded carrots
2 stalks celery, chopped
1 medium onion, chopped
2½ cups grated beets
1 cup shredded potatoes

2 cups puréed fresh or low-sodium
*   canned tomatoes*
2 quarts vegetable stock or water
Pinch of ground ginger
¼ cup chopped fresh parsley
Pinch of black pepper
1 tablespoon honey
1½ tablespoons lemon juice

1. Heat ½ cup water, chicken broth, or vegetable stock in a large, heavy
   soup pot over medium heat. Add cabbage, carrots, celery, and onion.
   Cook and stir until tender and lightly browned. Add more water
   during this process if necessary.
2. Add beets, tomatoes, potatoes, vegetable stock or water, ginger, parsley, and pepper. Heat to boiling.
3. Reduce heat to low. Cover and simmer for 40 minutes or until the
   vegetables are tender.
4. Transfer 2 cups of borscht into a blender or food processor and process
   until smooth. Stir into borscht. Stir in honey and lemon juice. Cover
   and simmer 5 minutes.

Calories Per Serving: 79
Fat: .3 g
Cholesterol: 0 mg
Protein: 2.3 g

Carbohydrates: 18 g
Dietary Fiber: 3.3 g
Sodium: 152 mg

✳ *Cantonese Vegetable Soup* ✳

YIELD: 6 servings (2 cups each) • *PREPARATION TIME: 25 minutes*
plus rice cooking time • *COOKING TIME: 20 minutes*

The crisp vegetables in this oriental soup are combined with rice and chicken or vegetable broth. Serve with Wonton Chips (page 76).

6 cups nonfat chicken broth or vegetable
   broth
1 onion, finely chopped
2 cloves garlic, minced
1 tablespoon minced gingerroot
1 teaspoon light soy sauce
1/2 cup chopped water chestnuts
1/2 cup bamboo shoots
3/4 cup chopped broccoli florets
1 green bell pepper, seeded and chopped

1 carrot, shredded
3/4 cup sliced mushrooms
1 cup sliced celery
1/2 cup chopped snow peas or frozen
   green peas
1/4 cup shredded spinach
1 cup cooked long-grain white or
   brown rice
Pinch of black pepper
3 scallions, thinly sliced

1. Heat 1/2 cup of the broth in a large, heavy soup pot over high heat. When broth is boiling, add onion, garlic, and gingerroot. Cook for 3 minutes.
2. Add soy sauce and the remaining 5 1/2 cups broth. Bring stock to a gentle boil.
3. Add water chestnuts, bamboo shoots, broccoli, green pepper, carrot, mushrooms, celery, snow peas or green peas, spinach, cooked rice and black pepper. Bring to a simmer and cook for 10 minutes.
4. Garnish with scallions and serve.

Calories Per Serving: 166
Fat: .5 g
Cholesterol: 0 mg
Protein: 6.4 g

Carbohydrates: 34 g
Dietary Fiber: 2.8 g
Sodium: 200 mg

✳ *Apple-Zucchini Soup* ✳

YIELD: 8 servings (1 cup each) • *PREPARATION TIME: 20 minutes* •
COOKING TIME: 40 minutes

This soup is flavored with curry and works well with a meal that includes Indian dishes, or serve with Egg Salad Sandwich Supreme (page 51).

Apple-Zucchini Soup *(cont'd)*

1/4 cup water, nonfat chicken broth, vegetable broth, or wine	4 cups nonfat chicken broth
1 onion, chopped	1/4 cup uncooked long-grain white rice
1 apple, peeled, cored, and chopped	2 cups diced zucchini
1 1/2 teaspoons curry powder	1 cup skim milk

1. Heat water, broth, or wine in soup pot over medium heat. Add onion and apple. Cook and stir until they are tender. Add more liquid during this process if necessary.
2. Sprinkle curry powder over onion and apple. Stir.
3. Add chicken broth and bring to a boil.
4. Add rice and zucchini. Cover, lower heat, and cook for 30 minutes.
5. Transfer soup to a food processor or blender and purée.
6. Transfer soup back to pot. Heat, slowly adding skim milk, until soup is warmed through.

Calories Per Serving: 61	Carbohydrates: 11 g
Fat: .3 g	Dietary Fiber: 1.3 g
Cholesterol: .5 mg	Sodium: 85 mg
Protein: 3 g	

✳ *Celery Soup* ✳

YIELD: 8 servings (1/4 cup each) • *PREPARATION TIME: 20 minutes* • *COOKING TIME: 25 minutes*

This soup is rich with the flavor of wine and herbs. If you wish, you can season it with a few drops of hot pepper sauce before serving. Serve with Rotelle-Fruit Salad (page 265).

1 cup vegetable broth or nonfat chicken broth	1/2 teaspoon dried thyme leaves
1/2 cup white wine	1/4 teaspoon black pepper
4 cups thinly sliced celery	4 cups skim milk
1 onion, finely chopped	2 tablespoons arrowroot or cornstarch
1/2 teaspoon dried marjoram leaves	

1. Combine the broth, wine, celery, onion, marjoram, thyme, and pepper in a soup pot. Bring to a boil.

2. Lower heat, cover, and simmer for 25 minutes.
3. Transfer the soup to a food processor or blender and purée.
4. Return the soup to the pot. Add 3½ cups of the milk to the pot.
5. Combine the arrowroot or cornstarch with the remaining ½ cup of milk. Slowly add to soup.
6. Stir the soup until it begins to boil. Lower heat at once and simmer, still stirring, for 5 minutes.

Calories Per Serving: 78
Fat: .3 g
Cholesterol: 2 mg
Protein: 5 g

Carbohydrates: 11 g
Dietary Fiber: 1.3 g
Sodium: 143 mg

✳ *Carrot Soup* ✳

YIELD: 6 servings (2 cups each) • *PREPARATION TIME: 20 minutes* •
COOKING TIME: 30 minutes

Carrots, turnips, and potato are combined in this soup, which is made rich with the addition of evaporated skim milk. Serve with White-Bean Sandwiches (page 63).

*¼ cup water, nonfat chicken broth,
    vegetable broth, or wine
1 onion, finely chopped
3 cups sliced carrots
2 cups diced turnips
1 cup diced potato
2 cups nonfat chicken broth or
    vegetable broth*

*¼ teaspoon dried thyme leaves
Pinch of black pepper
Pinch of ground nutmeg
1½ cups evaporated skim milk
1½ cups skim milk*

1. Heat ¼ cup water, broth, or wine in a large, heavy soup pot. Add onion. Cook and stir over medium heat until onion is tender. Add more liquid during this process if necessary.
2. Add carrots, turnips, potato, and broth. Bring to a boil. Lower heat.
3. Cover and cook over low heat for 20 minutes or until vegetables are quite tender.
4. Transfer soup to a food processor or blender and purée.
5. Return soup to pot. Add thyme, pepper, nutmeg, evaporated milk, and skim milk.

Carrot Soup *(cont'd)*

6. Cook over medium-low heat, stirring, until warmed through.

Calories Per Serving: 138	Carbohydrates: 25 g
Fat: .5 g	Dietary Fiber: 3.5 g
Cholesterol: 3.5 mg	Sodium: 197 mg
Protein: 9 g	

✳ *Summer Squash and Orzo Soup* ✳

YIELD: 6 servings (1³/4 cups each) ▪ *PREPARATION TIME: 20 minutes* ▪
COOKING TIME: 20 minutes

Summer squash and orzo are simmered with celery, onion, garlic, tomatoes, and Italian spices. Serve with Veggie Pita Melts (page 59).

*¹/4 cup water, nonfat chicken broth,
vegetable broth, or wine
1 onion, finely chopped
1 clove garlic, minced
1 stalk celery, chopped
1 medium yellow summer squash
1 medium pattypan squash or
zucchini
6 cups nonfat chicken broth or
vegetable broth*

*¹/4 teaspoon black pepper
2 cups chopped fresh or low-sodium
canned tomatoes
1 teaspoon dried basil leaves
1 teaspoon dried oregano leaves
¹/2 cup orzo or other tiny pasta
2 tablespoons chopped fresh parsley
¹/2 cup nonfat Parmesan cheese
(optional)*

1. Heat the water, broth, or wine in a large, heavy soup pot. Add the onion and garlic. Cook and stir until tender. Add the celery, summer squash, and pattypan squash or zucchini and cook for 3 minutes. Add more liquid during this process if necessary.
2. Add broth, pepper, tomatoes, basil, oregano, and orzo. Bring to a boil, cover, and simmer for 8 minutes or until orzo is tender.
3. Add parsley and Parmesan cheese, if using.

Calories Per Serving: 66	Carbohydrates: 13 g
Fat: .5 g	Dietary Fiber: 2.5 g
Cholesterol: 0 mg	Sodium: 155 mg
Protein: 4.7 g	

✳ *Minestrone Soup* ✳

YIELD: 6 servings (2 cups each) • *PREPARATION TIME: 30 minutes* •
COOKING TIME: 45 minutes plus bean cooking time

This traditional favorite is a meal in a bowl. Sprinkle with grated fat-free mozzarella and serve with thick slices of fat-free Italian bread. Serve with Cucumber and Onion Salad (page 233).

1/4 cup water, chicken broth, vegetable broth, or wine
1/2 cup chopped onion or leek
1/2 cup chopped celery
1 clove garlic, minced
2 cups chopped fresh or low-sodium canned tomatoes with liquid
1 cup low-sodium tomato sauce
1 cup home-cooked or canned red kidney beans, pinto beans, lima beans, or Great Northern beans, drained and rinsed

3 1/2 cups water
2 cups chopped broccoli
1 1/2 cups chopped fresh or frozen spinach
1 cup diced carrots
1/4 cup chopped fresh parsley
3/4 teaspoon dried basil leaves
1 bay leaf
Pinch of dried oregano leaves
1/2 teaspoon black pepper
1/2 cup dry elbow macaroni

1. Heat water, broth, or wine in a large soup pot over medium heat. Add onion or leek, celery, and garlic. Cook and stir over medium heat for 5 minutes or until lightly browned. Add more liquid during this process if necessary.
2. Add tomatoes, tomato sauce, beans, water, broccoli, spinach, carrots, parsley, basil, bay leaf, oregano, and black pepper. Simmer uncovered for 25 minutes.
3. Add macaroni and simmer for 15 minutes. Remove bay leaf before serving.

Variations

- Substitute 2 cups white or red cabbage for the chopped broccoli or spinach.
- Add 1 potato, peeled and diced in Step 2. Delete macaroni.

Calories Per Serving: 105
Fat: .7 g
Cholesterol: 0 mg
Protein: 6 g

Carbohydrates: 21 g
Dietary Fiber: 4 g
Sodium: 63 mg

✳ Lentil-Potato Soup ✳

YIELD: 5 servings (2 cups each) ▪ *PREPARATION TIME: 25 minutes* ▪
COOKING TIME: 45 minutes

Lentils are neither peas nor beans, but are related to both. They cook
more quickly than other dried legumes. Serve this zesty soup in warmed
soup bowls and garnish with nonfat plain yogurt and chopped scallions.
Serve with crusty French bread, a tossed salad with Parmesan-Mustard
Dressing (page 278), and baked apples.

2 cups uncooked brown lentils
8 cups water
³/₄ cup chopped onion
³/₄ cup chopped carrots
³/₄ cup chopped celery
1 cup peeled, chopped Idaho potatoes

1 bay leaf
¹/₂ teaspoon ground cumin
1 clove garlic, minced
Pinch of cayenne pepper
1 tablespoon lemon juice

1. Sort lentils, discarding any foreign material. Rinse well and drain.
2. Place lentils, water, onion, carrots, celery, potatoes, bay leaf, cumin,
   garlic, and cayenne pepper in a heavy soup pot. Cook for 45 minutes
   or until lentils are soft.
3. Add lemon juice, stir, and serve.

Variation
▪ Delete the lemon juice. Substitute a splash of dry sherry.

Calories Per Serving: 134
Fat: .2 g
Cholesterol: 0 mg
Protein: 7.7 g

Cabohydrates: 27 g
Dietary Fiber: 5.9 g
Sodium: 59.6 mg

✳ Succotash Soup ✳

YIELD: 6 servings (2 cups each) ▪ *PREPARATION TIME: 20 minutes* ▪
COOKING TIME: 20 minutes

This chowderlike soup features corn, red pepper, lima beans, and tomatoes. Serve with Vegetable-Cheese Bagels (page 57).

½ cup water, nonfat chicken broth, or vegetable broth
½ cup sliced onion
2 stalks celery, diced
2½ cups water or vegetable broth
1 cup chopped fresh or low-sodium canned tomatoes
2 potatoes, peeled and diced
1 red bell pepper, seeded and diced
1 cup frozen lima beans

Pinch of cayenne pepper
1 teaspoon honey
1 teaspoon Dijon mustard
1 clove garlic, minced
½ cup chopped fresh parsley
¼ teaspoon black pepper
3 cups fresh, frozen, or canned corn kernels
2½ cups skim milk

1. Heat the ½ cup water or broth in a large, heavy soup pot over medium heat. Add the onion and celery. Cook and stir for 5 minutes. Add more liquid during this process if necessary.
2. Add the 2½ cups water or vegetable broth, tomatoes, potatoes, red pepper, lima beans, cayenne pepper, honey, Dijon mustard, garlic, parsley, and black pepper, Reduce heat and simmer for 15 minutes.
3. Add the corn and milk and simmer for 5 minutes or until the potatoes and lima beans are tender.
4. Transfer 1 cup of the soup to a food processor or blender and purée. Stir into soup.

Calories Per Serving: 201
Fat: .6 g
Cholesterol: 1.7 mg
Protein: 9.5 g

Carbohydrates: 43 g
Dietary Fiber: 5.4 g
Sodium: 98 mg

✳ *Banana-Squash Soup* ✳

YIELD: *4 servings (1 cup each)* • PREPARATION TIME: *15 minutes* • COOKING TIME: *25 minutes*

Hubbard squash, honey, and banana are the main ingredients in this unusual soup. Hubbard squash has a fat, round middle, a tapering neck at the stem end, and comes to a point at the bottom. The skin may be dark green, bluish gray, or orange and is hard and bumpy. Serve with Rotini and Black-Eyed Pea Salad (page 263).

Banana-Squash Soup *(cont'd)*

1½ cups peeled and diced Hubbard squash, in 1½-inch cubes
¼ teaspoon black pepper
¼ teaspoon ground nutmeg

1½ cups skim milk
3 tablespoons honey
1 cup mashed ripe bananas

1. Bring 1 inch of water to boil in a steamer. Place squash in a steamer basket set over the boiling water and cover. Steam for 20 minutes.
2. Transfer steamed squash to a bowl and mash.
3. Add black pepper, nutmeg, milk, honey, and bananas.
4. Heat gently before serving. Add more skim milk for a thinner consistency.

Calories Per Serving: 135
Fat: .7 g
Cholesterol: 1.5 mg
Protein: 5 g

Carbohydrates: 30 g
Dietary Fiber: 2 g
Sodium: 53 mg

✳ Curried Broccoli-Apple Soup ✳

YIELD: *4 servings (2 cups each)* • PREPARATION TIME: *20 minutes* • COOKING TIME: *45 minutes*

This soup is made with a combination of broccoli, apples, onions, and celery, and can be served hot or cold. Garnish with chopped parsley and nonfat yogurt. Serve with Stuffed Pitas (page 63).

½ cup water, nonfat chicken broth, vegetable broth, or apple juice
2 cups broccoli stems and florets, chopped
1 cup chopped onion
1 cup peeled and diced red cooking apple

½ cup chopped celery
4 cups vegetable broth or nonfat chicken broth
1½ teaspoons curry powder
¼ teaspoon black pepper
¾ cup skim milk

1. Heat ½ cup water, broth, or apple juice in a heavy soup pot over medium heat. Add broccoli, onion, apple, and celery. Cook and stir over low heat for 10 minutes. Add more liquid during this process if necessary.

2. Add 4 cups vegetable or chicken broth, curry powder, and pepper. Bring to a boil.
3. Reduce heat, cover, and simmer for 30 minutes.
4. Purée soup in a food processor or blender.
5. Return purée to soup pot and stir in milk. Heat gently for 5 minutes.

Calories Per Serving: 76	Carbohydrates: 14.2 g
Fat: .6 g	Dietary Fiber: 3 g
Cholesterol: .7 mg	Sodium: 186 mg
Protein: 5.6 g	

✳ *Cauliflower Soup with Confetti Garnish* ✳

YIELD: *8 servings (2 cups each)* • PREPARATION TIME: *15 minutes* • COOKING TIME: *40 minutes*

The rice in this cauliflower soup helps to provide a rich, thick texture. Try adding ¹/₂ cup rice to other puréed soup recipes. Serve this soup hot or cold. Serve with Orange-Radish Salad (page 237).

¹/₄ cup water, nonfat chicken broth, vegetable broth, or wine	6 cups vegetable broth or water
1 cup chopped onion	2 cups skim milk
¹/₂ cup uncooked long-grain white rice	¹/₂ teaspoon white pepper
8 cups cauliflower florets	¹/₂ cup grated red bell pepper
	¹/₂ cup grated carrot
	¹/₂ cup chopped fresh parsley

1. Heat water, broth, or wine in a large, heavy soup pot over medium heat. Add onion. Cook and stir until tender. Add more liquid during this process if necessary.
2. Add rice, cauliflower, and 6 cups of vegetable broth or water. Simmer, covered, for 30 minutes or until the cauliflower and rice are tender.
3. Purée the soup in a food processor or blender.
4. Return the purée to the pot and add the skim milk and white pepper. Serve garnished with the grated red pepper, carrot, and parsley.

Calories Per Serving: 100	Carbohydrates: 20 g
Fat: .4 g	Dietary Fiber: 3.3 g
Cholesterol: 1 mg	Sodium: 57 mg
Protein: 5.3 g	

✳ *Black Bean–Vegetable Soup* ✳

Yield: 6 servings (2 cups each) • *Preparation Time: 15 minutes* •
Cooking Time: 1 hour plus bean cooking time

Serve this rich and flavorful black bean soup garnished with chopped
fresh tomatoes and chopped Spanish onions. Serve with Tex–Mex Pasta
Salad (page 263).

*5 cups nonfat chicken broth,
vegetable broth, or water
5 cloves garlic, minced
1 cup chopped onion
1 cup chopped celery
1/2 cup chopped carrots*

*1/2 cup chopped red bell pepper
1 teaspoon ground coriander
1/4 teaspoon cayenne pepper
5 cups home-cooked or canned black
beans, drained and rinsed*

1. Place broth or water, garlic, onion, celery, carrots, red pepper, coriander, and cayenne in a large, heavy soup pot. Bring to a boil, reduce
   heat, and simmer for 45 minutes.
2. In a blender or food processor, purée 1 1/2 cups of the black beans and
   add to broth with the remaining whole beans. Simmer for 15 minutes.

Variation
▪ Add 1 cup of cooked brown rice to soup with beans. Substitute cumin
  for coriander. Substitute oregano for cayenne pepper. Add 2 tablespoons cider vinegar.

Calories Per Serving: 221
Fat: .9 g
Cholesterol: 0 mg
Protein: 15 g

Carbohydrates: 39 g
Dietary Fiber: 7 g
Sodium: 136 mg

✳ *Old Country Mushroom-Barley Soup* ✳

Yield: 6 servings (2 cups each) • *Preparation Time: 20 minutes* •
Cooking Time: 1 hour

This easy soup is just the thing for a cold night. You can put it on the
stove, sit back and relax for an hour, and then enjoy its soothing warmth.

Serve with a salad of mixed greens and tomatoes with Lemon-Horse-radish Dressing (page 280).

4 cups mushrooms, sliced
1 cup shredded carrots
1 cup chopped fresh or low-sodium
  canned tomatoes
³/₄ cup chopped celery

¹/₂ cup pearl barley
¹/₂ cup chopped fresh parsley
¹/₂ teaspoon black pepper
5¹/₂ cups water

1. Combine the mushrooms, carrots, tomatoes, celery, barley, parsley, black pepper, and water in a large, heavy soup pot.
2. Bring soup to a boil, reduce heat, cover pan, and simmer for 1 hour.

Calories Per Serving: 86
Fat: .5 g
Cholesterol: 0 mg
Protein: 3g

Carbohydrates: 18 g
Dietary Fiber: 4 g
Sodium: 33 mg

✳ *Split Pea Soup with Carrots* ✳

YIELD: 4 servings (2 cups each) ▪ *PREPARATION TIME: 15 minutes*
plus cooling time ▪ *COOKING TIME: 1 hour*

Split peas can sit in a jar on your storage shelf for months and still retain their flavor and abundant nutrients. You'll find this classic soup soul-warming and easy to assemble. Serve with Wild Rice and Apple Salad (page 268).

4 cups water
³/₄ cup dry green split peas
³/₄ cup chopped carrots
¹/₄ cup chopped celery
¹/₄ cup chopped onion

¹/₄ teaspoon dried thyme leaves
Pinch of cayenne pepper
1 teaspoon lemon juice
1 large fresh tomato, chopped

1. Place water, split peas, carrots, celery, onion, thyme, and cayenne pepper in a large soup pot. Bring to a boil.
2. Reduce heat and simmer for 1 hour or until peas are tender.
3. Transfer to a blender or food processor and purée.
4. Return to pot and warm through. Stir in lemon juice.
5. Serve garnished with chopped tomato.

Split Pea Soup with Carrots *(cont'd)*

Calories Per Serving: 64
Fat: .3 g
Cholesterol: 0 mg
Protein: 3 g

Carbohydrates: 12 g
Dietary Fiber: 3.3 g
Sodium: 25 mg

✳ *Green Pea–Spinach Soup* ✳

YIELD: 4 servings (1¾ cups each) • *PREPARATION TIME: 15 minutes plus cooling time* • *COOKING TIME: 20 minutes*

Green peas are combined with nonfat buttermilk, spinach, and basil in this creamy soup. Serve with Vegetable-Tortilla Wraps (page 58).

2½ cups frozen green peas
⅓ cup chopped onion
2½ cups nonfat chicken broth
1 teaspoon dried basil leaves

¾ cup chopped fresh or thawed,
   frozen spinach
1½ cups nonfat buttermilk

1. Combine green peas, onion, chicken broth, basil, and spinach in a saucepan. Simmer for 15 minutes or until the onion is tender.
2. Transfer the green pea–spinach mixture to a blender or food processor and purée.
3. Return puréed mixture to saucepan. Add buttermilk. Heat for 5 minutes or until warmed through.

Calories Per Serving: 124
Fat: .4 g
Cholesterol: 1.9 mg
Protein: 9 g

Carbohydrates: 20 g
Dietary Fiber: 4 g
Sodium: 278 mg

✳ *Great Northern Bean Soup* ✳

YIELD: 12 servings (1½ cups each) • *PREPARATION TIME: 25 minutes* • *COOKING TIME: 45 minutes plus bean cooking time*

These white oval beans have a mild flavor and are perfect for soup recipes. Here they are cooked with kidney beans, green peppers, carrots, celery, zucchini, and onions. Serve with Pumpkin Quick Bread (page 315).

4 cups chopped fresh or low-sodium
   canned tomatoes, with liquid
4 cups home-cooked or canned white
   Great Northern beans, drained
   and rinsed
2 cups home-cooked or canned red
   kidney beans, drained and rinsed
2 cups water
1 cup chopped onions

1 cup chopped green bell pepper
1 cup sliced carrots
1 cup chopped celery
1 1/2 cups chopped zucchini
2 cloves garlic, minced
2 teaspoons chili powder
1 1/2 teaspoons dried basil leaves
1/2 teaspoon black pepper

1. Place tomatoes with their juice, Great Northern beans, kidney beans, water, onions, green pepper, carrots, celery, zucchini, garlic, chili powder, basil leaves, and pepper in a large, heavy soup pot. Bring to a boil.
2. Reduce heat, cover, and simmer for 45 minutes.

Calories Per Serving: 140
Fat: .9 g
Cholesterol: 0 mg
Protein: 8.6 g

Carbohydrates: 26 g
Dietary Fiber: 6.9 g
Sodium: 31 mg

Potato-Tomato Soup with Bell Peppers ✳ and Chiles ✳

YIELD: 6 servings (2 cups each) ▪ *PREPARATION TIME: 20 minutes* ▪
COOKING TIME: 40 minutes

Potatoes are the featured ingredient in this lively soup. Serve with Summer Squash Salad (page 241).

4 potatoes, peeled and cubed
5 1/4 cups water
1 cup chopped onion
2 cloves garlic, minced
1 green bell pepper, seeded and
   chopped
1 cup chopped fresh or low-sodium
   canned tomatoes

1 cup cooked fresh, frozen, or canned
   corn kernels
1/2 cup canned chopped, mild, green
   chiles, drained
1/2 teaspoon dried oregano leaves
1/2 teaspoon black pepper
1/2 cup nonfat grated cheese

Potato-Tomato Soup with Bell Peppers and Chiles *(cont'd)*

1. Place the potatoes in a large, heavy pot with 5 cups of the water. Bring to a boil, cover, reduce heat, and simmer for 15 minutes.
2. While the potatoes are cooking, heat the remaining ¼ cup of water in a skillet over medium heat. Add onion, garlic, and green pepper. Cook and stir over medium heat for 5 minutes or until lightly browned.
3. Remove 1 cup of potatoes from the pot and mash.
4. Return the mashed potatoes along with the onion mixture to the soup pot.
5. Add the tomatoes, corn, chiles, oregano, and black pepper. Simmer for 20 minutes
6. Stir in the cheese. Simmer for 5 minutes.

Calories Per Serving: 126
Fat: .4 g
Cholesterol: .4 mg
Protein: 4 g

Carbohydrates: 28 g
Dietary Fiber: 2.5 g
Sodium: 119 mg

✳ *Bean Bag Soup* ✳

YIELD: *8 servings (2 cups each)* ▪ PREPARATION TIME: *15 minutes plus bean soaking time* ▪ COOKING TIME: *3 hours*

This is a traditional bean soup, starting with dried beans and made the slow-cooking way. Serve with crusty bread and Carrot, Orange, and Celery Salad (page 229).

¼ *cup dried lima beans*
¼ *cup dried lentils*
¼ *cup dried yellow split peas*
¼ *cup dried green split peas*
¼ *cup dried pinto beans*
¼ *cup dried navy beans*
8 *cups water*

¼ *cup pearl barley*
1 *large onion, chopped*
1 *teaspoon chili powder*
½ *teaspoon black pepper*
2 *tablespoons lemon juice*
4 *cups chopped fresh or canned low-sodium tomatoes with liquid*

1. Rinse the lima beans, lentils, yellow split peas, green split peas, pinto beans, and dried navy beans. Depending on how much time you have, either cover with cold water and soak overnight; or cover with cold water, bring to a boil, cover tightly, and let sit for 1 hour.

2. Drain the beans and place in a large, heavy pot with the water. Bring to a boil, reduce heat, and cook for $2\frac{1}{2}$ hours.
3. Add the barley, onion, chili powder, black pepper, lemon juice, and canned tomatoes. Simmer for 30 more minutes.

Calories Per Serving: 96	Carbohydrates: 19.7 g
Fat: .6 g	Dietary Fiber: 4.3 g
Cholesterol: 0 mg	Sodium: 31 mg
Protein: 4.8 g	

❋ *Red Pepper–Plum Tomato Soup with Dill* ❋

YIELD: 6 servings ($1\frac{1}{2}$ cups each) • *PREPARATION TIME: 25 minutes* • *COOKING TIME: 30 minutes*

This rich tomato soup can be enjoyed warm or cold. Garnish with nonfat sour cream and additional dill. Serve with Black Bean Salad (page 257).

$\frac{1}{2}$ cup water, nonfat chicken broth, vegetable broth, or wine
1 large onion, finely chopped
1 cup diced red bell pepper
$\frac{1}{2}$ cup chopped celery
2 cloves garlic, minced
4 cups chopped low-sodium canned plum tomatoes

2 tablespoons low-sodium tomato purée or tomato paste
$\frac{1}{2}$ cup chopped mushrooms
3 cups vegetable broth
$\frac{1}{2}$ teaspoon dried dill leaves
$\frac{1}{4}$ teaspoon ground white pepper
$\frac{1}{4}$ teaspoon ground cumin

1. Heat water, broth, or wine in a large, heavy soup pot over medium heat. Add onion, red pepper, and celery. Cook and stir for 3 minutes. Stir in garlic. Cook for 2 more minutes. Add more liquid during this process if necessary.
2. Add tomatoes, tomato purée, mushrooms, and vegetable broth. Cover pan and bring to a boil.
3. Lower heat and simmer for 25 minutes.
4. Purée soup in a food processor or blender. Add dill, white pepper, and cumin. Reheat or cool as desired.

Calories Per Serving: 57	Carbohydrates: 11 g
Fat: .6 g	Dietary Fiber: 2.1 g
Cholesterol: 0 mg	Sodium: 101 mg
Protein: 3 g	

✳ *Potato-Leek Soup* ✳

YIELD: *4 servings (2 cups each)* • PREPARATION TIME: *20 minutes plus cooling time* • COOKING TIME: *30 minutes*

A leek is a variety of onion with a different mild flavor, but it looks like a very large scallion. In this soup, chopped leeks are combined with red potatoes, onion, and chicken or vegetable broth. Serve with Chili-Bean Heroes (page 62).

1 cup chopped onion	*¼ teaspoon ground white pepper*
2 cups chopped red potatoes	*1 tablespoon minced scallion*
1 cup chopped leeks	*¼ cup chopped fresh parsley*
4 cups nonfat chicken broth or vegetable broth	

1. Place onion, potatoes, leeks, broth, and white pepper in a large, heavy soup pot.
2. Cover and bring to a boil. Lower heat and simmer for 30 minutes.
3. Transfer to a food processor or blender and purée.
4. Stir in scallion and parsley. Serve.

Calories Per Serving: 107	Carbohydrates: 22 g
Fat: .3 g	Dietary Fiber: 2 g
Cholesterol: 0 mg	Sodium: 147 mg
Protein: 4 g	

✳ *Pinto Bean Chili Soup* ✳

YIELD: *8 servings (1½ cups each)* • PREPARATION TIME: *15 minutes* • COOKING TIME: *40 minutes plus bean cooking time*

This soup tastes like a great bowl of chili. It's a good dish to make the night before, refrigerate, and heat up quickly on a busy day. Serve with Sugar Snap Pea Salad (page 242).

2¼ cups water	*3½ cups chopped fresh or low-*
1 cup chopped onion	*sodium canned tomatoes, with*
3½ cups home-cooked or canned	*liquid*
pinto beans, drained and rinsed	*1 tablespoon chili powder*

³/₄ cup tomato purée or low-sodium   *1 teaspoon ground cumin*
  tomato paste

1. Heat ¹/₄ cup of the water in a large soup pot over medium heat. Add the onion. Cook and stir the onion over medium heat for 5 minutes or until tender. Add more liquid during this process if necessary.
2. Place the beans in a blender or food processor and process for 30 seconds. Set aside.
3. Place the tomatoes in the blender or food processor and process for 30 seconds.
4. Add the remaining 2 cups of water, beans and tomatoes, tomato purée or tomato paste, chili powder, and ground cumin to the onions in the saucepan. Stir well.
5. Bring to a boil, reduce heat, and simmer for 30 minutes.

Calories Per Serving: 142   Carbohydrates: 27 g
Fat: 1 g   Dietary Fiber: 7.4 g
Cholesterol: 0 mg   Sodium: 33 mg
Protein: 8.3 g

✳ *Butternut-Zucchini-Apple Soup* ✳

YIELD: 6 servings (1 cup each) • *PREPARATION TIME: 20 minutes* •
COOKING TIME: 35 minutes

This soup combines winter and summer squash with apple, ginger, nutmeg, cumin, cinnamon, and coriander. Soften the butternut squash before cutting by microwaving on HIGH for 1 minute. Serve with Whole-Grain Veggie Sandwiches (page 61).

¹/₂ cup dry sherry   *2 cups cubed zucchini*
¹/₂ cup chopped onion   *1 apple, peeled, cored, and chopped*
1 clove garlic, minced   *¹/₂ teaspoon ground coriander*
1 tablespoon grated fresh gingerroot *¹/₂ teaspoon ground nutmeg*
1 cup nonfat chicken broth or   *¹/₄ teaspoon ground cumin*
  vegetable broth   *¹/₄ teaspoon ground cinnamon*
1 cup apple juice   *1 tablespoon lemon juice*
1 cup peeled and cubed butternut
  squash

Butternut-Zucchini-Apple Soup *(cont'd)*

1. Warm dry sherry in a heavy soup pot over medium heat. Add onion, garlic, and gingerroot. Cook and stir over medium heat for 5 minutes or until lightly browned.
2. Add broth, apple juice, butternut squash, zucchini, apple, coriander, nutmeg, cumin, and cinnamon. Simmer for 25 minutes.
3. Place in a food processor or blender and purée. Return to pot, stir in lemon juice, and heat for 5 minutes or until warmed through.

Variations
- Delete apple juice in Step 2. Increase broth to 2 cups. Stir in 1 cup of buttermilk after soup is puréed in Step 3.
- Stir in ¹/₂ cup cooked rice in Step 3.
- Delete coriander, nutmeg, cumin, and cinnamon. Substitute 1 tablespoon curry powder.

Calories Per Serving: 77
Fat: .4g
Cholesterol: 0 mg
Protein: 1 g

Carbohydrates: 15 g
Dietary Fiber: 2 g
Sodium: 27 mg

COLD SOUPS

::

✳ Gazpacho ✳

YIELD: 6 servings (1½ cups each) • *PREPARATION TIME: 20 minutes
plus 1 hour chilling time*

This tomato-based gazpacho is made without oil. It should be served
chilled in chilled bowls. Serve with croutons made with whole wheat
bread, toasted until dry, rubbed with garlic, and cut into cubes. Garnish
with lemon slices.

*1 medium cucumber, peeled and
   seeded
1 small zucchini, diced
3 large ripe tomatoes, peeled
2 medium oranges, chopped
1 stalk celery, diced
½ cup chopped green bell pepper
½ cup chopped red onion
2 cloves garlic, minced*

*5 tablespoons lime or lemon juice
2 cups low-sodium tomato or
   vegetable juice such as V-8
½ cup fresh chopped parsley
1 tablespoon dried basil leaves
Pinch of cayenne pepper
½ teaspoon ground cumin
½ teaspoon chili powder*

1. Combine cucumber, zucchini, tomatoes, oranges, celery, green pepper, red onion, garlic, lime or lemon juice, tomato or vegetable juice, parsley, basil leaves, cayenne pepper, ground cumin, and chili powder in a large bowl.
2. Transfer to a food processor or blender and process until partially puréed. Chill for at least 1 hour.

Variations
- Substitute ⅓ cup red wine vinegar for the lime juice.
- Add 1 small green chile, seeded and chopped in Step 1.
- Substitute 1 cup nonfat chicken broth for 1 cup of the tomato juice in Step 1.
- Add 2 teaspoons dried mint, ½ teaspoon ground coriander, and

Gazpacho *(cont'd)*

¼ teaspoon ground allspice in Step 1. Delete cayenne pepper and cumin.

- Substitute 1½ cups cooked corn for the oranges. Do not purée the gazpacho before chilling.

Calories Per Serving: 72
Fat: .5 g
Cholesterol: 0 mg
Protein: 2.5 g

Carbohydrates: 17 g
Dietary Fiber: 4 g
Sodium: 19 mg

✷ Chilled Yellow Squash Soup ✷

YIELD: 4 servings (1¾ cup each) • PREPARATION TIME: 20 minutes plus 1 hour chilling time • COOKING TIME: 15 minutes

Squash is one of a trio of vegetables—corn and beans being the other two—that sustained Indians of North and South America, and also the American colonists. Yellow squash, green peas, carrot, and celery are combined with chicken broth and nonfat sour cream in this soup. Serve with Black Bean Sandwiches Deluxe (page 58).

2⅓ cups nonfat chicken broth or
    vegetable broth
1 clove garlic, minced
3 cups chopped yellow summer
    squash
¾ cup chopped carrot

½ cup chopped celery
¾ cup frozen green peas
½ cup water
½ teaspoon dried dill leaves
⅓ cup nonfat sour cream

1. Place broth, garlic, yellow summer squash, carrot, celery, green peas, water, and dill in a large soup pot. Bring to a boil.
2. Cover, reduce heat, and simmer for 15 minutes.
3. Transfer soup to a blender or food processor and process until smooth.
4. Transfer to a bowl, stir in sour cream, and chill for at least 1 hour.

Calories Per Serving: 59
Fat: .3 g
Cholesterol: .2 mg
Protein: 4 g

Carbohydrates: 10 g
Dietary Fiber: 3.5 g
Sodium: 131 mg

❈ *Sweet Potato—Carrot Soup* ❈

YIELD: 6 servings (2 cups each) • *PREPARATION TIME: 25 minutes* •
COOKING TIME: 20 minutes plus 4 hours chilling time

Sweet potatoes, carrots, and onion are accented with ginger in this refreshing chilled soup. Serve with Big Bean Salad Bowl (page 259).

1 onion, thinly sliced
3 cups thinly sliced carrots
3 cups sliced sweet potatoes
1/2 teaspoon ground ginger

6 cups nonfat chicken broth or
vegetable broth
1/3 cup plain nonfat yogurt
1/4 teaspoon ground white pepper

1. Place onion, carrots, sweet potatoes, ginger, and broth in a heavy soup pot. Cover and bring to a boil.
2. Reduce heat and simmer for 20 minutes or until carrots and sweet potatoes are tender.
3. Strain the soup, reserving both the solids and the liquid.
4. Place the solids in a food processor or blender and purée for 2 minutes.
5. Combine purée with reserved liquid, yogurt, and white pepper. Chill for 4 hours.

Calories Per Serving: 85
Fat: .2 g
Cholesterol: 0 mg
Protein: 3.5 g

Carbohydrates: 18 g
Dietary Fiber: 3 g
Sodium: 159 mg

❈ *Apple-Plum Soup* ❈

YIELD: 4 servings (1 cup each) • *PREPARATION TIME: 10 minutes plus 4 hours*
chilling time • *COOKING TIME: 12 minutes*

Juicy plums are the stars in this chilled soup. Shop for plums that are firm but resilient with a deep color. They should be ready to eat when you buy them. Serve with Vegetable-Macaroni Salad (page 261).

1/2 cup apple juice concentrate
5 large plums, pitted and chopped

1/4 teaspoon ground cinnamon
1 1/2 cups nonfat plain yogurt

Apple-Plum Soup *(cont'd)*

1. Bring apple juice concentrate to a boil in a heavy saucepan. Add plums and cinnamon.
2. Cover saucepan, reduce heat, and simmer for 12 minutes.
3. Place plums and juice in a food processor or blender and process until smooth.
4. Transfer to a bowl and stir in yogurt. Chill for 4 hours.

Calories Per Serving: 101	Carbohydrates: 21 g
Fat: .2 g	Dietary Fiber: .7 g
Cholesterol: 1.5 mg	Sodium: 70 mg
Protein: 5 g	

✳ *Blueberry-Orange Soup* ✳

YIELD: 4 servings (1 cup each) • *PREPARATION TIME: 10 minutes plus 4 hours chilling time*

Fresh or frozen blueberries are blended with orange juice, yogurt, and brown sugar in this soup. When shopping for fresh blueberries, avoid those that look dull, shriveled, or sticky. Watch for those that are completely blue, clean, and very dry. Serve with Penne Primavera with Garlic-Tomato Dressing (page 267).

3 cups fresh or frozen blueberries	*1/3 cup nonfat plain yogurt*
1 cup skim milk	*2 tablespoons brown sugar, firmly*
1/3 cup orange juice	*packed*

1. Combine 2 1/2 cups of the blueberries, milk, orange juice, yogurt, and brown sugar in a food processor or blender. Process until smooth.
2. Pour soup into a large bowl and stir in remaining 1/2 cup of blueberries. Chill for 4 hours.

Calories Per Serving: 128	Carbohydrates: 28 g
Fat: .6 g	Dietary Fiber: 2.7 g
Cholesterol: 1.3 mg	Sodium: 55 mg
Protein: 4 g	

✹ *Nectarine Soup* ✹

YIELD: 6 servings (1 cup each) • *PREPARATION TIME: 10 minutes*
plus 4 hours chilling time

Nectarines are not only delicious—they're also loaded with vitamin A. Here nectarines and strawberries are blended in a delicate cold soup. Serve with Green Bean and Red Pepper Salad (page 236).

5 nectarines, pitted and sliced
1 cup plain nonfat yogurt
2 cups skim milk

¼ teaspoon curry powder
½ cup fresh, hulled strawberries, sliced

1. Set aside ¾ cup nectarine slices.
2. Combine remaining nectarine, yogurt, milk, and curry powder in a food processor or blender and process until smooth.
3. Transfer to a serving bowl and stir in reserved nectarines and strawberries. Chill for 4 hours.

Calories Per Serving: 110
Fat: .8 g
Cholesterol: 2 mg
Protein: 6 g

Carbohydrates: 21 g
Dietary Fiber: 2 g
Sodium: 71 mg

✹ *Pear Soup* ✹

YIELD: 6 servings (1 cup each) • *PREPARATION TIME: 15 minutes*
plus 4 hours chilling time

Serve this chilled pear soup with a scoop of fruit-flavored nonfat frozen yogurt.

4 large pears, peeled, cored, and sliced
½ teaspoon grated orange peel
2 tablespoons lime juice

¼ teaspoon ground ginger
¼ teaspoon ground nutmeg
2 tablespoons maple syrup
2 cups nonfat buttermilk

1. Place pears, orange peel, and lime juice in a blender or food processor. Purée until smooth.

Pear Soup *(cont'd)*

2. Pass the purée through a fine sieve, pushing down on solids to extract as much liquid as possible. Discard solids.

3. Add ginger, nutmeg, maple syrup, and buttermilk to pear mixture and chill for 4 hours.

Calories Per Serving: 114	Carbohydrates: 26 g
Fat: .5 g	Dietary Fiber 2.8 g
Cholesterol: 1.7 mg	Sodium: 99 mg
Protein: 3 g	

MAIN DISHES

Vegetable Stew with Herbes de Provence • Ratatouille with Red Wine • Cauliflower Curry • Couscous and Vegetables • Stuffed Eggplant • Chick-peas with Vegetables and Couscous • Lima Bean Stew • Zucchini and Pattypan Casserole • Vegetable Succotash • Greek Zucchini Casserole • Lentil-Vegetable Stew • Baked Mixed Vegetable Biriyani • Garden Burgers • Potato-Tomato Curry • Turkish Vegetables • Tropical Mixed Vegetables • Many Vegetable Medley • Vegetable Paella • Harvest Stew • Spiced Eggplant • Pasta-Vegetable Casserole • Vegetable Curry • Broccoli Roll-Ups • Broccoli Pizza with Quick and Easy Crust • Steamed Vegetables with Garlic-Lemon Sauce • Vegetable Risotto • Broccoli-Stuffed Shells • Grilled Garden Kabobs • Orzo with Red Peppers, Cauliflower, and Broccoli • Quinoa with Vegetables • Bow Ties with Eggplant Sauce • Conchiglie with Cauliflower and Sun-Dried Tomatoes • Angel Hair Pasta with Steamed Vegetables and Garlic Sauce • Multicolored Shells with Broccoli, Mushrooms, Red Peppers, and Ricotta Cheese • Vermicelli with Roasted Peppers • Cavatelli with Simmered Vegetable Sauce • Tomato Linguine • Ziti with Great Northern Beans • Spinach Fettucine with Shiitake-Tomato Sauce • Fusilli with Lentil Sauce • Spinach-Mushroom Lasagna • Eggplant Del Rio • Black Bean Lasagna • Potato-Broccoli Chili • Cannellini–

Northern Bean Chili • Three-Bean Chili • Chili with Vegetables and Bulgur • Acorn Squash with Black Beans • New Year's Black-Eyed Peas and Rice • Lentils with Rice and Curry • Havana Beans with Rice • Tostadas • Bean Tortilla Bake • Baked Potatoes with Baked Beans • Apple-Bean Jumble

MAIN DISHES

::

✳ *Vegetable Stew with Herbes de Provence* ✳

YIELD: *6 servings* • PREPARATION TIME: *20 minutes* •
COOKING TIME: *20 minutes*

Eggplant, summer squash, onion, green bell pepper, and mushrooms are prepared with basil, thyme, rosemary, and parsley in this dish. Serve with rice, pasta, or steamed new potatoes and Cranberry Poached Peaches (page 213).

3/4 cup water, nonfat chicken broth, or vegetable broth
1 clove garlic, minced
1 tablespoon low-sodium tomato paste
1 cup diced zucchini squash
1 cup diced yellow summer squash
2 cups diced eggplant
1 cup diced green bell pepper

1/2 cup diced onion
1 cup sliced mushrooms
1 tablespoon dried basil leaves
1/2 teaspoon dried thyme leaves
1/2 teaspoon dried rosemary leaves
1/4 teaspoon black pepper
1/4 cup chopped fresh parsley
1 teaspoon balsamic vinegar

1. Place 1/4 cup of the water or broth in a large, heavy soup pot. Add garlic and tomato paste. Cook and stir over medium heat for 5 minutes. Add more liquid if necessary during this process.
2. Add the remaining 1/2 cup water or broth, zucchini, yellow summer squash, eggplant, green pepper, onion, and mushrooms to the pot.
3. Cover and simmer for 15 minutes or until vegetables are tender.
4. Stir in basil, thyme, rosemary, black pepper, parsley, and balsamic vinegar.

Calories Per Serving: 35
Fat: .4 g
Cholesterol: 0 mg
Protein: 1.6 g

Carbohydrates: 7.7 g
Dietary Fiber: 2.4 g
Sodium: 7 mg

✳ *Ratatouille with Red Wine* ✳

YIELD: *6 servings* • PREPARATION TIME: *25 minutes* •
COOKING TIME: *40 minutes*

This ratatouille is made in a red wine sauce with yellow summer squash
and cucumber. Serve with Whole Wheat Baguettes (page 310).

1 medium eggplant, diced	½ cup low-sodium tomato purée or
1 cup chopped onion	tomato paste
3 cups sliced yellow summer squash	1 garlic clove, crushed
1 large green bell pepper, seeded and	1 cup red wine or red grape juice
diced	1 teaspoon sugar
1 cup peeled, sliced cucumber	1 teaspoon dried basil leaves
2 cups fresh or low-sodium canned	Pinch of cayenne pepper
chopped tomatoes	

1. Place eggplant, onion, squash, green pepper, cucumber, tomatoes,
   tomato paste or purée, garlic, red wine or grape juice, sugar, basil, and
   cayenne pepper in a large, heavy saucepan.
2. Simmer over low heat for 40 minutes or until vegetables are tender.

Calories Per Serving: 83	Carbohydrates: 15 g
Fat: .7 g	Dietary Fiber: 4.9 g
Cholesterol: 0 mg	Sodium: 35 mg
Protein: 3 g	

✳ *Cauliflower Curry* ✳

YIELD: *4 servings* • PREPARATION TIME: *25 minutes* •
COOKING TIME: *25 minutes*

Cauliflower, potatoes, carrots, red bell pepper, onion, and peas are simmered in a curry-flavored, sauce. Serve with Green Bean and Tomato
Salad with Lemon-Garlic Dressing (page 235).

2 cups nonfat chicken broth or	1 white potato, cut into large chunks
vegetable broth	2 large carrots, cut into chunks
1 cup cauliflower florets	½ red bell pepper, seeded and diced

½ onion, diced
½ cup fresh or frozen green peas
1 tablespoon curry powder
1 clove garlic, minced

3 tablespoons seedless raisins
2 tablespoons honey
½ cup plain nonfat yogurt

1. Bring chicken broth to a boil in a large pot.
2. Add cauliflower, potato, carrots, red pepper, onion, peas, curry powder, garlic, raisins, and honey. Cover partially and simmer for 20 minutes, or until vegetables are tender.
3. Remove from heat, stir in yogurt, and serve.

Variation
• Substitute 1 can chopped tomatoes for 1 cup of the broth in Step 1. Delete the potato, red bell pepper, and peas. Substitute 2 cups green beans, cut in 1-inch pieces. Delete raisins and honey in Step 2. Substitute ¾ teaspoon ground cumin and ½ teaspoon cinnamon. Delete yogurt in Step 3.

Calories Per Serving: 156
Fat: .6 g
Cholesterol: .5 mg
Protein: 5.9 g

Carbohydrates: 34 g
Dietary Fiber: 4.2 g
Sodium: 128 mg

✳ *Couscous and Vegetables* ✳

YIELD: 4 servings • *PREPARATION TIME: 25 minutes* •
COOKING TIME: 25 minutes

Couscous is a tiny pasta that is shaped by pushing wheat flour dough through a screen. Both whole wheat and refined instant couscous are ready in five minutes or less. This recipe features couscous with onion, corn, tomato purée, green peppers, and mushrooms. Serve with Fruit Salad with Pineapple-Spice Dressing (page 218).

1¾ cup nonfat chicken broth,
    vegetable broth, or water
½ cup chopped onion
1 clove garlic, minced
¾ cup fresh, frozen, or canned corn
    kernels

½ cup chopped green bell peppers
½ cup chopped mushrooms
3 cups low-sodium tomato purée
1 teaspoon chili powder
1 teaspoon balsamic vinegar
1 cup instant couscous

Couscous and Vegetables *(cont'd)*

1. Heat ¹/₄ cup of the broth or water in a large skillet over medium heat. Add onion and garlic. Cook and stir over medium heat for 5 minutes. Add more liquid if necessary during this process.
2. Add corn, green pepper, and mushrooms. Cook and stir for 5 more minutes.
3. Add tomato purée, chili powder, and balsamic vinegar. Simmer for 15 minutes.
4. While vegetables are simmering, bring the remaining 1¹/₂ cups broth or water to a boil in a saucepan. Add the couscous. Cover the pan and remove from heat. Let stand for 5 minutes.
5. Spoon vegetables over couscous and serve.

Calories Per Serving: 158	Carbohydrates: 36 g
Fat: .6 g	Dietary Fiber: 5.9 g
Cholesterol: 0 mg	Sodium: 81 mg
Protein: 6.4 g	

✳ *Stuffed Eggplant* ✳

YIELD: 6 servings • *PREPARATION TIME: 25 minutes* •
COOKING TIME: 45 minutes

Here eggplant is stuffed with onion, celery, green pepper, tomatoes, and herbs. Serve with Puffed Potato Casserole (page 192).

*2 medium eggplants
(about 1 pound each)*
*¹/₄ cup water, chicken broth,
vegetable broth, or wine*
1 onion, chopped
1 stalk celery, chopped
2 cloves garlic, minced
1 small green bell pepper, chopped
*1 cup chopped fresh or low-sodium
canned tomatoes*

¹/₄ cup chopped fresh parsley
¹/₂ teaspoon dried basil leaves
¹/₂ teaspoon dried thyme leaves
¹/₄ teaspoon black pepper
Pinch of cayenne pepper
*¹/₄ cup low-sodium tomato juice or
water*
*¹/₂ cup nonfat whole-grain bread
crumbs*

1. Preheat oven to 375 degrees.
2. Cut the stem ends off of the eggplants and cut the eggplants in half

lengthwise. Remove pulp, leaving a shell of ¼ inch. Chop the eggplant pulp and set aside.

3. Heat the water, broth, or wine in a large skillet over medium heat. Add onion, celery, and garlic. Cook and stir over medium heat for 5 minutes. Add more liquid during this process if necessary.

4. Add reserved eggplant pulp, green pepper, tomatoes, parsley, basil leaves, thyme, black pepper, cayenne pepper, and tomato juice or water.

5. Simmer until eggplant is tender, about 5 minutes. Stir in bread crumbs.

6. Place eggplant shells close together on a nonstick baking dish. Stuff eggplant shells with vegetable mixture.

7. Bake for 35 minutes or until shells are tender.

Calories Per Serving: 84	Carbohydrates: 18 g
Fat: .9 g	Dietary Fiber: 4 g
Cholesterol: 0 mg	Sodium: 138 mg
Protein: 2.9 g	

✳ *Chick-peas with Vegetables and Couscous* ✳

YIELD: 8 servings • *PREPARATION TIME: 25 minutes plus 10 minutes standing time and bean cooking time* • *COOKING TIME: 40 minutes*

Chick-peas, zucchini, red onion, bell peppers, new potatoes, and raisins are prepared in a wine sauce and served over instant couscous in this dish.

½ cup water, nonfat chicken broth, or vegetable broth
¾ cup thinly sliced red onion
3 yellow, green, or red bell peppers, seeded and thinly sliced
1½ cups sliced new potatoes
¾ cup home-cooked or canned chick-peas, rinsed and drained
¼ cup raisins
2 cups sliced zucchini

2 tablespoons low-sodium tomato paste
1 teaspoon ground coriander
1 teaspoon ground cumin
Pinch of cayenne pepper
1 clove garlic, minced
½ teaspoon paprika
¼ cup white wine
1½ cups instant couscous

1. Heat water or broth in a skillet over medium heat. Add onion. Cook and stir over medium heat for 5 minutes or until lightly browned. Add

Chick-Peas with Vegetables and Couscous *(cont'd)*

    bell peppers, cook and stir for 5 minutes more. Add more liquid during this process if necessary.
2. Add the potatoes, chick-peas, raisins, zucchini, tomato paste, coriander, cumin, cayenne pepper, garlic, paprika, and wine.
3. Cover and simmer for 35 minutes. Let stand 10 minutes before serving.
4. Bring 2¼ cups water to a boil in a medium pan. Add couscous, cover and remove from heat. Let stand for 5 minutes.
5. Transfer couscous to a serving platter. Top with vegetables.

Calories Per Serving: 120　　Carbohydrates: 23 g
Fat: .8 g　　Dietary Fiber: 1.9 g
Cholesterol: 0 mg　　Sodium: 17 mg
Protein: 3.6 g

✳ *Lima Bean Stew* ✳

Yield: 6 servings • *Preparation Time: 20 minutes plus lima bean thawing time* • *Cooking Time: 30 minutes*

This creole recipe joins lima beans and tomatoes. Serve with hot basmati rice and Pineapple-Watercress Salad (page 240).

¼ cup water, chicken broth, vegetable broth, or wine
1 medium onion, chopped
2 cloves garlic, minced
2 teaspoons unbleached all-purpose flour
1 medium green or yellow bell pepper, seeded and chopped

2 cups chopped fresh or low-sodium canned tomatoes
¼ cup water
4 cups frozen lima beans, thawed
¼ cup chopped fresh parsley
½ teaspoon dried thyme leaves
Pinch of cayenne pepper
¼ teaspoon black pepper

1. Heat water, broth, or wine in a large skillet over medium heat. Add onion and garlic. Cook and stir over medium heat for 5 minutes. Add more liquid during this process if necessary.
2. Sprinkle the flour over the onions and stir.
3. Add the bell pepper and the tomatoes to the skillet. Simmer, covered, for 10 minutes.

4. Add ¼ cup water, lima beans, parsley, thyme, cayenne pepper, and black pepper. Cover and simmer for 15 minutes over very low heat.

Calories Per Serving: 139   Carbohydrates: 26 g
Fat: .6 g   Dietary Fiber: 6.8 g
Cholesterol: 0 mg   Sodium: 66 mg
Protein: 7.8 g

❋ *Zucchini and Pattypan Casserole* ❋

YIELD: *6 servings* • PREPARATION TIME: *15 minutes plus rice cooking time* •
COOKING TIME: *30 minutes*

Here zucchini and scalloped pattypan squash are baked with rice and bread crumbs in a dill-yogurt sauce. Serve with Cranberry Applesauce (page 206).

2 cups nonfat plain yogurt
⅓ cup grated nonfat cheddar cheese
2 egg whites, lightly beaten
¼ cup chopped onions
3 cups cooked white or brown rice
2 cups diced zucchini

2 cups diced pattypan or yellow
*   summer squash*
1 cup diced red bell pepper
½ teaspoon dried dill leaves
½ cup nonfat whole-grain bread
*   crumbs*

1. Preheat oven to 350 degrees.
2. Combine yogurt and cheese in a small saucepan. Heat over very low heat until cheese melts.
3. Stir in egg whites and onions. Remove from heat, cover and set aside.
4. Spread the rice on the bottom of a medium-sized baking dish.
5. Combine the zucchini, pattypan or yellow summer squash, red pepper, and dill. Place on top of the rice.
6. Pour the yogurt-cheese mixture over the squash and rice and top with bread crumbs.
7. Bake for 30 minutes or until crumbs are lightly browned and squash is just tender.

Calories Per Serving: 216   Carbohydrates: 41 g
Fat: .9 g   Dietary Fiber: 2.9 g
Cholesterol: 1.6 mg   Sodium: 116 mg
Protein: 10 g

✳ *Vegetable Succotash* ✳

YIELD: 6 servings • *PREPARATION TIME: 25 minutes plus potato and corn cooking time* • *COOKING TIME: 30 minutes*

Here green bell peppers, potatoes, corn, lima beans, and tomatoes make a simple, hearty dish. Serve with Pears with Red Wine (page 212).

¼ cup water, chicken broth, vegetable broth, or wine
1 medium onion, chopped
1 green bell pepper, seeded and diced
2 medium potatoes, cooked, peeled, and diced
2 cups fresh or frozen lima beans

2 cups fresh, frozen, or canned corn kernels
2 cups chopped fresh or low-sodium canned tomatoes
1 teaspoon paprika
¼ teaspoon black pepper

1. Heat water in a large, heavy pot over medium heat. Add onion. Cook and stir over medium heat for 5 minutes. Add more liquid if necessary during this process.
2. Add green pepper. Cook and stir for 5 more minutes, adding liquid if necessary.
3. Add the potatoes, lima beans, corn, tomatoes, paprika, and black pepper. Simmer, covered, for 20 minutes.

Calories Per Serving: 173
Fat: .5 g
Cholesterol: 0 mg
Protein: 7 g

Carbohydrates: 38 g
Dietary Fiber: 6.7 g
Sodium: 18 mg

✳ *Greek Zucchini Casserole* ✳

YIELD: 6 servings • *PREPARATION TIME: 25 minutes plus 10 minutes standing time* • *COOKING TIME: 1 hour and 10 minutes*

In this dish broiled zucchini slices are baked in a casserole with tomato sauce and nonfat cottage cheese flavored with rosemary and mint. Serve with Mashed Potatoes and Carrots (page 191).

¼ cup water, nonfat chicken broth, or vegetable broth

1 cup chopped onion
1 clove garlic, minced

2 cups chopped fresh or low-sodium
   canned tomatoes
1/2 teaspoon dried rosemary leaves
1 teaspoon dried mint leaves
1/4 cup chopped fresh parsley
1 teaspoon honey
1/4 teaspoon black pepper
1 cup low-sodium tomato sauce

2 cups nonfat cottage cheese
2 egg whites, lightly beaten
2 large zucchini, sliced 1/2 inch thick
1/2 cup nonfat grated Parmesan
   cheese

1. Heat water or broth in a heavy saucepan over medium heat. Add onion and garlic. Cook and stir over medium heat for 5 minutes or until vegetables are lightly browned. Add more liquid during this process if necessary.
2. Add tomatoes, rosemary, mint, parsley, honey, black pepper, and tomato sauce. Cover and simmer for 15 minutes.
3. In a bowl combine cottage cheese and egg white. Chill until ready to assemble casserole.
4. Broil zucchini on both sides until lightly browned.
5. Preheat oven to 375 degrees.
6. To assemble, place half of the sauce in the bottom of a 9-by-13-inch baking dish. Sprinkle with half of the Parmesan cheese. Place a layer of zucchini on top of the sauce and Parmesan, and top with the cottage cheese–egg mixture. Layer with the remaining zucchini slices and top with the rest of the tomato sauce and Parmesan cheese.
7. Bake for 45 minutes. Let stand for 10 minutes before cutting.

Calories Per Serving: 74
Fat: .4 g
Cholesterol: 1 mg
Protein: 6 g

Carbohydrates: 12.8 g
Dietary Fiber: 3 g
Sodium: 79 mg

✳ *Lentil-Vegetable Stew* ✳

YIELD: *6 servings* • PREPARATION TIME: *25 minutes* •
COOKING TIME: *1 hour and 15 minutes*

In this stew lentils, onions, carrots, leeks, turnips, potatoes, and celery are simmered in a tomato sauce. Serve with Harvest Quick Bread (page 316).

Lentil-Vegetable Stew *(cont'd)*

1 cup brown lentils
4 cups water or vegetable broth
1 onion, chopped
2 cloves garlic, chopped
4 carrots, diced
1 leek, sliced
2 turnips, diced
2 medium potatoes, peeled and diced

2 stalks celery, chopped
1/2 teaspoon dried rosemary leaves
4 cups chopped fresh or low-sodium canned plum tomatoes
1/2 teaspoon black pepper
1 tablespoon lemon juice
3 tablespoons chopped fresh parsley

1. Place lentils, water, onion, garlic, carrots, leek, turnips, potatoes, celery, and rosemary in a large, heavy soup pot. Bring to a boil, cover, and simmer for 50 minutes, or until lentils are tender.
2. Add tomatoes and black pepper. Simmer for 25 minutes.
3. Stir in lemon juice and garnish with parsley.

Calories Per Serving: 163
Fat: .8g
Cholesterol: 0 mg
Protein: 6.7 g

Carbohydrates: 36 g
Dietary Fiber: 2.7 g
Sodium: 98 mg

✳ *Baked Mixed Vegetable Biriyani* ✳

YIELD: 8 servings ▪ *PREPARATION TIME: 20 minutes plus rice-cooking time* ▪
COOKING TIME: 55 minutes

This spicy Indian dish is a symphony of vegetables and accent flavors. Serve with Broiled Pineapple (page 215).

1/4 teaspoon powdered saffron
1/2 cup lemon juice
6 cups cooked long-grain white or brown rice
1/2 cup water, nonfat chicken broth, or vegetable broth
1/2 teaspoon ground cumin
Pinch of cayenne pepper
3/4 cup chopped broccoli
3/4 cup chopped cauliflower

3/4 cup chopped yellow summer squash
3/4 cup chopped onion
1 cup potato chunks
1/2 cup sliced carrots
1/2 cup chopped green bell pepper
1 cup frozen green peas
1/2 cup raisins
2 cups plain nonfat yogurt

1. Preheat oven to 325 degrees.
2. Dissolve the saffron in the lemon juice. Stir the saffron–lemon juice mixture into the cooked rice.
3. Heat the water or broth in a skillet over medium heat. Add cumin, cayenne, broccoli, cauliflower, yellow summer squash, onion, potato, carrots, green pepper, and green peas. Cover and simmer for 10 minutes or until vegetables are just tender.
4. Toss the rice and vegetables together. Transfer to a 9-by-13-inch baking dish. Sprinkle with raisins. Spoon yogurt over the top.
5. Cover and bake for 35 minutes.

Calories Per Serving: 272
Fat: .7 g
Cholesterol: 1 mg
Protein: 9 g

Carbohydrates: 57 g
Dietary Fiber: 3.7 g
Sodium: 72 mg

✳ *Garden Burgers* ✳

YIELD: 6 servings ▪ *PREPARATION TIME: 25 minutes plus potato baking time* ▪
COOKING TIME: 10 minutes

These delicious patties are a mixture of five vegetables and mashed potatoes. Serve them with Simple Tomato Sauce (page 288).

¼ cup water, nonfat chicken broth, or vegetable broth
½ cup chopped fresh or canned low-sodium tomatoes
½ cup finely chopped red bell pepper
½ cup finely chopped green bell pepper
½ cup finely chopped zucchini
1 cup finely chopped onion

½ cup frozen peas, thawed
½ cup frozen corn, thawed
½ teaspoon dried thyme leaves
3 large potatoes, cooked and peeled
3 egg whites, lightly beaten
¼ cup skim milk
1 cup nonfat whole wheat bread crumbs

1. Heat water or broth in a large nonstick skillet over medium heat. Add tomatoes, red pepper, green pepper, celery, zucchini, and onions. Cook and stir for 10 minutes or until vegetables are tender.
2. Drain vegetables. Stir in peas, corn, and thyme.
3. Mash the cooked potatoes in a large bowl. Stir in egg whites and skim milk.

Garden Burgers *(cont'd)*

4. Stir potato mixture into vegetable mixture and shape into 12 burgers.
5. Place crumbs in a shallow bowl. Dip burger in crumbs to coat.
6. Brown burgers in a nonstick skillet, or in a skillet sprayed lightly with vegetable cooking spray, for 5 minutes. Turn and saute for 5 minutes more.

Calories Per Serving: 149

Fat: .7 g

Cholesterol: .1 mg

Protein: 6.3 g

Carbohydrates: 30 g

Dietary Fiber: 4.5 g

Sodium: 115 mg

✳ *Potato-Tomato Curry* ✳

YIELD: 6 servings ▪ *PREPARATION TIME: 20 minutes* ▪
COOKING TIME: 40 minutes

Here fresh tomatoes, potatoes, and mushrooms are simmered in a spicy curry sauce. Serve with Ginger-Lime Mangoes (page 210).

¼ cup water, nonfat chicken broth,
  or vegetable broth
2 onions, sliced
Pinch of ground ginger
1 teaspoon dried thyme leaves
1 teaspoon dried marjoram leaves
2 tablespoons fresh chopped parsley
1 teaspoon dried basil leaves

1 teaspoon dried dill leaves
½ teaspoon ground turmeric
2 cups chopped mushrooms
6 small potatoes, quartered
3 fresh tomatoes, thickly sliced
1 tablespoon lemon juice
2 teaspoons curry powder

1. Heat water or broth in a large skillet or heavy pot. Add onions, ginger, thyme, marjoram, parsley, basil, dill, and turmeric. Cook and stir onions and spices for 5 minutes, adding liquid as needed.
2. Add mushrooms. Cook and stir for 5 minutes.
3. Add potatoes. Cook and stir for 3 more minutes, adding liquid as needed.
4. Add tomatoes and cook, uncovered, for 20 minutes.
5. Add lemon juice and cook for 5 to 7 minutes more or until potatoes are tender.

Calories Per Serving: 161
Fat: .7 g
Cholesterol: 0 mg
Protein: 4.4 g

Carbohydrates: 36 g
Dietary Fiber: 1.3 g
Sodium: 15 mg

✳ *Turkish Vegetables* ✳

YIELD: 8 servings • *PREPARATION TIME: 25 minutes* •
COOKING TIME: 35 minutes

This dish, which can be enjoyed either hot or cold, features zucchini, okra, eggplant, green beans, and tomatoes. Serve with Fruit Mélange in Red Wine (page 362).

¹/₄ *cup water, nonfat chicken broth, or vegetable broth*
2 onions, sliced
2 cups diced zucchini
2 chopped green bell peppers
2 cups diced eggplant
2 cups green beans, cut in 1-inch pieces

2 cups fresh or partially thawed, frozen whole okra
4 cups chopped low-sodium canned tomatoes, including juice
¹/₄ *teaspoon black pepper*

1. Place water or broth in a large, heavy soup pot over medium heat. Add onions. Cook and stir until the onions are tender. Add more liquid during this process if necessary.
2. Add zucchini, green peppers, and eggplant. Cook and stir for 2 minutes, adding more liquid as needed.
3. Add green beans, okra, tomatoes with juice, and black pepper. Heat until liquid comes to a boil.
4. Lower heat, cover, and simmer for 30 minutes or until vegetables are tender.

Calories Per Serving: 77
Fat: .7 g
Cholesterol: 0 mg
Protein: 3.6 g

Carbohydrates: 16 g
Dietary Fiber: 1.9 g
Sodium: 22 mg

✳ *Tropical Mixed Vegetables* ✳

YIELD: 4 servings • *PREPARATION TIME: 20 minutes* •
COOKING TIME: 45 minutes

Here pineapple, carrots, water chestnuts, mushrooms, onion, and green pepper are combined and seasoned with basil, ginger, curry, and brown sugar. Serve with long-grain white or brown rice and Papaya-Honey Bake (page 211).

½ cup water, nonfat chicken broth, vegetable broth, or wine
½ cup sliced mushrooms
½ cup chopped green bell pepper
1 cup chopped onion
1 cup juice-packed canned pineapple chunks, juice reserved
2 cups sliced carrots

Pinch of dried basil leaves
¼ teaspoon ground ginger
Pinch of curry powder
1 tablespoon brown sugar, firmly packed
1 cup water chestnuts, drained and sliced

1. Heat ¼ cup of the water, broth, or wine in a skillet. Add mushrooms and green pepper. Cook and stir for 5 minutes. Add more liquid if necessary during this process.
2. Remove mushrooms and green pepper from skillet with a slotted spoon and set aside.
3. Heat the remaining ¼ cup of water, broth, or wine in the skillet. Add onions. Cook and stir for 5 minutes.
4. Add reserved pineapple juice, carrots, basil, ginger, curry, and brown sugar to skillet. Simmer for 35 minutes or until carrots are tender.
5. Add reserved mushrooms and green pepper, pineapple chunks, and water chestnuts. Simmer for 5 minutes or until all ingredients are warmed through.

Calories Per Serving: 111
Fat: .8 g
Cholesterol: 4.5 mg
Protein: 3 g

Carbohydrates: 23 g
Dietary Fiber: 1 g
Sodium: 24 mg

✳ *Many Vegetable Medley* ✳

YIELD: 8 servings ▪ *PREPARATION TIME: 30 minutes* ▪
COOKING TIME: 30 minutes

This combination of eleven vegetables is easy to fix and can be served over hot rice or pasta, with Lemon-Spiced Nectarines (page 207).

1¼ *cups water, nonfat chicken*
   broth, vegetable broth, or wine
½ *cup finely chopped onion*
2 *garlic cloves, minced*
1 *green bell pepper, seeded and*
   chopped
1 *cup diced potato*
1 *cup chopped cauliflower*
1 *cup chopped broccoli*
1 *cup diced eggplant*
1 *cup chopped celery*

1 *teaspoon ground cumin*
1 *teaspoon ground turmeric*
1 *teaspoon ground coriander*
½ *cup chopped string beans*
½ *cup chopped snow peas*
1 *cup chopped cabbage*
1 *cup chopped fresh or low-sodium*
   canned tomatoes
½ *teaspoon cayenne pepper*
⅓ *cup lemon juice*

1. In a large, heavy pot, heat ¼ cup of the water, broth, or wine over medium heat. Add the onion, garlic, and green pepper. Cook and stir over medium heat until vegetables are tender. Add liquid during this process if necessary.
2. Add the potato and ½ cup of the water or other liquid. Cover, reduce heat, and cook for 10 minutes.
3. Add cauliflower, broccoli, eggplant, celery, cumin, turmeric, coriander, and the remaining ½ cup of water. Cover and cook for 10 minutes.
4. Add string beans, snow peas, cabbage, tomatoes, and cayenne. Cook for 5 minutes.
5. Stir in lemon juice.

Calories per serving: 51
Fat: .4 g
Cholesterol: 0 mg
Protein: 2 g

Carbohydrates: 11 g
Dietary Fiber: 1 g
Sodium: 26 mg

❋ *Vegetable Paella* ❋

YIELD: *6 servings* • PREPARATION TIME: *20 minutes* •
COOKING TIME: *55 minutes*

Here yellow summer squash, peppers, and tomato are simmered with rice in a sauce flavored with paprika, garlic, and thyme.

*¼ cup water, nonfat chicken broth,
    vegetable broth, or wine
1 dry red chile pepper, crushed
1 large onion, thinly sliced
2 large green or red bell peppers,
    seeded and thinly sliced
2 cloves garlic, minced
1½ teaspoons paprika*

*½ teaspoon dried thyme leaves
1 medium yellow summer squash,
    diced
4 cups chopped fresh or low-sodium
    canned tomatoes, drained
¼ teaspoon black pepper
1 cup long-grain white rice
2 cups water or nonfat chicken
    broth*

1. Heat water, broth, or wine in a large, heavy pot over medium heat. Add chile pepper, onion, and bell peppers. Cook and stir for 10 minutes or until vegetables are tender and lightly browned. Add more liquid during this process if necessary.
2. Add garlic, paprika, thyme, yellow summer squash, tomatoes, and pepper. Cover the pot and simmer for 15 minutes.
3. Add rice and 2 cups water or chicken broth. Bring to a boil. Reduce heat, cover, and simmer for 30 minutes.

Calories Per Serving: 155
Fat: .7 g
Cholesterol: 0 mg
Protein: 4 g

Carbohydrates: 33 g
Dietary Fiber: 1.3 g
Sodium: 14 mg

❋ *Harvest Stew* ❋

YIELD: *8 servings* • PREPARATION TIME: *25 minutes* •
COOKING TIME: *35 minutes*

This dish is made with vegetables that are easy to find in the fall and winter months. Sprinkle with parsley and nonfat Parmesan cheese.

¼ cup water, nonfat chicken broth,
   vegetable broth, or wine
4 onions, chopped
4 cloves garlic, minced
4 leeks, cut into ¾-inch pieces
4 potatoes, cut into 1-inch cubes
4 carrots, cut into 1-inch cubes
½ turnip, cut into 1-inch cubes
1 sweet potato, cut into 1-inch cubes

5 cups water or nonfat chicken broth
2 teaspoons dried oregano leaves
2 teaspoons dried thyme leaves
1 cup broccoli florets
1 cup green beans, cut into 1-inch
   pieces
¼ teaspoon pepper
½ cup chopped fresh parsley
¼ cup nonfat Parmesan cheese

1. Heat water, broth, or wine in a large, heavy soup pot over medium heat. Add onions and garlic. Cook and stir until tender. Add more liquid during this process if necessary.
2. Add leeks, potatoes, carrots, turnip, sweet potato, 5 cups water or broth, oregano, and thyme. Cover and simmer for 30 minutes or until vegetables are tender.
3. Add broccoli, green beans, and pepper. Cook for 10 minutes, or until broccoli and green beans are tender, adding more water if needed.

Calories Per Serving: 172
Fat: .7 g
Cholesterol: .2 mg
Protein: 5 g

Carbohydrate: 39 g
Dietary Fiber: 5.8 g
Sodium: 60 mg

✳ *Spiced Eggplant* ✳

YIELD: 4 servings • *PREPARATION TIME: 15 minutes* •
COOKING TIME: 25 minutes

Here eggplant and sliced onions are cooked in a tomato-yogurt sauce. Serve with Stuffed Baked Potatoes (page 189).

¼ cup water, nonfat chicken broth, or
   vegetable broth
2 onions, sliced
1 large eggplant, cut into 2-inch cubes
2 cups plain nonfat yogurt
¼ cup low-sodium tomato purée or 1
   tablespoon low-sodium tomato paste

½ teaspoon ground ginger
½ teaspoon ground cloves
½ teaspoon ground cumin
1 cup water

Spiced Eggplant *(cont'd)*

1. Heat water or broth in a large saucepan over medium heat. Add onions. Cook and stir until onion is tender. Add more liquid during this
   process if necessary.
2. Add eggplant, yogurt, tomato purée, ginger, cloves, cumin, and 1 cup
   water.
3. Cook over low heat for 20 minutes or until eggplant is tender.

Calories Per Serving: 120
Fat: .7 g
Cholesterol: 2 mg
Protein: 8 g

Carbohydrates: 21 g
Dietary Fiber: 3.6 g
Sodium: 98 mg

✳ *Pasta-Vegetable Casserole* ✳

YIELD: 6 servings • *PREPARATION TIME: 25 minutes plus pasta cooking time and broccoli steaming time* • *COOKING TIME: 45 minutes*

Broccoli and red bell pepper are baked with pasta shells, nonfat ricotta
cheese, and nonfat Parmesan cheese in a tomato sauce. Serve with Spinach and Orange Salad (page 240).

*¹/₄ cup water, nonfat chicken broth,
    vegetable broth, or wine
1 small onion, chopped
¹/₄ cup chopped fresh parsley
1 clove garlic, minced
2 cups chopped fresh or low-sodium
    canned tomatoes with juice
6 ounces low-sodium tomato purée
    or low-sodium tomato paste
¹/₂ teaspoon dried oregano leaves
¹/₂ teaspoon dried marjoram leaves*

*2 pinches black pepper
2¹/₂ cups shell pasta, cooked until al
    dente and well drained in a
    colander
1 cup chopped broccoli, steamed
³/₄ cup chopped red bell pepper
2 cups nonfat ricotta cheese
¹/₂ cup nonfat grated Parmesan
    cheese
Pinch of ground nutmeg*

1. Preheat oven to 375 degrees.
2. Heat water, broth, or wine in a saucepan over medium heat. Add
   onion, parsley, and garlic. Cook and stir over medium heat for 5
   minutes or until onion is tender.
2. Stir in tomatoes, tomato purée, oregano, ¹/₄ teaspoon of the marjoram,
   and a pinch of black pepper. Simmer, covered, for 5 minutes.

3. Stir together the cooked pasta, steamed broccoli, red pepper, ricotta cheese, $1/4$ cup of the Parmesan cheese, the remaining $1/4$ teaspoon marjoram, nutmeg, and a pinch of black pepper. Transfer to a large oven-proof casserole.
4. Pour tomato mixture over pasta mixture in casserole. Top with remaining $1/4$ cup Parmesan.
5. Bake, uncovered, for 35 minutes or until casserole bubbles.

Calories Per Serving: 114
Fat: .6 g
Cholesterol: 1 mg
Protein: 6.7 g

Carbohydrates: 25 g
Dietary Fiber: 2 g
Sodium: 51 mg

✳ *Vegetable Curry* ✳

YIELD: 4 servings • *PREPARATION TIME: 25 minutes* •
COOKING TIME: 20 minutes

Vegetables are steamed and stir-fried, then topped with a sauce of curry powder, lime juice, red pepper, garlic, and gingerroot. Serve with long-grain white or brown rice, and Poached Pears in Orange Sauce (page 213).

1 apple, coarsely chopped
1 cup cauliflower florets
2 carrots, sliced
1 cup broccoli florets
1 red bell pepper, seeded and
   chopped
1 onion, cut in chunks
1 cup frozen green peas

2 tomatoes, cut in wedges
1 tablespoon curry powder
1 tablespoon minced gingerroot
2 cloves garlic, minced
$1/4$ teaspoon cayenne pepper
$1/2$ cup vegetable broth or nonfat
   chicken broth
2 tablespoons lime juice

1. Bring 1 inch of water to a boil in a steamer. Place apple, cauliflower, carrots, and broccoli in a steamer basket or colander and cover steamer. Steam about 5 minutes.
2. Add red pepper, onion, peas, and tomatoes. Steam for 3 more minutes.
3. Place curry powder, gingerroot, garlic, cayenne pepper, and broth in a saucepan. Simmer for 5 minutes.
4. Stir in lime juice.
5. Pour sauce over vegetables and serve.

Vegetable Curry *(cont'd)*

Calories Per Serving: 119
Fat: 1 g
Cholesterol: 0 mg
Protein: 5 g

Carbohydrates: 25 g
Dietary Fiber: 2.9 g
Sodium: 66 mg

✳ *Broccoli Roll-Ups* ✳

YIELD: *6 servings* • PREPARATION TIME: *25 minutes plus lasagna cooking time and broccoli steaming time* • COOKING TIME: *30 minutes*

Broccoli and nonfat ricotta cheese are rolled in lasagna noodles and baked in tomato sauce. Serve with Amaretto Fruit Delight (page 361).

1/4 cup water, nonfat chicken broth, or vegetable broth
1/4 cup chopped green bell pepper
1/4 cup chopped onion
1/2 cup chopped mushrooms
1 teaspoon chopped fresh parsley
1/2 teaspoon dried basil leaves
1/2 teaspoon dried oregano leaves
1/2 teaspoon dried thyme leaves

2 cups low-sodium tomato sauce
3 cups chopped broccoli, steamed
1/4 cup nonfat Parmesan cheese
1 cup nonfat skim ricotta cheese or cottage cheese
1/2 teaspoon black pepper
6 lasagne noodles, cooked until al dente and well drained in a colander

1. Heat water or broth in a saucepan over medium heat. Add green pepper, onion, and mushrooms. Cook and stir over medium heat for 5 minutes or until vegetables are lightly browned. Add more liquid during this process if necessary.
2. Add parsley, basil, oregano, thyme, and tomato sauce. Simmer over very low heat for 10 minutes.
3. Preheat oven to 350 degrees.
4. Combine broccoli, Parmesan cheese, ricotta cheese, and black pepper.
5. Spread broccoli filling in an even layer over each lasagne noodle. Roll up each lasagne noodle like a jelly roll. Place rolled-up noodles in a 9-by-13-inch baking dish.
6. Pour tomato sauce over roll-ups. Bake for 20 minutes.

Calories Per Serving: 145
Fat: .7 g
Cholesterol: .5 mg
Protein: 7 g

Carbohydrates: 28 g
Dietary Fiber: 3.6 g
Sodium: 53 mg

✳ *Broccoli Pizza with Quick and Easy Crust* ✳

YIELD: *6 servings (¹⁄₆ pizza each)* • PREPARATION TIME: *25 minutes plus broccoli steaming time* • COOKING TIME: *35 minutes*

The crust of this quick homemade pizza, which is made with beer, requires no separate rising time. Serve with a salad of red leaf lettuce, cucumbers, tomatoes, and Balsamic-Dijon Dressing (page 282).

SAUCE

¹⁄₄ cup water
1 clove garlic, minced
¹⁄₂ cup onion, finely chopped
¹⁄₄ cup chopped fresh parsley
¹⁄₄ cup finely chopped green bell pepper
1¹⁄₂ cups low-sodium tomato sauce

3 tablespoons low-sodium tomato paste
¹⁄₂ teaspoon dried oregano leaves
¹⁄₂ teaspoon dried marjoram leaves
¹⁄₂ teaspoon sugar
Pinch of black pepper

DOUGH

2 cups unbleached all-purpose flour
1 cup whole wheat flour

1 tablespoon baking powder
12 ounces beer

TOPPING

1¹⁄₂ cup nonfat grated mozzarella cheese
¹⁄₄ cup nonfat grated Parmesan cheese

¹⁄₂ cup sliced mushrooms
³⁄₄ cup broccoli florets, steamed
¹⁄₂ cup chopped scallions

1. For the sauce, heat water in a saucepan over medium heat. Add garlic and onion. Cook and stir for 5 minutes or until onion is tender. Add more liquid during this process if necessary.
2. Add the parsley, green pepper, tomato sauce, tomato paste, oregano, marjoram, sugar, and black pepper.
3. Bring sauce to a boil. Reduce heat and simmer, uncovered, for 10 minutes. Set aside.
4. Preheat oven to 425 degrees.
5. For the dough, combine flours, baking soda, and beer in a large bowl.
6. Spread dough in a 9-by-13-inch pan.
7. Spread sauce over the dough.
8. Top the sauce with the mozzarella cheese and Parmesan cheese. Sprin-

Broccoli Pizza with Quick and Easy Crust *(cont'd)*
kle the mushrooms over the pizza. Top with the steamed broccoli and
the scallions.

9. Bake for 25 minutes or until crust is crispy and golden. Cut into 6
   wedges.

Calories Per Serving: 272
Fat: .7
Cholesterol: 7.6 mg
Protein: 19 g

Carbohydrates: 43 g
Dietary Fiber: 4 g
Sodium: 516 mg

Steamed Vegetables with
✳ Garlic-Lemon Sauce ✳

YIELD: 6 servings • PREPARATION TIME: 20 minutes •
COOKING TIME: 18 minutes

Here carrots, yellow summer squash, broccoli, red potatoes, and green
beans are steamed and dressed with a garlic-lemon sauce.

1 cup thinly sliced carrots
1½ cups thinly sliced yellow
*   summer squash*
2 cups broccoli florets
1½ cups green beans, trimmed and
*   cut into 1-inch pieces*

1 cup sliced red potatoes
1 clove garlic, minced
⅓ cup fresh lemon juice
¼ teaspoon black pepper

1. Bring 1 inch of water to a boil in a steamer. Place carrots, yellow
   summer squash, and broccoli in a steamer basket or colander and
   steam, covered, for 8 minutes, or until just tender. Remove from
   steamer and set aside.
2. Bring 1 inch of water to a boil in steamer. Place green beans and
   potatoes in a steamer basket or colander, cover, and steam for 10
   minutes or until just tender.
3. While beans and potatoes are steaming, place garlic, lemon juice, and
   pepper in a saucepan and simmer for 8 minutes.
4. Combine beans and potatoes with other vegetables and toss with
   garlic-lemon sauce.

Note: To save time, you can use your microwave to steam some of the vegetables while you are steaming the rest on your stovetop.

Calories Per Serving: 60
Fat: .4 g
Cholesterol: 0 mg
Protein: 2.5 g

Carbohydrates: 13 g
Dietary Fiber: 2.9 g
Sodium: 17 mg

✳ *Vegetable Risotto* ✳

YIELD: *4 servings* • PREPARATION TIME: *25 minutes plus asparagus steaming time* • COOKING TIME: *40 minutes*

This creamy risotto requires constant stirring but is well worth the effort. Serve with nonfat Parmesan cheese and a side dish of Nutmeg-Cinnamon Baked Pears (page 214).

3³/₄ cups nonfat chicken broth or vegetable broth
¹/₂ cup chopped leeks
1 cup diced zucchini
¹/₂ cup diced carrot
1 cup asparagus tips, steamed

¹/₂ cup diced yellow or red bell pepper
1¹/₂ cups chopped fresh or low-sodium canned tomatoes
2 tablespoons chopped fresh parsley
¹/₄ teaspoon dried marjoram leaves
1 cup Arborio rice

1. Simmer 3¹/₂ cups of the broth in a small saucepan over low heat. Keep warm.
2. Heat the remaining ¹/₄ cup broth in a large saucepan over medium heat. Add leeks. Cook and stir for 3 minutes over medium heat. Add more liquid if necessary during this process.
3. Add zucchini, carrot, asparagus tips, and yellow pepper. Cook over low heat for 5 minutes, stirring.
4. Stir in tomatoes, parsley, and marjoram. Cook for 10 minutes, stirring several times.
5. Add rice and ¹/₂ cup of the warm broth. Cook for 3 minutes or until liquid is nearly absorbed, stirring constantly.
6. Add remaining broth ¹/₂ cup at a time, stirring constantly for 3 minutes or until each portion of broth is absorbed before adding the next. Serve immediately.

Vegetable Risotto *(cont'd)*

Calories Per Serving: 243
Fat: .9 g
Cholesterol: 0 mg
Protein: 9 g

Carbohydrates: 50 g
Dietary Fiber: 3.6 g
Sodium: 154 mg

✳ *Broccoli-Stuffed Shells* ✳

YIELD: 8 servings (3 shells each) • *PREPARATION TIME: 20 minutes plus broccoli steaming time and pasta cooking time* • *COOKING TIME: 30 minutes*

In this dish jumbo shell macaroni are stuffed with broccoli and nonfat ricotta cheese, then baked with tomato sauce. Serve with Eggplant-Tomato Salad (page 234).

1/4 cup water, nonfat chicken broth, or vegetable broth
1 cup chopped mushrooms
1/2 cup chopped onions
1 clove garlic, minced
1/2 teaspoon dried oregano leaves
1/2 teaspoon dried basil leaves
1/4 teaspoon black pepper

2 cups nonfat ricotta or cottage cheese
2 1/4 cups chopped broccoli, steamed
3 egg whites, lightly beaten
24 jumbo shell macaroni, cooked until al dente and well drained in a colander
2 cups low-sodium tomato sauce

1. Place 1/4 cup water or broth in a skillet and heat over medium heat. Add mushrooms, onions, and garlic. Cook and stir over medium heat for 5 minutes or until lightly browned. Add more liquid during this process if necessary.
2. Remove from heat and stir in oregano, basil, pepper, ricotta or cottage cheese, broccoli, and egg whites.
3. Preheat oven to 350 degrees.
4. Stuff drained shells with ricotta-broccoli mixture.
5. Spread 1/2 cup tomato sauce on the bottom of a 9-by-13-inch baking dish.
6. Arrange stuffed shells over sauce. Top with remaining tomato sauce.
7. Bake for 30 minutes or until shells are hot.

Calories Per Serving: 176
Fat: .7 g
Cholesterol: .5 mg
Protein: 10.5 g

Carbohydrates: 40 g
Dietary Fiber: 3 g
Sodium: 84 mg

✳ *Grilled Garden Kabobs* ✳

YIELD: 4 servings (2 skewers each) ▪ *PREPARATION TIME: 25 minutes plus*
45 minutes chilling time ▪ *COOKING TIME: 15 minutes*

Serve these grilled kabobs over a bed of hot, cooked basmati rice, and
Grilled Nectarines with Strawberry Purée (page 211).

½ cup Basic Italian Dressing (page
274) or commercial fat-free
Italian dressing
1 tablespoon minced fresh parsley
1 teaspoon dried basil leaves
½ teaspoon dried thyme leaves

2 medium zucchini, cut into 1-inch
chunks
8 cherry tomatoes
8 medium fresh mushrooms
2 medium yellow bell peppers, cut
into 1-inch chunks

1. Mix dressing with parsley, basil, and thyme in a small bowl. Chill for
   45 minutes.
2. Thread zucchini, tomatoes, mushrooms, and yellow bell peppers on
   8 skewers.
3. Place on grill rack over medium heat. Grill, turning and basting with
   dressing mixture, for 15 minutes or until tender.

Calories Per Serving: 43
Fat: .5 g
Cholesterol: 0 mg
Protein: 2.4 g

Carbohydrates: 9.4 g
Dietary Fiber: 3 g
Sodium: 43 mg

Orzo with
✳ *Red Peppers, Cauliflower, and Broccoli* ✳

YIELD: 4 servings ▪ *PREPARATION TIME: 20 minutes* ▪
COOKING TIME: minutes plus vegetable steaming time

Here orzo is tossed with vegetables in a lemon–dill sauce. Serve with
Mixed Berries with Whipped Topping (page 356).

1 cup orzo
¾ cup broccoli florets, steamed and
chopped
¾ cup cauliflower florets, steamed
and chopped

½ cup chopped red bell pepper
1 teaspoon dried dill leaves
2 tablespoons lemon juice
¼ teaspoon black pepper

Orzo with Red Peppers, Cauliflower, and Broccoli *(cont'd)*

1. Bring a large pot of water to a roiling boil. Stir in orzo and return to boiling. Cook, stirring occasionally, for 10 minutes or until the orzo is tender.
2. Drain orzo.
3. Toss orzo with steamed broccoli and cauliflower, red pepper, dill, lemon juice, and black pepper.

Calories Per Serving: 121
Fat: .9 g
Cholesterol: 0 mg
Protein: 6.4 g

Carbohydrates: 24 g
Dietary Fiber: 6.6 g
Sodium: 29 mg

❋ *Quinoa with Vegetables* ❋

YIELD: *4 servings* • PREPARATION TIME: *20 minutes* •
COOKING TIME: *40 minutes*

Quinoa (pronounced keen-wa) has the highest protein content of any grain. A grain eaten by the ancient Peruvians, quinoa has a sweet, nutty flavor. You can find it in some supermarkets, gourmet grocers, and health food stores. Serve with Apricot Upside Down Cake (page 342).

2 cups nonfat chicken broth, vegetable broth, or water
1 clove garlic, minced
1/2 cup chopped scallions
1/2 cup chopped green bell pepper
1/2 cup chopped mushrooms
Pinch of cayenne pepper
1 cup quinoa
1/2 cup chopped fresh or low-sodium canned plum tomatoes
3 tablespoons chopped parsley

1. Heat 1/4 cup of the broth or water in a heavy saucepan over medium heat. Add garlic and scallions. Cook and stir for 5 minutes. Add more liquid during this process if necessary.
2. Add green pepper and mushrooms and sauté for 5 more minutes.
3. Add the remaining 1 3/4 cups broth and bring to a boil. Stir in cayenne, quinoa, and tomatoes. Return to a boil. Reduce heat. Cover and simmer for 30 minutes or until the liquid has been absorbed.
4. Let sit for 5 minutes. Add parsley and serve.

Calories Per Serving: 188
Fat: 5 g
Cholesterol: 0 mg
Protein: 5 g

Carbohydrates: 40 g
Dietary Fiber: 1 g
Sodium: 75 mg

✳ *Bow Ties with Eggplant Sauce* ✳

YIELD: 6 servings • *PREPARATION TIME: 20 minutes* •
COOKING TIME: 30 minutes plus pasta cooking time

Cooked bow tie pasta is served with a spicy eggplant sauce in this dish. Serve with Corn and Green Bean Salad (page 231).

¼ cup water, nonfat chicken broth, vegetable broth, or wine
2 cloves garlic, minced
¼ cup chopped onion
¼ teaspoon cayenne pepper
3 cups unpeeled eggplant chunks
3 cups fresh or low-sodium canned tomatoes

½ teaspoon dried basil leaves
½ teaspoon dried oregano leaves
12 ounces bow ties, cooked until al dente, and well drained in a colander

1. Heat water, broth, or wine in a large heavy saucepan over medium heat. Add garlic, onion, and cayenne pepper. Cook and stir over medium heat for 5 minutes. Add the eggplant, reduce heat to low, and continue cooking and stirring until it begins to soften. Since the eggplant tends to absorb liquid, be prepared to add additional water during this process.
2. Add the tomatoes, basil, and oregano. Cover and simmer for 20 minutes or until the eggplant is tender.
3. Toss eggplant sauce with the bow tie pasta and serve.

Calories Per Serving: 145
Fat: .8 g
Cholesterol: 0 mg
Protein: 6 g

Carbohydrates: 35 g
Dietary Fiber: 2.3 g
Sodium: 19 mg

Conchiglie with Cauliflower and
✳ Sun-Dried Tomatoes ✳

YIELD: 4 servings • *PREPARATION TIME: 20 minutes* •
COOKING TIME: 18 minutes plus pasta cooking time

Conchiglie are pasta shells shaped like conch shells. In this recipe they're combined with a white wine sauce, cauliflower, and sun-dried tomatoes. Serve with Asparagus Salad (page 225).

¹/₄ cup water, nonfat chicken broth, vegetable broth, or wine
2 cloves garlic, minced
2 cups cauliflower florets, cut into ¹/₂-inch pieces
1 cup nonfat chicken broth
1 cup dry white wine

1¹/₂ cups chopped sun-dried tomatoes
¹/₂ teaspoon dried basil leaves
¹/₂ teaspoon dried thyme leaves
¹/₄ teaspoon black pepper
8 ounces conchiglie, cooked until al dente and well drained in a colander

1. Heat water, broth, or wine in a large saucepan. Add garlic and cauliflower. Cook and stir for 2 minutes. Add more water if necessary during this process.
2. Add 1 cup each chicken broth and white wine and bring to a boil.
3. Add sun-dried tomatoes, basil, thyme, and black pepper. Simmer over low heat for 12 minutes or until cauliflower is tender.
4. Serve over cooked conchiglie.

Calories Per Serving: 225
Fat: .8 g
Cholesterol: 0 mg
Protein: 8.8 g

Carbohydrates: 46 g
Dietary Fiber: 2 g
Sodium: 84 mg

Angel Hair Pasta with
✳ Steamed Vegetables and Garlic Sauce ✳

YIELD: 6 servings • *PREPARATION TIME: 25 minutes* •
COOKING TIME: 25 minutes plus pasta cooking time

In this recipe delicate angel hair pasta is tossed with steamed zucchini, yellow summer squash, red bell pepper, scallions, cherry tomatoes, and a mellow garlic sauce. Serve accompanied by a tossed salad with Honey-Mustard Dressing (page 281).

1¼ cups nonfat chicken broth
10 cloves garlic, peeled and chopped
2 cups zucchini, sliced
1 cup yellow summer squash, sliced
1 large red bell pepper, seeded and cut into chunks
2 tablespoons plus 1 teaspoon balsamic vinegar

12 ounces angel hair pasta, cooked al dente and well drained in a colander
½ cup chopped scallions
2 cups halved cherry tomatoes

1. Combine chicken broth and garlic in a small saucepan. Bring to boil, reduce heat to low, and simmer, covered, for 20 minutes.
2. Heat 1 inch of water in a steamer. Place zucchini, yellow summer squash, and red pepper in a steamer basket or collander, cover, and steam until squash are tender.
3. Pour broth-garlic mixture into a blender or food processor and add balsamic vinegar. Process until smooth. Return to saucepan over low heat until ready to serve.
4. Toss together cooked pasta, steamed vegetables, scallions, cherry tomatoes, and garlic purée in a large bowl.

Calories Per Serving: 188
Fat: .9 g
Cholesterol: 0 mg
Protein: 6.7 g

Carbohydrates: 39 g
Dietary Fiber: 1.8 g
Sodium: 30 mg

Multicolored Shells with Broccoli, Mushrooms, Red Peppers, ✳ *and Ricotta Cheese* ✳

Yield: 4 servings • Preparation Time: 15 minutes • Cooking Time: 10 minutes plus pasta cooking time

This colorful, simple dish is dressed with nonfat ricotta cheese. Look for tomato and spinach pasta shells on the pasta shelf at your supermarket. If they are not available, you can substitute plain shells. Serve with Baked Bananas and Pineapple (page 208).

Multicolored Shells with Broccoli, Mushrooms, Red Peppers, and Ricotta Cheese *(cont'd)*

2 cups broccoli florets

2 cups sliced mushrooms

1 large red pepper, seeded and cut
into 1/2-inch chunks

8 ounces spinach and tomato shells,
cooked al dente and well drained
in a colander

1/4 cup nonfat ricotta cheese

1/2 teaspoon dried dill leaves

1. Heat 1 inch of water in a steamer and place broccoli, mushrooms, and red pepper in a steamer basket or colander. Cover and steam until broccoli is just tender.
2. Toss steamed vegetables with cooked shells, ricotta cheese, and dill leaves.

Calories Per Serving: 182

Fat: 1 g

Cholesterol: .1 mg

Protein: 9 g

Carbohydrates: 44 g

Dietary Fiber: 1.9 g

Sodium: 15 mg

✳ *Vermicelli with Roasted Peppers* ✳

YIELD: *4 servings* • PREPARATION TIME: *30 minutes* •
COOKING TIME: *10 minutes plus pasta cooking time*

Here vermicelli is topped with a sauce of roasted peppers and balsamic vinegar. Serve alongside a tossed salad with Balsamic-Dijon Dressing (page 282).

4 medium bell peppers: 1 green,
1 red, 1 yellow, and 1 orange or
purple (or any combination
available)

1/4 cup water, nonfat chicken broth,
vegetable broth, or wine

2 cloves garlic, minced

2 tablespoons balsamic vinegar

Pinch of red pepper flakes

1/2 teaspoon ground basil leaves

8 ounces vermicelli, cooked al dente
and well drained in a colander

2 tablespoons chopped fresh parsley

1. Preheat oven to 500 degrees.
2. Place peppers on broiler-pan rack. Roast peppers on upper third of

oven until skins are blackened all over, about 20 minutes, turning peppers halfway through the cooking period. Transfer peppers to a bowl; cover until cool enough to handle.

3. Peel and seed peppers, cutting them into ½-inch-wide strips, and reserving liquid.

4. Heat water, broth, or wine in skillet over medium heat. Add garlic. Cook and stir over medium heat for 3 minutes. Add pepper strips, reserved liquid from peppers, balsamic vinegar, red pepper flakes, and basil. When the liquid begins to sizzle, serve over the cooked vermicelli and sprinkle with parsley.

Calories Per Serving: 178
Fat: 1 g
Cholesterol: 0 mg
Protein: 5.6 g

Carbohydrates: 37 g
Dietary Fiber: 1 g
Sodium: 6.7 mg

✳ *Cavatelli with Simmered Vegetable Sauce* ✳

YIELD: 6 servings • *PREPARATION TIME: 25 minutes* •
COOKING TIME: 20 minutes plus pasta cooking time

Here narrow rippled shells are served with a sauce of asparagus, snow peas, carrot, pattypan squash, mushrooms, and tomatoes. Serve with Pineapple and Apple Salad (page 238).

½ cup nonfat chicken broth
2 garlic cloves, minced
1 small onion, chopped
2 cups chopped fresh or low-sodium canned tomatoes
1 tablespoon low-sodium tomato paste
½ teaspoon sugar
½ teaspoon dried oregano leaves
1 teaspoon dried basil leaves

½ cup asparagus, cut in ½-inch slices
½ cup sliced snow peas
½ cup chopped carrots
½ cup chopped pattypan squash or zucchini
½ cup chopped mushrooms
12 ounces cavatelli, cooked al dente and well drained in a colander

1. Heat ¼ cup of the chicken broth in a large saucepan over medium heat. Add garlic and onions. Cook and stir over medium heat for 5 minutes. Add liquid if necessary during this process.

Cavatelli with Simmered Vegetable Sauce *(cont'd)*

2. Add tomatoes, the remaining ¼ cup broth, tomato paste, sugar, oregano, and basil.
3. When the tomato sauce begins to simmer, add the asparagus, snow peas, carrots, pattypan squash, and mushrooms. Simmer for 10 minutes.
4. Serve over cooked cavatelli.

Calories Per Serving: 197	Carbohydrates: 48 g
Fat: 1 g	Dietary Fiber: 1.8 g
Cholesterol: 0 mg	Sodium: 39 mg
Protein: 8.9 g	

✳ *Tomato Linguine* ✳

YIELD: *8 servings* • PREPARATION TIME: *15 minutes* • COOKING TIME: *20 minutes plus pasta cooking time*

A sauce made from fresh tomatoes, tomato purée, and canned Italian plum tomatoes, garlic, green bell pepper, basil, and oregano is served here with linguine. Top with nonfat Parmesan cheese. Serve with Corn and Zucchini Salad (page 232).

3½ cups canned low-sodium Italian plum tomatoes, undrained	*½ teaspoon dried basil leaves*
2 cups low-sodium canned tomato purée	*½ teaspoon dried oregano leaves*
3 cloves garlic, minced	*1 green bell pepper, seeded and finely chopped*
4 medium fresh tomatoes, chopped	*1 pound linguine, cooked al dente and well drained in a colander*

1. Combine canned plum tomatoes, tomato purée, garlic, and fresh tomatoes in a food processor or blender and process until smooth.
2. Transfer tomato sauce to a large saucepan and bring to a boil. Reduce heat and simmer for 12 minutes.
3. Add basil, oregano, and green pepper. Simmer for 8 minutes.
4. Serve tomato sauce with the cooked linguine.

Calories Per Serving: 252	Carbohydrates: 53 g
Fat: 1.5 g	Dietary Fiber: 5.2 g
Cholesterol: 0 mg	Sodium: 33 mg
Protein: 9.7 g	

✳ *Ziti with Great Northern Beans* ✳

YIELD: 6 servings ▪ *PREPARATION TIME: 20 minutes* ▪ *COOKING TIME: 20 minutes plus pasta cooking time and bean cooking time*

Here cooked ziti is served with Great Northern beans in a garlic–parsley sauce. Serve accompanied by Fruit Cup with Mango Sauce (page 360).

1/4 cup water, chicken broth, vegetable broth, or wine
1/2 cup chopped onion
2 cloves garlic, minced
2 1/2 cups fresh or low-sodium canned tomatoes, chopped and drained
1 cup home-cooked or canned Great Northern beans, drained and rinsed

1/4 teaspoon black pepper
1/2 teaspoon ground thyme leaves
1/2 teaspoon ground basil leaves
10 ounces ziti, cooked al dente and well drained in a colander
1/2 cup chopped fresh parsley

1. Heat water, broth, or wine in a large saucepan. Add onions and garlic. Cook and stir for 5 minutes over medium heat or until soft. Add more water if necessary during this process.
2. Add tomatoes and simmer for 10 minutes.
3. Add beans, black pepper, thyme and basil. Simmer for 10 more minutes.
4. Serve over cooked ziti and sprinkle with parsley.

Calories Per Serving: 192
Fat: 1 g
Cholesterol: 0 mg
Protein: 9 g

Carbohydrates: 45 g
Dietary Fiber: 2.8 g
Sodium: 19 mg

Spinach Fettucini with ✳ *Shiitake–Tomato Sauce* ✳

YIELD: 4 servings ▪ *PREPARATION TIME: 5 minutes plus 15 minutes mushroom soaking time* ▪ *COOKING TIME: 35 minutes plus pasta cooking time*

The rich taste of shiitake mushrooms makes this sauce a satisfying replacement for tomato sauce with meat. Serve alongside Green Salad with Fruit (page 251).

Spinach Fettucini with Shiitake-Tomato Sauce *(cont'd)*

¹/₄ cup water, nonfat chicken broth,
  vegetable broth, or wine
1 small onion, finely chopped
1 garlic clove, minced
¹/₂ ounce dried shiitake mushrooms,
  soaked for 15 minutes in warm
  water until well softened, stems
  discarded, caps finely minced

¹/₂ pound mushrooms, finely minced
2 cups fresh or low-sodium canned
  chopped tomatoes
¹/₂ teaspoon crushed oregano leaves
¹/₂ teaspoon crushed basil leaves
8 ounces spinach fettucini, cooked al
  dente and well drained in a
  colander

1. Heat water, broth, or wine in a large, heavy saucepan. Add onion and garlic. Cook and stir over medium heat for 5 minutes. Add more liquid during this process if necessary.
2. Add both kinds of mushrooms and sauté for 15 minutes.
3. Add tomatoes, oregano, and basil. Simmer for 15 minutes. Serve with the cooked spinach fettucini.

Calories Per Serving: 183
Fat: 1 g
Cholesterol: 0 mg
Protein: 6.4 g

Carbohydrates: 37 g
Dietary Fiber: 1 g
Sodium: 11 mg

✳ *Fusilli with Lentil Sauce* ✳

Yield: 6 servings • *Preparation Time: 15 minutes* •
Cooking Time: 35 minutes plus pasta cooking time

Here fusilli is served with a paprika-accented sauce of lentils and carrots. Sprinkle with nonfat Parmesan cheese and serve with Romaine Salad with Scallion Dressing (page 251).

1 ¹/₄ cups nonfat chicken broth
3 garlic cloves, chopped
1 small onion, chopped
1 medium carrot, chopped
1 teaspoon ground cumin
1 teaspoon ground ginger
¹/₄ teaspoon cayenne pepper
¹/₂ teaspoon ground paprika

1 teaspoon dried basil leaves
2 ³/₄ cups fresh or canned low-sodium
  chopped tomatoes
³/₄ cup brown lentils
1 tablespoon sugar
¹/₂ cup plain nonfat yogurt
12 ounces fusilli, cooked al dente and
  well drained in a colander

1. Heat ¼ cup of the chicken broth in a large saucepan over medium heat. Add garlic, onion, and carrot. Cook and stir over medium heat for 5 minutes. Add more liquid during this process if necessary.
2. Add the remaining cup of broth, cumin, ginger, cayenne pepper, paprika, basil, tomatoes, lentils, and sugar. Simmer for 30 minutes.
3. Remove from heat and stir in yogurt. Serve sauce over cooked fusilli.

Calories Per Serving: 213	Carbohydrates: 49 g
Fat: 1 g	Dietary Fiber: 2.6 g
Cholesterol: .3 mg	Sodium: 72 mg
Protein: 10 g	

✳ *Spinach-Mushroom Lasagna* ✳

YIELD: 6 servings • PREPARATION TIME: 30 minutes plus 15 minutes standing time • COOKING TIME: 35 minutes plus lasagna cooking time

Spinach, mushrooms, red bell peppers, and carrots are baked with layers of nonfat ricotta cheese, tomato sauce, and lasagna noodles. Serve alongside Green Salad with Raw Vegetables (page 253).

3 cups crushed fresh or low-sodium canned tomatoes
½ cup chopped mushrooms
½ cup chopped red bell pepper
½ cup chopped carrot
½ cup chopped onion
½ cup red wine or red grape juice
2 cloves garlic, minced
2 tablespoons honey
½ teaspoon dried basil leaves
½ teaspoon dried rosemary leaves
½ teaspoon dried oregano leaves

½ teaspoon dried thyme leaves
¼ teaspoon black pepper
4 egg whites, lightly beaten
1½ cups nonfat ricotta cheese or cottage cheese
8 ounces lasagna noodles, cooked until al dente and well drained in a colander
1 pound fresh spinach, well washed, drained, and chopped
4 ounces nonfat mozzarella cheese, grated

1. Place tomatoes, mushrooms, red peppers, carrot, onion, wine or grape juice, garlic, honey, basil, rosemary, oregano, thyme, and black pepper in a large, heavy saucepan. Simmer for 20 minutes.
2. Preheat oven to 350 degrees.

Spinach-Mushroom Lasagna *(cont'd)*

3. Mix together the egg whites and the ricotta or cottage cheese. Set aside.
4. To assemble, place a layer of tomato sauce in the bottom of a 9-by-13-inch casserole. Cover the sauce with a layer of cooked lasagna noodles. Spread ricotta-egg mixture over noodles and top with a layer of spinach. Add another layer of noodles, another layer of sauce, and finish with grated mozzarella.
5. Bake for 35 minutes. Let stand for 15 minutes before cutting.

Calories Per Serving: 227
Fat: 1 g
Cholesterol: 3.8 mg
Protein: 15 g

Carbohydrates: 36 g
Dietary Fiber: 4.3 g
Sodium: 264 mg

✳ *Eggplant Del Rio* ✳

YIELD: 8 servings • PREPARATION TIME: 15 minutes plus bean cooking time • COOKING TIME: 30 minutes

This hearty dish is made with corn, carrots, celery, tomatoes, pinto beans, and eggplant. Serve with Roasted Red Potatoes with Lemon-Oregano Sauce (page 191).

8 ¼ cups water, nonfat chicken broth, or vegetable broth
4 cloves garlic, minced
1 ½ cups chopped onions
3 cups chopped fresh or low-sodium canned tomatoes
1 cup sliced carrots
1 cup sliced celery

2 cups diced eggplant
2 cups home-cooked or canned pinto beans, drained and rinsed
2 cups fresh, frozen, or canned corn kernels
1 teaspoon ground cumin
1 teaspoon ground chili powder
½ cup grated nonfat cheese

1. Place ¼ cup of the water or broth in a heavy soup pot over medium heat. Add garlic and onion to pot. Cook and stir over medium heat for 5 minutes or until lightly browned. Add more liquid during this process if necessary.
2. Add remaining 8 cups of water, tomatoes, carrots, and celery. Bring mixture to a boil. Cook for 10 minutes.

3. Add eggplant. Cook for 10 minutes or until eggplant is tender.
4. Add the pinto beans, corn, cumin, and chili powder. Cook for 5 minutes.
5. Transfer 2 cups of the vegetable stew to a food processor or blender and purée.
6. Stir puréed mixture and cheese into the stew and serve.

Calories Per Serving: 141
Fat: .8 g
Cholesterol: .3 mg
Protein: 7.4 g

Carbohydrates: 29 g
Dietary Fiber: 6.5 g
Sodium: 73 mg

✳ *Black Bean Lasagna* ✳

YIELD: 8 servings • *PREPARATION TIME: 20 minutes* •
COOKING TIME: 50 minutes plus lasagna cooking time and 15 minutes standing time

This meatless lasagna is made with black beans and mushrooms. Serve with Oranges and Tomatoes with Honey Dressing (page 237).

¼ cup water, nonfat chicken broth, or vegetable broth
1 cup chopped onions
3 cloves garlic, minced
2 cups sliced mushrooms
1 teaspoon ground oregano leaves
1 teaspoon ground basil leaves
¼ cup chopped fresh parsley
½ cup low-sodium tomato juice
1 cup home-cooked or canned black beans, drained and rinsed

3 cups chopped fresh or low-sodium canned tomatoes
2 tablespoons low-sodium tomato purée or tomato paste
12 ounces lasagna noodles, cooked until al dente, rinsed, and well drained in a colander
3 cups nonfat ricotta cheese
½ cup grated nonfat mozzarella cheese
¼ cup nonfat Parmesan cheese

1. Heat water or broth in a skillet over medium heat. Add onions, garlic, and mushrooms. Cook and stir over medium heat for 5 minutes or until vegetables are lightly browned. Add liquid if necessary during this process.
2. Stir in oregano, basil, and parsley.
3. Add tomato juice and cook for 10 minutes.
4. Add beans, tomatoes, and tomato purée or paste. Simmer for 15 minutes.

Black Bean Lasagna *(cont'd)*

5. Preheat oven to 375 degrees.
6. To assemble, place a layer of noodles in a 9-by-13-inch baking dish. Top with a layer of tomato–black bean sauce. Top with a layer of ricotta cheese, followed by a layer of mozzarella cheese. Repeat with another layer each of noodles, sauce, ricotta, and mozzarella. Top with Parmesan cheese.
7. Bake for 20 minutes. Let stand 15 minutes before serving.

Calories Per Serving: 145
Fat: .7 g
Cholesterol: 3.4 mg
Protein: 12 g

Carbohydrates: 25 g
Dietary Fiber: 3 g
Sodium: 146 mg

✳ *Potato-Broccoli Chili* ✳

YIELD: 8 servings (2 cups each) • *PREPARATION TIME: 20 minutes* • *COOKING TIME: 45 minutes plus bean cooking time*

Potatoes, broccoli, corn, red onion, green bell pepper, and yellow summer squash are combined with beans and beer in this robust chili. Serve with Cucumber and Onion Salad (page 233).

1/4 cup water, nonfat chicken broth, or vegetable broth
1 cup diced yellow summer squash
1/2 cup diced green bell pepper
1/2 cup diced red onion
3 potatoes, diced
1 1/2 cups broccoli florets
1 tablespoon chili powder
Pinch of cayenne pepper

3 1/2 cups chopped fresh or low-sodium canned tomatoes
2 cups fresh, frozen, or canned corn kernels
12 ounces beer or nonalcoholic beer
1/4 cup low-sodium tomato purée or tomato paste
2 1/2 cups home-cooked or canned pinto beans, drained and rinsed

1. Heat 1/4 cup water or broth in a large, heavy soup pot. Add yellow summer squash, green pepper, and red onion. Cook and stir for 10 minutes or until vegetables are tender.
2. Add potatoes, broccoli, chili powder, cayenne pepper, tomatoes, corn, beer, and tomato purée or paste. Bring to a boil.
3. Reduce heat, cover, and cook over low heat for 25 minutes.
4. Add beans and cook for 10 more minutes.

Calories Per Serving: 205
Fat: 1 g
Cholesterol: 0 mg
Protein: 9 g

Carbohydrates: 41 g
Dietary Fiber: 7 g
Sodium: 41 mg

Cannelinni—
✳ *Northern Bean Chili* ✳

YIELD: 8 servings (1 cup each) ▪ *PREPARATION TIME: 20 minutes plus bean cooking time* ▪ *COOKING TIME: 30 minutes*

White beans are the featured players in this spicy chili. Serve with Blueberry Delight (page 359).

1³/₄ cups water, nonfat chicken broth, or vegetable broth
1 cup diced onions
2 cups diced carrots
1 cup diced celery
1 clove garlic, minced
1 jalapeño pepper, seeded and diced
¹/₂ cup chopped fresh parsley
2¹/₂ cups home-cooked or canned cannellini beans, drained and rinsed

2¹/₂ cups home-cooked or canned Great Northern beans, drained and rinsed
1 teaspoon dried thyme leaves
1 tablespoon ground cumin
¹/₂ teaspoon black pepper
¹/₂ teaspoon dried oregano leaves

1. Heat ¹/₄ cup of the water or broth in a large, heavy soup pot over medium heat. Add onions, carrots, celery, and garlic. Cook and stir for 10 minutes or until vegetables are tender.
2. Stir in the remaining cup water, jalapeño pepper, parsley, cannellini beans, Great Northern beans, thyme, cumin, black pepper, and oregano.
3. Simmer for 30 minutes.

Calories Per Serving: 159
Fat: 1 g
Cholesterol: 0 mg
Protein: 9.6 g

Carbohydrates: 29 g
Dietary Fiber: 7.7 g
Sodium: 67 mg

✳ *Three-Bean Chili* ✳

YIELD: *10 servings (1½ cups each)* • PREPARATION TIME: *20 minutes plus*
bean cooking time • COOKING TIME: *50 minutes*

This robust chili is packed with vegetables, kidney beans, pinto beans, and lentils. Serve with brown or white rice, and Beet and Pepper Salad (page 226).

⅓ *cup water, nonfat chicken broth,*
  vegetable broth, or wine
1 *medium onion, chopped*
2 *garlic cloves, minced*
1 *medium carrot, chopped*
7 *cups water*
⅓ *cup low-sodium tomato purée or*
  tomato paste
2 *cups brown lentils, rinsed*
1 *green bell pepper, chopped*
1 *yellow or red bell pepper, chopped*
2½ *cups home-cooked or canned*
  low-sodium dark red kidney
  beans, drained and rinsed

1 *cup home-cooked or canned low-*
  sodium pinto beans, drained and
  rinsed
2 *cups chopped fresh or low-sodium*
  canned tomatoes with juice
1 *tablespoon chili powder*
1 *tablespoon ground cumin*
¼ *teaspoon cayenne pepper*
¼ *teaspoon black pepper*

1. Heat water or broth in a large, heavy soup pot over medium heat. Add the onion, garlic, and carrot. Cook and stir over medium heat about 5 minutes. Add more liquid if necessary during this process.
2. Add 7 cups water, tomato purée or paste, lentils, green pepper, yellow pepper, red kidney beans, pinto beans, tomatoes, chili powder, cumin, cayenne pepper, and black pepper.
3. Bring to a boil. Reduce heat, cover, and simmer for 45 minutes until lentils are tender, adding more water if necessary.

Calories Per Serving: 151
Fat: .7 g
Cholesterol: 0 mg
Protein: 9 g

Carbohydrates: 28 g
Dietary Fiber: 7.6 g
Sodium: 33 mg

✳ *Lentils with Rice and Curry* ✳

YIELD: 4 servings ▪ *PREPARATION TIME: 10 minutes* ▪
COOKING TIME: 40 minutes

Lentils are rich in vitamins and high in protein. Here they're combined with rice, onions, parsley, and curry powder. Serve with Mushroom–Red Pepper Salad (page 235).

1 cup brown lentils
4¼ cups nonfat chicken broth,
  vegetable broth, or water
2 medium onions, thinly sliced
¼ teaspoon black pepper

½ cup uncooked long-grain
  white rice
2 teaspoons curry powder
1 tablespoon chopped fresh parsley

1. Place lentils and 4 cups of the broth or water in a large, heavy pot. Cover, bring to a boil, lower heat, and let lentils simmer gently for 20 minutes.
2. While the lentils are cooking, heat the remaining ¼ cup broth in a skillet over medium heat. Add the onions. Cook and stir for 5 minutes. Add more liquid during this process if necessary.
3. Add the cooked onions to the lentils along with the pepper, rice, and curry powder. Simmer, covered, for 20 more minutes or until rice is tender and liquid is absorbed, checking frequently to be sure lentils and rice don't stick to pan.
4. Sprinkle with parsley and serve.

Calories Per Serving: 168
Fat: .5 g
Cholesterol: 0 mg
Protein: 6.7 g

Carbohydrates: 34 g
Dietary Fiber: 4.4 g
Sodium: 19 mg

✳ *Chili with Vegetables and Bulgur* ✳

YIELD: 8 servings (1 cup each) ▪ *PREPARATION TIME: 25 minutes plus*
bean cooking time ▪ *COOKING TIME: 25 minutes*

Bulgur wheat makes a good substitute for meat in this chili. Serve with Simple Chopped Salad with Lemon Juice (page 245).

Chili with Vegetables and Bulgur *(cont'd)*

¼ cup water, nonfat chicken broth,
   or vegetable broth
½ cup chopped onion
2 cloves garlic, minced
½ cup sliced mushrooms
1 cup chopped green bell pepper
1 tablespoon chili powder
1 teaspoon ground cumin

3½ cups chopped fresh or low-
   sodium canned plum tomatoes
½ cup diced yellow squash
2 cups home-cooked or canned pinto
   beans or kidney beans, drained
   and rinsed
½ cup bulgur (cracked wheat)

1. Heat water or broth in a large nonstick saucepan over medium heat. Add onion and garlic. Cook and stir for 5 minutes. Add more liquid during this process if necessary.
2. Add mushrooms, green pepper, chili powder, cumin, tomatoes, and squash. Cover and simmer for 15 minutes.
3. Add the pinto or kidney beans and the bulgur. Cover and cook for 5 minutes or until warmed through.

Variation
• Delete chili powder and cumin. Substitute 1 teaspoon dried cilantro and 2 teaspoons lime juice.

Calories Per Serving: 119
Fat: .9 g
Cholesterol: 0 mg
Protein: 6 g

Carbohydrates: 23 g
Dietary Fiber: 6.6 g
Sodium: 31 mg

✳ *Acorn Squash with Black Beans* ✳

YIELD: *6 servings* • PREPARATION TIME: *20 minutes plus bean cooking time* •
COOKING TIME: *35 minutes*

Acorn squash and black beans are combined here with carrots, green bell pepper, and onion. Serve over hot brown rice with Snow Pea–Pineapple Salad (page 238).

2½ cups peeled acorn squash in
   1½-inch chunks
1¼ cups water, nonfat chicken
   broth, or white wine

2½ cups chopped onions
1 cup sliced carrots
½ cup diced green bell pepper
3 cloves garlic, minced

1 teaspoon ground cumin
¹/₂ teaspoon ground ginger
Pinch of cayenne pepper

¹/₂ teaspoon black pepper
2 cans home-cooked or canned black
*   beans, drained and rinsed*

1. Place 1 inch of water in a steamer. Bring to a boil. Place squash chunks in a steamer basket or colander. Cover and steam for 15 minutes or until squash is tender.
2. Place ¹/₄ cup of the water, broth, or wine in a skillet and heat over medium heat. Add onions, carrots, green pepper, and garlic. Cook and stir over medium heat for 10 minutes. Add more liquid during this process if necessary.
3. Add acorn squash, remaining cup of water, cumin, ginger, cayenne pepper, black pepper, and beans. Heat for 10 minutes.

Calories Per Serving: 160
Fat: .8 g
Cholesterol: 0 mg
Protein: 7 g

Carbohydrates: 34 g
Dietary Fiber: 6 g
Sodium: 15 mg

✳ *New Year's Black-Eyed Peas and Rice* ✳

YIELD: 6 servings ▪ *PREPARATION TIME: 15 minutes plus rice and bean cooking time* ▪ *COOKING TIME: 25 minutes*

This dish, also known as hopping John, is traditionally eaten in the Deep South on New Year's Day but it can be enjoyed the rest of the year as well. Serve with a tossed salad with Creamy Lemon-Mustard Dressing (page 277).

¹/₂ cup water
1 cup chopped onions
1 clove garlic, minced
2 cups chopped fresh or low-sodium
*   canned tomatoes*
¹/₂ teaspoon dried basil leaves

¹/₄ teaspoon dried thyme leaves
3 cups cooked long-grain white or
*   brown rice*
2 cups home-cooked or canned black-
*   eyed peas, rinsed and drained*
¹/₄ teaspoon black pepper

1. Place ¹/₄ cup of the water in a large skillet over medium heat. Add onions and garlic. Cook and stir for 5 minutes. Add more liquid if necessary during this process.

New Year's Black-Eyed Peas and Rice *(cont'd)*

2. Add the tomatoes, the remaining ¹/₄ cup water, basil leaves, and thyme leaves. Simmer for 5 minutes.
3. Stir in the rice, black-eyed peas, and black pepper.
4. Simmer for 15 minutes.

Calories Per Serving: 218
Fat: .8 g
Cholesterol: 0 mg
Protein: 8 g

Carbohydrates: 44 g
Dietary Fiber: 2 g
Sodium: 214 mg

✳ *Havana Beans with Rice* ✳

Yield: 4 servings • *Preparation Time: 25 minutes plus rice and bean cooking time* • *Cooking Time: 30 minutes*

This Cuban favorite makes a very satisfying meal. Garnish with salsa and serve with Yogurt Fruit Parfaits (page 360).

Beans

¹/₄ cup water, chicken broth, vegetable broth, or wine
1 medium red onion, chopped
2 cloves garlic, minced
1 green bell pepper, seeded and chopped

2 medium tomatoes, chopped
¹/₄ teaspoon black pepper
2 cups home-cooked or canned black beans, drained and rinsed

Rice

¹/₄ cup water, chicken broth, vegetable broth, or wine
¹/₄ cup chopped mushrooms
¹/₄ cup chopped scallions
¹/₄ cup chopped celery

1 clove garlic, minced
1 cup cooked long-grain white or brown rice
¹/₂ cup chopped fresh parsley

1. For the beans, heat the water, broth, or wine in a heavy saucepan over medium heat. Add onion, garlic, and green pepper. Cook and stir for 3 minutes.
2. Add tomatoes and black pepper. Cook and stir for 4 minutes.

3. Add the beans, cover, and simmer for 20 minutes.
4. While the beans are cooking, prepare the rice. Heat the water, broth or wine in a skillet over medium heat. Add the mushrooms, scallions, celery, and garlic. Cook and stir for 5 minutes. Add rice, stir, and heat until warmed through. Add more liquid during this process if necessary.
5. Serve the beans on a bed of rice.

Variations
- Serve the beans and rice at room temperature. Combine 3 tablespoons balsamic vinegar and ½ teaspoon dried thyme leaves. Toss with beans and rice.
- Stir 1 teaspoon dried cilantro, 2 tablespoons red wine vinegar, 3 tablespoons orange juice, 1 teaspoon ground cumin, and 1 teaspoon chili powder into beans at the end of Step 3. Toss with rice in a large bowl.

Calories Per Serving: 236
Fat: 1 g
Cholesterol: 0 mg
Protein: 10 g
Carbohydrates: 47 g
Dietary Fiber: 6.2 g
Sodium: 19 mg

✳ *Tostadas* ✳

YIELD: 4 servings (1 tostada each) • *PREPARATION TIME: 20 minutes plus bean and corn cooking time* • *COOKING TIME: 20 minutes*

These corn tortillas are baked and then topped with mashed beans, shredded lettuce, tomatoes, onions, and corn. Serve with a tomato or green chile salsa and Garden Tomato Soup (page 89).

4 nonfat corn tortillas
2 cups home-cooked or canned pinto beans, rinsed and drained
1 teaspoon chili powder
1 teaspoon ground cumin
1 clove garlic, minced
½ cup shredded romaine lettuce
2 tomatoes, chopped
1 onion, diced
½ cup finely diced green bell pepper or zucchini
½ cup cooked fresh, frozen, or canned corn kernels
½ cup nonfat grated cheese

1. Preheat oven to 375 degrees.

Tostadas *(cont'd)*

2. Place corn tortillas on a nonstick baking sheet and bake for 10 minutes or until crisp.
3. Mash beans and mix with chili powder, cumin, and garlic. Place in a small saucepan and heat until warmed through.
4. Spread bean mixture on baked corn tortillas. Top with lettuce, tomatoes, onions, green pepper, corn, and cheese.

Calories Per Serving: 201	Carbohydrates: 40 g
Fat: .9 g	Dietary Fiber: 8.3 g
Cholesterol: .6 mg	Sodium: 83 mg
Protein: 10.8 g	

✳ *Bean Tortilla Bake* ✳

YIELD: 6 servings (2 tortillas each) • *PREPARATION TIME: 15 minutes plus bean cooking time* • *COOKING TIME: 25 minutes*

Serve this dish with salsa and nonfat sour cream. Add a side dish of Shredded Carrot Salad (page 229).

1¹/₂ cups home-cooked or canned pinto beans, drained and rinsed	*¹/₂ teaspoon ground cumin*
1 cup home-cooked or canned navy beans, drained and rinsed	*1 clove garlic, minced*
	12 6-inch nonfat flour or corn tortillas
1¹/₂ cups home-cooked or canned kidney beans, drained and rinsed	*¹/₂ cup chopped scallions*
	2 tomatoes, chopped
¹/₂ cup low-sodium tomato juice	*1 cup shredded nonfat cheddar cheese*
2 teaspoons chili powder	*1¹/₄ cups low-sodium tomato sauce*

1. Combine pinto beans, navy beans, kidney beans, tomato juice, chili powder, cumin, and garlic in a saucepan. Simmer for 10 minutes.
2. Mash beans until chunky.
3. Preheat oven to 350 degrees.
4. Place 2 tablespoons of the bean mixture on each tortilla. Sprinkle scallions, tomatoes, and ¹/₂ cup of the cheddar cheese over bean mixture.
5. Roll tortillas up and place seam side down in a 9-by-13-inch baking dish.

6. Pour tomato sauce over tortillas. Cover and bake for 20 minutes.
7. Uncover, top with remaining ¹/₂ cup of cheese, and bake for 5 minutes more.

Calories Per Serving: 292
Fat: .9 g
Cholesterol: .8 mg
Protein: 14.8 g

Carbohydrates: 60 g
Dietary Fiber: 9.5 g
Sodium: 139 mg

❋ Baked Potatoes with Baked Beans ❋

YIELD: 4 servings (1 potato each) • *PREPARATION TIME: 10 minutes plus potato baking or microwaving time* • *COOKING TIME: 6 to 10 minutes*

These baked potatoes are topped with canned baked beans, nonfat cottage cheese, nonfat mozzarella cheese, and chopped scallions. Serve with Celery Soup (page 92).

4 warm baked potatoes, cut in half lengthwise
¹/₂ cup nonfat cottage cheese
1 cup canned vegetarian baked beans, drained and rinsed
¹/₂ cup grated nonfat mozzarella cheese
¹/₂ cup chopped scallions

1. Preheat oven to 375 degrees.
2. Spread 1 tablespoon cottage cheese over each potato half.
3. Add ¹/₄ cup baked beans to each potato half.
4. Top the baked beans on each potato half with 1 tablespoon cheese and 1 tablespoon scallions.
5. Bake until cheese melts, about 5 to 10 minutes.

Calories Per Serving: 244
Fat: .4 g
Cholesterol: 4 mg
Protein: 14 g

Carbohydrates: 46 g
Dietary Fiber: 6.9 g
Sodium: 255 mg

✳ *Apple-Bean Jumble* ✳

YIELD: 6 servings • *PREPARATION TIME: 15 minutes plus bean cooking time* • *COOKING TIME: 20 minutes*

Pinto beans, bell peppers, apples, tomatoes, and raisins are combined with chili powder and cinnamon in this recipe. Serve with Carrot Corn Bread (page 313) and Red Potato–Spinach Salad (page 239).

1¼ cups water, nonfat chicken broth, or vegetable broth
1 green bell pepper, seeded and chopped
½ cup chopped onion
1 apple, cored and chopped
1 clove garlic, chopped
1 tablespoon chili powder
¼ teaspoon ground cinnamon
1 cup chopped fresh or low-sodium canned tomatoes
¼ teaspoon black pepper
3 cups home-cooked or canned pinto beans, drained and rinsed
3 tablespoons raisins

1. Heat ¼ cup of the water or broth in a skillet over medium heat. Add green pepper, onion, apple, and garlic to skillet. Cook and stir for 5 minutes over medium heat or until tender. Add water if necessary during this process.
2. Stir in remaining cup of water, chili powder, ground cinnamon, tomatoes, and black pepper. Cover and cook over low heat for 10 minutes.
3. Add beans and raisins. Cook for 5 minutes or until warmed through.

Calories Per Serving: 163
Fat: 1 g
Cholesterol: 0 mg
Protein: 8.5 g

Carbohydrates: 32 g
Dietary Fiber: 8 g
Sodium: 26 mg

SIDE DISHES

VEGETABLE SIDE DISHES

Asparagus with Orange Sauce • Beets in Orange Flavor • Broccoli in Ginger-Mustard Sauce • Broccoli with Wine Sauce • Caraway Brussels Sprouts • Cabbage and Apples • Carrot–Mandarin Orange Casserole • Pineapple Carrots • Cauliflower and Tomatoes • Celery with Tomatoes • Creamy Baked Corn with Zucchini and Red Bell Peppers • Garlic, Chili, Corn, and Summer Squash • Corn on the Cob in Wine Sauce • Green Beans with Tomatoes and Cinnamon • Lemon-Mint Green Beans • Jalapeño Green Beans • Green Beans with Paprika Sauce • Green Peas with Mushrooms • Lima Beans and Bell Peppers • Lima Beans with Corn and Tomatoes • Maple Baked Sweet Potatoes • Green Peas and Bell Peppers • Vegetable-Stuffed Peppers • Orange–Acorn Squash • Sweet Potato Soufflé • Sherried Sweet Potatoes with Apples and Onion • Butternut-Apple Casserole • Swiss Chard with Balsamic Vinegar • Zucchini with Tomatoes

POTATO SIDE DISHES

Baked Potatoes • Baked Potatoes with Mustard-Dill Topping • Stuffed Baked Potatoes • Mashed Potatoes • Mashed Potatoes and Carrots • Roasted Red Potatoes with Lemon-Oregano Sauce • Puffed

Potato Casserole • Rosemary Potatoes • Wine-Parsley Potatoes • Baked Potato Slices with Onion Sauce and Parmesan Cheese • Oven Fries

GRAIN SIDE DISHES

Mexicali Rice • Lemon-Thyme Vegetable Rice • Curried Tangerine Rice • Tomato-Carrot Rice • Oriental Rice with Asparagus • Dried Apricots and Wild Rice • Spicy Rice with Dried Fruit • Peach-Blueberry Rice • Barley and Apples

BEAN SIDE DISHES

Eight-Flavor Baked Beans • Lentils in Tomato Sauce • Black Beans and Corn • Molasses-Apple Baked Beans

FRUIT SIDE DISHES

Chunky Spiced Applesauce • Cranberry Applesauce • Lemon Spiced Nectarines • Spiced Bananas and Mandarin Oranges • Baked Bananas and Pineapple • Strawberry-Banana Salad • Honeyed Cranberries • Ginger-Lime Mangoes • Grilled Nectarines with Strawberry Purée • Papaya-Honey Bake • Pears with Red Wine • Cranberry Poached Peaches • Poached Pears in Orange Sauce • Nutmeg-Cinnamon Baked Pears • Baked Pineapple • Broiled Pineapple • Raspberry-Pear Toss • Melon and Blueberry Salad with Frozen Raspberry Purée • Prunes with Brown Sugar and Vanilla • Strawberries in Orange Flavor • Strawberries with Sugar and Balsamic Vinegar • Fruit Salad with Pineapple-Spice Dressing • Rainbow Fruit Bowl • Maple Fruit • Curried Fruit • Pears and Cranberries

These side dishes can be served in addition to main dishes or combined with each other and/or salads to make a complete meal. All of these recipes offer delicious nonfat choices to serve with lean meat, poultry, or fish if you are including them in your diet.

VEGETABLE SIDE DISHES

::

✳ Asparagus with Orange Sauce ✳

YIELD: 4 servings • PREPARATION TIME: 15 minutes •
COOKING TIME: 18 minutes

Here steamed asparagus is topped with a sauce of orange juice, lime juice, scallions, garlic, and orange zest. When buying asparagus be sure the tiny buds at the tip fit together tightly and smoothly. The tip should be firm and free of any damage.

1/2 cup orange juice
1 tablespoon lime juice
1 tablespoon chopped scallions
1 clove garlic, minced

1 tablespoon grated orange peel
2 pounds fresh asparagus, trimmed
1 tablespoon red wine vinegar

1. Combine orange juice, lime juice, scallions, garlic, and orange peel. Let stand while you cook the asparagus.
2. Bring 1 inch of water to a boil in a steamer. Place the asparagus in a steamer basket or colander and cover. Steam for 4 to 8 minutes until just tender.
3. Add the wine vinegar to the orange juice mixture.
4. Pour the orange juice mixture over the asparagus before serving.

Calories Per Serving: 73
Fat: .8 g
Cholesterol: 0 mg
Protein: 6 g

Carbohydrates: 14 g
Dietary Fiber: 2.9 g
Sodium: 10.6 mg

❋ Beets in Orange Flavor ❋

YIELD: 4 servings • *PREPARATION TIME: 15 minutes plus beet cooling time* •
COOKING TIME: 30 minutes

Fresh beets are a delicious change of pace. When you see them at the supermarket, pick up a bunch and try this easy recipe. Look for beets that are clean and free of cuts and soft spots. Smaller beets are less likely to have unusable, woody cores.

5 or 6 fresh beets, tops removed
1 teaspoon brown sugar, firmly
   packed

¹/₂ teaspoon grated orange peel
³/₄ cup orange juice

1. Heat 1 inch of water in a steamer basket and bring to a boil. Place beets in a colander or steamer basket, cover, and steam for 20 minutes or until tender. Cool. Peel and slice.
2. Combine the brown sugar, orange peel, and orange juice in a medium saucepan and bring to a boil. Boil for 1 minute.
3. Stir in the sliced beets and simmer for 5 minutes.

Calories Per Serving: 45
Fat: .1 g
Cholesterol: 0 mg
Protein: .9 g

Carbohydrates: 10 g
Dietary Fiber: 1.6 g
Sodium: 31 mg

❋ Broccoli in Ginger-Mustard Sauce ❋

YIELD: 4 servings • *PREPARATION TIME: 15 minutes* •
COOKING TIME: 12 minutes

Here broccoli is simmered in orange juice, soy sauce, mustard, ginger, and sugar.

4 cups broccoli florets, and peeled,
   chopped stalks
¹/₄ cup orange juice
1 tablespoon light soy sauce

2 teaspoons Dijon mustard
¹/₂ teaspoon ground ginger
¹/₂ teaspoon brown sugar, firmly
   packed

1. Place 1 inch of water in a steamer. Place broccoli in a colander or steamer basket, cover, and steam for 7 to 8 minutes or until tender.
2. Place orange juice, soy sauce, Dijon mustard, ground ginger, and brown sugar in a skillet and heat over medium heat. When mixture is hot, add the steamed broccoli. Simmer for 3 to 4 minutes.

Calories Per Serving: 137
Fat: .4 g
Cholesterol: 0 mg
Protein: 3.9 g

Carbohydrates: 34 g
Dietary Fiber: 2.6 g
Sodium: 215 mg

✳ *Broccoli with Wine Sauce* ✳

YIELD: 4 servings • *PREPARATION TIME: 15 minutes* •
COOKING TIME: 15 minutes

In this dish broccoli florets and red peppers are steamed in a wine sauce seasoned with garlic.

¹/₄ cup water, nonfat chicken broth, or vegetable broth
1 garlic clove, minced
6 cups broccoli florets
¹/₂ cup chopped red bell pepper

¹/₂ cup white wine
Pinch of black pepper
1 tablespoon nonfat Parmesan cheese (optional)

1. Heat water or broth in a skillet over medium heat. Add garlic. Cook and stir for 30 seconds.
2. Add broccoli and red pepper. Cook and stir for 1 minute.
3. Add ¹/₄ cup of the wine and the black pepper.
4. Cook and stir the vegetables for 4 to 6 minutes or until the broccoli is crisp-tender. Add the remaining ¹/₄ cup wine during this process.
5. Sprinkle with Parmesan, if desired, before serving.

Calories Per Serving: 59
Fat: .5 g
Cholesterol: 0 mg
Protein: 4 g

Carbohydrates: 7.9 g
Dietary Fiber: 1.6 g
Sodium: 55 mg

✳ *Caraway Brussels Sprouts* ✳

YIELD: *4 servings* • PREPARATION TIME: *15 minutes* •
COOKING TIME: *15 minutes*

Fresh brussels sprouts are prepared with a mustard–caraway sauce in this dish. Buy brussels sprouts that are firm, deep green in color, with tight-fitting leaves.

1 pound brussels sprouts
½ cup plain nonfat yogurt
1½ tablespoons Dijon mustard

½ teaspoon crushed caraway seeds
¼ teaspoon black pepper

1. Remove any discolored outer leaves from brussels sprouts and cut off stem ends. Slash bottom of each sprout with a shallow **X**.
2. Heat 1 inch of water in a steamer and bring to a boil. Place brussels sprouts in a colander or steamer basket, cover, and steam for 10 minutes or until tender.
3. Combine yogurt, Dijon mustard, caraway seeds, and black pepper.
4. Toss yogurt sauce with brussels sprouts.

Calories Per Serving: 83
Fat: 1 g
Cholesterol: .5 mg
Protein: 5.7 g

Carbohydrates: 16 g
Dietary Fiber: 6.7 g
Sodium: 129 mg

✳ *Cabbage and Apples* ✳

YIELD: *6 servings* • PREPARATION TIME: *25 minutes* •
COOKING TIME: *35 minutes*

Here red cabbage and apples are simmered in red wine. Store whole unwashed heads of cabbage in your refrigerator for one to two weeks. Don't chop cabbage until ready to cook to avoid losing nutrients.

¼ cup water, chicken broth,
vegetable broth, or red wine
1 large onion, cut in half and thinly
sliced

5 cups chopped red cabbage
1 large apple, peeled, cored,
quartered, and sliced
½ cup dry red wine

2 tablespoons apple cider vinegar   ¹/₄ teaspoon black pepper
1 teaspoon honey

1. Heat the water, broth, or wine in a large heavy pot over medium heat. Add the onion. Cook and stir over medium heat for 5 minutes. Add more water during this process if necessary.
2. Add the cabbage, apple, wine, vinegar, honey, and black pepper, and stir.
3. Simmer for 30 minutes or until cabbage is tender.

Variation
▪ Add 2 teaspoons Dijon mustard in Step 2.

Calories Per Serving: 58   Carbohydrates: 11 g
Fat: .3 g   Dietary Fiber: 2.4 g
Cholesterol: 0 mg   Sodium: 20 mg
Protein: 1.3 g

✳ *Carrot–Mandarin Orange Casserole* ✳

YIELD: *8 servings* • PREPARATION TIME: *20 minutes* • COOKING TIME: *1 hour*

Sweet potatoes, carrots, prunes, pineapple, and mandarin oranges are baked with orange juice, brown sugar, and cinnamon in this traditional dish.

6 sweet potatoes, peeled and diced   ¹/₂ teaspoon cinnamon
4 cups diced carrots   2 ¹/₂ cups juice-packed canned
¹/₂ cup pitted prunes   pineapple chunks
1 cup orange juice   1 cup mandarin orange slices,
¹/₄ cup brown sugar, firmly packed   drained

1. Preheat oven to 350 degrees.
2. Bring water to a boil in a large pot. Add sweet potatoes and carrots. Simmer for 15 minutes or until tender.
3. Drain and mash. Stir in prunes. Place in a large nonstick casserole or a casserole sprayed with vegetable cooking spray.
4. Combine orange juice, brown sugar, cinnamon, pineapple, and mandarin orange slices.

Carrot–Mandarin Orange Casserole *(cont'd)*

5. Pour juice and fruit mixture over sweet potatoes and prunes. Bake, covered, for 45 minutes.

Calories Per Serving: 206
Fat: .4 g
Cholesterol: 0 mg
Protein: 2.9 g

Carbohydrates: 50 g
Dietary Fiber: 6 g
Sodium: 32 mg

✳ *Pineapple Carrots* ✳

YIELD: 4 servings • *PREPARATION TIME: 15 minutes* •
COOKING TIME: 15 minutes

When shopping for carrots, look for those that are vivid orange, since they are more nutritious than pale carrots. In this recipe, carrots are simmered in pineapple juice, cinnamon, and pepper.

*8 medium carrots, scrubbed and cut
   into julienne strips
1½ cups pineapple juice*

*1½ teaspoons ground cinnamon
¼ teaspoon black pepper*

1. Place carrot strips, pineapple juice, ground cinnamon, and black pepper in a saucepan.
2. Bring to a boil, reduce heat, and simmer, covered, for 15 minutes.

Calories Per Serving: 108
Fat: .4 g
Cholesterol: 0 mg
Protein: 1.5 g

Carbohydrates: 26 g
Dietary Fiber: 4.8 g
Sodium: 53 mg

✳ *Cauliflower and Tomatoes* ✳

YIELD: 6 servings • *PREPARATION TIME: 20 minutes* •
COOKING TIME: 40 minutes

This dish is accented with Indian spices.

½ cup water, nonfat chicken broth, or vegetable broth

1 cup chopped onions

1 ½ cups low-sodium canned tomato purée

2 tablespoons chopped canned green chiles

2 tablespoons chopped fresh parsley

2 teaspoons ground ginger

2 teaspoons ground cumin

1 teaspoon ground coriander

½ teaspoon turmeric

¼ teaspoon cayenne pepper

6 cups cauliflower florets

1. Heat ¼ cup of the water or broth in a heavy saucepan. Add onions. Cook and stir until onions are tender. Add more liquid during this process if necessary.
2. Add tomato purée, chiles, parsley, ginger, cumin, coriander, turmeric, and cayenne pepper. Simmer for 5 minutes.
3. Add cauliflower. Simmer, covered, for 20 minutes or until cauliflower is tender.

Calories Per Serving: 52
Fat: .6 g
Cholesterol: 0 mg
Protein: 3 g

Carbohydrates: 10 g
Dietary Fiber: 3.3 g
Sodium: 46 mg

✳ *Celery with Tomatoes* ✳

YIELD: 4 servings •
PREPARATION TIME: 15 minutes • *COOKING TIME: 30 minutes*

This dish of cooked celery flavored with white wine provides an interesting change of pace.

¼ cup water, nonfat chicken broth, vegetable broth, or wine

2½ cups sliced celery

1 onion, finely chopped

¾ cup low-sodium tomato juice

½ cup white wine

½ teaspoon dried basil leaves

½ teaspoon dried oregano leaves

Pinch of white pepper

1½ cups chopped fresh or low-sodium canned tomatoes

1. Heat water, broth, or wine in a saucepan over medium heat. Add celery and onion. Cook and stir until the onion is soft. Add more liquid during this process if necessary.

Celery with Tomatoes *(cont'd)*

2. Add tomato juice, wine, basil, oregano, and pepper. Cook over low heat for 20 minutes or until celery is tender.
3. Stir in tomatoes. Cook for 5 minutes more.

Variation
- Substitute reserved liquid from canned tomatoes for all or part of tomato juice or wine.

Calories Per Serving: 72
Fat: .5 g
Cholesterol: 0 mg
Protein: 2.2 g

Carbohydrates: 11.9 g
Dietary Fiber: 1.3 g
Sodium: 102 mg

Creamy Baked Corn with Zucchini and Red ❋ Bell Peppers ❋

YIELD: *6 servings* • PREPARATION TIME: *15 minutes* • COOKING TIME: *40 minutes*

Here cream-style corn is baked with vegetables and whole-grain bread crumbs.

¹/₂ cup chopped scallions
¹/₂ cup chopped red bell pepper
¹/₂ cup chopped zucchini
2 cups cream-style corn

¹/₄ teaspoon white pepper
¹/₂ cup nonfat whole-grain bread crumbs

1. Preheat oven to 350 degrees.
2. Combine scallions, red pepper, and zucchini. Add corn and white pepper. Mix well.
3. Transfer corn mixture to an 11-by-7-inch baking dish. Sprinkle with bread crumbs.
4. Bake for 40 minutes.

Calories Per Serving: 76
Fat: .6 g
Cholesterol: 0 mg
Protein: 2 g

Carbohydrates: 18 g
Dietary Fiber: 1.4 g
Sodium: 22 mg

❋ *Garlic, Chile, Corn, and Summer Squash* ❋

YIELD: *4 servings* • PREPARATION TIME: *15 minutes plus corn cooking time* •
COOKING TIME: *15 minutes*

Canned green chiles are added to corn and yellow summer squash here.
Look for small, lemon-colored summer squash, harvested young with
soft skin and tender seeds. They may be straight-necked or crook-
necked.

1/4 cup water, nonfat chicken broth,
   vegetable broth, or wine
1 medium onion, chopped
2 cloves garlic, minced
2 1/2 cups diced yellow summer
   squash

1/4 cup canned mild or hot green
   chiles, drained and minced
1 1/2 cups cooked fresh, frozen, or
   canned corn kernels
2 tablespoons fresh chopped parsley
1/4 teaspoon black pepper

1. Heat water, broth, or wine in a large skillet over medium heat. Add
   onion and garlic. Cook and stir for 5 minutes over low heat.
2. Add squash and chiles. Cook and stir for 8 minutes, adding more
   liquid if necessary.
3. Add corn, parsley, and pepper. Cook and stir for 2 additional minutes.

Calories: 91
Fat: .5 g
Cholesterol: 0 mg
Protein: 3.5 g

Carbohydrates: 21 g
Dietary Fiber: 3.7 g
Sodium: 67 mg

❋ *Corn on the Cob in Wine Sauce* ❋

YIELD: *8 servings (1 ear each)* • PREPARATION TIME: *10 minutes* •
COOKING TIME: *8 minutes*

If you're having trouble adjusting to the idea of corn on the cob without
butter, try preparing it with this wine sauce.

8 ears fresh sweet corn, shucked and
   silked
2 tablespoons lemon juice
1/4 cup dry white wine

1 teaspoon dried thyme leaves
1 teaspoon dried basil leaves
1/4 teaspoon black pepper

Corn on the Cob in Wine Sauce *(cont'd)*

1. Bring a large pot of water to a boil. Plunge ears of corn into boiling water and when water returns to a boil, cook for 3 minutes.
2. Drain corn and place on serving platter.
3. Combine lemon juice, wine, thyme leaves, basil leaves, and pepper in a small saucepan and warm through.
4. Pour sauce over corn.

Calories Per Serving: 90
Fat: 1 g
Cholesterol: 0 mg
Protein: 2.6 g

Carbohydrates: 19 g
Dietary Fiber: 6.6 g
Sodium: 18 mg

Green Beans with Tomatoes
❋ *and Cinnamon* ❋

YIELD: *6 servings* • PREPARATION TIME: *25 minutes* •
COOKING TIME: *20 minutes*

Shop for green beans that are slim and smooth. Those with bulges will be too mature to be tender. Here, green beans and tomatoes are enhanced with a combination of flavors including onions, garlic, allspice, and cinnamon.

¹/₄ cup water, nonfat chicken broth,
* vegetable broth, sherry, or wine*
1 medium onion, diced
2 cloves garlic, minced
6 medium tomatoes, diced
4 cups diced green beans

2 teaspoons ground cinnamon
¹/₂ teaspoon ground allspice
¹/₄ teaspoon black pepper

1. Heat water, broth, wine or sherry in a skillet over medium heat. Add onion and garlic. Cook and stir over medium heat for 5 minutes, adding more liquid if necessary.
2. Add tomatoes, green beans, cinnamon, allspice, and black pepper to skillet. Cover and simmer for 20 minutes or until green beans are tender.

Calories Per Serving: 66
Fat: .6 g
Cholesterol: 0 mg
Protein: 3 g

Carbohydrates: 14 g
Dietary Fiber: 3.5 g
Sodium: 14 mg

✳ *Lemon-Mint Green Beans* ✳

YIELD: 4 servings • *PREPARATION TIME: 15 minutes* •
COOKING TIME: 12 minutes

You can store unwashed raw green beans in your refrigerator in a plastic bag for three to five days. Green beans take on new character when steamed and then tossed with lemon juice, dry mustard, mint leaves, garlic, black pepper, and yogurt.

1 pound trimmed green beans
1 tablespoon lemon juice
¹/₂ teaspoon dry mustard
¹/₂ teaspoon dried mint leaves

1 clove garlic, minced
¹/₄ teaspoon black pepper
¹/₃ cup plain nonfat yogurt

1. Bring 1 inch of water to a boil in a steamer. Place beans in a steamer basket or colander. Cover and steam for 12 minutes or until tender.
2. Combine green beans, lemon juice, dry mustard, dried mint leaves, garlic, black pepper, and yogurt.
3. Toss beans with lemon-mint sauce.

Calories Per Serving: 57
Fat: .4 g
Cholesterol: .3 mg
Protein: 3.5 g

Carbohydrates: 12 g
Dietary Fiber: 2 g
Sodium: 19 mg

✳ *Jalapeño Green Beans* ✳

YIELD: 6 servings • *PREPARATION TIME: 25 minutes* •
COOKING TIME: 25 minutes

Here green beans are simmered with tomatoes and jalapeño pepper.

Jalapeño Green Beans *(cont'd)*

$^1/_3$ cup water, nonfat chicken broth,
  vegetable broth, or wine
1 medium onion, chopped
2 cloves garlic, minced
4 cups string beans, trimmed and cut
  in half
3 medium tomatoes, chopped

1 jalapeño pepper, minced and
  seeded (leave seeds in if you want
  dish to be hot)
$^1/_4$ cup water
1 tablespoon white wine vinegar
$^1/_4$ teaspoon black pepper

1. Heat water, broth, or wine in a large, heavy pot over medium heat.
   Add onion and garlic. Cook and stir for 5 minutes. Add string beans.
   Cook and stir for 5 minutes, adding liquid if necessary.
2. Add tomatoes, jalapeño, water, vinegar, and pepper.
3. Cover pot and simmer for 15 minutes or until beans are tender.

Calories Per Serving: 53
Fat: .5 g
Cholesterol: 0 mg
Protein: 2.5 g

Carbohydrates: 11 g
Dietary Fiber: 2.7 g
Sodium: 51 mg

❋ Green Peas with Paprika Sauce ❋

Yield: 4 servings • Preparation Time: 10 minutes •
Cooking Time: 20 minutes

Fresh or frozen green peas are steamed and topped with a paprika and
onion–accented tomato sauce in this recipe. If using fresh peas, you can
store them in their pods in plastic bags in your refrigerator for three or
four days. Don't shell them until you are ready to cook them.

3 cups fresh or frozen green peas
$^1/_4$ cup water, nonfat chicken broth,
  vegetable broth, sherry, or wine
1 medium onion, chopped
1 clove garlic, minced

2 teaspoons ground paprika
2 cups chopped fresh or low-sodium
  canned tomatoes with juice
$^1/_4$ teaspoon black pepper

1. Bring 1 inch of water to a boil in a steamer. Place peas in steamer
   basket or colander. Cover and steam for 5 to 7 minutes. Remove peas
   from heat and set aside.

2. Heat water, broth, sherry, or wine in a skillet over medium heat. Add onion and garlic. Cook and stir over medium heat for 5 minutes. Add more liquid if necessary during this process.
3. Stir in paprika and cook for 1 minute.
4. Add tomatoes with juice and black pepper. Bring to a boil, lower heat, and simmer for 10 minutes.
5. Transfer steamed green peas to a serving bowl and top with tomato sauce.

Calories Per Serving: 130
Fat: 1 g
Cholesterol: 0 mg
Protein: 7 g

Carbohydrates: 25 g
Dietary Fiber: 6.7 g
Sodium: 20 mg

✳ *Green Peas with Mushrooms* ✳

YIELD: 4 servings • *PREPARATION TIME: 10 minutes* •
COOKING TIME: 25 minutes

Green peas, mushrooms, and onions are combined with curry powder and yogurt in this Indian-style dish.

*¹/₂ cup water, nonfat chicken broth,
   vegetable broth, sherry, or wine
2 cups sliced fresh mushrooms
1 medium onion, chopped*

*1 teaspoon curry powder
2 cups fresh or frozen green peas
¹/₂ cup plain nonfat yogurt*

1. Place water, broth, sherry, or wine in a saucepan and bring to a boil.
2. Add mushrooms, onion, and curry powder. Cook over medium heat for 15 minutes or until most of the liquid is absorbed.
3. Add green peas. Simmer for 5 more minutes or until peas are warmed through.
4. Remove from heat. Stir in yogurt and serve.

Calories Per Serving: 103
Fat: .6 g
Cholesterol: .5 mg
Protein: 7 g

Carbohydrates: 18 g
Dietary Fiber: 4.3 g
Sodium: 95 mg

✳ *Lima Beans and Bell Peppers* ✳

YIELD: *4 servings* • PREPARATION TIME: *15 minutes* •
COOKING TIME: *20 minutes*

Here lima beans and red bell peppers are simmered with onion.

*¼ cup water, nonfat chicken broth,
  or vegetable broth
2 tablespoons chopped onion
⅔ cup diced red bell pepper*

*¾ cup water
Pinch of black pepper
1 ¾ cups fresh or frozen lima beans*

1. Heat water or broth in a saucepan over medium heat. Add onion and red pepper. Cook and stir for 5 minutes or until vegetables are tender.
2. Add ¾ cup water, black pepper, and lima beans. Bring to a boil. Lower heat and simmer for 15 minutes or until the lima beans are tender. Add more water if necessary during this process.

Calories Per Serving: 79
Fat: .3 g
Cholesterol: 0 mg
Protein: 4.6 g

Carbohydrates: 15 g
Dietary Fiber: 1.5 g
Sodium: 42 mg

✳ *Lima Beans with Corn and Tomatoes* ✳

YIELD: *4 servings* • PREPARATION TIME: *20 minutes* •
COOKING TIME: *22 minutes*

This satisfying and attractive dish is seasoned with garlic, parsley, and onions. You may find fresh limas still in their pods or shelled and pre-packaged in plastic-wrapped trays. If they are unshelled, look for pods that are full and green with no browning. They should look moist, feel firm, and show no signs of withering.

*1¼ cups nonfat chicken broth,
  vegetable broth, or water
1 small onion, chopped
1 clove garlic, minced
½ cup chopped fresh or low-sodium
  canned tomatoes with their juice*

*1 tablespoon chopped fresh parsley
1 cup fresh or frozen lima beans
¾ cup fresh, frozen, or canned corn
  kernels
¼ teaspoon black pepper*

1. Heat ¼ cup of the broth or water in a large saucepan over medium heat. Add onion and garlic. Cook and stir over medium heat for 5 minutes. Add liquid during this process if necessary.
2. Add parsley and tomatoes. Simmer for 2 minutes.
3. Add lima beans and the remaining cup of broth. Bring to a boil, cover, and simmer for 10 minutes.
4. Add the corn and the black pepper. Simmer for 5 minutes more.

Calories Per Serving: 86
Fat: .3 g
Cholesterol: 0 mg
Protein: 4.7 g

Carbohydrates: 17 g
Dietary Fiber: 3.3 g
Sodium: 71 mg

✳ *Maple Baked Sweet Potatoes* ✳

YIELD: *4 servings* • PREPARATION TIME: *20 minutes plus sweet potato baking time* • COOKING TIME: *40 minutes*

Sweet potatoes and apples are baked in a maple-flavored sauce. Rome Beauty, Golden Delicious, or Granny Smith apples work well in this recipe.

3 medium sweet potatoes, baked and cut into ½-inch slices
½ cup maple syrup
2 large apples, peeled, cored, quartered, and thinly sliced

Ground cinnamon
Ground cloves
¾ cup apple juice

1. Preheat oven to 350 degrees.
2. Arrange half the sweet potato slices in the bottom of a 1½-quart non-stick casserole or in a casserole lightly sprayed with vegetable cooking spray. Pour ¼ cup of the maple syrup over the sweet potato slices.
3. Arrange half of the apple slices on top of the sweet potato slices. Sprinkle with cinnamon and cloves.
4. Add a second layer of sweet potato slices and top with the remaining ¼ cup maple syrup.
5. Add the remaining apple slices and sprinkle with cinnamon and cloves.
6. Pour apple juice over the top of the apples and sweet potatoes.
7. Cover and bake for 30 minutes. Remove cover and bake for 10 additional minutes.

Maple Baked Sweet Potatoes *(cont'd)*

Calories Per Serving: 272

Fat: .4 g

Cholesterol: 0 mg

Protein: 1.6 g

Carbohydrates: 66 g

Dietary Fiber: 4 g

Sodium: 81 mg

✳ *Green Peas and Bell Peppers* ✳

YIELD: 4 servings • *PREPARATION TIME: 15 minutes* •
COOKING TIME: 12 minutes

This quick and easy dish combines frozen green peas, onion, chopped bell peppers, and marjoram, a sweet mild herb that is similar to oregano.

1/2 cup water

2 1/4 cups fresh or frozen green peas

3 tablespoons chopped onion

*1/4 cup chopped red, green, or yellow
  bell pepper*

1/4 teaspoon dried marjoram leaves

1/4 teaspoon black pepper

1. Bring water to a boil. Add peas. Return to boil and simmer for 3 to 4 minutes.
2. Stir in onion, bell peppers, marjoram, and black pepper. Simmer for 3 minutes.

Calories Per Serving: 75

Fat: .3 g

Cholesterol: 0 mg

Protein: 4.7 g

Carbohydrates: 13 g

Dietary Fiber: 3.6 g

Sodium: 80 mg

✳ *Vegetable Stuffed Peppers* ✳

YIELD: 4 servings (1 pepper each) • *PREPARATION TIME: 25 minutes* •
COOKING TIME: 35 minutes

Here green, red, yellow, orange, or purple bell peppers are stuffed with a mixture of onion, parsley, green beans, corn, and tomato. When buying sweet bell peppers, watch for those that are firm with smooth skins.

1 cup green beans, cut into ¹/₂-inch
   pieces
4 large bell peppers, of different
   colors if possible
¹/₄ cup water, nonfat chicken broth,
   vegetable stock, sherry, or wine
¹/₄ cup chopped onion
1 tablespoon chopped fresh parsley
1 cup fresh, frozen, or canned corn
   kernels

1 medium tomato, chopped
¹/₄ teaspoon dried marjoram leaves
¹/₄ teaspoon dried basil leaves
Pinch of dried dill weed
Pinch of black pepper
¹/₂ cup nonfat grated cheddar cheese
   (optional)

1. Bring 1 inch of water to a boil in a steamer. Place green beans in a steamer basket or colander. Cover and steam for 6 to 8 minutes.
2. Preheat oven to 350 degrees.
3. Slice the tops off the peppers and scoop out their insides.
4. Heat water, broth, sherry, or wine in a skillet over medium heat. Add onion and parsley. Cook and stir over medium heat for 3 minutes. Add more liquid during this process if necessary.
5. Add corn, tomato, marjoram, basil, dill weed, and black pepper to skillet. Cook and stir for 2 minutes.
6. Stuff vegetables into peppers and place peppers in a shallow baking dish. Bake for 20 minutes.
7. If using cheese, sprinkle peppers with cheese and bake for 5 more minutes.

Calories Per Serving: 78
Fat: .5 g
Cholesterol: .6 mg
Protein: 3.8 g

Carbohydrates: 17 g
Dietary Fiber: 3.2 g
Sodium: 45 mg

✳ *Orange–Acorn Squash* ✳

YIELD: *4 servings* • PREPARATION TIME: *15 minutes* •
COOKING TIME: *25 minutes*

Here slices of acorn squash are simmered in orange juice, brown sugar, and ground nutmeg. Acorn squash have dark green rinds. They are spherical in shape with evenly spaced ridges running from the stem and to a point at the bottom.

Orange–Acorn Squash *(cont'd)*

1 1-pound acorn squash, peeled
½ cup orange juice
1 tablespoon brown sugar, firmly
packed

¼ teaspoon ground nutmeg

1. Cut acorn squash into ½-inch-thick slices, discarding seeds.
2. Combine orange juice, brown sugar, and ground nutmeg.
3. Place squash and orange juice mixture in a large skillet.
4. Bring juice to boil and reduce heat. Simmer for 25 minutes or until squash slices are tender.

Calories Per Serving: 114
Fat: .3 g
Cholesterol: 0 mg
Protein: 1.9 g

Carbohydrates: 29 g
Dietary Fiber: no data
Sodium: 8 mg

✳ *Sweet Potato Soufflé* ✳

YIELD: 4 servings • *PREPARATION TIME: 15 minutes* •
COOKING TIME: 25 minutes

This easy soufflé is an easy and attractive way to use up leftover sweet potatoes.

5 egg whites
1 tablespoon ground cinnamon
1 tablespoon finely grated orange
peel

2 cups cooked, mashed sweet
potatoes

1. Beat egg whites until they form soft peaks.
2. Gently fold egg whites, cinnamon, and orange peel into mashed sweet potatoes.
3. Fill four individual soufflé dishes with the sweet potato mixture.
4. Bake for 25 minutes and serve at once.

Calories Per Serving: 199
Total Fat: .5 g
Cholesterol: 0 mg
Protein: 7 g

Carbohydrates: 41 g
Dietary Fiber: 4.9 g
Sodium: 90 mg

Sherried Sweet Potatoes with
❋ *Apples and Onion* ❋

YIELD: *6 servings* • PREPARATION TIME: *25 minutes* •
COOKING TIME: *20 minutes*

This purée is a harmonious mix of sweet potatoes, apple, spices, and dry sherry.

3 sweet potatoes, diced	*3 tablespoons nonfat sour cream*
1 apple, cored, peeled, and diced	*2 tablespoons finely chopped*
¹/₂ teaspoon ground cinnamon	*scallions*
¹/₂ teaspoon ground tarragon leaves	*2 tablespoons dry sherry*
¹/₂ teaspoon ground coriander	*2 tablespoons chopped fresh parsley*

1. Bring a large saucepan of water to a boil. Add sweet potatoes and cook for 12 minutes. Add apple and keep cooking at a boil until potatoes are tender.
2. Drain sweet potatoes and apples. Return to saucepan and place over moderate heat. Toss with a large spoon until all moisture is gone.
3. Remove saucepan from heat. Add cinnamon, tarragon, coriander, and sour cream. Mash.
4. Stir in scallions, dry sherry, and parsley. Reheat over gentle heat.

Variations
- The potato-apple mixture can be placed in a baking dish after Step 4 and baked at 400 degrees for 20 minutes.
- Use white potatoes or yams, or a combination of all three instead of just sweet potatoes.

Calories Per Serving: 76	Carbohydrates: 17 g
Fat: .2 g	Dietary Fiber: 2 g
Cholesterol: .1 mg	Sodium: 7.6 mg
Protein: 1 g	

❋ *Butternut-Apple Casserole* ❋

YIELD: 4 servings • *PREPARATION TIME: 15 minutes* • *COOKING TIME: 1 hour*

Butternut squash contains large amounts of beta carotene and stars as the main ingredient in this colorful casserole.

1 butternut squash, peeled, seeded,
   and cut into chunks
3 apples, cored, peeled, and sliced
1 tablespoon lemon juice

³/₄ teaspoon ground cinnamon
1 tablespoon brown sugar, firmly
   packed
¹/₂ cup apple juice

1. Preheat oven to 350 degrees.
2. Combine squash and apples with lemon juice and cinnamon.
3. Place squash-apple mixture in a 1-quart casserole and sprinkle with brown sugar.
4. Pour apple juice over mixture and cover casserole.
5. Bake for 1 hour or until squash is fork-tender.

Calories Per Serving: 129
Fat: .4 g
Cholesterol: 0 mg
Protein: 1.3 g

Carbohydrates: 33 g
Dietary Fiber: 4 g
Sodium: 6.4 mg

❋ *Swiss Chard with Balsamic Vinegar* ❋

YIELD: 4 servings • *PREPARATION TIME: 20 minutes* •
COOKING TIME: 8 minutes

Swiss chard, an often-ignored vegetable, is high in vital nutrients. Here it's combined with chopped onion, bell pepper, garlic, and balsamic vinegar. Buy Swiss chard that is crisp and evenly green without yellowing.

1 bunch Swiss chard, trimmed, and
   cut in 2-inch pieces
¹/₂ cup nonfat chicken broth
¹/₂ cup finely chopped onion

1 red or yellow bell pepper, chopped
2 cloves garlic, minced
¹/₄ teaspoon black pepper
1 tablespoon balsamic vinegar

1. Place Swiss chard, chicken broth, onion, bell pepper, garlic, and black pepper in a large saucepan over medium heat and cook about 8 minutes or until greens are tender.
2. Add the balsamic vinegar and toss.

Calories Per Serving: 22

Fat: .2 g

Cholesterol: 0 mg

Protein: 1.3 g

Carbohydrates: 4.6 g

Dietary Fiber: 1 g

Sodium: 94 mg

✳ *Zucchini with Tomatoes* ✳

YIELD: 4 servings ▪ *PREPARATION TIME: 15 minutes* ▪
COOKING TIME: 30 minutes

This traditional dish is a great way to use a bumper crop of zucchini and tomatoes. It can be eaten hot or cold.

¹/₄ cup water, nonfat chicken broth, vegetable broth, or wine
1 onion, sliced
1 green bell pepper, sliced

3 cups sliced zucchini
¹/₄ teaspoon black pepper
4 large tomatoes, chopped
2 tablespoons fresh chopped parsley

1. Heat water, broth, or wine in a large skillet over medium heat. Add onion and green pepper. Cook until vegetables are tender. Add more liquid if necessary during this process.
2. Add zucchini, black pepper, tomatoes, and parsley. Simmer for 30 minutes.

Variation

▪ Delete the tomatoes. Substitute 3 cups tomato juice in Step 2. Simmer for 40 minutes or until tomato juice forms a thick sauce.

Calories Per Serving: 57

Fat: .6 g

Cholesterol: 0 mg

Protein: 2.9 g

Carbohydrates: 12 g

Dietary Fiber: 4 g

Sodium: 15 mg

POTATO SIDE DISHES

::

✳ Baked Potatoes ✳

*YIELD: 4 servings (1 potato each) • PREPARATION TIME: 5 minutes •
COOKING TIME: 45 minutes*

Baked potatoes are the basis of a wide variety of exciting nonfat dishes. Here's a quick refresher on the finer points of preparing perfect baked potatoes. You can also microwave baked potatoes. See recipe, page 412.

*4 medium white potatoes, yams, or
   sweet potatoes*

1. Preheat oven to 400 degrees.
2. Scrub the potatoes and pierce them several times with a fork to allow steam to escape.
3. Place potatoes in oven and bake for 45 minutes.
4. The potato is done when it can be easily pierced with a fork.

Calories Per Serving: 145	Carbohydrates: 33 g
Fat: .2 g	Dietary Fiber: 3.7 g
Cholesterol: 0 mg	Sodium: 8 mg
Protein: 3 g	

✳ Baked Potatoes with Mustard-Dill Topping ✳

*YIELD: 4 servings (1 potato each) • PREPARATION: 5 minutes plus potato baking or
microwaving time*

There are an endless number of ways to top baked potatoes that will make you forget about fat-laden sour cream and butter toppings forever. For instance, in this recipe Dijon mustard, scallions, and yogurt make a zesty topping for a warm-from-the-oven baked potato.

1 cup plain nonfat yogurt
2 tablespoons Dijon mustard

2 tablespoons chopped scallions
4 warm baked potatoes

1. Combine the yogurt, Dijon mustard, and scallions.
2. Slit the baked potatoes down the middle and push from both ends to form a hollow.
3. Top each potato with a quarter of the yogurt mixture.

Variations
- Top potatoes with steamed asparagus; leftover soup; fresh lemon juice with Dijon mustard; chopped tomato, green pepper, and onion; a few splashes of herb vinegar; baked beans; zucchini, tomatoes, and onions sautéed in vegetable broth; stewed tomatoes; salsa; tomato sauce; vegetarian chili; or vegetable stew.

Calories Per Serving: 180
Fat: .3 g
Cholesterol: 1 mg
Protein: 6 g

Carbohydrates: 38 g
Dietary Fiber: 3.6 g
Sodium: 84 mg

❊ Stuffed Baked Potatoes ❊

YIELD: 4 servings (1 potato each) • *PREPARATION TIME: 20 minutes plus 10 minutes cooling time* • *COOKING TIME: 1 hour and 10 minutes*

Here baked potatoes are stuffed with a blend of cottage cheese, scallions, paprika, and grated nonfat cheese.

4 medium baking potatoes
1 cup nonfat cottage cheese
1/4 cup skim milk
2 tablespoons chopped scallions

1/2 teaspoon paprika
1/2 teaspoon black pepper
1/4 cup grated nonfat cheese

1. Preheat oven to 400 degrees.
2. Pierce potatoes with a fork and bake for 1 hour. Cool for 10 minutes.
3. Cut potatoes in half. Scoop out pulp, leaving a 1/4-inch shell, and place in a medium bowl. Mash the pulp with a fork or potato masher.
4. Place cottage cheese and milk in a blender or food processor and process until smooth.

Stuffed Baked Potatoes *(cont'd)*

5. Add blended cottage cheese, scallions, paprika, black pepper, and cheese to potatoes and mix well.
6. Stuff potato shells with mixture.
7. Bake at 400 degrees for 10 minutes.

Calories Per Serving: 196
Fat: .2 g
Cholesterol: 3.6 mg
Protein: 12 g

Carbohydrates: 38 g
Dietary Fiber: 3.8 g
Sodium: 284 mg

✳ *Mashed Potatoes* ✳

YIELD: 4 servings ▪ *PREPARATION TIME: 25 minutes* ▪
COOKING TIME: 20 minutes

You can still enjoy this old favorite without the fat calories!

*4 large potatoes, peeled and
    quartered*
*½ cup skim milk or evaporated skim
    milk*

¼ teaspoon black pepper
Natural butter substitute (optional)
Ground nutmeg (optional)

1. Place potatoes in a large, heavy pot. Cover with water. Boil, covered, for 20 minutes or until tender.
2. Drain potatoes and mash with a potato masher or large fork.
3. Beat milk in with a wire whisk.
4. Sprinkle with pepper, and natural butter substitute and nutmeg, if desired.

Variation
▪ Substitute ½ cup nonfat buttermilk for the skim milk.

Calories Per Serving: 133
Fat: .3 g
Cholesterol: .5 mg
Protein: 3.6 g

Carbohydrates: 29 g
Dietary Fiber: 1.5 g
Sodium: 44 mg

✳ *Mashed Potatoes and Carrots* ✳

YIELD: 4 servings • *PREPARATION TIME: 15 minutes* •
COOKING TIME: 40 minutes

Here potatoes and carrots are mashed together with skim milk and dill. Smooth-skinned round red potatoes and round white potatoes with tannish skins are both good for boiling.

*4 boiling potatoes, peeled and cut
  into chunks*
*2 large carrots, scrubbed and cut into
  chunks*

6 tablespoons skim milk
1 teaspoon dried dill leaves
1/4 teaspoon black pepper

1. Bring water to a boil in a large saucepan. Add potatoes and carrots and cook for 25 minutes or until tender.
2. Drain potatoes and carrots and return to pot. Mash with a large fork or potato masher.
3. Stir in milk, dill, and black pepper.

Calories Per Serving: 144
Fat: .3 g
Cholesterol: .4 mg
Protein: 3.7 g

Carbohydrates: 32 g
Dietary Fiber: 2.6 g
Sodium: 31 mg

Roasted Red Potatoes
✳ *with Lemon-Oregano Sauce* ✳

YIELD: 4 servings • *PREPARATION TIME: 10 minutes* •
COOKING TIME: 40 minutes

In this dish small red potatoes are roasted in lemon juice.

*1 pound small red potatoes, cut
  in half*
1/3 cup lemon juice

2 teaspoons dried oregano leaves
1/4 teaspoon black pepper

1. Preheat oven to 350 degrees.
2. Arrange potatoes in a shallow oven-proof dish.

Roasted Red Potatoes with Lemon-Oregano Sauce *(cont'd)*

3. Combine lemon juice, oregano, and pepper.
4. Pour lemon-oregano sauce over potatoes.
5. Roast for 40 minutes, turning several times. Check to see if potatoes are tender before removing from oven.

Calories Per Serving: 80	Carbohydrates: 19 g
Fat: .2 g	Dietary Fiber: 1.9 g
Cholesterol: 0 mg	Sodium: 4.3 mg
Protein: 1.7 g	

✳ *Puffed Potato Casserole* ✳

YIELD: 4 servings ▪ *PREPARATION TIME: 15 minutes* ▪
COOKING TIME: 1 hour and 10 minutes

In this recipe, mashed potatoes are baked with skim milk, nonfat cheese, mustard, scallions, and egg whites.

6 potatoes, peeled and quartered	*2 teaspoons Dijon mustard*
³/₄ cup skim milk	*¹/₄ cup chopped scallions*
¹/₃ cup nonfat grated cheese	*2 egg whites*

1. Place potatoes in a large, heavy pot. Cover with water.
2. Boil, covered, for 20 minutes or until tender. Drain potatoes.
3. Preheat oven to 375 degrees.
4. Mash potatoes with a potato masher or large fork.
5. Beat milk into mashed potatoes and mash again until smooth.
6. Stir in cheese, mustard, and scallions.
7. Place in a nonstick baking dish or a baking dish lightly sprayed with vegetable cooking spray.
8. Just before baking, beat egg whites until stiff and spread on top of the potatoes. Bake for 50 minutes.

Calories Per Serving: 236	Carbohydrates: 44 g
Fat: .4 g	Dietary Fiber: 78 g
Cholesterol: 4.5 mg	Sodium: 278 mg
Protein: 13 g	

✳ *Rosemary Potatoes* ✳

YIELD: *6 servings* • PREPARATION TIME: *15 minutes* •
COOKING TIME: *50 minutes*

When a potato is harvested young, it is called a new potato. The skin is thin and fragile. New potatoes are low in starch and high in moisture. They are often referred to as waxy potatoes. Here, red-skinned new potatoes are roasted with rosemary.

2 pounds small red new potatoes   ¹/₄ *teaspoon black pepper*
1 teaspoon dried rosemary leaves

1. Preheat oven to 450 degrees.
2. Scrub potatoes and cut them into halves or quarters.
3. Use a nonstick baking dish, or a baking dish lightly sprayed with vegetable cooking spray or lined with a baking pan liner. Place potatoes on baking sheet and sprinkle with rosemary and black pepper.
4. Bake for 50 minutes or until potatoes are tender. Stir potatoes once or twice during baking period.

Calories Per Serving: 117   Carbohydrates: 27 g
Fat: .2 g   Dietary Fiber: 1.5 g
Cholesterol: 0 mg   Sodium: 7.1 mg
Protein: 2.3 g

✳ *Wine-Parsley Potatoes* ✳

YIELD: *6 servings* • PREPARATION TIME: *15 minutes* •
COOKING TIME: *15 minutes*

Here red potato slices are tossed with fresh tomatoes in a wine and parsley dressing.

3 cups sliced red potatoes   *1 tablespoon chopped fresh parsley*
¹/₂ *cup dry white wine*   ¹/₄ *teaspoon black pepper*
1 cup sliced mushrooms   *1 large tomato, diced*

Wine-Parsley Potatoes *(cont'd)*

1. Bring 1 inch of water to a boil in a steamer. Place potato slices in a colander or steamer basket, cover, and steam for 15 minutes or until tender.
2. While potatoes are steaming, heat 1/4 cup of the white wine in a skillet over medium heat. Add mushrooms. Cook and stir for 5 minutes over medium heat. Add more wine if necessary during this process.
3. Place warm steamed potato slices, warm mushrooms and any remaining liquid from the skillet, the remaining 1/4 cup of white wine, parsley, pepper, and tomato in a large bowl, toss, and serve.

Calories Per Serving: 80

Carbohydrates: 15 g

Fat: .2 g

Dietary Fiber: 1.2 g

Cholesterol: 0 mg

Sodium: 17 mg

Protein: 1.7 g

Baked Potato Slices with Onion Sauce ✳ *and Parmesan Cheese* ✳

YIELD: *4 servings* • PREPARATION TIME: *25 minutes* •
COOKING TIME: *50 minutes*

This traditional scalloped potato dish is usually packed with fat grams. Here layers of potatoes are baked in an onion-flavored sauce.

1 cup skim milk

2 teaspoons arrowroot or cornstarch

1/4 teaspoon cayenne pepper

1/4 teaspoon black pepper

1/4 cup chopped onion

2 large potatoes, peeled and sliced very thin

1/4 cup nonfat Parmesan cheese

1. Place milk, arrowroot, cayenne, and black pepper in a small saucepan. Cook and stir over medium heat until the mixture thickens and begins to bubble. Stir onions into sauce.
2. Use a nonstick baking dish or lightly spray the sides of a baking dish with vegetable cooking spray. Place layers of thinly sliced potatoes in the casserole.
3. Pour the onion sauce over the potatoes. Sprinkle with Parmesan cheese.

4. Cover and bake for 40 minutes. Remove the cover and bake for 10 more minutes. Check to be sure potatoes are tender.

Calories Per Serving: 106
Fat: .2 g
Cholesterol: 1.3 mg
Protein: 4 g

Carbohydrates: 21 g
Dietary Fiber: 2 g
Sodium: 62 mg

✳ *Oven Fries* ✳

YIELD: 4 servings ▪ *PREPARATION TIME: 20 minutes* ▪
COOKING TIME: 35 minutes

One of the hardest things for many fat abstainers to give up is the taste of french fried potatoes. These oven fries are great sprinkled with catsup, paprika, or vinegar.

4 large baking potatoes
Black pepper

1. Preheat oven to 450 degrees.
2. Peel the potatoes and soak them in ice water.
3. Cut each potato into slices, 1/4 inch thick. Cut each slice into strips, 1/4 inch thick. Return to ice water until ready to cook. Drain strips and dry them on paper towels.
4. Arrange the potatoes without overlapping them on nonstick baking sheets with rims, or on baking sheets lightly sprayed with vegetable cooking spray or lined with nonstick baking pan liners.
5. Bake in the top half of the oven for 15 minutes. Turn potatoes over. Bake for 20 more minutes or until potatoes are golden brown and tender.
6. Sprinkle with pepper and serve hot.

Calories Per Serving: 97
Fat: .1 g
Cholesterol: 0 mg
Protein: 2 g

Carbohydrates: 22 g
Dietary Fiber: 2.5 g
Sodium: 5.3 mg

GRAIN
SIDE DISHES

::

✳ Mexicali Rice ✳

YIELD: 6 servings • PREPARATION TIME: 20 minutes • COOKING TIME: 1 hour

This rice makes a great accompaniment to bean dishes.

1/4 cup water, chicken broth,
    vegetable broth, or wine
1 large onion, chopped
2 cloves garlic, minced
1 green bell pepper, seeded and
    chopped
1 cup chopped fresh or canned low-
    sodium tomatoes, drained

1 teaspoon dried oregano leaves
1 teaspoon ground cumin
1/4 teaspoon cayenne pepper
1/3 cup water, chicken broth,
    vegetable broth, or wine
1 1/2 cups uncooked long-grain rice
3 1/2 cups water

1. Heat 1/4 cup water, broth, or wine in a large skillet over medium heat. Add onion and garlic. Cook and stir over medium heat for 5 minutes. Add liquid if necessary during this process.
2. Add green pepper, tomato, oregano, cumin, and cayenne pepper. Cook and stir over low heat for 10 minutes. Transfer to a bowl.
3. Heat 1/3 cup water, broth, or wine in the skillet. Add rice. Cook rice for 5 minutes, stirring constantly.
4. Add reserved vegetable mixture and 3 cups water.
5. Cover tightly and cook over very low heat for 25 minutes. Check to see if rice is done. If not, add 1/2 cup more liquid and cook uncovered.

Variation
- Substitute 1 cup brown rice. In Step 4 add 3 1/2 cups water. Cover tightly and cook over very low heat for 40 minutes. Check to see if rice is done. If not, add 1/2 cup more water and cook uncovered.

Calories Per Serving: 202
Fat: .7 g
Cholesterol: 0 mg
Protein: 4.6 g

Carbohydrates: 44 g
Dietary Fiber: 1.8 g
Sodium: 23 mg

✳ *Lemon-Thyme Vegetable Rice* ✳

YIELD: *4 servings* • PREPARATION TIME: *20 minutes* •
COOKING TIME: *25 minutes*

Peas, scallions, and red bell pepper are added to this lemon and thyme–flavored rice dish.

2 cups nonfat chicken broth, vegetable broth, or water
2/3 cup uncooked long-grain white rice
1/2 teaspoon ground thyme leaves
1/4 teaspoon black pepper

1 red bell pepper, seeded and chopped
1/4 cup chopped scallions
1 cup frozen peas
2 tablespoons fresh chopped parsley
1 teaspoon finely grated lemon peel

1. Bring broth or water to a boil in a large saucepan. Stir in the rice, thyme, and pepper. Simmer over low heat for 10 minutes.
2. Stir in red pepper and scallions. Simmer for 5 minutes.
3. Stir in frozen peas, parsley, and lemon peel. Simmer for 5 more minutes or until rice is tender.

Calories Per Serving: 81
Fat: .5 g
Cholesterol: 0 mg
Protein: 4 g

Carbohydrates: 15 g
Dietary Fiber: 2.5 g
Sodium: 106 mg

✳ *Curried Tangerine Rice* ✳

YIELD: *4 servings* • PREPARATION TIME: *10 minutes* •
COOKING TIME: *25 minutes*

Curry powder, sliced scallions, and parsley are cooked with long-grain rice in this dish.

Curried Tangerine Rice *(cont'd)*

2 cups nonfat chicken broth,
  vegetable broth, or water
1 teaspoon curry powder
²/₃ cup uncooked long-grain white
  rice
2 medium tangerines, peeled,
  sectioned, seeded, and diced
  (reserve any juice produced by the
  tangerine)

2 tablespoons chopped scallions
2 tablespoons chopped fresh parsley

1. Bring the chicken broth to a boil in a medium saucepan. Stir in the curry powder and rice. Return to boiling. Reduce heat and simmer, covered, for 20 minutes or until the rice is tender.
2. Stir the tangerines, scallions, and parsley into the rice. Warm through and serve.

Variation

- Substitute brown rice. Increase liquid to 2 ½ cups and increase cooking time in Step 1 to 40 minutes.

Calories Per Serving: 63
Total Fat: .5 g
Cholesterol: 0 mg
Protein: 2 g

Carbohydrates: 13 g
Dietary Fiber: 1.6 g
Sodium: 71 mg

✳ *Tomato-Carrot Rice* ✳

YIELD: *4 servings* • PREPARATION TIME: *20 minutes* •
COOKING TIME: *25 minutes*

Carrots, corn, lima beans, and onion are featured in this rice dish that is steamed in tomato juice.

¼ cup water, chicken broth,
  vegetable broth, or wine
½ cup diced carrots
½ cup fresh, frozen, or canned corn
  kernels
½ cup frozen lima beans

½ cup chopped onion
1 cup uncooked long-grain white rice
2 cups tomato juice
1 teaspoon dried oregano leaves
¼ teaspoon black pepper

1. Heat water, broth, or wine in a medium skillet over medium heat. Add carrots, corn, lima beans, and onion. Cook and stir for 5 minutes. Add more liquid during this process if necessary.
2. Add rice, tomato juice, oregano, and pepper. Bring to a boil. Reduce heat, cover pan, and cook for 20 minutes or until rice is tender.

Calories Per Serving: 128
Fat: .7 g
Cholesterol: 0 mg
Protein: 4.6 g

Carbohydrates: 27 g
Dietary Fiber: 4.5 g
Sodium: 41 mg

✳ *Oriental Rice with Asparagus* ✳

YIELD: *6 servings* ▪ PREPARATION TIME: *25 minutes plus asparagus steaming time* ▪ COOKING TIME: *25 minutes*

Here long-grain rice is tossed with soy sauce, parsley, rice vinegar, sugar, asparagus, plum tomatoes, red onion, and green bell pepper.

1 ½ cups uncooked long-grain white rice
3 cups water
2 tablespoons light soy sauce
¼ cup chopped fresh parsley
2 tablespoons rice vinegar
1 teaspoon sugar

½ pound asparagus, trimmed, cut into 1-inch pieces, and steamed
1 cup sliced canned low-sodium plum tomatoes
¾ cup chopped red onion
1 green bell pepper, seeded and chopped

1. Place rice and water in a saucepan and bring to a boil. Reduce heat, cover, and simmer for 20 minutes or until rice is tender. Transfer to a colander and rinse.
2. Combine soy sauce, parsley, rice vinegar, and sugar.
3. Toss sauce with rice, steamed asparagus, tomatoes, red onions, and green pepper.

Calories Per Serving: 196
Fat: .6 g
Cholesterol: 0 mg
Protein: 5.3 g

Carbohydrates: 43 g
Dietary Fiber: 1.8 g
Sodium: 217 mg

✳ Dried Apricots and Wild Rice ✳

YIELD: *4 servings* • PREPARATION TIME: *20 minutes* • COOKING TIME: *50 minutes*

Dried apricots, orange rind, scallions, and balsamic vinegar add an unexpected twist to this wild rice dish.

1 cup uncooked wild rice	2 tablespoons fresh chopped parsley
3 cups plus 3 tablespoons water	2 tablespoons balsamic vinegar
1/2 cup chopped scallions	1/2 teaspoon grated orange rind
1/2 cup dried apricots, cut into slivers	1/4 teaspoon black pepper

1. Rinse wild rice in hot water and drain several times.
2. Place rice and 3 cups of the water in a large saucepan and bring to a boil. Cover, reduce heat, and simmer for 45 minutes.
3. Drain rice. Toss with scallions, apricots, and parsley.
4. Combine the remaining 3 tablespoons water, vinegar, orange rind, and black pepper.
5. Pour vinegar sauce over rice and toss.

Calories Per Serving: 95	Carbohydrates: 22 g
Fat: .5 g	Dietary Fiber: 2 g
Cholesterol: 0 mg	Sodium: 10 mg
Protein: 1.9 g	

✳ Spicy Rice with Dried Fruit ✳

YIELD: *4 servings* • PREPARATION TIME: *20 minutes* • COOKING TIME: *30 minutes*

Rice is cooked here with apple juice, allspice, vanilla, lemon peel, raisins, dried apricots, and dried pineapple.

1 cup uncooked long-grain white rice	1 teaspoon grated lemon peel
1 1/2 cups apple juice	1/4 cup raisins
1 1/2 cups water	1/4 cup chopped dried apricots
1/2 teaspoon ground allspice	1/4 cup chopped dried pineapple
1 teaspoon vanilla extract	

1. In a large skillet, stir the rice over medium heat for 5 minutes.
2. Add apple juice, water, allspice, vanilla, and lemon peel. Bring to a boil and boil for 5 minutes.
3. Add raisins, apricots, and pineapple. Cover with lid slightly ajar and simmer for 20 minutes or until the rice is tender. Add more liquid if needed.

Variation
- Substitute brown rice for the white rice. Substitute ¹/₂ teaspoon curry powder for the allspice. Substitute ¹/₄ cup chopped onions and ¹/₄ cup chopped fresh apple for the apricots and pineapple.

Calories Per Serving: 283	Carbohydrates: 65 g
Fat: .5 g	Dietary Fiber: 2.4 g
Cholesterol: 0 mg	Sodium: 10 mg
Protein: 4 g	

✳ *Peach-Blueberry Rice* ✳

Yield: 4 servings • *Preparation Time: 20 minutes* •
Cooking Time: 25 minutes

Rice is tossed with fresh peaches and blueberries with a spicy mint-ginger dressing in this dish.

1 cup uncooked long-grain white rice	*Pinch of ground cloves*
1³/₄ cups water	*3 tablespoons plain nonfat yogurt*
2 scallions, minced	*1 teaspoon brown sugar, firmly*
2 tablespoons minced fresh parsley	*packed*
1 teaspoon dried mint leaves	*1 large peach or nectarine, chopped*
1 teaspoon minced fresh gingerroot	*³/₄ cup fresh or thawed frozen*
¹/₂ teaspoon grated lemon rind	*blueberries*
Pinch of ground cinnamon	

1. Place rice and water in a medium saucepan. Bring water to a boil. Reduce heat to simmer, cover, and cook for 25 minutes or until rice is tender. Drain rice.
2. Toss rice with scallions, parsley, mint, gingerroot, lemon rind, cinnamon, cloves, yogurt, brown sugar, peach or nectarine, and blueberries.

Peach-Blueberry Rice *(cont'd)*

Calories Per Serving: 213
Fat: .6 g
Cholesterol: .2 mg
Protein: 4.5 g

Carbohydrates: 47 g
Dietary Fiber: 1.7 g
Sodium: 16 mg

✳ *Barley and Apples* ✳

YIELD: 6 servings • PREPARATION TIME: 20 minutes •
COOKING TIME: 50 minutes

This barley is combined with mushrooms, apple, raisins, honey, and lemon juice.

2 cups nonfat chicken broth
1 cup water
³/₄ cup barley
¹/₂ cup chopped onion
¹/₄ cup chopped celery
1 cup chopped mushrooms

1 cup peeled and diced apple
¹/₃ cup raisins
1 tablespoon honey
1 tablespoon lemon juice
2 tablespoons chopped fresh parsley

1. Place 1³/₄ cups of the broth and ³/₄ cup of the water in large saucepan. Bring to a boil.
2. Add barley and reduce heat. Simmer for 45 minutes or until barley is tender.
3. Place remaining ¹/₄ cup broth in a skillet over medium heat. Add onion, celery, and mushrooms. Cook and stir for 5 minutes over medium heat.
4. Add remaining ¹/₄ cup water, apple, and raisins. Simmer for 20 minutes or until apples are tender.
5. Combine barley and apple mixture. Stir in honey, lemon juice, and parsley.

Calories Per Serving: 147
Fat: .5 g
Cholesterol: 0 mg
Protein: 3.9 g

Carbohydrates: 33 g
Dietary Fiber: 5 g
Sodium: 55 mg

BEAN
SIDE DISHES

::

✳ *Eight-Flavor Baked Beans* ✳

Yield: 6 servings • Preparation Time: 15 minutes plus bean cooking time •
Cooking Time: 1 hour and 15 minutes

These navy beans are baked in a tangy sauce flavored with onion, garlic,
brown sugar, cider vinegar, dry mustard, paprika, ginger, and cayenne.

*1/4 cup water, chicken broth,
  vegetable broth, or wine
1 medium onion, chopped
2 cloves garlic, minced
1 cup chopped fresh or low-sodium
  canned tomatoes, drained
1/4 cup brown sugar, firmly packed*

*2 tablespoons cider vinegar
1 1/2 teaspoons dry mustard
1 teaspoon ground paprika
1/4 teaspoon ground ginger
Pinch of cayenne pepper
4 cups cooked or canned navy beans,
  drained and rinsed*

1. Preheat oven to 325 degrees.
2. Heat water, broth, or wine in a large, heavy pot over medium heat.
   Add onion and garlic and cook, stirring, over medium heat for 5
   minutes. Add more water during this process if necessary.
3. Add tomatoes, sugar, vinegar, mustard, paprika, ginger, and cayenne.
   Simmer for 10 minutes.
4. Place sauce and beans in a 1 1/2-quart oven-proof casserole and bake,
   covered, for 45 minutes.
5. Remove cover and bake for 15 additional minutes.

Calories Per Serving: 205
Fat: .9 g
Cholesterol: 0 mg
Protein: 10.9 g

Carbohydrates: 40 g
Dietary Fiber: 6.9 g
Sodium: 18 mg

✳ *Lentils in Tomato Sauce* ✳

YIELD: 4 servings • PREPARATION TIME: 15 minutes •
COOKING TIME: 37 minutes

These lentils are simmered in a garlic-tomato sauce.

*¹/₄ cup chicken broth, vegetable
    broth, water, or wine
4 garlic cloves, minced
2 cups chopped and drained fresh or
    low-sodium canned tomatoes*

*1 cup lentils, rinsed
2¹/₂ cups water
1 tablespoon lemon juice*

1. Heat the broth, water, or wine in a skillet and sauté the garlic over medium heat for 2 minutes.
2. Add the tomatoes and cook, stirring, for 5 minutes.
3. Add lentils and water. Stir and bring to a boil.
4. Cover, lower heat, and simmer for 30 minutes.
5. Stir in lemon juice.

Calories Per Serving: 82
Fat: .3 g
Cholesterol: 0 mg
Protein: 5.4 g

Carbohydrates: 16 g
Dietary Fiber: 3.3 g
Sodium: 44 mg

✳ *Black Beans and Corn* ✳

*YIELD: 4 servings • PREPARATION TIME: 15 minutes plus bean and corn
    cooking time • COOKING TIME: 10 minutes*

Black beans and corn are cooked with garlic, onion, and red bell pepper in this dish.

*¹/₄ cup water, nonfat chicken broth,
    or vegetable broth
¹/₂ cup onion, chopped
1 clove garlic, chopped
¹/₂ cup chopped green bell pepper
2 cups home-cooked or canned black
    beans, drained and rinsed*

*1 cup cooked fresh, frozen, or canned
    corn kernels
¹/₂ teaspoon ground cumin
¹/₂ teaspoon ground coriander*

1. Heat water or broth in a skillet over medium heat. Add onion, garlic,

and green bell pepper. Cook and stir over medium heat for 5 minutes. Add water during this process if necessary.
2. Add black beans, corn, cumin, and coriander. Cook for 5 minutes or until beans and corn are warmed through.

Variation
- Let beans and corn cool to room temperature and toss with a dressing of 2 tablespoons apple cider vinegar, 1 tablespoon sugar, and 1 tablespoon water.

Calories Per Serving: 159
Fat: .6 g
Cholesterol: 0 mg
Protein: 9 g

Carbohydrates: 31 g
Dietary Fiber: 4.9 g
Sodium: 12.5 mg

✳ *Molasses-Apple Baked Beans* ✳

YIELD: 8 servings • *PREPARATION TIME: 15 minutes plus bean-cooking time* • *COOKING TIME: 60 minutes*

Here Great Northern beans are baked with apples, molasses, tomato sauce, and dry mustard.

1¼ cups water or vegetable broth
¾ cup chopped onion
2 medium apples, peeled, cored, and grated
1 teaspoon dry mustard

1 cup low-sodium tomato sauce
2 tablespoons molasses
6 cups home-cooked or canned Great Northern beans, drained and rinsed

1. Preheat oven to 350 degrees.
2. Heat ¼ cup of the water or broth in a skillet over medium heat. Add onion. Cook and stir over medium heat for 3 minutes or until lightly browned. Add water if necessary during this process.
3. Add apples, cover, lower heat, and cook for 5 minutes.
4. Transfer apples and onion to a 1½-quart oven-proof casserole.
5. Add dry mustard, tomato sauce, molasses, and beans. Mix well.
6. Bake, covered, for 45 minutes.

Calories Per Serving: 207
Fat: .9 g
Cholesterol: 0 mg
Protein: 11 g

Carbohydrates: 40 g
Dietary Fiber: 8.7 g
Sodium: 20 mg

FRUIT
SIDE DISHES

::

✳ Chunky Spiced Applesauce ✳

YIELD: 8 servings • PREPARATION TIME: 20 minutes •
COOKING TIME: 40 minutes

Homemade applesauce is a special treat that's easy to prepare.

10 large cooking apples, peeled,
   cored, and cut into chunks
1/2 cup apple juice
1/4 cup brown sugar, firmly packed

1/2 teaspoon ground cinnamon
1/4 teaspoon ground ginger
1/4 teaspoon ground cloves

1. Place apples and apple juice in a large, heavy pot. Cover and simmer for 10 minutes, stirring often until apples are crisp-tender.
2. Stir in sugar and continue cooking for 30 minutes.
3. Stir in cinnamon, ginger, and cloves. Serve warm or cold.

Calories Per Serving: 147
Fat: .8 g
Cholesterol: 0 mg
Protein: .5 g

Carbohydrates: 37 g
Dietary Fiber: 5 g
Sodium: 3.9 mg

✳ Cranberry Applesauce ✳

YIELD: 6 servings • PREPARATION TIME: 20 minutes •
COOKING TIME: 15 minutes

Fresh cranberries give this applesauce a special taste.

6 apples, cored and cut into chunks
1 cup raw cranberries
1/2 cup apple cider
1 cinnamon stick

2 tablespoons brown sugar, firmly
   packed
Pinch of ground nutmeg

1. Combine the apples, cranberries, apple cider, and cinnamon in a large, heavy saucepan. Bring to a boil, reduce heat, cover, and simmer for 15 minutes, stirring several times.
2. Remove the cinnamon stick. Transfer the apple-cranberry mixture to a blender or food processor and purée.
3. Stir sugar and nutmeg into purée.

Calories Per Serving: 122

Fat: .6 g

Cholesterol: 0 mg

Protein: .4 g

Carbohydrates: 31 g

Dietary Fiber: 3.6 g

Sodium: 5 mg

✳ *Lemon-Spiced Nectarines* ✳

YIELD: 4 servings • *PREPARATION TIME: 10 minutes plus chilling time* • *COOKING TIME: 12 minutes*

Here nectarines are simmered with spices and accented with lemon juice. When selecting nectarines, a sweet scent is almost always a guarantee of good fruit.

1¹/₂ cups water
¹/₄ teaspoon ground cinnamon
¹/₂ teaspoon ground cloves
¹/₄ teaspoon ground ginger
4 large nectarines, peeled and thinly sliced

3 tablespoons lemon juice
1 tablespoon brown sugar, firmly packed

1. Place water, cinnamon, cloves, and ginger in a large skillet. Heat until water begins to boil.
2. After water has boiled for 2 minutes, add nectarines. Simmer for 10 minutes.
3. Transfer nectarines and juice to a bowl. Stir in lemon juice and sugar. Chill before serving.

Calories Per Serving: 84

Fat: .7 g

Cholesterol: 0 mg

Protein: 1 g

Carbohydrates: 20 g

Dietary Fiber: 2 g

Sodium: 1.8 mg

✳ *Spiced Bananas and Mandarin Oranges* ✳

YIELD: 4 servings ▪ *PREPARATION TIME: 10 minutes* ▪
COOKING TIME: 6 minutes

This simple dish features bananas and mandarin oranges simmered with ginger and cloves. Look for plump rather than skinny bananas that still have some stem attached. Don't buy bananas with bruises or those that look dull and gray.

3 ripe bananas, peeled and cut into   *¹/₄ teaspoon ground ginger*
1-inch chunks   *¹/₄ teaspoon ground cloves*
1 8-ounce can juice-packed mandarin
oranges, juice reserved

1. Place bananas, mandarin oranges and their juice, ginger, and cloves in a saucepan.
2. Simmer until bananas are heated through.

Calories Per Serving: 101   Carbohydrates: 25 g
Fat: .5 g   Dietary Fiber: 2 g
Cholesterol: 0 mg   Sodium: 1.1 mg
Protein: 1 g

✳ *Baked Bananas and Pineapple* ✳

YIELD: 4 servings ▪ *PREPARATION TIME: 10 minutes* ▪
COOKING TIME: 30 minutes

Here bananas and crushed pineapple are baked with honey. The best way to store bananas is to leave them in the open at room temperature. Keep them away from direct sunlight and high heat.

3 large bananas, peeled and cut in   *¹/₂ cup honey*
half lengthwise   *1 tablespoon orange juice*
1 8-ounce can juice-packed crushed
pineapple

1. Preheat oven to 350 degrees.

2. Place bananas in a nonstick baking dish.
3. Combine pineapple, honey, and orange juice. Pour over the bananas.
4. Bake for 30 minutes.

Calories Per Serving: 237   Carbohydrates: 61 g
Fat: .5 g   Dietary Fiber: 2.5 g
Cholesterol: 0 mg   Sodium: 3.9 mg
Protein: 1 g

✳ *Strawberry-Banana Salad* ✳

YIELD: 4 servings ▪ *PREPARATION TIME: 15 minutes*

Strawberries and bananas are served with a creamy dressing in this dish.

3 medium bananas   2 tablespoons nonfat mayonnaise
1 teaspoon lemon juice   5 tablespoons nonfat plain yogurt
3 cups whole, hulled fresh   2 tablespoons skim milk
  strawberries or thawed, frozen
  strawberries

1. Peel and slice bananas. Sprinkle with lemon juice.
2. Toss bananas with strawberries.
3. Combine mayonnaise, yogurt, and skim milk.
4. Serve bananas and strawberries in bowls topped with dressing.

Calories Per Serving: 135   Carbohydrates: 321 g
Fat: .9 g   Dietary Fiber: 4.2 g
Cholesterol: .4 mg   Sodium: 125 mg
Protein: 2.8 g

✳ *Honeyed Cranberries* ✳

YIELD: 4 servings ▪ *PREPARATION TIME: 10 minutes plus 2 hours chilling time* ▪
COOKING TIME: 10 minutes

You can enjoy apple and honey–flavored cranberries with or without a
turkey dinner. Store this sauce in the refrigerator for up to ten days. If

Honeyed Cranberries *(cont'd)*

you buy fresh cranberries, they should look shiny and plump. They should be bright in color whether they are light or dark red. Don't buy soft or shriveled berries or any with brown spots.

> 2 cups fresh or frozen cranberries ²/₃ cup honey
> ¹/₂ cup apple juice

1. Place cranberries, apple juice, and honey in a saucepan over medium heat.
2. Bring to a boil and simmer for 5 minutes or until the cranberries burst their skins.
3. Allow to cool to room temperature and chill for at least 2 hours.

Calories Per Serving: 230
Fat: .3 g
Cholesterol: 0 mg
Protein: .5 g

Carbohydrates: 59 g
Dietary Fiber: 1.8 g
Sodium: 8 mg

✳ *Ginger-Lime Mangoes* ✳

YIELD: *4 servings* • PREPARATION TIME: *10 minutes*

These sliced mangoes are served with fresh ginger and lime juice. Ripen mangoes at room temperature until they feel fairly soft. Once they are ripe—yellow and orange-red, softened, and sweetly scented—store in a plastic bag in the refrigerator for no more than two or three days.

> 2 large, ripe mangoes, peeled ²/₃ cup lime juice
> 2 teaspoons minced fresh gingerroot

1. Cut mango away from the center pit in slices ¹/₄ inch thick.
2. Toss the mango slices with the gingerroot and lime juice.

Calories Per Serving: 79
Fat: .3 g
Cholesterol: 0 mg
Protein: .7 g

Carbohydrates: 21 g
Dietary Fiber: 2.3 g
Sodium: 2.4 mg

✳ *Grilled Nectarines with Strawberry Purée* ✳

YIELD: 4 servings (1 nectarine half each) ▪ *PREPARATION TIME: 10 minutes* ▪
COOKING TIME: 15 minutes

Grilled fresh nectarines are topped with a purée made from frozen berries
in this succulent side dish or dessert.

6 ounces frozen strawberries,
  slightly thawed
1 tablespoon lemon juice
2 large nectarines, peeled, halved,
  and pitted

1 tablespoon brown sugar, firmly
  packed
¼ teaspoon ground cinnamon

1. Place strawberries and lemon juice in a blender or food processor and
   purée. Strain, cover, and chill.
2. Cut a 16-inch square of heavy-duty aluminum foil. Place nectarine
   halves on foil, hollow side up.
3. Combine brown sugar and cinnamon. Sprinkle over nectarines.
4. Seal foil over nectarines. Grill on rack over medium heat for 15
   minutes.
5. Remove nectarines from foil and place on small plates. Spoon cold
   strawberry purée over each nectarine half.

Calories Per Serving: 70
Fat: .6 g
Cholesterol: 0 mg
Protein: 1 g

Carbohydrates: 17 g
Dietary Fiber: 3 g
Sodium: 2 mg

✳ *Papaya-Honey Bake* ✳

YIELD: 6 servings (1 papaya half each) ▪ *PREPARATION TIME: 10 minutes* ▪
COOKING TIME: 35 minutes

Here ripe papaya halves are baked with honey and vanilla. When buying
fresh papayas, select fruit that is at least half-yellow and still firm. A firm
papaya will ripen completely at room temperature in three to five days.

3 papayas, peeled, halved, and
  seeded

6 teaspoons vanilla extract
6 tablespoons honey

Papaya-Honey Bake *(cont'd)*
1. Preheat oven to 350 degrees.
2. Place papaya halves hollow side up in a baking dish with ½ inch water.
3. Top each papaya half with 1 teaspoon vanilla and 1 tablespoon honey.
4. Bake for 35 minutes or until tender.

Calories Per Serving: 102
Fat: 0 g
Cholesterol: 0 mg
Protein: .3 g

Carbohydrates: 24 g
Dietary Fiber: .5 g
Sodium: 2.6 mg

❋ *Pears with Red Wine* ❋

Yield: 4 servings (1 pear each) • *Preparation Time: 10 minutes* • *Cooking Time: 15 minutes*

Pears are a delicacy when steamed with red wine and brown sugar. Choose pears that are well colored, firm, and clear skinned. Avoid those with wrinkled skin or overly soft flesh. Pears meant for cooking should be slightly firm.

2 cups red wine
½ teaspoon ground cinnamon
½ teaspoon ground cloves
1 teaspoon vanilla extract

2 tablespoons brown sugar, firmly packed
4 large firm pears, peeled

1. Heat wine, cinnamon, cloves, vanilla, and sugar in a steamer.
2. Place pears in steamer basket or colander, cover, and steam for 8 minutes.
3. Remove pears and reduce steaming liquid over high heat to half its volume.
4. Pour reduced steaming liquid over peas before serving.

Variations
- Replace pears with ripe peaches.
- Replace red wine with white wine.

Calories Per Serving: 208
Fat: .7 g
Cholesterol: 0 mg
Protein: 1 g

Carbohydrates: 33 g
Dietary Fiber: 4 g
Sodium: 79 mg

✳ *Cranberry Poached Peaches* ✳

YIELD: 6 servings (1 peach each) • *PREPARATION TIME: 5 minutes* •
COOKING TIME: 20 minutes

In this dish fresh peaches are poached to rosy perfection in cranberry
sauce.

6 peaches	*1¼ cups water*
1 cup cranberry juice	*⅓ cup sugar*

1. Bring a large pot of water to a boil. Drop peaches in boiling water.
   Boil for 3 minutes. Remove peaches and peel skin off. Cut peaches in
   half and discard pits.
2. Place cranberry juice, 1¼ cups water, and sugar in a large saucepan.
3. Bring to a boil, lower heat, and simmer for 5 minutes.
4. Add peaches to cranberry mixture. Simmer for 6 minutes or until
   peaches are just tender, spooning cranberry mixture over peaches.
5. Remove peaches and place in glass bowl.
6. Bring cranberry mixture to a boil and boil rapidly until the mixture is
   reduced by half. Pour over peaches.

Calories Per Serving: 101	Carbohydrates: 26 g
Fat: .1 g	Dietary Fiber: 1.3 g
Cholesterol: 0 mg	Sodium: 1.7 mg
Protein: .6 g	

✳ *Poached Pears in Orange Sauce* ✳

YIELD: 4 servings (1 pear each) • *PREPARATION TIME: 10 minutes plus 1 hour
chilling time* • *COOKING TIME: 20 minutes*

Pears poached in citrus juices and honey are a quick and elegant dish.

1½ cups orange juice	*3 tablespoons grated orange peel*
2 tablespoons lemon juice	*4 pears, peeled, halved, and cored*
½ cup honey	

1. Combine orange juice, lemon juice, honey, and orange peel in a small
   saucepan. Bring to a simmer.

Poached Pears in Orange Sauce *(cont'd)*

2. Add pear halves, cover and simmer for 15 minutes or until pears are tender. Remove pears from pan.
3. Simmer sauce for 5 more minutes.
4. Pour sauce over pears and chill until serving time.

Calories Per Serving: 274
Fat: .9 g
Cholesterol: 0 mg
Protein: 1 g

Carbohydrates: 70 g
Dietary Fiber: 5 g
Sodium: 3.8 mg

✳ *Nutmeg-Cinnamon Baked Pears* ✳

YIELD: 4 servings • *PREPARATION TIME: 10 minutes* •
COOKING TIME: 30 minutes

Here pears are baked in apple juice, nutmeg, and cinnamon.

*4 large pears, peeled, cored, and
  quartered*
½ cup apple juice

1 teaspoon ground nutmeg
1 teaspoon ground cinnamon

1. Preheat oven to 350 degrees.
2. Place pears in a baking dish with apple juice.
3. Sprinkle with nutmeg and cinnamon.
4. Cover baking dish with aluminum foil. Bake for 30 minutes.

Calories Per Serving: 116
Fat: .9 g
Cholesterol: 0 mg
Protein: .7 g

Carbohydrates: 29 g
Dietary Fiber: 4 g
Sodium: 3.3 mg

✳ *Baked Pineapple* ✳

YIELD: 6 servings • *PREPARATION TIME: 10 minutes* •
COOKING TIME: 25 minutes

The next time you see a fresh pineapple at the market, bring it home and prepare this simple but tantalizing dish. Look for a full ripe pineapple that yields slightly to finger pressure and has flat, shiny eyes on its rind.

1 fresh pineapple, cut in half   4 tablespoons honey
   lengthwise

1. Preheat oven at 400 degrees.
2. Score the pineapple flesh deeply in a crisscross pattern with a sharp knife point.
3. Spread 2 tablespoons honey over each pineapple half.
3. Bake for 25 minutes. Cut each half in three sections and serve.

Calories Per Serving: 81   Carbohydrates: 20 g
Fat: .3 g   Dietary Fiber: .9 g
Cholesterol: 0 mg   Sodium: 1.1 mg
Protein: .3 g

❋ *Broiled Pineapple* ❋

Yield: 4 servings ▪ *Preparation Time: 15 minutes* ▪
Cooking Time: 3 minutes

Here's another way to make fresh pineapple a special treat.

1 medium-size pineapple   ⅓ cup brown sugar, firmly packed

1. Preheat broiler.
2. Cut pineapple skin away with sharp knife. Remove eyes with the knife tip. Cut pineapple into 8 round slices.
3. Arrange pineapple slices on a broiling pan. Sprinkle with brown sugar.
4. Broil for 3 minutes.

Calories Per Serving: 126   Carbohydrates: 32 g
Fat: .5 g   Dietary Fiber: 1.3 g
Cholesterol: 0 mg   Sodium: 6.2 mg
Protein: .4 g

❋ *Raspberry-Pear Toss* ❋

Yield: 4 servings ▪ *Preparation Time: 15 minutes*

This is a perfect dish to serve when you spot fresh raspberries at your market.

Raspberry-Pear Toss (cont'd)

1 16-ounce can juice-packed canned
    pears, juice reserved
2½ cups raspberries

1 tablespoon lime juice
½ cup orange juice

1. Dice the pears and place them, with their juice, in a bowl.
2. Add the raspberries, lime juice, and orange juice.

Calories Per Serving: 89
Fat: .5 g
Cholesterol: 0 mg
Protein: 1 g

Carbohydrates: 22 g
Dietary Fiber: .5 g
Sodium: 4.8 mg

Melon and Blueberry Salad with
✳ Frozen Raspberry Purée ✳

YIELD: 6 servings • PREPARATION TIME: 15 minutes

Serve this dish garnished with lime wedges when melon, peaches, and blueberries are in season.

1 ripe cantaloupe or honeydew
    melon
2 peaches or nectarines, peeled and
    sliced

2 tablespoons lemon juice
2 cups blueberries
1½ cups frozen raspberries
1½ tablespoons honey

1. Cut the melon into 6 slices and place on individual plates or in bowls.
2. Toss peaches or nectarines with 1 teaspoon of the lemon juice, then toss with blueberries.
3. Fill centers of melon wedges with peaches and blueberries.
4. Place frozen raspberries and honey in a blender or food processor and purée.
5. Spoon over peaches and blueberries.

Calories Per Serving: 101
Fat: .6 g
Cholesterol: 0 mg
Protein: 1 g

Carbohydrates: 25 g
Dietary Fiber: 4 g
Sodium: 9 mg

✳ *Prunes with Brown Sugar and Vanilla* ✳

YIELD: *4 servings* • PREPARATION TIME: *15 minutes* •
COOKING TIME: *25 minutes*

Dried prunes are simmered with brown sugar, vanilla, and cinnamon.
Serve alone or with a bowl of citrus fruit sections. Also try this method
of cooking dried fruit with dried apricots, peaches, and pears.

4 cups water	*4 navel orange slices*
¹/₂ cup brown sugar, firmly packed	*1 cinnamon stick*
1 cup pitted prunes	*1 teaspoon vanilla extract*

1. Combine water, brown sugar, prunes, orange slices, cinnamon stick,
   and vanilla in a saucepan.
2. Bring to a boil, stirring until sugar dissolves.
3. Reduce heat and simmer for 20 minutes or until prunes are soft.
4. Remove prunes and set aside.
5. Bring liquid in saucepan to a boil and boil rapidly until reduced to
   1 cup of liquid. Remove cinnamon stick and pour liquid over prunes.

Calories Per Serving: 210	Carbohydrates: 54 g
Fat: .2 g	Dietary Fiber: 3 g
Cholesterol: 0 mg	Sodium: 9.8 mg
Protein: 1.2 g	

✳ *Strawberries in Orange Flavor* ✳

YIELD: *4 servings* • PREPARATION TIME: *10 minutes plus 1 hour marinating time*

Here strawberries are marinated in orange juice and tossed with a
yogurt–brown sugar sauce.

4 cups whole, hulled, fresh	*¹/₃ cup brown sugar, firmly packed*
strawberries	*2 cups plain nonfat yogurt*
³/₄ cup orange juice	

1. Place strawberries and orange juice in a glass bowl and marinate for
   1 hour.

Strawberries in Orange Flavor *(cont'd)*
2. Combine yogurt and brown sugar.
3. Stir yogurt into marinated strawberries.

Calories Per Serving: 198
Fat: .8 g
Cholesterol: 2 mg
Protein: 7 g

Carbohydrates: 41 g
Dietary Fiber: 4 g
Sodium: 95 mg

Strawberries with Sugar and ❋ *Balsamic Vinegar* ❋

YIELD: *4 servings* • PREPARATION TIME: *15 minutes plus 3 hours standing time*

An unlikely trio of ingredients produces a unique and distinctive collaboration.

4 cups strawberries, hulled and sliced   *1 tablespoon balsamic vinegar*
2 tablespoons sugar

1. Place strawberries in a glass pie pan and sprinkle with sugar.
2. Cover with plastic wrap and let stand for 3 hours at room temperature. Stir several times.
3. Sprinkle with vinegar immediately before serving.

Calories Per Serving: 68
Fat: .5 g
Cholesterol: 0 mg
Protein: .9 g

Carbohydrates: 16 g
Dietary Fiber: 3.8 g
Sodium: 2 mg

❋ *Fruit Salad with Pineapple-Spice Dressing* ❋

YIELD: *6 servings* • PREPARATION TIME: *20 minutes plus 45 minutes chilling time*

Oranges, grapefruit, strawberries, and pear are tossed with a dressing of pineapple juice, white wine, cinnamon, and nutmeg.

2 navel oranges, peeled and cut in   *1 medium grapefruit, peeled and cut*
   chunks   *in chunks*

1 cup strawberries, sliced
1 pear, cored and cut in chunks
2 cups juice-packed canned
  pineapple chunks, 1/2 cup juice
  reserved

2 tablespoons dry white wine or
  white grape juice
Pinch of ground cinnamon
Pinch of ground nutmeg

1. Combine oranges, grapefruit, strawberries, and pear.
2. Combine reserved pineapple juice, white wine or white grape juice, cinnamon, and nutmeg in a jar with a tight lid. Shake until blended.
3. Toss dressing over fruit.
4. Cover and chill for 45 minutes.

Calories Per Serving: 99
Fat: .4 g
Cholesterol: 0 mg
Protein: 1.3 g

Carbohydrates: 24 g
Dietary Fiber: 3.7 g
Sodium: 4.8 mg

✳ *Rainbow Fruit Bowl* ✳

YIELD: *6 servings* • PREPARATION TIME: *15 minutes*

Here a rainbow of fruit is combined with a honey–poppy seed dressing.

1 1/2 cups raspberries
1 cup blueberries
2 kiwis, peeled and sliced
1 cup peeled mango chunks
1 cup papaya chunks
1/2 cup juice-packed canned mandarin
  oranges

1/4 cup orange juice
1 tablespoon red wine vinegar
1 tablespoon honey
1/2 teaspoon poppy seeds

1. Combine raspberries, blueberries, kiwis, mango, papaya, and mandarin oranges.
2. Combine orange juice, red wine vinegar, honey, and poppy seeds in a jar with a tight lid. Shake until blended.
3. Pour dressing over fruit salad.

Calories Per Serving: 98
Fat: .6 g
Cholesterol: 0 mg
Protein: 1 g

Carbohydrates: 24 g
Dietary Fiber: 4 g
Sodium: 4.5 mg

❋ *Maple Fruit* ❋

YIELD: 8 servings • *PREPARATION TIME: 20 minutes plus 1 hour chilling time*

Pears, oranges, grapes, pineapple, and dried apricots are served with a ginger-maple dressing. Navel oranges are a good choice for the cook in a hurry since their skins zip off, each segment separates neatly and they contain no seeds.

3 cored and diced pears
2 navel oranges, sectioned
1 cup red seedless grapes
1/2 cup dried apricots
2 cups juice-packed pineapple
  chunks, drained

1/4 cup maple syrup
1/2 teaspoon grated fresh gingerroot
2 teaspoons lemon juice

1. Toss together pears, oranges, grapes, apricots, pineapple chunks, maple syrup, gingerroot, and lemon juice.
2. Chill for 1 hour.

Calories Per Serving: 109
Fat: .4 g
Cholesterol: 0 mg
Protein: 1 g

Carbohydrates; 28 g
Dietary Fiber: 3 g
Sodium: 5.8 mg

❋ *Curried Fruit* ❋

YIELD: 6 servings • *PREPARATION TIME: 25 minutes*

Red and green apples, oranges, grapes, and strawberries are united in this whirl of color and taste.

2 cups coarsely chopped red apples
2 cups coarsely chopped green apples
3 tablespoons lime juice
1 cup navel orange sections
3/4 cup green or red seedless grapes

1/2 cup sliced strawberries
2/3 cup plain nonfat yogurt
1 tablespoon honey
1 1/4 teaspoons curry powder

1. Toss red and green apples with lime juice.
2. Toss apples with oranges, grapes, and strawberries.

3. Combine yogurt, honey, and curry powder.
4. Combine yogurt sauce with fruit.

Calories Per Serving: 116
Fat: .6 g
Cholesterol: .5 mg
Protein: 2 g

Carbohydrates: 30 g
Dietary Fiber: 2.8 g
Sodium: 21 mg

✳ *Pears and Cranberries* ✳

YIELD: 8 servings ▪ *PREPARATION TIME: 10 minutes* ▪
COOKING TIME: 35 minutes

These pears are brushed with lime juice and baked with cranberries, apple juice, honey, and spices.

8 firm pears, cored and cut in half
1 tablespoon lime juice
2 cups fresh or frozen cranberries
1 cup apple juice

2 tablespoons honey
½ teaspoon ground cinnamon
Pinch of ground cloves

1. Preheat oven to 350 degrees.
2. Brush pear halves with lime juice and place in a baking dish.
3. Combine cranberries, apple juice, honey, cinnamon, and cloves.
4. Cook over medium heat until the cranberries burst their skins.
5. Pour cranberry mixture over pears.
6. Bake for 30 minutes or until pears are tender.

Calories Per Serving: 150
Fat: .8 g
Cholesterol: 0 mg
Protein: .9 g

Carbohydrates: 38 g
Dietary fiber: 2.8 g
Sodium: 5 mg

SALADS

FRUIT AND VEGETABLE SALADS

Apple-Celery Salad · Asparagus Salad · Beet Salad · Beet and Pepper Salad · Carrot-Apple-Pineapple Salad · Carrot-Apple-Raisin Salad · Curried Carrot Salad · Carrot, Orange, and Celery Salad · Marinated Carrots and Green Beans · Shredded Carrot Salad · Cauliflower-Mushroom Salad with Balsamic Dressing · Corn and Green Bean Salad · Corn and Zucchini Salad · Middle Eastern Cucumber Salad · Cucumber and Onion Salad · Eggplant-Tomato Salad · Mushroom–Red Pepper Salad · Green Bean and Tomato Salad with Lemon-Garlic Dressing · Green Bean and Red Pepper Salad · Orange-Radish Salad · Oranges and Tomatoes with Honey Dressing · Snow Pea–Pineapple Salad · Pineapple and Apple Salad · Red Potato–Spinach Salad · Pineapple-Watercress Salad · Spinach and Orange Salad · Summer Squash Salad · Strawberry-Cucumber Salad · Strawberry-Spinach Salad · Sugar Snap Pea Salad · Tomato Salad · Tomato-Jalapeño Salad · Tomato-Yogurt Salad · Turnip and Red Grape Salad · Simple Chopped Salad with Lemon Juice

P O T A T O   S A L A D S

Very Fast Potato Salad • Mexicali Potato Salad • Potato–Green Bean
Salad • Potato Salad with Parsley Dressing • Red Pepper–Potato
Salad • Lemon-Dill Potato Salad

G R E E N   S A L A D S

Green Salad with Fruit • Romaine Salad with Scallion Dressing •
Tossed Salad with Balsamic Dressing • Green Salad with
Raw Vegetables

S L A W S   A N D   M I X E D   F R U I T
A N D   V E G E T A B L E   S A L A D S

Zippy Coleslaw • Apple-Honey Slaw • Island Salad •
Red Cabbage Slaw

B E A N   S A L A D S

Black Bean Salad • Black-Eyed Pea Salad • Red, White, and Black
Bean Salad • Kidney Bean and Corn Salad • Big Bean Salad Bowl

G R A I N   S A L A D S

Independence Day Macaroni Salad • Vegetable-Macaroni Salad •
Asparagus–Plum Tomato Pasta Salad • Tex-Mex Pasta Salad •
Rotini and Black-Eyed Pea Salad • Rigatoni-Vegetable Salad with
Pinto Beans • Rotelle-Fruit Salad • Shell Pasta Slaw • Cannelini
Beans, Rice, and Vegetable Salad • Penne Primavera with Garlic-
Tomato Dressing • Wild Rice and Apple Salad • Couscous Salad

The salads in this section are all made with nonfat dressings. They can be
served on their own for lunches or snacks, or in concert with other grain,
fruit, and vegetable dishes for main meals on a nonfat diet. They also
make an excellent nonfat addition for a meal featuring lean meat, poultry,
or fish if these foods remain in your diet.

FRUIT AND VEGETABLE SALADS

::

✳ Apple-Celery Salad ✳

YIELD: 4 servings • *PREPARATION TIME: 15 minutes plus 1 hour chilling time*

Honey and lemon flavor this salad of apples and celery.

2 medium apples, cored and diced
2 stalks celery, chopped

2 tablespoons lemon juice
1 tablespoon honey

1. Combine the apples, celery, lemon juice, and honey.
2. Chill for 1 hour before serving.

Calories Per Serving: 62
Fat: .3 g
Cholesterol: 0 mg
Protein:. 3 g

Carbohydrates: 16 g
Dietary Fiber: 1.8 g
Sodium: 18 mg

✳ Asparagus Salad ✳

YIELD: 6 servings • *PREPARATION TIME: 20 minutes plus asparagus steaming time*
and 1 hour asparagus chilling time

Steamed, chilled asparagus is served with a watercress-lemon dressing. If you're being very conservative with your sodium intake, be aware of the rather high sodium count found in nonfat mayonnaise.

3 pounds asparagus, trimmed,
steamed, and chilled for 1 hour
³/₄ cup chopped watercress

½ cup nonfat mayonnaise
2 tablespoons skim milk
1 tablespoon lemon juice

Asparagus Salad *(cont'd)*
1. Arrange chilled asparagus on a serving platter.
2. Combine watercress, mayonnaise, skim milk, and lemon juice.
3. Spoon dressing over asparagus.

Calories Per Serving: 85
Fat: .7 g
Cholesterol: 0 mg
Protein: 6 g

Carbohydrates: 17 g
Dietary Fiber: 2.7 g
Sodium: 294 mg

✳ *Beet Salad* ✳

YIELD: *4 servings* • PREPARATION TIME: *10 minutes*

Canned beets make a quick salad when you have to throw dinner together in a hurry.

1/2 *cup cider vinegar*
1/4 *cup sugar*
1/2 *cup water*
2 *cups sliced low-sodium canned*
    beets

1 *onion, thinly sliced*
1/2 *teaspoon dried dill leaves*

1. Combine cider vinegar, sugar, and water.
2. Toss vinegar mixture with beets, onion, and dill.

Calories Per Serving: 94
Fat: .2 g
Cholesterol: 0 mg
Protein: 1 g

Carbohydrates: 25 g
Dietary Fiber: 2 g
Sodium: 58 mg

✳ *Beet and Pepper Salad* ✳

YIELD: *4 servings* • PREPARATION TIME: *10 minutes plus 3 hours chilling time*

This sweet-and-sour beet salad accented with green bell pepper and cloves is a great addition to any meal.

2 cups sliced low-sodium canned
   beets, with ½ cup juice reserved
½ cup red wine vinegar
2 tablespoons sugar
1 small green bell pepper, thinly
   sliced

½ teaspoon black pepper
¼ teaspoon ground cloves
1 small onion, thinly sliced

1. Place the beets in a glass bowl. Place the reserved beet juice and the vinegar in a medium saucepan and bring to a boil.
2. Add the sugar, green pepper, black pepper, cloves, and onion. Bring to a boil again.
3. Pour sugar-vinegar mixture over beets in bowl. Chill for 3 hours.

Calories Per Serving: 73
Fat: .3 g
Cholesterol: 0 mg
Protein: 1 g

Carbohydrates: 18 g
Dietary Fiber: 2 g
Sodium: 58 mg

✳ *Carrot-Apple-Pineapple Salad* ✳

YIELD: *4 servings* • PREPARATION TIME: *25 minutes plus 1 hour chilling time*

Here carrots, apples, green bell pepper, and pineapple are dressed with fruit juice and yogurt.

2 medium apples, cored and chopped
2 medium carrots, thinly sliced
1 medium green bell pepper, seeded
   and chopped
1 cup fresh or juice-packed canned
   pineapple chunks

¾ cup plain nonfat yogurt
4 tablespoons orange juice
¼ teaspoon ground cinnamon

1. Combine apples, carrots, green pepper, and pineapple.
2. Combine yogurt, orange juice, and cinnamon.
3. Toss dressing with fruit.
4. Chill for 1 hour before serving.

Calories Per Serving: 129
Fat: .6 g
Cholesterol: .75 mg
Protein: 3 g

Carbohydrates: 30 g
Dietary Fiber: 3.5 g
Sodium: 47 mg

✳ *Carrot-Apple-Raisin Salad* ✳

YIELD: 6 servings • *PREPARATION TIME: 20 minutes*

Carrots and raisins make a winning combination with a lemon-flavored dressing. If you are watching your sodium intake, be aware of the high sodium count in nonfat mayonnaise.

2 cups grated carrots	*1 teaspoon sugar*
1 cup grated apple	*2 tablespoons evaporated skim milk*
³/₄ cup raisins	*1 tablespoon lemon juice*
¹/₃ cup nonfat mayonnaise	

1. Combine carrots, apple, and raisins in a bowl.
2. Combine mayonnaise, sugar, evaporated skim milk, and lemon juice.
3. Toss carrot mixture with dressing.

Calories Per Serving: 106	Carbohydrates: 26 g
Fat: .2 g	Dietary Fiber: 2.5 g
Cholesterol: .2 mg	Sodium: 207 mg
Protein: 1 g	

✳ *Curried Carrot Salad* ✳

YIELD: 4 servings • *PREPARATION TIME: 15 minutes plus 6 hours chilling time* • *COOKING TIME: 20 minutes*

These steamed carrots are marinated in a curry-flavored dressing.

2 cups sliced carrots	*1¹/₂ tablespoons honey*
¹/₃ cup white wine or white grape juice	*2 teaspoons curry powder*
	1 teaspoon ground ginger
¹/₄ cup white wine vinegar	

1. Place carrots in a saucepan with white wine or white grape juice, vinegar, honey, curry power, and ground ginger.
2. Bring to a boil, reduce heat, and simmer for 15 minutes.
3. Place carrots and liquid in a glass bowl, cover, and chill for 6 hours.

Calories Per Serving: 70
Fat: .3 g
Cholesterol: 0 mg
Protein: .7 g

Carbohydrates: 13 g
Dietary Fiber: 2 g
Sodium: 34 mg

✳ *Carrot, Orange, and Celery Salad* ✳

YIELD: 6 servings • *PREPARATION TIME: 25 minutes plus 30 minutes chilling time*

This attractive salad is rich in beta carotene and Vitamin C.

4 cups shredded carrots
1¼ cups navel orange sections,
   chopped
½ cup chopped celery

1 tablespoon all-fruit marmalade
1 tablespoon honey
¼ cup orange juice
1 teaspoon dried dill leaves

1. Combine carrots, orange sections, celery, marmalade, honey, orange juice, and dill in a glass bowl.
2. Refrigerate for 30 minutes before serving.

Calories Per Serving: 69
Fat: .2 g
Cholesterol: 0 mg
Protein: 1 g

Carbohydrates: 16 g
Dietary Fiber: 3.3 g
Sodium: 36 mg

✳ *Shredded Carrot Salad* ✳

YIELD: 4 servings • *PREPARATION TIME: 20 minutes plus 1 hour standing time*

Shredded carrots are tossed here with a zesty dressing.

6 large carrots, shredded
2 scallions, chopped
2 tablespoons sugar
½ teaspoon ground cumin

Pinch of cayenne pepper
¼ teaspoon black pepper
3 tablespoons lemon juice
½ cup minced parsley

1. Toss the carrots with the scallions.

Shredded Carrot Salad *(cont'd)*

2. Combine the sugar, ground cumin, cayenne pepper, black pepper, and lemon juice.
3. Toss carrot-scallion mixture with spices. Let stand for 1 hour. Sprinkle with parsley before serving.

Variation
- Delete the sugar, cumin, and cayenne pepper. Substitute 1 teaspoon grated fresh gingerroot and 1 clove garlic, minced.

Calories Per Serving: 76
Fat: .3 g
Cholesterol: 0 mg
Protein: 1.4 g

Carbohydrates: 19 g
Dietary Fiber: 3.9 g
Sodium: 41 mg

❋ Marinated Carrots and Green Beans ❋

YIELD: 6 servings • PREPARATION TIME: 25 minutes plus green bean steaming time and 5 hours chilling time

Crunchy carrots, steamed green beans, cabbage, and cucumber are marinated in a multiflavored dressing in this colorful salad.

6 grated carrots
1½ cups green beans, trimmed and steamed
1½ cups shredded white cabbage
1 grated cucumber
2 cloves garlic, minced

½ teaspoon cayenne pepper
3 tablespoons brown sugar, firmly packed
3 tablespoons cider vinegar
1 tablespoon lemon juice
1 teaspoon ground turmeric

1. Combine carrots, steamed green beans, white cabbage, and cucumber in a glass bowl.
2. Combine garlic, cayenne pepper, brown sugar, cider vinegar, lemon juice, and turmeric.
3. Toss dressing with vegetables.
4. Chill, covered, for 5 hours.

Calories Per Serving: 82
Fat: .4 g
Cholesterol: 0 mg
Protein: 1.9 g

Carbohydrates: 20 g
Dietary Fiber: 3.7 g
Sodium: 33 mg

Cauliflower-Mushroom Salad with
✳ Balsamic Dressing ✳

YIELD: *4 servings* • PREPARATION TIME: *25 minutes plus 3 hours chilling time* • COOKING TIME: *10 minutes*

Here cauliflower, green bell peppers, carrots, and mushrooms are tossed with a balsamic-tomato dressing. Serve in salad bowls over shredded romaine lettuce.

³/₄ cup sliced cauliflower florets
1 cup diced green bell peppers
¹/₂ cup sliced carrots
³/₄ cup sliced mushrooms
¹/₄ cup low-sodium tomato juice
¹/₂ teaspoon cornstarch

2 tablespoons balsamic vinegar
2 tablespoons red wine vinegar
1 tablespoon minced onion
¹/₂ teaspoon dried oregano leaves
2 tablespoons chopped fresh parsley

1. Heat 1 inch of water in a steamer. Place cauliflower, green peppers, and carrots in a steamer basket or colander, cover, and steam for 4 minutes.
2. Place steamed vegetables in a glass bowl and toss with mushrooms.
3. Heat tomato juice and cornstarch in a saucepan over low heat, stirring until juice thickens.
4. Combine tomato juice with balsamic vinegar, red wine vinegar, onion, oregano, and parsley.
5. Pour dressing over vegetables and chill, covered, for 3 hours.

Calories Per Serving: 28
Fat: .3 g
Cholesterol: 0 mg
Protein: 1 g

Carbohydrates: 6 g
Dietary Fiber: 1.8 g
Sodium: 11 mg

✳ Corn and Green Bean Salad ✳

YIELD: *6 servings* • PREPARATION TIME: *15 minutes plus vegetable cooking time*

Steamed green beans and cooked corn are tossed with tomato dressing in this dish.

Corn and Green Bean Salad (cont'd)

2 cups steamed green beans, cut into
2-inch pieces
1 cup cooked fresh, frozen, or canned
corn kernels
2 fresh large tomatoes, seeded and
finely chopped

1/4 cup nonfat mayonnaise
1/4 cup plain nonfat yogurt
1/4 teaspoon ground white pepper

1. Combine green beans and corn.
2. Beat together the chopped tomatoes, mayonnaise, yogurt, and white pepper.
3. Combine the green beans and corn with the tomato dressing.

Calories Per Serving: 64
Fat: .2 g
Cholesterol: .2 mg
Protein: 2.5 g

Carbohydrates: 14 g
Dietary Fiber: 1.8 g
Sodium: 153 mg

✸ Corn and Zucchini Salad ✸

YIELD: 4 servings • PREPARATION TIME: 25 minutes plus corn cooking time
and 2 hours chilling time

In this dish corn, scallions, zucchini, and red bell pepper are marinated in a parsley dressing.

2 cups cooked fresh, frozen, or
canned corn kernels
1/2 cup chopped scallions
1/2 cup chopped zucchini
1/2 cup chopped red bell pepper
1/2 cup chopped celery
2 tablespoons finely chopped fresh
parsley

1 clove garlic, minced
Pinch of black pepper
1 teaspoon sugar
1/2 teaspoon ground cumin
1 teaspoon Dijon mustard
3 tablespoons cider vinegar

1. Combine corn, scallions, zucchini, red pepper, and celery in a glass bowl.
2. Combine parsley, garlic, pepper, sugar, cumin, mustard, and cider vinegar.

3. Toss dressing with vegetables.
4. Cover and chill for at least 2 hours.

Calories Per Serving: 85
Fat: .3 g
Cholesterol: 0 mg
Protein: 3 g

Carbohydrates: 21 g
Dietary Fiber: 2.7 g
Sodium: 36 mg

✳ *Middle Eastern Cucumber Salad* ✳

YIELD: 4 servings • PREPARATION TIME: 15 minutes plus 1 hour chilling time

Crunchy cucumbers are tossed here with a yogurt dressing flavored with mint and scallions.

¼ cup skim milk
1 cup plain nonfat yogurt
1 tablespoon lemon juice
½ cup chopped scallions

1 clove garlic, minced
½ teaspoon dried mint leaves
2 cucumbers, peeled and sliced

1. Place skim milk, yogurt, and lemon juice in a blender or food processor and process until smooth.
2. Toss together scallions, garlic, mint leaves, and cucumbers.
3. Pour yogurt sauce over cucumbers and chill for 1 hour before serving.

Variations
- Add ¼ teaspoon ground cumin in Step 2.
- Delete milk. Replace lemon juice with balsamic vinegar.

Calories Per Serving: 60
Fat: .3 g
Cholesterol: 1.25 mg
Protein: 4 g

Carbohydrates: 10 g
Dietary Fiber: 1.6 g
Sodium: 55 mg

✳ *Cucumber and Onion Salad* ✳

YIELD: 4 servings • PREPARATION TIME: 15 minutes plus 2 hours chilling time

This traditional cucumber and onion salad is dressed with rice vinegar.

Cucumber and Onion Salad *(cont'd)*

1 large cucumber, thinly sliced

1 medium onion, thinly sliced into
rings

1/3 cup rice vinegar

1 1/2 tablespoons sugar

1/4 teaspoon red pepper flakes

1/4 teaspoon ground white pepper

1. Combine cucumber and onion in a glass bowl.
2. Combine vinegar, sugar, red pepper flakes, and black pepper.
3. Pour dressing over cucumber and onions. Chill for 2 hours and drain.

Variations

- Use red onion. Add 1/2 cup red bell pepper and 1 carrot cut into julienne strips in Step 1. Add 1 teaspoon dried coriander in Step 2.
- Add 1 teaspoon soy sauce in Step 2.
- Delete red pepper flakes and add 1/2 teaspoon dried dill.

Calories Per Serving: 43

Fat: .2 g

Cholesterol: 0 mg

Protein: .8 g

Carbohydrates: 10 g

Dietary Fiber: 1.4 g

Sodium: 3 mg

✳ *Eggplant-Tomato Salad* ✳

YIELD: *4 servings* ▪ PREPARATION TIME: *25 minutes plus 30 minutes chilling time*
▪ COOKING TIME: *15 minutes*

Steamed eggplant chunks are tossed here with tomatoes, green bell pepper, scallions, and a variety of spices.

1 medium eggplant, peeled and cut
into chunks

1/4 cup water, nonfat chicken broth,
vegetable broth, or wine

2 cloves garlic, minced

1/4 cup finely chopped onion

1 teaspoon grated fresh gingerroot

1 teaspoon ground cumin

1 teaspoon ground coriander

1/4 teaspoon red pepper flakes

2 medium tomatoes, chopped

1 green bell pepper, seeded and
chopped

1. Heat 1 inch of water in a steamer. Place eggplant chunks in a steamer basket or colander. Cover and steam for 8 minutes or until eggplant is tender.

2. Heat the water, broth, or wine in a skillet over medium heat. Add the garlic, onion, ginger, cumin, coriander, red pepper flakes, tomatoes, and green pepper. Cook and stir over medium heat for 5 minutes. Add more liquid during this process if necessary.
3. Toss the eggplant with the tomato mixture.
4. Chill for 30 minutes before serving.

Calories Per Serving: 53	Carbohydrates: 11 g
Fat: .7 g	Dietary Fiber: 3.9 g
Cholesterol: 0 mg	Sodium: 10 mg
Protein: 1.8 g	

✳ Mushroom–Red Pepper Salad ✳

YIELD: 4 servings ▪ *PREPARATION TIME: 20 minutes*

Fresh mushrooms are the featured ingredient in this refreshing, easy-to-assemble salad.

12 large mushroom caps, thinly
   sliced
1 cup chopped celery
1/4 cup minced onion

1/4 cup chopped red bell pepper
1/4 teaspoon black pepper
3 tablespoons lemon juice

1. Toss mushrooms with celery, onion, red pepper, black pepper, and lemon juice.

Calories Per Serving: 27	Carbohydrates: 5.8 g
Fat: .3 g	Dietary Fiber: 1.5 g
Cholesterol: 0 mg	Sodium: 29 mg
Protein: 1.5 g	

Green Bean and Tomato Salad with ✳ Lemon-Garlic Dressing ✳

YIELD: 4 servings ▪ *PREPARATION TIME: 20 minutes plus bean steaming time*

These tomatoes and green beans are dressed with a lemon-yogurt-garlic dressing.

Green Bean and Tomato Salad with Lemon-Garlic Dressing *(cont'd)*

2 cups trimmed, steamed green beans	1 tablespoon lemon juice
2 medium tomatoes, quartered	1 clove garlic, minced
2 tablespoons chopped fresh parsley	1/4 teaspoon black pepper
3/4 cup plain nonfat yogurt	

1. Toss green beans, tomatoes, and parsley.
2. Combine yogurt, lemon juice, garlic, and black pepper.
3. Combine green beans and tomatoes with dressing.

Calories Per Serving: 61   Carbohydrates: 11 g
Fat: .4 g   Dietary Fiber: 2 g
Cholesterol: .75 mg   Sodium: 41 mg
Protein: 4 g

✳ *Green Bean and Red Pepper Salad* ✳

YIELD: 4 servings • *PREPARATION TIME: 15 minutes plus bean cooking time plus 1 hour chilling time*

Green beans and red peppers are served with a tomato dressing in this recipe.

2 cups cooked fresh or frozen green beans, cut into 1-inch slices	1 tablespoon white wine vinegar
	1/4 teaspoon dried basil leaves
1 red bell pepper, seeded and chopped	Pinch of dry mustard
	1 clove garlic, minced
1 tablespoon chopped onion	1/4 teaspoon black pepper
1 cup low-sodium tomato juice	

1. Toss string beans with red pepper and onion in a large glass bowl.
2. Combine tomato juice, white wine vinegar, basil, mustard, garlic, and black pepper.
3. Pour tomato dressing over string bean mixture. Chill for 1 hour.

Calories Per Serving: 40   Carbohydrates: 9 g
Fat: .3 g   Dietary Fiber: 2 g
Cholesterol: 0 mg   Sodium: 9 mg
Protein: 1.9 g

❋ *Orange-Radish Salad* ❋

YIELD: 4 servings ▪ *PREPARATION TIME: 15 minutes plus 3 hours chilling time*

Here navel oranges and radishes are combined with lemon juice, sugar, and cinnamon.

4 large navel oranges, peeled and sectioned
½ cup sliced radishes

¼ cup lemon juice
½ teaspoon sugar
Pinch of ground cinnamon

1. Toss oranges and radishes with lemon juice, sugar, and cinnamon.
2. Marinate in refrigerator for 3 hours before serving.

Calories Per Serving: 69
Fat: .2 g
Cholesterol: 0 mg
Protein: 1 g

Carbohydrates: 17 g
Dietary Fiber: 3 g
Sodium: 1.5 mg

Oranges and Tomatoes with ❋ *Honey Dressing* ❋

YIELD: 4 servings ▪ *PREPARATION TIME: 25 minutes*

Here green peppers, sliced oranges, and tomatoes are dressed with orange juice and honey.

2 green bell peppers, seeded and sliced in rings
3 medium tomatoes, sliced
1 large navel orange, peeled and sliced
1 medium cucumber, peeled and sliced

½ teaspoon grated orange peel
¼ cup orange juice
1 tablespoon minced scallion
1 tablespoon honey
¼ teaspoon black pepper

1. Arrange green pepper slices, tomato slices, orange slices, and cucumber slices on a serving platter.
2. Combine orange peel, orange juice, scallion, honey, and black pepper.

Oranges and Tomatoes with Honey Dressing *(cont'd)*

3. Spoon dressing over oranges and vegetables.

Calories Per Serving: 76	Carbohydrates: 18 g
Fat: .5 g	Dietary Fiber: 3.5 g
Cholesterol: 0 mg	Sodium: 10 mg
Protein: 1.9 g	

✳ *Snow Pea–Pineapple Salad* ✳

YIELD: *8 servings* • PREPARATION TIME: *20 minutes plus vegetable steaming time*

Pineapple chunks, snow peas, carrots, and red peppers are served with a pineapple-ginger dressing in this dish.

3 cups juice-packed pineapple
  chunks, with ¼ cup juice reserved
2 cups trimmed, steamed snow peas
1½ cups sliced, steamed carrots
2 cups diced red bell pepper

3 tablespoons white wine vinegar
1 tablespoon light soy sauce
½ teaspoon minced fresh gingerroot
1 bunch watercress, trimmed, or
  3 cups shredded romaine lettuce

1. Toss pineapple with snow peas, carrots, and red pepper.
2. Combine reserved pineapple juice, white wine vinegar, soy sauce, and gingerroot.
3. Transfer pineapple–snow pea mixture to a bowl lined with watercress or romaine, and spoon dressing over salad.

Calories Per Serving: 74	Carbohydrates: 19 g
Fat: .4 g	Dietary Fiber: 2.9 g
Cholesterol: 0 mg	Sodium: 167 mg
Protein: 3.4 g	

✳ *Pineapple and Apple Salad* ✳

YIELD: *6 servings* • PREPARATION TIME: *15 minutes*

This pineapple and apple salad is flavored with lime juice, raisins, wine vinegar, and honey.

4 apples, peeled, cored, and diced   ¼ cup raisins
¾ cup chopped pineapple   ¼ cup white wine vinegar
2 tablespoons lime juice   ¼ cup honey

1. Combine apples, pineapple, and lime juice.
2. Add raisins, vinegar, and honey to the pineapple and apple. Serve immediately.

Calories Per Serving: 128   Carbohydrates: 33 g
Fat: .4 g   Dietary Fiber: .9 g
Cholesterol: 0 mg   Sodium: 3 mg
Protein: .5 g

✳ Red Potato–Spinach Salad ✳

YIELD: 4 servings • PREPARATION TIME: 15 minutes plus potato cooling time • COOKING TIME: 20 minutes

New potatoes and fresh raw spinach leaves are combined with a lemon-yogurt dressing.

1½ pounds new red potatoes,   3 tablespoons lemon juice
   scrubbed and halved   ½ cup plain nonfat yogurt
2 cups fresh spinach leaves, chopped   ¼ teaspoon black pepper
½ cup chopped scallions

1. Drop potatoes in boiling water and cook over medium heat for 20 minutes or until tender. Drain and allow potatoes to cool.
2. Toss cooled potatoes with spinach leaves and scallions.
4. Combine lemon juice, yogurt, and black pepper.
5. Toss dressing with potatoes, spinach, and scallions.

Calories Per Serving: 204   Carbohydrates: 45 g
Fat: .4 g   Dietary Fiber: 3 g
Cholesterol: .5 mg   Sodium: 53 mg
Protein: 6 g

✳ *Pineapple-Watercress Salad* ✳

YIELD: 4 servings ▪ *PREPARATION TIME: 15 minutes*

Pineapple, watercress, and red bell pepper are dressed with soy sauce here.

1 bunch watercress, coarse stems
  removed and chopped
2 cups fresh or juice-packed canned
  pineapple chunks
1 medium red bell pepper, halved,
  seeded, and cut into thin strips

1 small green bell pepper, halved,
  seeded, and cut into thin strips
1 teaspoon light soy sauce
2 tablespoons pineapple juice or
  orange juice

1. Toss together watercress, pineapple chunks, red and green pepper strips, soy sauce, and juice.

Calories Per Serving: 56
Fat: .3 g
Cholesterol: 0 mg
Protein: 1.8 g

Carbohydrates: 13 g
Dietary Fiber: 1.9 g
Sodium: 168 mg

✳ *Spinach and Orange Salad* ✳

YIELD: 6 servings ▪ *PREPARATION TIME: 25 minutes*

Spinach leaves and orange segments are tossed in an orange-buttermilk dressing.

6 cups torn spinach leaves
2 navel oranges, peeled and diced
²/₃ cup nonfat buttermilk
1 teaspoon grated fresh gingerroot

¹/₄ cup orange juice
2 teaspoons ground cumin
2 teaspoons ground coriander
2 teaspoons ground paprika

1. Toss the spinach leaves and oranges together in a salad bowl.
2. Combine the buttermilk, gingerroot, orange juice, cumin, coriander, and paprika.
3. Toss the dressing with the spinach and oranges.

Calories Per Serving: 52
Fat: .5 g
Cholesterol: .6 mg
Protein: 3 g

Carbohydrates: 10 g
Dietary Fiber: 2.5 g
Sodium: 75 mg

✳ *Summer Squash Salad* ✳

YIELD: 4 servings • PREPARATION TIME: 15 minutes plus 1 hour standing time and 2 hours chilling time

This salad combines zucchini and yellow summer squash in a dill-vinegar dressing.

1½ cups zucchini, very thinly sliced
1½ cups yellow summer squash,
    very thinly sliced
1½ teaspoon salt

1 teaspoon dried dill leaves
⅓ cup white wine vinegar
¾ teaspoon sugar

1. Toss zucchini and yellow summer squash with salt. Place vegetables in a colander in the sink for 1 hour. Rinse in cold water and drain well.
2. Combine squash with dill, vinegar, and sugar in a glass bowl. Cover and refrigerate for 2 hours.

Calories Per Serving: 20
Fat: .2 g
Cholesterol: 0 mg
Protein: 1 g

Carbohydrates: 4 g
Dietary Fiber: 1 g
Sodium: 70 mg

✳ *Strawberry-Cucumber Salad* ✳

YIELD: 4 servings • PREPARATION TIME: 15 minutes

Strawberries and cucumber are paired and flavored with lime juice in this quick and easy salad.

1 cucumber, peeled and very thinly
    sliced
2 cups fresh or thawed, frozen
    strawberries, quartered

4 tablespoons lime juice
¼ teaspoon black pepper

Strawberry-Cucumber Salad *(cont'd)*

1. Toss cucumbers and strawberries with lime juice and pepper.

Variation

- Make a cucumber-orange salad by substituting 3 chopped navel oranges for the strawberries. Dress with orange juice instead of lime juice.

Calories Per Serving: 37	Carbohydrates: 8 g
Fat: .4 g	Dietary Fiber: 2.7 g
Cholesterol: 0 mg	Sodium: 2.7 mg
Protein: .9 g	

✳ *Strawberry-Spinach Salad* ✳

YIELD: 4 servings • *PREPARATION TIME: 25 minutes*

Here strawberries and spinach are served with a balsamic vinegar dressing.

2 tablespoons balsamic vinegar	*1/2 teaspoon black pepper*
2 tablespoons rice vinegar	*8 cups torn fresh spinach leaves*
1 1/2 tablespoons honey	*1 cup sliced strawberries*
2 teaspoons Dijon mustard	*1/2 cup chopped red onions*

1. Combine balsamic vinegar, rice vinegar, honey, mustard, and black pepper.
2. Toss spinach, strawberries, and red onions with dressing.

Calories Per Serving: 71	Carbohydrates: 15 g
Fat: .6 g	Dietary Fiber: 4 g
Cholesterol: 0 mg	Sodium: 122 mg
Protein: 3.7 g	

✳ *Sugar Snap Pea Salad* ✳

YIELD: 4 servings • *PREPARATION TIME: 15 minutes plus 1 hour chilling time* •
COOKING TIME: 1 minute

These sugar snap peas are tossed with cucumber and onion in a dill-flavored dressing.

²/₃ cup water
¹/₃ cup cider vinegar
1 tablespoon sugar
¹/₄ teaspoon salt
¹/₄ teaspoon black pepper
1 large cucumber, peeled, seeded,
  and sliced

1 onion, sliced
1 teaspoon dried dill leaves
4 cups sugar snap peas, stems and
  strings removed

1. Combine water, vinegar, sugar, salt, and black pepper in a glass bowl.
2. Add cucumber, onion, and dill and toss.
3. Cover and refrigerate for at least 1 hour.
4. Fill a large saucepan with water and bring to a boil. Drop sugar snap peas in for 1 minute. Drain, rinse in ice water, and drain again.
5. Refrigerate until ready to use.
6. When ready to use, toss sugar snap peas with cucumber–onion mixture.

Calories Per Serving: 99
Fat: .5 g
Cholesterol: 0 mg
Protein: 5 g

Carbohydrates: 20 g
Dietary Fiber: 5 g
Sodium: 143 mg

✳ *Tomato Salad* ✳

YIELD: 4 servings ▪ *PREPARATION TIME: 15 minutes plus 30 minutes standing time*

This salad is dressed with lemon juice and cayenne pepper.

4 tomatoes, chopped
1 green bell pepper, chopped
¹/₄ cup fresh parsley, finely chopped

¹/₄ cup chopped scallions
2 tablespoons lemon juice
¹/₄ teaspoon cayenne pepper

1. Combine tomatoes, green pepper, parsley, scallions, lemon juice, and cayenne pepper in a glass bowl.
2. Chill for 30 minutes before serving.

Calories Per Serving: 33
Fat: .4 g
Cholesterol: 0 mg
Protein: 1.4 g

Carbohydrates: 7.5 g
Dietary Fiber: 2 g
Sodium: 12 mg

✳ *Tomato-Jalapeño Salad* ✳

YIELD: 6 servings ▪ *PREPARATION TIME: 15 minutes plus 1 hour chilling time*

Jalapeño pepper, red onions, and tomatoes are tossed together here with lemon juice and black pepper.

1 jalapeño pepper, seeded and finely chopped
½ cup chopped red onions

5 tomatoes, chopped
3 tablespoons lemon juice
½ teaspoon black pepper

1. Combine jalapeño pepper, red onions, tomatoes, lemon juice, and black pepper.
2. Refrigerate for 1 hour.

Calories Per Serving: 27
Fat: .3 g
Cholesterol: 0 mg
Protein: 1 g

Carbohydrates: 6 g
Dietary Fiber: 1.6 g
Sodium: 40 mg

✳ *Tomato-Yogurt Salad* ✳

YIELD: 4 servings ▪ *PREPARATION TIME: 15 minutes*

Here fresh tomatoes and onion are mixed with cumin, mint, and yogurt.

3 medium tomatoes, quartered
1 small onion, chopped
¾ cup plain nonfat yogurt
Pinch of cayenne pepper

½ teaspoon ground cumin
1 teaspoon dried mint leaves
¼ teaspoon black pepper

1. Combine tomatoes and onion.
2. Combine yogurt, cayenne, cumin, mint, and black pepper.
3. Gently toss tomatoes and onions with dressing.

Calories Per Serving: 50
Fat: .4 g
Cholesterol: .75 mg
Protein: 3 g

Carbohydrates: 8.9 g
Dietary Fiber: 1.5 g
Sodium: 41 mg

✳ *Turnip and Red Grape Salad* ✳

YIELD: 4 servings ▪ *PREPARATION TIME: 15 minutes plus 3 hours chilling time*

Crunchy, shredded, raw turnips and juicy seedless red grapes are tossed with a dressing of mayonnaise, yogurt, orange juice, and cayenne pepper.

2½ cups shredded raw turnips
1½ cups seedless red grapes
⅓ cup nonfat mayonnaise

⅓ cup plain nonfat yogurt
2 tablespoons orange juice
Pinch of cayenne pepper

1. Mix together turnips and red grapes.
2. Combine mayonnaise, yogurt, orange juice, and cayenne pepper.
3. Combine turnips, grapes, and dressing.

Calories Per Serving: 81
Fat: .4 g
Cholesterol: .3 mg
Protein: 2 g

Carbohydrates: 19 g
Dietary Fiber: 2 g
Sodium: 321 mg

✳ *Simple Chopped Salad with Lemon Juice* ✳

YIELD: 4 servings ▪ *PREPARATION TIME: 20 minutes*

This Mediterranean classic is quick and easy to prepare and tastes wonderful when made with vegetables fresh from the garden.

1 red bell pepper, finely chopped
1 cucumber, peeled, seeded, and
 finely chopped
2 carrots, finely chopped

2 ripe tomatoes, seeded and chopped
4 scallions, chopped
1 tablespoon lemon juice
¼ teaspoon black pepper

1. Combine the red pepper, cucumber, carrots, tomatoes, scallions, lemon juice, and black pepper.

Calories Per Serving: 44
Fat: .4 g
Cholesterol: 0 mg
Protein: 1.5 g

Carbohydrates: 10 g
Dietary Fiber: 3 g
Sodium: 20 mg

POTATO SALADS

::

✳ *Very Fast Potato Salad* ✳

YIELD: 6 servings ▪ *PREPARATION TIME: 15 minutes plus 1 hour refrigeration time*

You can make this potato salad in a jiffy on a hot day when you don't feel like cooking, stick it in the refrigerator for an hour, and serve with an all-salad supper.

2 pounds red potatoes, cut into chunks
¼ cup chopped scallions
1 green bell pepper, seeded and chopped

2 tablespoons nonfat mayonnaise
6 tablespoons plain nonfat yogurt
1 tablespoon Dijon mustard

1. Bring a large pot of water to a boil. Add potatoes and cook for 15 minutes or until tender. Drain potatoes.
2. Toss potatoes with scallions, green pepper, mayonnaise, yogurt, and mustard.
3. Refrigerate for 1 hour.

Calories Per Serving: 138
Fat: .2 g
Cholesterol: .3 mg
Protein: 3.5 g

Carbohydrates: 30 g
Dietary Fiber: 1.7 g
Sodium: 98 mg

✳ *Mexicali Potato Salad* ✳

YIELD: 8 servings ▪ *PREPARATION TIME: 25 minutes plus 30 minutes chilling time*
▪ *COOKING TIME: 15 minutes*

This potato salad has a south-of-the-border taste thanks to the addition of cilantro, jalapeños, lime juice, and cumin.

2 pounds red potatoes, cut into
   chunks
2 medium chopped tomatoes
1 green bell pepper, seeded and
   chopped
1 red bell pepper, seeded and
   chopped

1 teaspoon dried cilantro
1 tablespoon chopped fresh jalapeño
   peppers
$1/3$ cup nonfat mayonnaise
$2/3$ cup plain nonfat yogurt
3 tablespoons lime juice
1 teaspoon ground cumin

1. Bring a large pot of water to a boil. Add potatoes and cook for 15 minutes or until tender. Drain and chill potatoes for 30 minutes.
2. Toss potatoes with tomatoes, green bell pepper, and red bell pepper.
3. Combine cilantro, jalapeños, mayonnaise, yogurt, lime juice, and cumin.
4. Toss dressing with potato mixture.

Calories Per Serving: 129
Fat: .4 g
Cholesterol: .3 mg
Protein: 3.5 g

Carbohydrates: 28 g
Dietary Fiber: 1.8 g
Sodium: 203 mg

✳ *Potato–Green Bean Salad* ✳

YIELD: *4 servings* • PREPARATION TIME: *20 minutes plus egg cooking time and 30 minutes chilling time* • COOKING TIME: *15 minutes*

Here red potatoes, green beans, red bell peppers, and egg whites are tossed with a lemon–mustard dressing.

1 pound red potatoes, cut into chunks
$1/2$ pound green beans, trimmed and
   cut into 1-inch pieces
$1/2$ cup chopped red bell pepper
2 hard-cooked egg whites, chopped
3 tablespoons plain nonfat yogurt

2 tablespoons nonfat mayonnaise
2 tablespoons chopped red onion
1 tablespoon lemon juice
1 teaspoon Dijon mustard
$1/4$ teaspoon black pepper

1. Bring a large pot of water to a boil. Cook potatoes for 15 minutes or until tender. Drain and chill for 30 minutes.
2. Bring 1 inch of water to a boil in a steamer. Place green beans in a steamer basket or colander. Cover and steam for 5 minutes or until the beans are just tender. Rinse in cold water and drain.

Potato–Green Bean Salad *(cont'd)*

3. Combine cooled potatoes, beans, red pepper, and egg whites in a bowl.
4. Combine yogurt, mayonnaise, red onion, lemon juice, mustard, and black pepper.
5. Toss dressing with potato mixture.

Calories Per Serving: 173
Fat: .5 g
Cholesterol: .2 mg
Protein: 6.6 g

Carbohydrates: 37 g
Dietary Fiber: 4.7 g
Sodium: 166 mg

✳ *Potato Salad with Parsley Dressing* ✳

YIELD: 6 servings • *PREPARATION TIME: 15 minutes plus potato and egg cooking time*

Here potatoes are combined with egg whites, scallions, pickle relish, and parsley.

3 cups cooked potatoes, peeled and sliced
2 hard-boiled egg whites
½ cup chopped scallions
2 tablespoons pickle relish
½ tablespoon Dijon mustard
1 tablespoon nonfat mayonnaise

½ teaspoon white wine vinegar
1 tablespoon nonfat buttermilk or skim milk
¼ cup fresh chopped parsley
Pinch of cayenne pepper
¼ teaspoon black pepper

1. Combine potatoes, egg whites, scallions, and pickle relish.
2. Combine Dijon mustard, mayonnaise, white wine vinegar, buttermilk, parsley, cayenne pepper, and black pepper.
3. Combine dressing with potato mixture.

Calories Per Serving: 79
Fat: .1 g
Cholesterol: 0 mg
Protein: 2.6 g

Carbohydrates: 16 g
Dietary Fiber: .9 g
Sodium: 118 mg

✳ *Red Pepper–Potato Salad* ✳

YIELD: 6 servings ▪ *PREPARATION TIME: 20 minutes plus potato cooking time*

Here red bell pepper, potatoes, and onion are seasoned with paprika and caraway seeds.

*1½ pounds potatoes, cooked and
   diced
1 small onion, chopped
1 large red bell pepper, seeded and
   diced*

*¼ cup nonfat mayonnaise
½ cup plain nonfat yogurt
2 teaspoons paprika
½ teaspoon caraway seeds
½ cup chopped fresh parsley*

1. Combine the potatoes, onion, and red pepper.
2. Combine the mayonnaise, yogurt, paprika, and caraway seeds.
3. Toss the potato mixture with the dressing. Garnish with chopped parsley.

Calories Per Serving: 135
Fat: .4 g
Cholesterol: .33 mg
Protein: 3.7 g

Carbohydrates: 30 g
Dietary Fiber: 1.9 g
Sodium: 163 mg

✳ *Lemon-Dill Potato Salad* ✳

YIELD: 4 servings ▪ *PREPARATION TIME: 20 minutes plus potato cooking time and
1 hour chilling time*

Potatoes, scallions, radishes, and celery are combined with a lemon-dill dressing in this salad.

*3 medium potatoes, cooked and sliced
½ cup chopped scallions
½ cup chopped radishes
¾ cup chopped celery
1 cup plain nonfat yogurt*

*½ teaspoon Dijon mustard
1 clove garlic, minced
1 teaspoon dill leaves
2 tablespoons lemon juice
1 cup diced cucumber*

1. Combine potatoes, scallions, radishes, and celery in a large bowl.

Lemon-Dill Potato Salad *(cont'd)*

2. Combine yogurt, mustard, garlic, dill, and lemon juice. Chill for 1 hour.
3. Garnish with diced cucumber and serve.

Calories Per Serving: 33   Carbohydrates: 6 g
Fat: 0 g   Dietary Fiber: .5 g
Cholesterol: .3 mg   Sodium: 20 mg
Protein: 1 g

GREEN SALADS

::

✳ Green Salad with Fruit ✳

YIELD: 4 servings • PREPARATION TIME: 20 minutes

In this salad romaine lettuce, apple, pear, celery, and seedless red grapes are tossed with a honey-yogurt dressing.

4 cups romaine lettuce leaves, rinsed and torn
1 apple, cored and diced
1 pear, cored and diced
1 stalk celery, chopped

1 cup seedless red grapes
1/3 cup plain nonfat yogurt
1 1/2 tablespoons lemon juice
1 tablespoon honey
1/4 teaspoon ground cinnamon

1. Toss together romaine lettuce with apple, pear, celery, and grapes.
2. Combine yogurt, lemon juice, honey, and cinnamon.
3. Toss salad with dressing.

Calories Per Serving: 118
Fat: .5 g
Cholesterol: .3 mg
Protein: 2.7 g

Carbohydrates: 30 g
Dietary Fiber: 3.6 g
Sodium: 29 mg

✳ Romaine Salad with Scallion Dressing ✳

YIELD: 6 servings • PREPARATION TIME: 25 minutes

Here crisp romaine lettuce, red cabbage, cucumber, and plum tomatoes are served with a zesty scallion dressing.

2 cups torn romaine lettuce
1 cup shredded red cabbage
3/4 cup diced cucumber
3/4 cup sliced plum or cherry tomatoes
1/4 cup sliced radishes

2/3 cup plain nonfat yogurt
1/4 cup chopped scallions or chives
1 teaspoon red wine vinegar
1/2 teaspoon Dijon mustard
1/4 teaspoon black pepper

Romaine Salad with Scallion Dressing *(cont'd)*

1. Toss together romaine lettuce, red cabbage, cucumber, tomatoes, and radishes in a large salad bowl.
2. Combine yogurt, scallions or chives, red wine vinegar, Dijon mustard, and black pepper.
3. Toss dressing with salad.

Calories Per Serving: 25
Fat: .2 g
Cholesterol: .4 mg
Protein: 2 g

Carbohydrates: 4 g
Dietary Fiber: .9 g
Sodium: 30 mg

✳ *Tossed Salad with Balsamic Dressing* ✳

YIELD: 6 servings ▪ *PREPARATION TIME: 15 minutes*

In this recipe spinach and raw vegetables are tossed with a balsamic-oregano dressing.

2 cups torn spinach leaves
2 cups torn romaine lettuce
1 cup torn green or red leaf lettuce
1/2 cup chopped tomatoes
1 cup chopped green bell pepper
1 cup peeled, seeded, and chopped cucumber

1/3 cup sliced red onion
1/4 cup balsamic vinegar
1 1/2 teaspoons dried oregano leaves
3 tablespoons sherry
2 tablespoons water

1. Toss together spinach, romaine, green or red leaf lettuce, tomatoes, green pepper, cucumber, and red onion.
2. Combine balsamic vinegar, oregano, sherry, and water.
3. Toss dressing with salad.

Calories Per Serving: 28
Fat: 3 g
Cholesterol: 0 mg
Protein: 1.5 g

Carbohydrates: 5 g
Dietary Fiber: 1.7 g
Sodium: 19 mg

✳ *Green Salad with Raw Vegetables* ✳

YIELD: 6 servings ▪ *PREPARATION TIME: 20 minutes*

Green leaf lettuce is tossed with carrots, red onion, mushrooms, tomatoes, broccoli, and red bell pepper.

6 cups green leaf lettuce, rinsed and
  torn
2 grated carrots
1 medium red onion, sliced
8 mushrooms, sliced
2 medium tomatoes, sliced
1¹/₂ cups broccoli florets

1 cup diced red bell pepper
2 teaspoons lemon juice
2 teaspoons Dijon mustard
Pinch of cayenne pepper
1 cup plain nonfat yogurt
2 tablespoons chopped fresh parsley
¹/₄ teaspoon black pepper

1. Toss together lettuce, carrots, red onion, mushrooms, tomatoes, broccoli, and red pepper.
2. Combine lemon juice, mustard, cayenne pepper, yogurt, parsley, and black pepper.
3. Toss salad with dressing.

Calories Per Serving: 94
Fat: .7 g
Cholesterol: .7 mg
Protein: 5 g

Carbohydrates: 20 g
Dietary Fiber: 3.8 g
Sodium: 77 mg

SLAWS AND MIXED FRUIT AND VEGETABLE SALADS

::

✳ *Zippy Coleslaw* ✳

YIELD: 4 servings • *PREPARATION TIME: 20 minutes*

This nonfat version of a perennial favorite is accented with horseradish.

5 cups grated white cabbage
1 cup grated green bell pepper
1 cup grated carrot
⅓ cup plain nonfat yogurt

2 tablespoons skim milk
1 teaspoon prepared horseradish
1 clove garlic, minced
½ teaspoon white pepper

1. Place cabbage, green pepper, and carrot in a mixing bowl.
2. Combine yogurt, skim milk, horseradish, garlic, and white pepper.
3. Toss the cabbage mixture with the yogurt mixture.

Variations
- For a slaw with a mustard-flavored dressing, place cabbage, green bell pepper, and carrot in a mixing bowl. Add 1 grated onion. Toss with a dressing of 4 tablespoons nonfat mayonnaise, 3 tablespoons nonfat yogurt, 3 tablespoons cider vinegar, 1 tablespoon Dijon mustard, 1 teaspoon sugar, and 2 teaspoons celery seed. Thin dressing with skim milk if necessary.
- Place cabbage, green bell pepper, and carrot in a mixing bowl. Toss with a dressing of ½ cup nonfat sour cream, ¼ cup plain nonfat yogurt, 1 tablespoon cider vinegar, ½ teaspoon dry mustard, and ¼ teaspoon paprika.

Calories Per Serving: 59
Fat: .4 g
Cholesterol: .5 mg
Protein: 3 g

Carbohydrates: 12 g
Dietary Fiber: 3 g
Sodium: 63 mg

There's something about an old friend...
Someone who's known you through
so many phases of your life...
Someone who's been there for you
through wonderful times and tearful
times... Someone who loves you
like a sister.

There's something about an
old friend who holds a
place in your heart
that no new friend could
ever quite replace...

✳ *Apple-Honey Slaw* ✳

YIELD: *4 servings* • PREPARATION TIME: *20 minutes*

This slaw is made with grated apple and a honey-flavored dressing.

2 cups shredded white cabbage
1 red apple, cored and grated
2 stalks celery, chopped
1/2 cup plain nonfat yogurt

1 tablespoon honey
1 tablespoon white wine vinegar
1/2 teaspoon Dijon mustard
1/4 teaspoon ground paprika

1. Combine cabbage, apple, and celery.
2. Combine yogurt, honey, white wine vinegar, mustard, and paprika.
3. Toss cabbage mixture with dressing.

Calories Per Serving: 66
Fat: .3 g
Cholesterol: .5 mg
Protein: 2 g

Carbohydrates: 14 g
Dietary Fiber: 2 g
Sodium: 40 mg

✳ *Island Salad* ✳

YIELD: *4 servings* • PREPARATION TIME: *15 minutes*

Here oranges, bananas, green peppers, and cucumbers are combined with yogurt.

1 small cucumber, peeled and
  coarsely chopped
2 medium bananas, thinly sliced
2 medium green bell peppers, seeded
  and diced

2 navel oranges, peeled, sectioned,
  and diced
1/2 cup plain nonfat yogurt

1. Toss together cucumber, bananas, green peppers, oranges, and yogurt.

Calories Per Serving: 118
Fat: .7 g
Cholesterol: .5 mg
Protein: 3 g

Carbohydrates: 27 g
Dietary Fiber: 3.8 g
Sodium: 25 mg

✳ Red Cabbage Slaw ✳

YIELD: 8 servings • PREPARATION TIME: 25 minutes

This unusual slaw is made with red cabbage and a nonfat dressing featuring pickle relish.

2 cups shredded red cabbage
2 cups shredded white cabbage
1 cup shredded carrots
¼ cup pickle relish
¾ cup minced scallions

½ cup nonfat mayonnaise
2 teaspoons Dijon mustard
2 tablespoon lemon juice
¼ teaspoon black pepper

1. Combine red cabbage, white cabbage, and carrots.
2. Combine pickle relish, scallions, mayonnaise, mustard, lemon juice, and black pepper.
3. Toss dressing with cabbage mixture.

Calories Per Serving: 47
Fat: .1 g
Cholesterol: 0 mg
Protein: .6 g

Carbohydrates: 11 g
Dietary Fiber: 1.3 g
Sodium: 298 mg

BEAN SALADS

::

✳ Black Bean Salad ✳

YIELD: 10 servings • PREPARATION TIME: 25 minutes plus bean and corn cooking time

This salad, which is a meal in itself, unites black beans with tomatoes, corn, and cucumber.

*4 cups home-cooked or canned black
  beans, drained and rinsed
1 small red onion, chopped
1 medium tomato, diced
1 tablespoon ground coriander
2 cups cooked fresh, canned, or
  frozen corn kernels*

*1 medium cucumber, peeled, seeded,
  and diced
¼ teaspoon black pepper
3 tablespoons red wine vinegar
2 tablespoons water
½ teaspoon Dijon mustard*

1. Combine the black beans, red onion, tomato, coriander, corn, and cucumbers in a large bowl.
2. Combine the black pepper, red wine vinegar, water, and Dijon mustard in a small bowl with a wire whisk.
3. Toss the bean mixture with the dressing.

Calories Per Serving: 128
Fat: .5 g
Cholesterol: 0 mg
Protein: 7 g

Carbohydrates: 25 g
Dietary Fiber: 4 g
Sodium: 7.5 mg

✳ Black-Eyed Pea Salad ✳

YIELD: 6 servings • PREPARATION TIME: 15 minutes plus bean cooking time and 8 hours chilling time

This Southwestern salad will keep in the refrigerator for ten days. Garnish with chopped bell peppers and scallions.

Black-Eyed Pea Salad *(cont'd)*

2 cups home-cooked or canned black-
   eyed peas, rinsed and drained
1 large onion, chopped
1/4 cup red wine vinegar

1/4 cup water
1/4 teaspoon cayenne pepper
1/4 teaspoon black pepper
1 clove garlic, peeled

1. Combine black-eyed peas, onion, red wine vinegar, water, cayenne pepper, black pepper, and garlic in a glass bowl. Refrigerate overnight.
2. Remove garlic clove and serve.

Calories Per Serving: 71
Fat: .5 g
Cholesterol: 0 mg
Protein: 4.8 g

Carbohydrates: 12 g
Dietary Fiber: 4 g
Sodium: 3 mg

✳ Red, White, and Black Bean Salad ✳

YIELD: 6 servings • PREPARATION TIME: 15 minutes plus bean cooking time and 1 hour chilling time

This salad is made with pinto, cannellini, and black beans.

5 cloves garlic, chopped
1/4 cup lemon juice
1 teaspoon ground cumin
1/2 teaspoon dried oregano leaves
2 teaspoon hot chili oil
1/4 teaspoon black pepper
2 cups home-cooked or canned pinto
   beans, drained and rinsed

2 cups home-cooked or canned
   cannellini beans, drained and
   rinsed
2 cups home-cooked or canned black
   beans, drained and rinsed
1 medium onion, chopped

1. Purée garlic, lemon juice, cumin, oregano, chili oil, and black pepper in a blender or food processor.
2. Place pinto beans, cannellini beans, black beans, and onion in a glass bowl. Toss with garlic dressing.
3. Chill for 1 hour.

Calories Per Serving: 188
Fat: .9 g
Cholesterol: 0 mg
Protein: 12 g

Carbohydrates: 34 g
Dietary Fiber: 7 g
Sodium: 22 mg

✳ *Kidney Bean and Corn Salad* ✳

YIELD: 8 servings • *PREPARATION TIME: 20 minutes plus bean and corn cooking time*

You can prepare this salad of kidney beans, corn, green bell peppers, celery, and scallions a day ahead.

2 cups home-cooked or canned red kidney beans, drained and rinsed	½ cup chopped scallions
	¼ cup red wine vinegar
2 cups cooked fresh, frozen, or canned corn kernels	1 teaspoon lemon juice
	2 cloves garlic, minced
2 green bell peppers, seeded and diced	½ teaspoon sugar
½ cup diced celery	¼ teaspoon black pepper

1. Place beans, corn, green peppers, celery, scallions, vinegar, lemon juice, garlic, sugar, and black pepper in a glass bowl.
2. Toss and chill until ready to serve.

Calories Per Serving: 101
Fat: .4 g
Cholesterol: 0 mg
Protein: 5 g

Carbohydrates: 21 g
Dietary Fiber: 4.4 g
Sodium: 12 mg

✳ *Big Bean Salad Bowl* ✳

YIELD: 8 servings • *PREPARATION TIME: 20 minutes plus bean cooking time and 8 hours marinating time*

Here four kinds of beans are tossed with a sweet-and-sour dressing.

⅔ cup sugar	2 cups home-cooked or canned red kidney beans, drained and rinsed
¾ cup red wine vinegar	
½ teaspoon white pepper	1 yellow or green bell pepper, chopped
2 cups cooked fresh or frozen string beans, cut into 1-inch pieces	2 cups chopped celery
2 cups cooked fresh or frozen wax beans, cut into 1-inch pieces	3 small onions, thinly sliced
2 cups cooked fresh or frozen lima beans	

Big Bean Salad Bowl *(cont'd)*

1. Place sugar, wine vinegar, and white pepper in a small saucepan and bring to a boil for 1 minute. Remove from heat.
2. Combine string beans, wax beans, lima beans, kidney beans, yellow or green pepper, celery, and onions in a large glass bowl.
3. Pour the sugar and vinegar dressing over the bean mixture and toss.
4. Marinate in refrigerator for at least 8 hours.

Calories Per Serving: 208
Fat: .7 g
Cholesterol: 0 mg
Protein: 8 g

Carbohydrates: 45 g
Dietary Fiber: 8 g
Sodium: 40 mg

GRAIN SALADS

::

✳ Independence Day Macaroni Salad ✳

YIELD: 8 servings ▪ *PREPARATION TIME: 20 minutes plus macaroni cooking time*

This all-American classic can be enjoyed by everyone gathered around your picnic table, whether they're watching their fat calories or not.

4 cups macaroni, cooked al dente
   and well drained in a colander
2 cups chopped celery
2 cups chopped carrots
1 cup chopped red bell pepper
1/2 cup chopped scallions

1/4 teaspoon black pepper
1/4 cup nonfat buttermilk or skim
  milk
1/2 cup nonfat cottage cheese
1/2 cup plain nonfat yogurt
1 tablespoon Dijon mustard

1. Combine cooked macaroni, celery, carrots, red bell pepper, scallions, and black pepper in a large bowl. Toss to mix.
2. Place buttermilk or skim milk, cottage cheese, yogurt, and mustard in a blender or food processor and process until smooth.
3. Toss macaroni salad with dressing.

Calories Per Serving: 134
Fat: .6 g
Cholesterol: 1.1 mg
Protein: 6 g

Carbohydrates: 25 g
Dietary Fiber: 2.6 g
Sodium: 138 mg

✳ Vegetable-Macaroni Salad ✳

YIELD: 4 servings ▪ *PREPARATION TIME: 25 minutes plus macaroni and corn
cooking time and 1 hour chilling time*

Here corn, carrots, red onion, celery, and red bell pepper are tossed with macaroni and a simple nonfat mayonnaise–lemon juice dressing.

Vegetable-Macaroni Salad (*cont'd*)

1/2 pound elbow macaroni, cooked al dente and well drained in a colander
1/2 cup cooked fresh, frozen, or canned corn kernels
1/2 cup thinly sliced carrots
1/4 cup chopped red onion
1/2 cup chopped red bell pepper
1/2 cup chopped celery
1/4 cup nonfat mayonnaise
1/2 cup plain nonfat yogurt
1 tablespoon lemon juice
1 clove garlic, minced
1 teaspoon ground basil
Pinch of cayenne pepper

1. Combine macaroni, corn, carrots, red onion, red pepper, and celery.
2. Combine mayonnaise, yogurt, lemon juice, garlic, basil, and cayenne.
3. Toss dressing with macaroni mixture. Chill for 1 hour before serving.

Calories Per Serving: 186
Fat: .7 g
Cholesterol: .5 mg
Protein: 7.8 g

Carbohydrates: 45 g
Dietary Fiber: 1.4 g
Sodium: 252 mg

✳ *Asparagus–Plum Tomato Pasta Salad* ✳

YIELD: *8 servings* • PREPARATION TIME: *25 minutes* •
COOKING TIME: *8 minutes plus pasta cooking time and 3 hours chilling time*

Asparagus and Italian plum tomatoes are featured in this pasta salad.

3/4 pound asparagus, sliced in 1/2-inch pieces
1 large yellow bell pepper, seeded and chopped
2 cups zucchini, chopped
1 pound pasta spirals, cooked al dente and well drained in a colander
1/2 cup apple juice
1/4 cup cider vinegar
1 teaspoon Dijon mustard
1/4 cup nonfat mayonnaise
1/4 teaspoon black pepper
2 cups sliced fresh Italian plum tomatoes

1. Cook asparagus in boiling water for 4 minutes. Add yellow pepper and zucchini and cook for 4 additional minutes. Drain.
2. Combine asparagus, yellow pepper, and zucchini in a bowl with cooked pasta.

3. Combine apple juice, cider vinegar, Dijon mustard, mayonnaise, and black pepper.
4. Toss dressing with vegetable-pasta mixture. Chill for 3 hours.
5. Toss with plum tomatoes before serving.

Calories Per Serving: 197
Fat: .9 g
Cholesterol: 0 mg
Protein: 8 g

Carbohydrates: 48 g
Dietary Fiber: 1 g
Sodium: 120 mg

✳ *Tex-Mex Pasta Salad* ✳

YIELD: *6 servings* ▪ PREPARATION TIME: *25 minutes plus pasta cooking time*

This pasta salad is tossed with a tomato juice dressing, green chiles, tomatoes, scallions, green bell pepper, and Mexican spices.

1 cup tomato juice
2 tablespoons cider vinegar
1 teaspoon dried cilantro leaves
2 teaspoons chili powder
1 teaspoon ground cumin
Pinch of cayenne pepper
1 4-ounce can green chiles, drained

½ cup chopped scallions
10 ounces linguine, cooked al dente and well drained in a colander
1 cup chopped fresh or canned tomatoes
1 cup chopped green bell pepper

1. Combine tomato juice, cider vinegar, cilantro, chili powder, cumin, cayenne, chiles, and scallions.
2. Toss dressing with cooked linguine.
3. Top with tomatoes and green peppers.

Calories Per Serving: 155
Fat: .9 g
Cholesterol: 0 mg
Protein: 5 g

Carbohydrates: 32 g
Dietary Fiber: 1.3 g
Sodium: 101 mg

✳ *Rotini and Black-Eyed Pea Salad* ✳

YIELD: *6 servings* ▪ PREPARATION TIME: *25 minutes plus pasta and bean cooking time and 2 hours chilling time*

Here black-eyed peas are tossed with cooked rotini in a spicy dressing.

Rotini and Black-Eyed Pea Salad *(cont'd)*

1/4 cup nonfat mayonnaise

2 tablespoons tarragon vinegar or
    red wine vinegar plus 1 teaspoon
    crushed tarragon

2 tablespoons orange juice

1 tablespoon Dijon mustard

1 clove garlic, minced

1/2 teaspoon ground cumin

1/2 teaspoon sugar

Pinch of cayenne pepper

1/2 teaspoon dried cilantro leaves

6 ounces rotini, cooked al dente and
    well drained in a colander

2 cups home-cooked or canned black-
    eyed peas, drained and rinsed

1 tomato, diced

1 1/2 cups chopped green bell pepper

1/2 cup chopped scallions

1. Combine mayonnaise, tarragon vinegar, orange juice, Dijon mustard, garlic, cumin, sugar, cayenne pepper, and cilantro.
2. Combine rotini, black-eyed peas, tomato, green pepper, and scallions.
3. Toss dressing with rotini mixture. Chill for 2 hours.

Calories Per Serving: 182
Fat: .9 g
Cholesterol: 0 mg
Protein: 7.8 g

Carbohydrates: 35 g
Dietary Fiber: 1.7 g
Sodium: 377 mg

✳ Rigatoni-Vegetable Salad with Pinto Beans ✳

YIELD: 6 servings • PREPARATION TIME: 20 minutes plus bean, pea, and corn cooking time

Cooked rigatoni is combined with pinto beans, scallions, peas, tomato, and cucumber in a tarragon-flavored dressing.

8 ounces rigatoni, cooked al dente
    and well drained in a colander

1 cup home-cooked or canned pinto
    beans, drained and rinsed

2 tablespoons chopped scallions

1/2 cup cooked fresh or frozen peas,
    steamed

1/2 cup cooked fresh, frozen, or
    canned corn kernels

2 medium tomatoes, cut in half and
    thinly sliced

1 cucumber, peeled and thinly sliced

1/2 cup plain nonfat yogurt

1/4 cup nonfat mayonnaise

1/2 teaspoon dried tarragon leaves

1/4 teaspoon black pepper

1. Combine cooked rigatoni, pinto beans, scallions, peas, corn, tomatoes, and cucumber.
2. Combine yogurt, mayonnaise, tarragon, and black pepper.
3. Toss dressing with rigatoni and vegetables.

Calories Per Serving: 221
Fat: 1 g
Cholesterol: .3 mg
Protein: 9.5 g

Carbohydrates: 44 g
Dietary Fiber: 5 g
Sodium: 174 mg

✳ *Rotelle-Fruit Salad* ✳

YIELD: 4 servings ▪ *PREPARATION TIME: 20 minutes plus pasta cooking time and 2 hours chilling time*

Here wheel-shaped pasta is mixed with six different kinds of fruit in a creamy fruit-juice dressing.

8 ounces rotelle, cooked al dente and well drained in a colander
2 cups fresh or juice-packed canned pineapple chunks, drained
1 navel orange, peeled and sectioned
1 cup red seedless grapes, halved
1 cup seedless green grapes

1 apple, cored and chopped
1 banana, sliced
1 cup plain nonfat yogurt
¼ cup frozen orange juice or pineapple juice concentrate, thawed

1. Toss cooked rotelle with pineapple, orange, red grapes, green grapes, apple, and banana.
2. Combine yogurt and juice concentrate.
3. Toss yogurt dressing with rotelle and fruit.
4. Chill for 2 hours before serving.

Calories Per Serving: 183
Fat: .9 g
Cholesterol: .5 mg
Protein: 5.5 g

Carbohydrates: 39 g
Dietary Fiber: 2.9 g
Sodium: 23 mg

✳ *Shell Pasta Slaw* ✳

YIELD: 8 servings ▪ *PREPARATION TIME: 25 minutes plus pasta cooking time and 2 hours chilling time*

These pasta shells are tossed with cabbage, carrots, celery, cucumber, and a robust dressing.

8 ounces medium shell pasta, cooked al dente and well drained in a colander
3 cups shredded cabbage
2 cups shredded carrots
2 cups finely chopped celery
2 cups finely chopped cucumber

1¹/₄ cups plain nonfat yogurt
¹/₄ cup nonfat mayonnaise
2 tablespoons white wine vinegar
¹/₂ teaspoon dry mustard
¹/₄ teaspoon black pepper
Pinch of ground paprika

1. Toss cooked pasta shells with cabbage, carrots, celery, and cucumber.
2. Combine yogurt, mayonnaise, vinegar, dry mustard, black pepper, and paprika.
3. Toss dressing with vegetables. Chill for 2 hours before serving.

Calories Per Serving: 171
Fat: .7 g
Cholesterol: .5 mg
Protein: 7 g

Carbohydrates: 41 g
Dietary Fiber: 1.8 g
Sodium: 141 mg

Cannellini Beans, Rice, and ✳ *Vegetable Salad* ✳

YIELD: 5 servings ▪ *PREPARATION TIME: 20 minutes plus rice and bean cooking time and 30 minutes chilling time*

In this dish rice is combined with a lemon-parsley dressing, raw vegetables, and cannellini beans.

1 cup home-cooked or canned cannellini beans, drained and rinsed

2 cups long-grain white or brown rice, cooked, rinsed, and cooled
3 tablespoons nonfat mayonnaise

3 tablespoon cider vinegar
2 cloves garlic, crushed
1 tablespoon lemon juice
2 tablespoons chopped fresh parsley

1/4 teaspoon black pepper
1 medium carrot, thinly sliced
1 red bell pepper, seeded and diced
1 stalk celery, chopped

1. Toss beans and rice together.
2. Combine mayonnaise, cider vinegar, garlic, lemon juice, parsley, and black pepper.
3. Combine dressing with rice and beans. Chill for 30 minutes.
4. Toss with carrot, red pepper, and celery before serving.

Calories Per Serving: 338
Fat: .8 g
Cholesterol: 0 mg
Protein: 8.5 g

Carbohydrates: 73 g
Dietary Fiber: 3.6 g
Sodium: 145 mg

Penne Primavera with Garlic-Tomato ✳ *Dressing* ✳

YIELD: 4 servings ▪ *PREPARATION TIME: 20 minutes plus pasta cooking time, vegetable steaming time, and 2 hours chilling time*

Here cooked penne is tossed with vegetables in a dressing made with tomato juice, garlic, and herbs.

8 ounces penne or other medium
   tubular pasta, cooked al dente and
   well drained in a colander
1 cup cauliflower florets, steamed
1 cup broccoli florets, steamed
1 cup chopped yellow or red bell
   pepper

1 cup low-sodium tomato juice
1/2 teaspoon ground oregano leaves
1/2 teaspoon ground basil leaves
1 clove garlic, minced

1. Toss together cooked penne, steamed broccoli and cauliflower, and red bell pepper. Chill for 2 hours.
2. Combine tomato juice, oregano leaves, basil leaves, and garlic.
3. Toss with chilled penne and vegetables.

Penne Primavera with Garlic-Tomato Dressing *(cont'd)*

Calories Per Serving: 219
Fat: 1.2 g
Cholesterol: 0 mg
Protein: 8.6 g

Carbohydrates: 44 g
Dietary Fiber: 4.7 g
Sodium: 14 mg

✳ *Wild Rice and Apple Salad* ✳

YIELD: 4 servings ▪ *PREPARATION TIME: 15 minutes* ▪ *COOKING TIME: 1 hour*

In this salad apples, brown sugar, lemon juice, and wild rice are dressed with nonfat yogurt and mayonnaise.

2 cups water, nonfat chicken broth, or vegetable broth
1 cup uncooked wild rice
2 large apples, cored and diced
1 tablespoon lemon juice

1 tablespoon brown sugar, firmly packed
2 stalks celery, sliced
1/2 cup nonfat plain yogurt
1/4 cup nonfat mayonnaise

1. Bring water or broth to a boil in a medium saucepan. Stir in wild rice. Reduce heat. Cover and simmer for 1 hour or until rice is tender and kernels are slightly open. Drain rice.
2. Combine apples with lemon juice, brown sugar, and celery. Toss with brown rice, yogurt, and mayonnaise.

Calories Per Serving: 135
Fat: .5 g
Cholesterol: .5 mg
Protein: 3.5 g

Carbohydrates: 30 g
Dietary Fiber: 2.5 g
Sodium: 256 mg

✳ *Couscous Salad* ✳

YIELD: 4 servings ▪ *PREPARATION TIME: 25 minutes* ▪
COOKING TIME: 10 minutes

Here cooked couscous is mixed with onion, garlic, scallions, carrots, celery, apricots, and raisins. Garnish with shredded lettuce and red bell pepper strips.

¹/₄ cup water
1 medium onion, finely chopped
1 clove garlic, minced
2 scallions, chopped
3 carrots, chopped
2 stalks celery, chopped

¹/₄ teaspoon ground cinnamon
¹/₄ teaspoon ground cloves
10 dried or fresh apricots, chopped
¹/₂ cup raisins
1¹/₂ cups water
1 cup couscous

1. Heat water in skillet over medium heat. Add onion, garlic, scallions, carrots, and celery. Cook and stir for 5 minutes over medium heat. Add more liquid if necessary during this process.
2. Bring 1¹/₂ cups water to a boil in a saucepan. Add the couscous. Cover the pan and remove from heat. Let stand for 5 minutes.
3. Drain onion mixture and toss with cinnamon, cloves, apricots, and raisins. Toss with couscous.

Calories Per Serving: 203
Fat: .6 g
Cholesterol: 0 mg
Protein: 4 g

Carbohydrates: 46 g
Dietary Fiber: 3.7 g
Sodium: 31 mg

DRESSINGS, SAUCES, AND RELISHES

DRESSINGS

Sweet-and-Sour Dressing • Quick Garlic-French Dressing • Basic
Italian Dressing • Curried Dressing • Parsley-Tomato Dressing •
Mustard-Horseradish Dressing • Tangy Dressing • Creamy Lemon-
Mustard Dressing • Creamy Buttermilk Dressing • Parmesan-
Mustard Dressing • Tomato-Mustard Dressing • Creamy
Tomato-Relish Dressing • Caraway-Dill Dressing • Lemon-
Horseradish Dressing • Creamy Dijon Dressing • Honey-Mustard
Dressing • Balsamic-Dijon Dressing • Mustard-Dill Dressing •
Tomato-Herb Dressing • Oriental Dressing I • Oriental Dressing II •
Maple-Vanilla Dressing • Cottage Cheese–Dill Dressing • Honey-
Ricotta Dressing • Green Goddess Dressing • Banana Dressing

SAUCES AND TOPPINGS

Simple Tomato Sauce • Tomato-Wine Sauce • Raw Tomato Sauce •
White Sauce I • White Sauce II • Simple Pear Sauce • Simple
Strawberry Sauce • Fruit Sauce • Blueberry Topping • Orange-
Honey Sauce • Dijon-Horseradish Sauce • Chinese Dipping Sauce •
Alfredo Sauce • Mushroom Sauce • Herbed Nonfat Mayonnaise •
Prune Butter • Baked Potato Topping

R E L I S H E S ,   C H U T N E Y S , A N D   S A L S A S

Pepper Relish • Uncooked Tomato Relish • Apple Relish • Strawberry Relish • Raspberry-Cranberry Relish • Ginger-Pineapple Relish • Papaya Relish • Fresh Pineapple–Red Pepper Relish • Nectarine Chutney • Corn Relish • Tomato-Fruit Chutney

One of the hardest adjustments to make when cutting the fat out of a diet is giving up oil-based salad dressings. However, the following recipes will go a long way toward convincing you that there is life after oil and egg yolks.

DRESSINGS

::

✳ Sweet-and-Sour Dressing ✳

YIELD: 8 servings (¹/₄ cup each) • PREPARATION TIME: 5 minutes

Sugar, vinegar, and Dijon mustard join to create this zesty dressing for coleslaws, potato salads, pasta salads, or vegetable salads.

1 cup water
¹/₂ cup confectioners' sugar
2 teaspoons Dijon mustard

¹/₄ cup apple cider vinegar
1 teaspoon ground paprika
1 teaspoon celery seed

1. Combine water, sugar, mustard, and vinegar in a blender or food processor and process until well combined.
2. Whisk in paprika and celery seed.

Calories Per Serving: 27
Fat: .1 g
Cholesterol: 0 mg
Protein: .1 g

Carbohydrates: 7 g
Dietary Fiber: 0 g
Sodium: 18 mg

✳ Quick Garlic-French Dressing ✳

YIELD: 4 servings (3 tablespoons each) • PREPARATION TIME: 10 minutes
plus 20 minutes chilling time

You can whip up this dressing with ingredients that are on your refrigerator shelf in a jiffy. Use on mixed greens and vegetable salads.

¹/₂ cup plain nonfat yogurt
2 tablespoons catsup
2 teaspoons honey

1 teaspoon Dijon mustard
1 clove garlic, minced
¹/₄ teaspoon black pepper

Quick Garlic-French Dressing *(cont'd)*

1. Place yogurt, catsup, honey, mustard, garlic, and black pepper in a blender or food processor. Process until smooth.
2. Chill for 20 minutes before serving.

Variations

- Delete mustard and substitute honey. Delete black pepper and substitute ¹/₂ teaspoon chili powder and 1 teaspoon dried cilantro. Add ¹/₄ cup chopped tomato.
- Delete catsup and substitute 1 tablespoon honey.

Calories Per Serving: 33
Fat: .1 g
Cholesterol: .5 mg
Protein: 1.8 g

Carbohydrates: 6.3 g
Dietary Fiber: 0 g
Sodium: 84 mg

✳ *Basic Italian Dressing* ✳

YIELD: *12 servings (¹/₄ cup each)* • PREPARATION TIME: *15 minutes* •
COOKING TIME: *5 minutes*

This dressing is thickened with arrowroot or cornstarch to replace the missing oil. You can vary the seasonings as you wish. It can be refrigerated for two days. Use as a marinade for grilled foods and as a dressing for mixed green salads.

2 tablespoons arrowroot or cornstarch
2 cups water
¹/₂ cup white wine vinegar
¹/₄ cup minced green bell pepper
2 scallions, minced

2 cloves garlic, minced
2 tablespoons Dijon mustard
1 tablespoon honey
1 tablespoon chopped fresh parsley
¹/₂ teaspoon paprika
¹/₄ teaspoon black pepper

1. Dissolve arrowroot or cornstarch in ¹/₄ cup of the water.
2. Bring remaining 1³/₄ cups water to a boil. Stir in dissolved arrowroot or cornstarch and whisk until the liquid is clear.
3. Allow mixture to cool.
4. Stir in vinegar, green pepper, scallions, garlic, mustard, honey, parsley, paprika, and black pepper.

Calories Per Serving: 16
Fat: .1 g
Cholesterol: 0 mg
Protein: .1 g

Carbohydrates: 3.5 g
Dietary Fiber: .1 g
Sodium: 34 mg

✳ *Curried Dressing* ✳

YIELD: 4 servings (¹/₄ cup each) • *PREPARATION TIME: 10 minutes*
plus 30 minutes chilling time

This spicy dressing includes curry powder, tomato juice, and honey. Use on tossed raw vegetable salads including ingredients such as carrots, cauliflower, celery, and green bell pepper.

1 teaspoon curry powder
¹/₃ cup tomato juice
¹/₃ cup nonfat cottage cheese
1 tablespoon lemon juice

1 teaspoon honey
¹/₂ cup chopped fresh or low-sodium
  canned tomatoes

1. Place curry powder, tomato juice, cottage cheese, lemon juice, honey, and tomatoes in a food processor or blender and purée.
2. Chill, covered, for 30 minutes before serving.

Calories Per Serving: 29
Fat: .1 g
Cholesterol: 1.1 mg
Protein: 3.3 g

Carbohydrates: 4.6 g
Dietary Fiber: .6 g
Sodium: 97 mg

✳ *Parsley-Tomato Dressing* ✳

YIELD: 4 servings (3 tablespoons each) • *PREPARATION TIME: 15 minutes*

This light dressing works well with mixed-vegetable salads including ingredients such as zucchini, green beans, corn, and red bell pepper.

³/₄ cup tomato juice
¹/₄ cup red wine vinegar
1 tablespoon minced onion
¹/₄ cup chopped fresh parsley
1 clove garlic, minced

Pinch of cayenne pepper
¹/₂ teaspoon oregano leaves
¹/₂ teaspoon black pepper
¹/₂ cup fresh or canned tomatoes,
  chopped

Parsley-Tomato Dressing *(cont'd)*

1. Place tomato juice, vinegar, onion, parsley, garlic, cayenne pepper, oregano, black pepper, and canned tomatoes in a food processor or blender. Process until smooth.

Calories Per Serving: 20
Fat: .2 g
Cholesterol: 0 mg
Protein: .8 g

Carbohydrates: 5 g
Dietary Fiber: 1 g
Sodium: 56 mg

❋ Mustard-Horseradish Dressing ❋

YIELD: 6 servings (3 tablespoons each) • *PREPARATION TIME: 15 minutes*

This zesty yogurt dressing includes scallions, tomato paste, parsley, and basil. Use on steamed and raw vegetables.

1 cup plain nonfat yogurt
1 tablespoon Dijon mustard
1/2 teaspoon prepared horseradish
1 tablespoon lemon juice
1 teaspoon minced scallions

2 tablespoons low-sodium tomato paste
1 tablespoon chopped fresh parsley
1 teaspoon dried basil leaves
1/2 teaspoon black pepper

1. Combine yogurt, mustard, horseradish, lemon juice, scallions, tomato paste, parsley, basil, and pepper.

Calories Per Serving: 30
Fat: .2 g
Cholesterol: .7 mg
Protein: 2.5 g

Carbohydrates: 4.5 g
Dietary Fiber: .4 g
Sodium: 70 mg

❋ Tangy Dressing ❋

YIELD: 4 servings (1/4 cup each) • *PREPARATION TIME: 15 minutes*

This dressing works well with a salad of mixed greens such as red leaf lettuce, watercress, and spinach.

1/2 cup nonfat cottage cheese
1/3 cup nonfat buttermilk
2 tablespoons chopped fresh parsley

1 tablespoon cider vinegar
1 clove garlic, minced
Pinch of cayenne pepper

1. Place cottage cheese, buttermilk, parsley, vinegar, garlic, and cayenne in a blender or food processor and process until smooth.

Calories Per Serving: 28
Fat: 0 g
Cholesterol: 2 mg
Protein: 4.7 g

Carbohydrates: 3 g
Dietary Fiber: 0 g
Sodium: 148 mg

✳ *Creamy Lemon-Mustard Dressing* ✳

YIELD: 6 servings (¹/₃ cup each) • *PREPARATION TIME: 10 minutes plus 3 hours yogurt draining time*

This dressing has a wonderful creamy texture and is a great choice for tossed green salads with raw mushrooms, diced yellow peppers, and sliced onions.

2 cups plain nonfat yogurt
4 tablespoons lemon juice

2 teaspoons Dijon mustard

1. Line a small colander with a coffee filter or several layers of clean, dry cheesecloth. Place the yogurt in the colander and allow the liquid to drip into a bowl for 3 hours. Discard the liquid.
2. Combine the drained yogurt, lemon juice, and mustard.

Calories Per Serving: 46
Fat: .2 g
Cholesterol: 1.3 mg
Protein: 4.4 g

Carbohydrates: 6.7 g
Dietary Fiber: 0 g
Sodium: 80 mg

✳ *Creamy Buttermilk Dressing* ✳

YIELD: 10 servings (¹/₄ cup each) • *PREPARATION TIME: 10 minutes*

This tangy dressing can be used instead of mayonnaise. Season with dry mustard, dill weed, paprika, or black pepper.

¹/₂ cup nonfat buttermilk
1 cup nonfat cottage cheese

1 cup nonfat plain yogurt

Creamy Buttermilk Dressing (*cont'd*)

1. Place buttermilk, cottage cheese, and yogurt in a blender or food processor and process until smooth.

Calories Per Serving: 41
Fat: 0 g
Cholesterol: 1.4 mg
Protein: 3.9 g

Carbohydrates: 6.5 g
Dietary Fiber: 0 g
Sodium: 123 mg

❋ *Parmesan-Mustard Dressing* ❋

YIELD: 4 servings (¹/₃ cup each) • *PREPARATION TIME: 15 minutes plus 1 hour chilling time*

This buttermilk dressing is accented with nonfat Parmesan cheese, garlic, parsley, onion, and dry mustard. Serve with a salad of spinach, apple slices, and steamed potatoes.

1 cup nonfat buttermilk
¹/₄ cup nonfat sour cream
¹/₄ cup nonfat mayonnaise
1 tablespoon grated nonfat Parmesan cheese

1 tablespoon chopped fresh parsley
1 clove garlic, minced
1 teaspoon minced onion
¹/₄ teaspoon dry mustard

1. Combine buttermilk, sour cream, mayonnaise, Parmesan cheese, parsley, garlic, onion, and dry mustard in a bowl.
2. Cover and chill for 1 hour.

Calories Per Serving: 44
Fat: 0 g
Cholesterol: 1.5 mg
Protein: 2 g

Carbohydrates: 8 g
Dietary Fiber: 0 g
Sodium: 284 mg

❋ *Tomato-Mustard Dressing* ❋

YIELD: 8 servings (¹/₄ cup each) • *PREPARATION TIME: 10 minutes plus chilling time*

Try substituting this multi-accented dressing for French dressing on vegetable salads. Chill before serving to allow the flavors to mingle.

2 cups low-sodium tomato juice
2 tablespoons white wine vinegar
$^1/_4$ teaspoon dry mustard
1 clove garlic, minced

$^1/_4$ teaspoon dried basil leaves
2 teaspoons minced onion
$^1/_4$ teaspoon black pepper

1. Place tomato juice, white wine vinegar, dry mustard, garlic, basil leaves, onion, and black pepper in a blender or food processor and process until ingredients are well combined.

Calories Per Serving: 14
Fat: 0 g
Cholesterol: 0 mg
Protein: .5 g

Carbohydrates: 3.4 g
Dietary Fiber: .7 g
Sodium: 7 mg

✳ *Creamy Tomato-Relish Dressing* ✳

YIELD: 6 servings ($^1/_4$ cup each) • *PREPARATION TIME: 10 minutes*

Use this dressing as a substitute for Russian dressing on vegetable salads garnished with hard-cooked egg whites.

1 cup chopped fresh or low-sodium
   canned tomatoes with juice
$^1/_2$ cup nonfat cottage cheese

$^1/_4$ cup pickle relish or finely chopped
   sweet pickles
1 teaspoon Dijon mustard

1. Place tomatoes, cottage cheese, relish, and mustard in a blender or food processor and process until creamy.

Calories Per Serving: 31
Fat: .1 g
Cholesterol: 1 mg
Protein: 2.8 g

Carbohydrates: 5 g
Dietary Fiber: .2 g
Sodium: 178 mg

✳ *Caraway-Dill Dressing* ✳

YIELD: 4 servings ($^1/_4$ cup each) • *PREPARATION TIME: 10 minutes plus 1 hour chilling time*

Try this dressing with potato or vegetable salads. It tastes best when served chilled.

Caraway-Dill Dressing *(cont'd)*

1 cup plain nonfat yogurt
1 tablespoon red wine vinegar
1 clove garlic, minced
$^1/_2$ teaspoon caraway seeds

$^1/_2$ teaspoon dried dill leaves
2 teaspoons minced onion
$^1/_2$ teaspoon sugar

1. Place yogurt, wine vinegar, garlic, caraway seeds, dill leaves, onion, and sugar in a bowl and mix until well combined.
2. Chill for 1 hour.

Calories Per Serving: 37
Fat: .2 g
Cholesterol: 1 mg
Protein: 3.3 g

Carbohydrates: 5.6 g
Dietary Fiber: 0 g
Sodium: 44 mg

❋ *Lemon-Horseradish Dressing* ❋

YIELD: 4 servings ($^1/_4$ cup each) ▪ *PREPARATION TIME: 15 minutes plus 1 hour chilling time*

Lemon juice and horseradish are combined with Dijon mustard, paprika, garlic, and onion in this yogurt dressing. Serve chilled with raw vegetable salads.

1 cup plain nonfat yogurt
2 tablespoons lemon juice
$^1/_2$ teaspoon prepared horseradish
$^1/_2$ teaspoon Dijon mustard

$^1/_2$ teaspoon paprika
1 clove garlic, minced
1 tablespoon minced onion

1. Place yogurt, lemon juice, horseradish, Dijon mustard, paprika, garlic, and onion in a bowl and mix until well combined.
2. Chill for 1 hour.

Calories Per Serving: 63
Fat: .7 g
Cholesterol: 2.5 mg
Protein: 2.6 g

Carbohydrates: 12 g
Dietary Fiber: .3 g
Sodium: 49 mg

✳ *Creamy Dijon Dressing* ✳

YIELD: 4 servings (¹/₃ cup each) ▪ *PREPARATION TIME: 5 minutes*

Try this multipurpose dressing with grain and vegetable salads.

1 cup nonfat cottage cheese	¹/₄ cup water
2 tablespoons red wine vinegar	1¹/₂ teaspoons Dijon mustard
¹/₂ teaspoon black pepper	

1. Place the cottage cheese, red wine vinegar, black pepper, water, and mustard in a blender or food processor and process until smooth.

Calories Per Serving: 57	Carbohydrates: 9 g
Fat: 0 g	Dietary Fiber: .1 g
Cholesterol: 3 mg	Sodium: 275 mg
Protein: 8 g	

✳ *Honey-Mustard Dressing* ✳

YIELD: 4 servings (¹/₄ cup each) ▪ *PREPARATION TIME: 10 minutes plus 30 minutes chilling time*

This dressing combines the bite of Dijon mustard with the mellow flavor of honey. Toss with steamed cubed potatoes, steamed trimmed green beans, tomatoes, kidney beans, and chopped fresh parsley.

1 cup plain nonfat yogurt	4 teaspoons Dijon mustard
2 tablespoons honey	1 teaspoon cider vinegar

1. Combine yogurt, honey, mustard, and cider vinegar in a jar. Tighten lid and shake until blended.
2. Chill for 30 minutes before serving.

Calories Per Serving: 69	Carbohydrates: 12.9 g
Fat: .2 g	Dietary Fiber: .1 g
Cholesterol: 1 mg	Sodium: 109 mg
Protein: 3.3 g	

❋ *Balsamic-Dijon Dressing* ❋

YIELD: 4 servings (4 teaspoons each) • *PREPARATION TIME: 5 minutes*

Balsamic vinegar has such an intense flavor that a small serving of this dressing goes quite a long way. Try using it on a salad of chicory, Boston lettuce, romaine lettuce, escarole, and watercress with cucumbers and cherry tomatoes.

3 tablespoons balsamic vinegar	*¼ teaspoon black pepper*
2 tablespoons water	*1 teaspoon Dijon mustard*

1. Put the vinegar, water, pepper, and mustard in a small bowl.
2. Whisk until smooth.

Calories Per Serving: 3	Carbohydrates: .7 g
Fat: 0 g	Dietary Fiber: 0 g
Cholesterol: 0 mg	Sodium: 17 mg
Protein: 0 g	

❋ *Mustard-Dill Dressing* ❋

YIELD: 4 servings (¼ cup each) • *PREPARATION TIME: 10 minutes*

Here Dijon mustard and yogurt are mixed with black pepper, sugar, and dill. Serve with a salad of steamed cauliflower, peas, yellow summer squash, and cooked rice.

1 cup plain nonfat yogurt	*½ teaspoon sugar*
1 tablespoon dried dill leaves	*¼ teaspoon black pepper*
1 tablespoon Dijon mustard	

1. Combine yogurt, dill leaves, mustard, sugar, and black pepper in a bowl.

Calories Per Serving: 40	Carbohydrates: 5.4 g
Fat: .2 g	Dietary Fiber: .1 g
Cholesterol: 1 mg	Sodium: 94 mg
Protein: 3.5 g	

❋ Tomato-Herb Dressing ❋

YIELD: 6 servings (3 tablespoons each) • *PREPARATION TIME: 15 minutes*

This dressing is accented with red wine vinegar, oregano, scallions, parsley, and cayenne. Try it on a salad of broccoli, asparagus tips, snow peas, nonfat Swiss cheese strips, green bell peppers, and onions.

½ cup red wine vinegar
¾ cup low-sodium tomato juice
¼ teaspoon dried oregano leaves
1 tablespoon chopped scallions
1 tablespoon minced fresh parsley

1 garlic clove, minced
¼ teaspoon black pepper
Pinch of cayenne pepper
Pinch of sugar

1. Place the wine vinegar, tomato juice, oregano, scallions, parsley, garlic, black pepper, cayenne pepper, and sugar in a jar with a tight-fitting lid and shake until thoroughly mixed.

Calories Per Serving: 10
Fat: 0 g
Cholesterol: 0 mg
Protein: .3 g

Carbohydrates: 2.7 g
Dietary Fiber: .4 g
Sodium: 4 mg

❋ Oriental Dressing I ❋

YIELD: 4 servings (1½ tablespoons each) • *PREPARATION TIME: 5 minutes*

This dressing works well on salads featuring oriental vegetables or fruit such as apples.

2½ teaspoons prepared mustard
5 tablespoons rice vinegar

2 teaspoons light soy sauce
2½ teaspoons sugar

1. Mix the mustard, rice vinegar, soy sauce, and sugar together.

Calories Per Serving: 15
Fat: 0 g
Cholesterol: 0 mg
Protein: 2.3 g

Carbohydrates: 5.8 g
Dietary Fiber: 0 g
Sodium: 333 mg

✳ Oriental Dressing II ✳

YIELD: 4 servings (¼ cup each) ▪ *PREPARATION TIME: 10 minutes plus
45 minutes standing time*

This dressing features rice vinegar and low-sodium soy sauce infused
with the flavors of ginger and garlic. It goes well with a salad of mixed
greens and fruit.

1 clove garlic, cut in several pieces
1 cup rice vinegar
1 teaspoon light soy sauce

*1 slice fresh gingerroot, cut in several
    pieces*

1. Combine garlic, rice vinegar, gingerroot, and soy sauce.
2. Let stand for 45 minutes.
3. Strain dressing. Discard garlic and ginger.

Calories Per Serving: 9
Fat: 0 g
Cholesterol: 0 mg
Protein: .2 g

Carbohydrates: 3.4 g
Dietary Fiber: 0 g
Sodium: 87 mg

✳ Maple-Vanilla Dressing ✳

YIELD: 4 servings (¼ cup each) ▪ *PREPARATION TIME: 5 minutes plus 30 minutes
chilling time*

This dressing is a perfect topping for a bowl of strawberries, blueberries,
and oranges.

¾ cup plain nonfat yogurt
½ teaspoon vanilla extract

¼ cup maple syrup

1. Combine yogurt, vanilla, and maple syrup in a bowl.
2. Cover and chill for 30 minutes.

Calories Per Serving: 86
Fat: .1 g
Cholesterol: .75 mg
Protein: 2.4 g

Carbohydrates: 18 g
Dietary Fiber: 0 g
Sodium: 68 mg

✳ *Cottage Cheese–Dill Dressing* ✳

Yield: 4 servings (3½ tablespoons each) • *Preparation Time: 15 minutes plus 4 hours chilling time*

This creamy ranch-style dressing is made with nonfat buttermilk, nonfat cottage cheese, and nonfat Parmesan cheese. Serve with mixed greens, plum tomatoes, and sliced mushrooms.

⅓ cup nonfat buttermilk
½ cup nonfat cottage cheese
1 tablespoon lemon juice
1 tablespoon nonfat Parmesan cheese
1 scallion, chopped

1 clove garlic, minced
1 tablespoon fresh chopped parsley
½ teaspoon dried dill
¼ teaspoon black pepper

1. Combine buttermilk, cottage cheese, lemon juice, Parmesan cheese, scallion, garlic, parsley, dill, and black pepper in a food processor or blender. Process until smooth.
2. Chill in a covered container for 4 hours before serving.

Variation
- Substitute ⅓ cup nonfat plain yogurt for cottage cheese. Delete Parmesan cheese and dill. Add 2 tablespoons apple cider vinegar and 2 tablespoons honey.

Calories Per Serving: 31
Fat: 0 g
Cholesterol: 2 mg
Protein: 4.9 g

Carbohydrates: 3 g
Dietary Fiber: .1 g
Sodium: 154 mg

✳ *Honey-Ricotta Dressing* ✳

Yield: 4 servings (5 tablespoons each) • *Preparation Time: 10 minutes plus 1 hour chilling time*

This delicate dressing works very well with fruit and can also be used as a topping for baked desserts. Serve with a bowl of pear chunks and red grapes.

Honey-Ricotta Dressing *(cont'd)*

½ *cup nonfat ricotta cheese*   ½ *cup plain nonfat yogurt*
¼ *cup honey*

1. Combine ricotta cheese, honey, and yogurt in a bowl and stir until well combined.
2. Chill for 1 hour.

Calories Per Serving: 83   Carbohydrates: 19 g
Fat: 0 g   Dietary Fiber: 0 g
Cholesterol: .75 mg   Sodium: 23 mg
Protein: 2 g

✳ *Green Goddess Dressing* ✳

YIELD: 6 servings (2 tablespoons each) • *PREPARATION TIME: 15 minutes plus 1 hour chilling time*

This dressing works well over sliced steamed red-skinned potatoes and steamed green vegetables.

½ *cup plain nonfat yogurt*   *1 tablespoon minced onion*
¼ *cup nonfat mayonnaise*   *1 tablespoon chopped scallion*
¼ *cup chopped fresh parsley*   ½ *teaspoon dried tarragon leaves*
1 tablespoon white wine vinegar

1. Place yogurt, mayonnaise, parsley, vinegar, onion, scallion, and tarragon in a bowl.
2. Whisk until well combined.
3. Chill for 1 hour.

Calories Per Serving: 26   Carbohydrates: 5 g
Fat: .05 g   Dietary Fiber: .1 g
Cholesterol: .333 mg   Sodium: 156 mg
Protein: 1 g

✳ *Banana Dressing* ✳

YIELD: 4 servings (¹/₃ cup each) • *PREPARATION TIME: 10 minutes*

This dressing can be used on a variety of fruit and vegetable salads. Serve with a salad of mango, papaya, pineapple, and kiwi slices.

1 banana
¹/₂ cup water
2 tablespoons white wine vinegar

1 tablespoon Dijon mustard
1 tablespoon ground cumin
¹/₄ teaspoon black pepper

1. Place banana, water, white wine vinegar, mustard, cumin, and pepper in a blender or food processor.
2. Process until smooth.

Calories Per Serving: 37
Fat: .6 g
Cholesterol: 0 mg
Protein: .6 g

Carbohydrates: 7.9 g
Dietary Fiber: .5 g
Sodium: 53 mg

SAUCES AND TOPPINGS

::

❋ Simple Tomato Sauce ❋

YIELD: 4 servings (¹/₂ cup each) ▪ *PREPARATION TIME: 15 minutes* ▪
COOKING TIME: 25 minutes

This basic tomato sauce can be served hot or cold and enhanced with the addition of chiles, paprika, or sherry. Use it with grains, pasta, and vegetable dishes.

¹/₄ cup water, nonfat chicken broth, vegetable broth, or wine
1 medium onion, chopped
2 cloves garlic, minced
¹/₄ cup chopped red bell pepper
2 cups chopped fresh tomatoes or low-sodium canned plum tomatoes, drained

¹/₂ teaspoon dried thyme leaves
¹/₂ teaspoon dried oregano leaves
¹/₄ cup chopped fresh parsley
¹/₂ teaspoon dried basil leaves
1 stalk celery, finely chopped
¹/₄ teaspoon black pepper
¹/₂ teaspoon brown sugar, firmly packed

1. Place water, broth, or wine in a saucepan over medium heat. Add onion, garlic, and red pepper. Cook and stir over low heat for 5 minutes. Add more liquid if necessary during this process.
2. Add the tomatoes, thyme leaves, oregano leaves, parsley, basil, and celery. Cover and cook over low heat for 15 minutes.
3. Stir in pepper and brown sugar.

Calories Per Serving: 45
Fat: .5 g
Cholesterol: 0 mg
Protein: 1.9 g

Carbohydrates: 10 g
Dietary Fiber: 1.8 g
Sodium: 36 mg

❋ *Tomato-Wine Sauce* ❋

YIELD: 8 servings (¹/₂ cup each) • *PREPARATION TIME: 10 minutes* •
COOKING TIME: 45 minutes

This basic tomato sauce can be used with a wide variety of pasta and vegetable dishes. Here fresh or canned tomatoes are accented with red or white wine, onion, oregano, basil, and garlic.

¹/₂ cup red or white wine or nonfat chicken broth
¹/₂ cup chopped onion
3¹/₂ cups chopped fresh or low-sodium canned tomatoes

³/₄ teaspoon ground oregano leaves
³/₄ teaspoon ground basil leaves
1 clove garlic, minced
¹/₄ teaspoon black pepper

1. Heat the wine or broth in a large saucepan over medium heat. Add the onions. Cook and stir over medium heat until tender. Add more liquid if necessary during this process.
2. Add the tomatoes, oregano, basil, garlic, and pepper. Bring to a boil.
3. Reduce heat, cover, and simmer for 35 minutes.

Calories Per Serving: 71
Fat: .6 g
Cholesterol: 0 mg
Protein: 2.3 g

Carbohydrates: 11 g
Dietary Fiber: 1.8 g
Sodium: 46 mg

❋ *Raw Tomato Sauce* ❋

YIELD: 4 servings (¹/₂ cup each) • *PREPARATION TIME: 25 minutes*

This sauce is a real treat when tomatoes are at the peak of their season. Try serving it over hot pasta. The sauce can be thinned by adding skim milk.

4 medium tomatoes
2 tablespoons red wine vinegar
1 tablespoon fresh chopped parsley

1 teaspoon dried oregano leaves
¹/₄ teaspoon black pepper

1. Cut away the hard section of the tomatoes where their stalks were attached and place the tomatoes in boiling water for 30 seconds. Re-

Raw Tomato Sauce *(cont'd)*

move with a slotted spoon and cool under cold water. Slide the peel off the tomatoes. Cut tomatoes in half and squeeze seeds and excess liquid from them.
2. Place tomatoes, vinegar, parsley, oregano, and pepper in a blender or food processor and process until smooth.

Calories Per Serving: 26
Fat: .3 g
Cholesterol: 0 mg
Protein: 1 g

Carbohydrates: 6 g
Dietary Fiber: 1.6 g
Sodium: 11 mg

✳ *White Sauce I* ✳

YIELD: 8 servings (¹/₂ cup each) • *PREPARATION TIME: 5 minutes* •
COOKING TIME: 15 minutes

While creamy sauces with a butter base are off limits when you're avoiding fat, you can create a substitute fat-free sauce using skim milk. Add the spices of your choice to complement the dish that the sauce will be accompanying.

2 cups skim milk
1 tablespoon arrowroot

2 tablespoons nonfat chicken broth
¹/₄ teaspoon black pepper

1. Place skim milk, arrowroot, chicken broth, and black pepper in a saucepan over low heat.
2. Stir sauce for 15 minutes or until thickened.

Variation
• Substitute 2 tablespoons cornstarch dissolved in a small amount of cold liquid for the arrowroot. Delete the chicken broth.

Calories Per Serving: 26
Fat: .1 g
Cholesterol: 1 mg
Protein: 2 g

Carbohydrates: 3.9 g
Dietary Fiber: 0 g
Sodium: 34 mg

✳ *White Sauce II* ✳

YIELD: 4 servings (¹/₄ cup each) ▪ *PREPARATION TIME: 10 minutes* ▪
COOKING TIME: 6 minutes

Use this light white sauce as a substitute for heavier fat-laden white sauces.

2 tablespoons unbleached all-purpose flour	2 teaspoons lemon juice
³/₄ cup skim milk	¹/₄ teaspoon salt
¹/₄ cup nonfat chicken broth	Pinch of white pepper
	Pinch of paprika

1. Place flour and milk in a saucepan. Stir flour into milk until well blended into a smooth paste.
2. Place saucepan over low heat. Add chicken broth, lemon juice, salt, white pepper, and paprika.
3. Stir constantly until sauce has thickened.

Variations
▪ Add ¹/₂ teaspoon curry powder.
▪ Increase flour to 4 tablespoons. Increase milk to 1¹/₂ cups. Increase chicken broth to ¹/₂ cup. Add ¹/₄ teaspoon dry mustard and delete paprika. Add ¹/₂ cup chopped mushrooms in Step 2.

Calories Per Serving: 32	Carbohydrates: 5.6 g
Fat: .2 g	Dietary Fiber: .1 g
Cholesterol: .7 mg	Sodium: 165 mg
Protein: 2 g	

✳ *Simple Pear Sauce* ✳

YIELD: 10 servings (¹/₂ cup each) ▪ *PREPARATION TIME: 15 minutes* ▪
COOKING TIME: 50 minutes

This pear topping works well with pancakes, waffles, and fruit desserts. You can serve pear sauce cool or warm. It will keep for a week in the refrigerator.

Simple Pear Sauce *(cont'd)*

5 cups peeled pears, cut into 1-inch
    chunks
½ cup water

4 tablespoons brown sugar, firmly
    packed
½ teaspoon ground ginger

1. Place pears and water in a saucepan. Cover and cook over low heat
   until pears are tender.
2. Add brown sugar and ginger.
3. Mash pears.
4. Return to heat for 5 minutes, stirring.
5. Transfer to clean jars if not using immediately.

Calories Per Serving: 60
Fat: .3 g
Cholesterol: 0 mg
Protein: .3 g

Carbohydrates: 15 g
Dietary Fiber: 1.7 g
Sodium: 2.5 mg

✳ *Simple Strawberry Sauce* ✳

YIELD: 6 servings (½ cup each) • *PREPARATION TIME: 10 minutes*

This is a good topping for frozen yogurt, crêpes, and angel food cake.

3 cups sliced fresh strawberries
3 tablespoons brown sugar, firmly
    packed

¼ cup orange juice

1. Combine 2 cups of the strawberries, brown sugar, and orange juice in
   a bowl. Mash, leaving mixture slightly chunky.
2. Stir in sliced strawberries. Chill until ready to serve.

Calories Per Serving: 52
Fat: .3 g
Cholesterol: 0 mg
Protein: .5 g

Carbohydrates: 13 g
Dietary Fiber: 2 g
Sodium: 3.1 mg

✳ *Fruit Sauce* ✳

YIELD: 4 servings (¼ cup each) • *PREPARATION TIME: 15 minutes*

This sauce should be served chilled over bowls of mixed fruit.

1 small apple or pear, cored, peeled, and chopped
¹/₄ cup raisins or chopped dried apricots or prunes

¹/₂ cup nonfat plain yogurt
¹/₄ cup frozen apple, orange, or cranberry juice concentrate

1. Place apple or pear, raisins or other dried fruit, yogurt, and juice concentrate in a blender or food processor and process until smooth.

Calories Per Serving: 84
Fat: .2 g
Cholesterol: .5 mg
Protein: 2.3 g

Carbohydrates: 19 g
Dietary Fiber: 1.3 g
Sodium: 24 mg

✳ *Blueberry Topping* ✳

YIELD: 6 servings (¹/₂ cup each) • *PREPARATION TIME: 10 minutes* • *COOKING TIME: 8 minutes*

This cinnamon-nutmeg blueberry sauce is a perfect topping for frozen desserts, fruit salads, or angel food cake.

2¹/₂ cups fresh or thawed frozen blueberries
¹/₂ cup sugar
1 teaspoon ground cinnamon

¹/₂ teaspoon ground nutmeg
1 tablespoon cornstarch
¹/₃ cup orange juice

1. Combine blueberries, sugar, cinnamon, and nutmeg in a medium saucepan.
2. Stir cornstarch into orange juice. Pour into saucepan with blueberries and stir.
3. Cook, stirring, over medium heat for 8 minutes or until mixture thickens.
4. Cool to room temperature and store in refrigerator until ready to use.

Calories Per Serving: 107
Fat: .3 g
Cholesterol: 0 mg
Protein: .5 g

Carbohydrates: 27 g
Dietary Fiber: 1.5 g
Sodium: 4 mg

✳ *Orange-Honey Sauce* ✳

YIELD: 4 servings (3 tablespoons each) ▪ *PREPARATION TIME: 10 minutes*

Serve this sweet sauce warm over pancakes or French toast.

¼ cup water
½ teaspoon cornstarch
½ teaspoon grated orange peel

½ cup orange juice
1 teaspoon honey

1. Combine water and cornstarch in a small saucepan.
2. Stir in orange peel, orange juice, and honey.
3. Cook over medium heat until sauce begins to bubble.
4. Cook for 2 more minutes.

Calories Per Serving: 21
Fat: 0 g
Cholesterol: 0 mg
Protein: .2 g

Carbohydrates: 4.9 g
Dietary Fiber: 0 g
Sodium: 1 mg

✳ *Dijon-Horseradish Sauce* ✳

YIELD: 6 servings (¼ cup each) ▪ *PREPARATION TIME: 15 minutes*

This zesty sauce makes a good topping for a combination of steamed cauliflower, green beans, green bell pepper, and yellow summer squash.

¾ cup nonfat sour cream
¼ cup nonfat mayonnaise
⅓ cup plain nonfat yogurt
1 tablespoon dried dill leaves

3 tablespoons prepared horseradish
2 teaspoons Dijon mustard
2 teaspoons cider vinegar
½ teaspoon sugar

1. Combine sour cream, mayonnaise, yogurt, dill, horseradish, mustard, vinegar, and sugar together with a wire whisk.

Calories Per Serving: 28
Fat: 0 g
Cholesterol: .5 mg
Protein: .9 g

Carbohydrates: 5.8 g
Dietary Fiber: 0 g
Sodium: 255 mg

✳ *Chinese Dipping Sauce* ✳

YIELD: 4 servings (2 tablespoons each) • *PREPARATION TIME: 10 minutes*

This sauce can be used for oriental dumplings, baked egg rolls, or raw vegetables.

½ cup nonfat chicken broth
1 tablespoon dry sherry
1 teaspoon lemon juice

1 teaspoon sugar
2 scallions, chopped

1. Combine chicken broth, sherry, lemon juice, sugar, and scallions.

Calories Per Serving: 8
Fat: 0 g
Cholesterol: 0 mg
Protein: .3 g

Carbohydrates: 1.4 g
Dietary Fiber: no data
Sodium: 17 mg

✳ *Alfredo Sauce* ✳

YIELD: 4 servings (6 tablespoons each) • *PREPARATION TIME: 5 minutes* •
COOKING TIME: 10 minutes

Try this sauce over pasta or vegetables.

12 ounces evaporated skim milk
1 tablespoon arrowroot or cornstarch
1 teaspoon natural butter substitute such as Molly McButter

2 tablespoons nonfat Parmesan cheese
Pinch of white pepper

1. Reserve 2 tablespoons evaporated skim milk. Place the rest of the milk in a saucepan over medium heat.
2. Combine the reserved milk with the arrowroot or cornstarch.
3. Add arrowroot or cornstarch to the saucepan and mix well. Continue cooking, stirring until the sauce has thickened.
4. Stir in butter substitute, Parmesan cheese, and white pepper.

Calories Per Serving: 86
Fat: .2 g
Cholesterol: 3.9 mg
Protein: 7.5 g

Carbohydrates: 13 g
Dietary Fiber: .02 g
Sodium: 168 mg

✳ *Mushroom Sauce* ✳

YIELD: 8 servings (¹/₂ cup each) ▪ *PREPARATION TIME: 15 minutes* ▪
COOKING TIME: 15 minutes

This mushroom sauce is seasoned with garlic, onion, basil, and oregano.
Serve it over pasta or steamed green beans and carrots.

¹/₄ cup water, nonfat chicken broth,
    vegetable broth, or wine
1 small onion, finely chopped
¹/₂ cup mushrooms, finely chopped
1 clove garlic, minced

12 ounces evaporated skim milk
1 tablespoon arrowroot or cornstarch
¹/₂ teaspoon dried basil leaves
¹/₂ teaspoon dried oregano leaves

1. Heat water, broth, or wine in a skillet over medium heat. Add onion,
   mushrooms, and garlic. Cook and stir for 5 minutes. Add more liquid
   during this process if necessary.
2. Drain onion mixture and set aside.
3. Reserve 2 tablespoons evaporated skim milk. Place the rest of the milk
   in a saucepan over medium heat.
4. Combine the reserved milk with the arrowroot or cornstarch.
5. Add arrowroot or cornstarch to saucepan and mix well. Continue
   cooking, stirring until the sauce has thickened.
6. Stir in onion mixture, basil, and oregano.

Calories Per Serving: 48
Fat: .16 g
Cholesterol: 1.9 mg
Protein: 3.9 g

Carbohydrates: 7.8 g
Dietary Fiber: .2 g
Sodium: 56 mg

✳ *Herbed Nonfat Mayonnaise* ✳

YIELD: 16 servings (2 tablespoons each) ▪ *PREPARATION TIME: 15 minutes*

Dress up the taste of nonfat mayonnaise and yogurt by adding a variety
of herbs.

1 cup nonfat mayonnaise
1 cup plain nonfat yogurt

¹/₂ cup chopped fresh parsley
1 small onion, cut in chunks

1 tablespoon Dijon mustard
1 clove garlic, quartered

1 teaspoon dried thyme leaves

1. Place mayonnaise, yogurt, parsley, onion, mustard, garlic, and thyme in a food processor or blender.
2. Process until smooth.

Calories Per Serving: 31
Fat: .1 g
Cholesterol: .25 mg
Protein: .9 g

Carbohydrates: 6.7 g
Dietary Fiber: .1 g
Sodium: 234 mg

✳ *Prune Butter* ✳

YIELD: 8 servings (6 tablespoons each) • *PREPARATION TIME: 5 minutes* •
COOKING TIME: 40 minutes

Spread prune butter on whole-grain bread. It can also be used as a substitute for oil or shortening in many recipes. Store it in a tightly covered container for ten days in the refrigerator or six months in the freezer.

2 cups pitted prunes
3 cups water
¹/₂ cup honey
¹/₄ cup apple juice

1¹/₂ teaspoons grated lemon peel
1 teaspoon ground cinnamon
¹/₄ teaspoon ground allspice

1. Place prunes in a saucepan with water. Bring to a boil. Reduce heat to low.
2. Simmer for 25 minutes or until prunes are soft.
3. Drain prunes and combine in saucepan with honey, apple juice or apple cider vinegar, lemon peel, cinnamon, and allspice.
4. Simmer over low heat, stirring and breaking up the prunes with a spoon for 10 minutes or until the mixture is very thick.
5. Let cool before using or storing.

Calories Per Serving: 166
Fat: .2 g
Cholesterol: 0 mg
Protein: 1 g

Carbohydrates: 43 g
Dietary Fiber: 2.8 g
Sodium: 3 mg

✳ *Baked Potato Topping* ✳

YIELD: 4 servings (¹/₄ cup each) ▪ *PREPARATION TIME: 5 minutes*

This topping makes a good substitute for sour cream on baked potatoes and other dishes.

1 cup nonfat cottage cheese

1. Purée cottage cheese in a blender until creamy.

Variations
- Combine 1 teaspoon horseradish and 1 tablespoon chopped fresh parsley with the puréed cottage cheese.
- For a thinner sauce, purée the cottage cheese with ¹/₄ cup skim milk and 1 tablespoon lemon juice.

Calories Per Serving: 40	Carbohydrates: 2.9 g
Fat: 0 g	Dietary Fiber: no data
Cholesterol: 3 mg	Sodium: 250 mg
Protein: 7.9 g	

RELISHES, CHUTNEYS, AND SALSAS

::

Relishes and chutneys can add striking colors and vivid flavors to a wide variety of dishes. Relishes are sweet and chunky combinations of vegetables and fruits. Chutneys are sweet and sour blends of vinegar, fruit, onion, and sugar. These condiments can be used in place of butter on hot baked potatoes, vegetables, and baked goods.

✴ *Pepper Relish* ✴

YIELD: 16 servings (6 tablespoons each) • *PREPARATION TIME: 25 minutes plus overnight standing time*

This old-fashioned marinated vegetable relish is a combination of green and red bell peppers, cabbage, brown sugar, and mustard seeds. Pepper relish can be stored in the refrigerator for three days.

1 cup minced green bell pepper	*2 tablespoons whole mustard seeds*
1/2 cup minced red bell pepper	*2 tablespoons brown sugar, firmly*
4 cups minced green cabbage	*packed*
1 teaspoon salt	*1/2 cup apple cider vinegar*

1. Place green pepper, red pepper, cabbage, and salt in a glass bowl. Let stand overnight in the refrigerator.
2. Drain and discard the liquid from the vegetables and transfer them to a large glass jar.
3. Place mustard seeds, brown sugar, and vinegar in a nonreactive saucepan and bring to a boil. Pour over the vegetables in the glass jar. Stir well.
4. Let pepper relish cool to room temperature and then refrigerate.

Pepper Relish *(cont'd)*

Calories Per Serving: 29

Fat: .8 g

Cholesterol: 0 mg

Protein: .8 g

Carbohydrates: .6 g

Dietary Fiber: .3 g

Sodium: 269 mg

✳ *Uncooked Tomato Relish* ✳

YIELD: 14 servings (¹/₂ cup each) ▪ *PREPARATION TIME: 25 minutes plus corn cooking time and 4 hours chilling time*

This relish is a great way to combine tomatoes and corn at their seasonal peak, but you can also enjoy it during the winter with canned or frozen corn and canned tomatoes.

2 cups cooked fresh, frozen, or canned corn kernels

3¹/₂ cups chopped fresh or low-sodium canned tomatoes, drained

¹/₂ cup chopped onion

¹/₂ cup chopped green bell pepper

1 jalapeño pepper, seeded and finely chopped

¹/₄ cup lemon juice

1 teaspoon sugar

2 tablespoons fresh chopped parsley

¹/₂ teaspoon ground cumin

1. Combine the corn, tomatoes, onion, green pepper, jalapeño pepper, lemon juice, sugar, parsley, and cumin in a large glass bowl.
2. Chill for 4 hours before serving.

Calories Per Serving: 30

Fat: .13 g

Cholesterol: 0 mg

Protein: 1 g

Carbohydrates: 7.5 g

Dietary Fiber: 1 g

Sodium: 22 mg

✳ *Apple Relish* ✳

YIELD: 6 servings (¹/₂ cup each) ▪ *PREPARATION TIME: 15 minutes*

Try this apple relish with a curried vegetable or grain dish.

3 medium apples, peeled and grated
2 teaspoons sugar

1 tablespoon dried mint leaves
3 tablespoons white wine vinegar

1. Toss grated apples with sugar, mint, and white wine vinegar.

Calories Per Serving: 46
Fat: .2 g
Cholesterol: 0 mg
Protein: .1 g

Carbohydrates: 12 g
Dietary Fiber: 1.5 g
Sodium: .6 mg

✳ Strawberry Relish ✳

Yield: 6 servings (1 cup each) • *Preparation Time: 15 minutes plus 1 hour standing time*

Strawberries, raisins, ginger, lime juice, and scallions are the surprising ingredients in this relish.

2¹/₂ cups chopped fresh or thawed, frozen strawberries
3 cups seedless raisins
¹/₂ teaspoon ground ginger

2 tablespoons lime juice
2 tablespoons honey
1 tablespoon chopped scallions
¹/₄ teaspoon black pepper

1. Toss strawberries, raisins, ginger, lime juice, honey, scallions, and pepper in a glass bowl.
2. Let stand at room temperature for 1 hour. Chill until ready to serve.

Calories Per Serving: 260
Fat: .6 g
Cholesterol: 0 mg
Protein: 2.7 g

Carbohydrates: 68 g
Dietary Fiber: 5.5 g
Sodium: 10 mg

✳ Raspberry-Cranberry Relish ✳

Yield: 4 servings (¹/₂ cup each) • *Preparation Time: 10 minutes* • *Cooking Time: 5 minutes*

This double berry relish has a tart and tangy character.

Raspberry-Cranberry Relish *(cont'd)*

1 cup fresh or frozen cranberries

1 cup orange juice

1/2 cup sugar

2 cups fresh or frozen raspberries

1. Place cranberries and orange juice in a saucepan and bring to a boil.
2. Add sugar and stir until dissolved.
3. Add raspberries and stir. Lower heat and simmer for 3 minutes.

Calories Per Serving: 169

Fat: .6 g

Cholesterol: 0 mg

Protein: 1.2 g

Carbohydrates: 42 g

Dietary Fiber: 22 g

Sodium: 3 mg

✳ *Ginger-Pineapple Relish* ✳

YIELD: *4 servings (1/2 cup each)* • PREPARATION TIME: *10 minutes plus 15 minutes standing time*

This relish is a great side dish for oriental vegetable stir-fries or grain dishes with a tropical flavor.

2 tablespoons minced fresh
  gingerroot

2 cups diced fresh pineapple or juice-
  packed pineapple chunks

1/2 cup chopped scallions

1/2 teaspoon red pepper flakes

1. Combine gingerroot, pineapple, scallions, and red pepper flakes in a small bowl.
2. Let stand 15 minutes before serving.

Variation

- Replace gingerroot with 1 tablespoon lime juice. Add 2 kiwis, peeled and diced.

Calories Per Serving: 43

Fat: .4 g

Cholesterol: 0 mg

Protein: .4 g

Carbohydrates: 10 g

Dietary Fiber: 1 g

Sodium: 3.6 mg

✳ *Papaya Relish* ✳

YIELD: 4 servings (¹⁄₃ cup each) • *PREPARATION TIME: 15 minutes*

This relish tastes great spread on toasted whole-grain bread.

2 medium papayas, peeled, seeded, and cut into chunks	*1 tablespoon fresh lemon juice*
1 tablespoon sugar	*2 teaspoons fresh gingerroot*

1. Place papaya chunks, sugar, lemon juice, and gingerroot in a blender or food processor and purée.

Calories Per Serving: 33	Carbohydrates: 8.6 g
Fat: .1 g	Dietary Fiber: .4 g
Cholesterol: 0 mg	Sodium: 1.7 mg
Protein: .3 g	

✳ *Fresh Pineapple–Red Pepper Relish* ✳

YIELD: 10 servings (¹⁄₂ cup each) • *PREPARATION TIME: 25 minutes* •
COOKING TIME: 35 minutes

This relish can be stored in the refrigerator in an airtight container for as long as two months.

3 cups diced fresh pineapple	*¹⁄₂ cup brown sugar, firmly packed*
1 cup seeded and diced red bell peppers	*²⁄₃ cup cider vinegar*
1 cup chopped onions	*2 cinnamon sticks*
2 garlic cloves, minced	*¹⁄₄ teaspoon black pepper*
3 tablespoons peeled, chopped fresh gingerroot	*¹⁄₂ teaspoon ground cloves*
	¹⁄₄ teaspoon red pepper flakes
	¹⁄₂ cup raisins

1. Combine pineapple, red peppers, onions, garlic, gingerroot, brown sugar, cider vinegar, and cinnamon sticks in a large, heavy saucepan. Cook over low heat until sugar is dissolved.
2. Add black pepper, cloves, and red pepper flakes. Simmer for 25 minutes, stirring frequently.
3. Stir in raisins and cook for 5 more minutes. Cool.

Fresh Pineapple–Red Pepper Relish *(cont'd)*
Variation

- Delete cinnamon sticks, raisins, and 1½ cups pineapple. Add 1 apple, cored and diced; 1 pear, cored and diced; ½ tablespoon cumin; and 1 teaspoon curry powder.

Calories Per Serving: 96   Carbohydrates: 25 g
Fat: .3 g   Dietary Fiber: 1.3 g
Cholesterol: 0 mg   Sodium: 6 mg
Protein: .7 g

✳ *Nectarine Chutney* ✳

YIELD: *6 servings (½ cup each)* • PREPARATION TIME: *20 minutes* •
COOKING TIME: *45 minutes*

This fresh fruit chutney makes a terrific addition to a bowl of curried winter squash.

3 ripe nectarines, diced   *1 tablespoon minced fresh gingerroot*
1 apple, cored and diced   *3 cloves garlic, minced*
1 pear, cored and diced   *½ tablespoon ground cumin*
½ onion, diced   *1 teaspoon curry powder*
1 cup red wine vinegar   *¼ teaspoon black pepper*
¼ cup brown sugar, firmly packed   *Pinch of cayenne pepper*
½ cup raisins

1. Combine nectarines, apple, pear, onion, vinegar, sugar, raisins, gingerroot, garlic, cumin, curry powder, black pepper, and cayenne pepper in a heavy saucepan.
2. Simmer over low heat for 45 minutes. Cool to room temperature and refrigerate.

Calories Per Serving: 149   Carbohydrates: 38 g
Fat: .8 g   Dietary Fiber: 3.3 g
Cholesterol: 0 mg   Sodium: 7 mg
Protein: 1.6 g

❋ Corn Relish ❋

Yield: 12 servings (¹/₂ cup each) • Preparation Time: 15 minutes plus corn cooking time and overnight chilling time • Cooking Time: 2 minutes

This old-fashioned relish can be stored in the refrigerator for up to two weeks.

¹/₂ cup apple cider vinegar	¹/₂ teaspoon mustard seed
¹/₄ cup lemon juice	4¹/₂ cups cooked fresh, frozen, or
¹/₄ cup sugar	canned corn kernels
¹/₂ teaspoon celery seed	1 large red bell pepper, diced
¹/₂ teaspoon black pepper	6 scallions, chopped

1. Place vinegar, lemon juice, sugar, celery seed, black pepper, and mustard seed in a medium saucepan and bring to a boil. Cook for 2 minutes.
2. Place corn kernels, red pepper, and scallions in a medium bowl. Pour vinegar mixture over vegetables and stir. Chill overnight before serving.

Calories Per Serving: 69	Carbohydrates: 18 g
Fat: .14 g	Dietary Fiber: 1.4 g
Cholesterol: 0 mg	Sodium: 3.6 mg
Protein: 2 g	

❋ Tomato-Fruit Chutney ❋

Yield: 6 servings (¹/₂ cup each) • Preparation Time: 20 minutes • Cooking Time: 40 minutes

This tomato and apple chutney is spiced with jalapeño peppers.

3 ripe tomatoes, diced	2 jalapeño peppers, seeded and
2 apples, cored and diced	minced
¹/₂ onion, diced	¹/₄ cup brown sugar, firmly packed
1 cup red wine vinegar	¹/₂ tablespoon ground cumin
1 tablespoon minced fresh gingerroot	¹/₄ teaspoon ground black pepper
3 cloves garlic, minced	Pinch of cayenne pepper
¹/₂ cup raisins	

Tomato-Fruit Chutney *(cont'd)*

1. Combine tomatoes, apples, onion, vinegar, gingerroot, garlic, raisins, jalapeño peppers, brown sugar, cumin, black pepper, and cayenne pepper in a heavy saucepan.
2. Simmer over low heat for 40 minutes. Cool to room temperature and refrigerate.

Calories Per Serving: 125
Fat: .6 g
Cholesterol: 0 mg
Protein: 1.4 g

Carbohydrates: 32 g
Dietary Fiber: 2.6 g
Sodium: 95 mg

BREADS
AND
QUICK BREADS

Easy Whole Wheat–Raisin Bread ▪ Soda Bread ▪ Whole Wheat
Baguettes ▪ Applesauce Quick Bread ▪ Apricot-Orange Quick
Bread ▪ Carrot Corn Bread ▪ Banana Quick Bread ▪ Pumpkin Quick
Bread ▪ Harvest Quick Bread ▪ Flour Tortillas ▪ Garlic Bread

BREADS AND QUICK BREADS

::

One of the best ways to be sure you are eating fat-free bread is to make your own. Be sure to store nonfat baked goods tightly wrapped in the refrigerator.

✳ *Easy Whole Wheat—Raisin Bread* ✳

Yield: 10 servings (1 slice each) • *Preparation Time: 15 minutes plus
1 hour standing time* • *Cooking Time: 1 hour*

This simple nonfat bread is packed with raisins and molasses. Serve for breakfast spread with Prune Butter (page 297).

2 cups whole wheat flour
1 cup unbleached all-purpose flour
2 teaspoons baking soda
1/2 teaspoon salt

1 cup raisins
2 cups nonfat buttermilk
1/2 cup molasses

1. Combine whole wheat flour, white flour, baking soda, salt, and raisins.
2. Stir the buttermilk and molasses into the dry ingredients. Mix well.
3. Pour into a nonstick bread pan, or a bread pan lined with a baking pan liner, and let stand for 1 hour.
4. Preheat oven to 325 degrees.
5. Bake bread for 1 hour or until a wooden pick inserted in the center of the bread comes out dry.
6. Cool in pan for 10 minutes, then transfer to a wire rack to cool. Cut into 10 slices.

Calories Per Serving: 189
Fat: .5 g
Cholesterol: .9 mg
Protein: 5.5 g

Carbohydrates: 42 g
Dietary Fiber: 3.4 g
Sodium: 229 mg

✳ *Soda Bread* ✳

YIELD: *9 servings (1 wedge each)* • PREPARATION TIME: *15 minutes* •
COOKING TIME: *40 minutes*

This simple bread requires no rising time. Serve with Bean Bag Soup
(page 104).

2 cups whole wheat flour	*1 teaspoon baking soda*
1 cup unbleached all-purpose flour	*1½ cups nonfat buttermilk*
1 teaspoon baking powder	

1. Preheat oven to 375 degrees.
2. Mix together whole wheat flour, all-purpose flour, baking soda, and
   baking powder.
3. Stir in the buttermilk and mix until dry ingredients are just moist.
4. Knead the dough on a floured surface for 2 minutes. Shape into a ball.
5. Place dough on a nonstick baking sheet, or on a baking sheet lined
   with a baking sheet liner. Flatten into a 7-inch round, 1½ inches thick.
   Cut an **X** across the loaf.
6. Bake for 40 minutes or until the loaf sounds hollow when the bottom
   is tapped. Cool on a rack.
7. Cut into 9 wedges.

Variation
• Add cinnamon, nutmeg, caraway seeds, raisins, applesauce, chopped
  apples, or dried apricots in Step 2.

Calories Per Serving: 139	Carbohydrates: 28 g
Fat: .6 g	Dietary Fiber: 3.3 g
Cholesterol: .7 mg	Sodium: 155
Protein: 5.7 g	

✳ *Whole Wheat Baguettes* ✳

YIELD: *18 servings (2 2-inch slices each)* • PREPARATION TIME: *25 minutes plus
3 hours rising time* • COOKING TIME: *25 minutes*

Here's a delicious whole wheat French loaf that is free of fat and preserva-
tives. This recipe yields four loaves, so you can freeze several loaves for

later use. Bake those loaves you plan to freeze for only 15 minutes, cool, and wrap in foil. When ready to eat, remove from freezer, thaw, and bake at 350 degrees for 10 minutes, still wrapped in foil. Then remove foil and bake for 5 minutes more. Serve with Lima Bean Stew (page 122).

1 tablespoon active dry yeast
1 tablespoon sugar
½ teaspoon salt
2½ cups warm water (105 to 115 degrees)

3 cups unbleached all-purpose flour
2 to 3 cups whole wheat flour
Cornmeal
1 egg white mixed with 1 tablespoon cold water

1. Combine yeast, sugar, salt, and water in a large bowl.
2. Add the all-purpose and whole wheat flours a little bit at a time, mixing well. Expect the dough to be sticky and add enough flour to make it possible for you to move the dough to a lightly floured surface.
3. Knead the dough for 10 minutes, or until smooth and elastic, adding flour until the dough no longer sticks to your hands.
4. Place dough in a bowl, coated with vegetable cooking spray. Cover and let rise in a warm place (85 degrees), free from drafts, for 2 hours or until it doubles in bulk.
5. Punch the dough down. Move dough back to the floured surface and divide into 4 equal portions. Shape each part into a long loaf. Sprinkle cornmeal on the bottom of 4 nonstick baguette pans. Place each loaf on a pan.
6. Gently slash top of dough with a sharp knife, making 5 diagonal cuts. Brush the tops of the loaves with the egg white and water. Let dough rise for 1 hour or until it doubles in size.
7. Preheat oven to 350 degrees.
8. Bake the bread for 13 minutes and then cover the loaves with foil. Continue baking for 12 minute more or until loaves sound hollow when thumped.
9. Let loaves cool in pans until the bread shrinks from the sides of the pans. Remove from pans and cool on racks. Cut into 2-inch slices.

Calories Per Serving: 143
Fat: .6 g
Cholesterol: 0 mg
Protein: 4.8 g

Carbohydrates: 30 g
Dietary Fiber: 3 g
Sodium: 66 mg

✳ *Applesauce Quick Bread* ✳

YIELD: 10 servings (1 slice each) • *PREPARATION TIME: 15 minutes plus 1 hour standing time* • *COOKING TIME: 50 minutes*

A slice of this moist loaf makes a good breakfast on the run, lunch, snack-time treat, or dessert. Serve with Banana-Squash Soup (page 97).

2½ cups unbleached all-purpose
   flour
2 teaspoons baking powder
½ teaspoon salt
½ cup brown sugar, firmly packed

1 tablespoon ground cinnamon
1 cup applesauce
2 egg whites
1 cup skim milk

1. Combine the white flour, baking powder, salt, sugar, and cinnamon.
2. Stir in the applesauce, egg whites, and milk.
3. Pour into a nonstick loaf pan, or a pan lined with a baking pan liner or lightly sprayed with vegetable cooking spray. Let stand for 1 hour.
4. Preheat oven to 325 degrees.
5. Bake bread for 50 minutes or until a wooden pick inserted in center of the bread comes out dry.
6. Cool in pan for 10 minutes, then transfer to a wire rack to cool. Cut into 10 slices.

Calories Per Serving: 189
Fat: .4 g
Cholesterol: .4 mg
Protein: 4.8 g

Carbohydrates: 41 g
Dietary Fiber: 1 g
Sodium: 201 mg

✳ *Apricot-Orange Quick Bread* ✳

YIELD: 12 servings (1 slice each) • *PREPARATION TIME: 25 minutes* • *COOKING TIME: 40 minutes*

Dried apricots are the featured ingredient in this orange-accented cake. Serve with Chilled Yellow Squash Soup (page 110).

2½ cups cake flour
¾ cup brown sugar, firmly packed
1½ tablespoons baking powder

¼ teaspoon salt (optional)
3 tablespoons applesauce or prune
   purée (see page 23)

½ cup skim milk
2 egg whites, lightly beaten
¼ cup orange juice

2 teaspoons grated orange peel
¾ cup chopped dried apricots

1. Preheat oven to 350 degrees. Use a nonstick 9-by-5-inch loaf pan or line a loaf pan with a baking pan liner or lightly spray with vegetable cooking spray. Sprinkle pan with flour.
2. Place cake flour, brown sugar, baking powder, salt, if using, apple-sauce or prune purée, skim milk, egg whites, orange juice, orange peel, and apricots in the bowl of an electric mixer. Beat on medium, scraping the sides and bottom of the bowl, until just blended.
3. Pour into baking pan. Bake for 40 minutes or until a wooden pick inserted in the center of the cake comes out clean.
4. Let stand in pan for 5 minutes. Remove. Cool on rack. Slice into 12 slices.

Calories Per Serving: 165
Fat: .3 g
Cholesterol: .2 mg
Protein: 3 g

Carbohydrates: 37 g
Dietary Fiber: 1 g
Sodium: 143 mg

✳ *Carrot Corn Bread* ✳

YIELD: 8 servings (1 square each) • *PREPARATION TIME: 15 minutes* •
COOKING TIME: 20 minutes

This corn bread is made with cornmeal, corn, buttermilk, and brown sugar. Serve it warm from the oven.

½ cup whole wheat or unbleached
   all-purpose flour
1½ cups yellow cornmeal
2 teaspoons baking powder
¼ teaspoon salt
½ teaspoon baking soda
1 cup plain nonfat yogurt or
   nonfat buttermilk

¾ cup cream-style corn
½ cup shredded carrots
1 tablespoon brown sugar,
   firmly packed
2 egg whites

1. Preheat oven to 400 degrees.
2. Combine flour, cornmeal, baking powder, salt, and baking soda.

Carrot Corn Bread *(cont'd)*

3. In a separate bowl, combine buttermilk, corn, carrots, brown sugar, and egg whites.
4. Add the wet ingredients to the dry ingredients. Mix until well combined.
5. Use a nonstick square baking pan or line a square baking pan with a baking pan liner or spray with vegetable cooking spray.
6. Bake for 22 minutes or until a wooden pick inserted in center of the bread comes out dry. Slice into 8 squares.

Variations
- Substitute maple syrup for brown sugar. Omit carrots. Increase cream-style corn to 1 cup.
- Add dried herbs or spice such as basil, dill, or cumin to batter.

Calories Per Serving: 154	Carbohydrates: 32 g
Fat: 1 g	Dietary Fiber: 4.7 g
Cholesterol: .5 mg	Sodium: 245 mg
Protein: 6.2 g	

✳ *Banana Quick Bread* ✳

YIELD: 12 servings (1 slice each) • *PREPARATION TIME: 20 minutes* •
COOKING TIME: 1 hour and 15 minutes

This moist, lemony banana loaf makes a great snack or dessert.

¹/₂ cup pitted prunes	*1¹/₂ cups all-purpose unbleached*
2 tablespoons water	*flour*
2¹/₂ very ripe bananas	*³/₄ cup sugar*
4 egg whites, lightly beaten	*1 teaspoon baking powder*
2 teaspoons lemon juice	*¹/₄ teaspoon salt (optional)*
¹/₄ cup skim milk	

1. Preheat oven to 350 degrees. Use a 9-by-5-inch nonstick loaf pan or line a loaf pan with a baking pan liner or lightly spray with vegetable cooking spray.
2. Place prunes and water in a food processor or blender and purée.
3. Place bananas in a large bowl and mash. Beat together the prune purée, egg whites, lemon juice, and milk.

4. In a separate bowl combine the flour, sugar, baking powder, and salt, if using.
5. Stir the wet ingredients into the dry ingredients until just moistened.
6. Transfer batter to loaf pan. Bake for 1 hour and 15 minutes or until a wooden pick inserted in the center of loaf comes out clean.
7. Cool in the pan for 10 minutes. Remove and finish cooling on a wire rack. Slice into 12 slices.

Variation
• Substitute 1 teaspoon vanilla and 1 teaspoon ground cinnamon for the lemon juice.

Calories Per Serving: 148
Fat: .3 g
Cholesterol: .01 mg
Protein: 3 g

Carbohydrates: 34 g
Dietary Fiber: 1 g
Sodium: 49 mg

✳ *Pumpkin Quick Bread* ✳

YIELD: 12 servings (1 slice each) • *PREPARATION TIME: 20 minutes* •
COOKING TIME: 50 minutes

Prune butter and pumpkin purée are key ingredients in this bread that is accented with cinnamon, cloves, ginger, and nutmeg. Serve with Old Country Mushroom–Barley Soup (page 100).

1/2 cup pitted prunes
2 tablespoons water
3/4 cup canned pumpkin purée
1/2 cup honey
4 egg whites, lightly beaten
1/2 cup apple juice
1 teaspoon cinnamon
1/4 teaspoon ground cloves
Pinch of ground nutmeg

1/4 teaspoon ground ginger
1 1/2 cups all-purpose unbleached flour
1 cup cornmeal
2 teaspoons baking powder
1 teaspoon baking soda
1/4 teaspoon salt (optional)
1/2 cup raisins

1. Preheat oven to 350 degrees. Use a nonstick 9-by-5-inch loaf pan, or line a loaf pan with a baking pan liner or lightly spray with vegetable cooking spray.
2. Place prunes and water in a food processor or blender and purée.

Pumpkin Quick Bread *(cont'd)*

3. Beat together prune purée, pumpkin purée, honey, egg whites, and apple juice in a bowl.
4. Combine cinnamon, cloves, nutmeg, ginger, flour, cornmeal, baking powder, baking soda, and salt, if using, in a separate bowl.
5. Stir the wet ingredients into the dry ingredients until just moistened. Fold in raisins.
6. Transfer to loaf pan. Bake for 50 minutes or until a wooden pick inserted in center comes out clean.
7. Cool in the pan for 10 minutes. Remove and finish cooling on a wire rack. Slice into 12 slices.

Note: You can substitute ¹/₃ cup commercially prepared baby food puréed prunes or prune butter (found in jam and jelly or baking section of your supermarket) for the prune purée.

Calories Per Serving: 186
Fat: .6 g
Cholesterol: 0 mg
Protein: 4 g

Carbohydrates: 42 g
Dietary Fiber: 2.8 g
Sodium: 148 mg

❋ *Harvest Quick Bread* ❋

YIELD: *12 servings (1 slice each)* • PREPARATION TIME: *20 minutes* •
COOKING TIME: *1 hour and 10 minutes*

Fresh or frozen cranberries and chopped apples are accented with cinnamon and nutmeg in this recipe. Serve with Curried Broccoli-Apple Soup (page 98).

¹/₂ cup pitted prunes
2 tablespoons water
1 cup fresh or frozen cranberries, chopped
1 cup grated apple
¹/₂ cup apple juice
1 tablespoon grated lemon peel
2 egg whites, lightly beaten

2 cups unbleached all-purpose flour
¹/₂ cup sugar
¹/₂ cup brown sugar, firmly packed
1 teaspoon baking powder
¹/₂ teaspoon baking soda
¹/₂ teaspoon ground cinnamon
¹/₂ teaspoon ground nutmeg

1. Preheat oven to 350 degrees. Use a nonstick 9-by-5-inch loaf pan or

line a loaf pan with a baking pan liner or lightly spray with vegetable cooking spray.
2. Place prunes and water in a food processor or blender and purée.
3. Mix together prune purée, cranberries, apples, apple juice, lemon peel, and egg whites in a bowl.
4. Combine flour, sugar, brown sugar, baking powder, baking soda, cinnamon, and nutmeg in a separate bowl.
5. Stir the wet ingredients into the dry ingredients until just moistened.
6. Transfer to loaf pan. Bake for 1 hour and 10 minutes or until a wooden pick inserted in center comes out clean.
7. Cool in the pan for 10 minutes. Remove and finish cooling on a wire rack. Slice into 12 slices.

Note: You can substitute ⅓ cup commercially prepared baby food puréed prunes or prune butter (found in jam and jelly or baking section of your supermarket) for the prune purée.

Calories Per Serving: 179	Carbohydrates: 42 g
Fat: .4 g	Dietary Fiber: 1.5 g
Cholesterol: 0 mg	Sodium: 75 mg
Protein: 3 g	

✳ *Flour Tortillas* ✳

YIELD: 12 servings (1 large tortilla each) • *PREPARATION TIME: 25 minutes* •
COOKING TIME: 20 minutes

Commercially baked fat-free wheat tortillas can be hard to find. Try making your own! Use to make Apple-Pear Tortilla Roll-Ups (page 60).

1½ cups unbleached all-purpose flour	*1½ cups whole wheat flour*
	1 cup water

1. Combine all-purpose flour, whole wheat flour, and water.
2. Move dough to a floured board and knead until a smooth but stiff dough results.
3. Divide dough into 12 equal parts. Shape into smooth, pliable balls.
4. Roll each ball out as thinly as possible on a floured surface.

318 ••• SARAH SCHLESINGER

Flour Tortillas *(cont'd)*

5. Drop tortilla on a very hot ungreased griddle. Cook until speckled on one side. Turn and cook on the reverse side.
6. As you cook each tortilla, place it between the folds of a clean cotton kitchen towel to keep warm and flexible until serving.
7. Repeat steps 4 through 6 for each tortilla, reflouring surface as needed.

Calories Per Serving: 112   Carbohydrates: 23 g
Fat: .3 g   Dietary Fiber: .8 g
Cholesterol: 0 mg   Sodium: 199 mg
Protein: 3 g

✳ *Garlic Bread* ✳

YIELD: 12 servings (1 slice each) • PREPARATION TIME: 10 minutes •
COOKING TIME: 4 to 6 minutes

You can enjoy garlic bread without olive oil by using Basic Italian Dressing (page 274) or a fat-free commercial Italian dressing, combined with paprika and garlic.

½ cup Basic Italian Dressing (page 274) or commercially prepared fat-free Italian dressing
½ teaspoon paprika
4 cloves garlic, peeled

1 loaf fat-free whole-grain French bread or Italian bread, sliced into 12 slices
¼ cup chopped fresh parsley

1. Preheat broiler.
2. Place dressing, paprika, and garlic cloves in a blender and process until well blended.
3. Spread mixture on one side of bread slices and sprinkle with parsley.
4. Broil slices until they are lightly golden, being careful not to allow bread to burn.

Calories Per Serving: 53   Carbohydrates: 12 g
Fat: 0 g   Dietary Fiber: 0 g
Cholesterol: 0 mg   Sodium: 114 mg
Protein: 2 g

DRINKS

COLD DRINKS

Veggie Pick-Me-Up • Fall Fruit Pick-Me-Up • Apricot-Orange-Grapefruit Chiller • Blueberry Shake • Apple Shake • Cantaloupe-Raspberry Fizz • Mango Freeze • Nectarine-Honey Refresher • Orange-Banana Freeze • Peach-Ginger-Grape Fizz • Orange-Papaya Drink • Peach-Banana Shake • Plum-Honey-Cinnamon Cooler • Strawberry-Orange Freeze • Tomato Zinger • Watermelon-Banana Shake • Generic Cooler • Lime-Yogurt Cooler • Honey-Vanilla Refresher • Apple-Carrot Pick-Me-Up • Orange-Cantaloupe-Beet Juice • Garden Cocktail • Carrot Refresher

WARM DRINKS

Hot Pineapple Spice Drink • Grapefruit Warmer • Mulled Apple Warmer • Spicy Cranberry Warmer • Hot Lemonade • Hot Tomato Cocktail

COLD DRINKS

::

Thirst-quenching chilled drinks can be mixed and matched by combining fruit (blueberries, strawberries, raspberries, cantaloupe, watermelon, honeydew melon, peaches, pears, apricots, plums, pineapple, banana, or cherries) with a mixer (water, sparkling water, skim milk, fruit juices) and extras (crushed ice, honey, sugar, cinnamon, vanilla extract, lemon or lime juice, nonfat yogurt, or lowfat frozen yogurt).

✳ *Veggie Pick-Me-Up* ✳

YIELD: 8 servings (1 cup each) ▪ *PREPARATION TIME: 25 minutes plus ice cube freezing time*

This lively mixed-vegetable drink is served over tomato-juice ice cubes. Season with hot pepper sauce and garnish with a slice of lemon or lime.

48 ounces canned low-sodium vegetable juice such as V-8
1 cup chopped fresh or low-sodium canned tomatoes
2 tablespoons chopped celery
2 tablespoons chopped cucumber
2 tablespoons lemon juice
2 tablespoons lime juice

1 tablespoon chopped onion
2 tablespoons chopped green bell pepper
2 tablespoons chopped carrot
2 tablespoons chopped fresh parsley
1 teaspoon dried dill leaves
2 cloves garlic, minced

1. Pour 1½ cups of the vegetable juice cocktail into an ice cube tray and freeze.
2. When cubes are frozen solid, place the remaining vegetable juice, tomatoes, celery, cucumber, lemon juice, lime juice, onion, green pepper, carrot, parsley, dill, and garlic in a food processor or blender and purée.
3. Serve vegetables puréed over frozen cubes.

Veggie Pick-Me-Up *(cont'd)*

Calories Per Serving: 40	Carbohydrates: 10 g
Fat: .2 g	Dietary Fiber: 2.4 g
Cholesterol: 0 mg	Sodium: 23 mg
Protein: 1.7 g	

✳ *Fall Fruit Pick-Me-Up* ✳

YIELD: 3 servings (1 cup each) ▪ *PREPARATION TIME: 10 minutes*

This drink requires no blending and features the extra taste sensation of thinly sliced pear.

1¹/₂ cups pear nectar
2 cups unsweetened apple juice

1 pear, halved, cored, and thinly
sliced

1. Combine the pear nectar and the apple juice.
2. Stir in the sliced pear.
3. Pour the drink into ice filled glasses.

Calories Per Serving: 185	Carbohydrates: 47 g
Fat: .4 g	Dietary Fiber: 2.6 g
Cholesterol: 0 mg	Sodium: 9.5 mg
Protein: .4 g	

✳ *Apricot-Orange-Grapefruit Chiller* ✳

YIELD: 4 servings (1¹/₃ cups each) ▪ *PREPARATION TIME: 5 minutes*

This combination of fruit juices and seltzer is a sure way to quench your thirst at any time of the year. Keep a pitcher of this delectable drink in your refrigerator and pour over ice cubes when ready to serve.

16 ounces seltzer water, chilled
12 ounces canned apricot nectar,
chilled
¹/₂ cup unsweetened orange juice,
chilled

¹/₄ cup unsweetened grapefruit juice,
chilled
2 tablespoons lemon juice

1. Pour the seltzer water, apricot nectar, orange juice, grapefruit juice, and lemon juice into a large pitcher.
2. Stir until thoroughly combined.

Calories Per Serving: 75
Fat: .2 g
Cholesterol: 0 mg
Protein: .7 g

Carbohydrates: 18 g
Dietary Fiber: .8 g
Sodium: 3.8 mg

✳ *Blueberry Shake* ✳

YIELD: 2 servings (1¾ cups each) • *PREPARATION TIME: 10 minutes*

This quick and easy shake is calcium rich and instantly refreshing.

1½ cups fresh or thawed, frozen blueberries
⅓ cup instant nonfat dry milk
1 cup plain nonfat yogurt

¾ cup water
1 teaspoon honey
1 teaspoon vanilla extract

1. Place blueberries, dry milk, yogurt, water, honey, and vanilla in a blender and process until smooth.

Calories Per Serving: 183
Fat: .7 g
Cholesterol: 4 mg
Protein: 11 g

Carbohydrates: 33 g
Dietary Fiber: 2.5 g
Sodium: 155 mg

✳ *Apple Shake* ✳

YIELD: 2 servings (1 cup each) • *PREPARATION TIME: 10 minutes*

Fresh apple, apple juice, banana, and cinnamon join forces for a cooling treat.

1 cup apple juice
1 large apple, cored, peeled, and sliced

1 banana, peeled and sliced
¼ teaspoon ground cinnamon

Apple Shake *(cont'd)*

1. Place apple juice, apple, banana, and cinnamon in blender or food processor and process until smooth.

Calories Per Serving: 152
Fat: .7 g
Cholesterol: 0 mg
Protein: .8 g

Carbohydrates: 38 g
Dietary Fiber: 2.6 g
Sodium: 4.5 mg

✳ *Cantaloupe-Raspberry Fizz* ✳

YIELD: 5 servings (1¹/₂ cups each) • *PREPARATION TIME: 15 minutes*

Here ripe melon and berries are blended with apple juice.

3¹/₂ cups apple juice, chilled
1 cup cubed cantaloupe
1 cup raspberries or blueberries
1 large peach, plum, or nectarine,
   peeled, halved, pitted, and cut
   into chunks

1¹/₂ cups seltzer water, chilled

1. Place apple juice, cantaloupe, raspberries or blueberries, and peach, plum, or nectarine in a blender or food processor and purée.
2. Combine fruit purée with seltzer water.

Calories Per Serving: 112
Fat: .4 g
Cholesterol: 0 mg
Protein: .7 g

Carbohydrates: 27 g
Dietary Fiber: 1.9 g
Sodium: 7.7 mg

✳ *Mango Freeze* ✳

YIELD: 4 servings (1 cup each) • *PREPARATION TIME: 10 minutes plus 30 minutes*
freezing time

Ripe mangoes, bananas, and lime juice are united in this memorable drink. Buy mangoes when they are still firm and allow them to ripen at room temperature until they are soft to the touch. After they have ripened, chill them until ready to use.

1½ cups chopped ripe mangoes	*2 tablespoons lime juice*
1½ cups chopped bananas	*½ teaspoon vanilla extract*
1 cup pineapple juice	*8 ice cubes, cracked*

1. Place chopped mangoes and bananas in the freezer for 30 minutes.
2. Place frozen fruit in a blender or food processor with pineapple juice, lime juice, and vanilla. Purée.
3. Gradually add ice cubes, blending until thick and icy. Serve immediately.

Calories Per Serving: 112	Carbohydrates: 28 g
Fat: .4 g	Dietary Fiber: 1.9 g
Cholesterol: 0 mg	Sodium: 1.9 mg
Protein: .9 g	

✳ *Nectarine-Honey Refresher* ✳

YIELD: 4 servings (1¼ cups each) • *PREPARATION TIME: 10 minutes plus 4 hours freezing time*

Nectarines, honey, lemon juice, and vanilla create this yogurt-based drink. Try this method with other fruit combinations.

2½ cups plain nonfat yogurt	*2 tablespoons lemon juice*
3 medium ripe nectarines or peaches,	*¼ cup honey*
peeled, pitted, and cut into chunks	*¼ teaspoon vanilla extract*

1. Using two 8-section ice-cube trays, divide 2 cups of the yogurt among the 16 sections. Freeze for 4 hours.
2. Place the remaining ½ cup yogurt, nectarines or peaches, lemon juice, honey, and vanilla in a food processor or blender. Purée.
3. Add frozen yogurt cubes and process until smooth.

Calories Per Serving: 175	Carbohydrates: 35 g
Fat: .3 g	Dietary Fiber: 1 g
Cholesterol: 2.5 mg	Sodium: 110 mg
Protein: 8 g	

✷ *Orange-Banana Freeze* ✷

YIELD: 4 servings (1¹/₄ cups each) • *PREPARATION TIME: 10 minutes*

This nutritious shake makes a great refresher at the end of a busy day or an instant breakfast on a morning when you're running late.

2 sliced, ripe bananas
2 egg whites

1¹/₂ cups orange juice
1 cup nonfat vanilla frozen yogurt

1. Place bananas, egg whites, orange juice, and frozen yogurt in a blender or food processor. Process until smooth.

Calories Per Serving: 134
Fat: .6 g
Cholesterol: 1 mg
Protein: 6 g

Carbohydrates: 27 g
Dietary Fiber: 1.6 g
Sodium: 72 mg

✷ *Peach-Ginger-Grape Fizz* ✷

YIELD: 4 servings (1¹/₂ cups each) • *PREPARATION TIME: 15 minutes*

Here ripe peaches, fresh ginger, and white grape juice are blended with sparkling cold seltzer water.

1¹/₂ teaspoons grated fresh gingerroot
3 cups white grape juice, chilled
3 large peaches or nectarines, peeled, pitted, and cut into chunks

³/₄ cup seltzer water, chilled

1. Place ginger, 1¹/₂ cups of the grape juice, and peaches or nectarines in a blender or food processor and purée.
2. Combine the remaining grape juice, the blended peaches, and the seltzer.

Calories Per Serving: 145
Fat: .2 g
Cholesterol: 0 mg
Protein: 1.5 g

Carbohydrates: 35 g
Dietary Fiber: 1 g
Sodium: 5.3 mg

✳ *Orange-Papaya Drink* ✳

YIELD: 5 servings (1 cup each) • *PREPARATION TIME: 15 minutes*

Papaya and orange juice here are accented with the taste of lime.

3 cups unsweetened orange juice,
    chilled
1 ripe papaya, peeled, seeded, and
    cut into chunks

2 tablespoons lime juice
1¼ cups seltzer water, chilled

1. Combine the orange juice and papaya in a blender in batches and purée.
2. Combine the orange-papaya purée with the lime juice and seltzer.

Calories Per Serving: 74
Fat: .3 g
Cholesterol: 0 mg
Protein: 1 g

Carbohydrates: 17 g
Dietary Fiber: 1.3 g
Sodium: 1.6 mg

✳ *Peach-Banana Shake* ✳

YIELD: 4 servings (1¼ cups each) • *PREPARATION TIME: 10 minutes plus
overnight banana freezing time*

Juicy peaches, frozen bananas, and orange juice mingle happily in this cooling drink.

2 bananas, peeled, wrapped in a
    plastic bag, and frozen overnight
2 cups orange juice

2 ripe peaches or nectarines, peeled,
    pitted, and cut into chunks

1. Place frozen bananas, orange juice, and peaches in a blender or food processor and process until smooth.

Variation
- Substitute blueberries, blackberries, or strawberries for the peaches.
- Add 2 teaspoons honey.
- Substitute apple juice for the orange juice.

Peach–Banana Shake *(cont'd)*

Calories Per Serving: 127	Carbohydrates: 31 g
Fat: .6 g	Dietary Fiber: 2.5 g
Cholesterol: 0 mg	Sodium: 1.5 mg
Protein: 1.7 g	

✳ *Plum-Honey-Cinnamon Cooler* ✳

YIELD: 4 servings (1½ cups each) • *PREPARATION TIME: 15 minutes*

Here plums and apple juice are flavored with honey and cinnamon, then lightened with seltzer water.

3 cups apple juice, chilled	*2 tablespoons honey*
3 large plums, peeled, halved, pitted	*¼ teaspoon cinnamon*
and cut into chunks	*1 cup seltzer water, chilled*

1. Place apple juice, plums, honey, and cinnamon in a blender or food processor and purée.
2. Combine apple-plum purée with seltzer water.

Calories Per Serving: 135	Carbohydrates: 34 g
Fat: .2 g	Dietary Fiber: .8 g
Cholesterol: 0 mg	Sodium: 5.8 mg
Protein: .1 g	

✳ *Strawberry-Orange Freeze* ✳

YIELD: 6 servings (1 cup each) • *PREPARATION TIME: 10 minutes*

This icy confection combines strawberries and orange juice in a vanilla-flavored shake.

2½ cups sliced fresh or thawed,	*1 tablespoon sugar*
frozen strawberries	*1 teaspoon vanilla extract*
1 6-ounce can frozen orange juice	*2 egg whites*
concentrate	*2 cups crushed ice*
1½ cups skim milk	

1. Place strawberries, orange juice concentrate, skim milk, sugar, vanilla, egg whites, and crushed ice in a blender or food processor. Process until smooth.

Calories Per Serving: 112
Fat: .4 g
Cholesterol: 1 mg
Protein: 4 g

Carbohydrates: 23 g
Dietary Fiber: 1.8 g
Sodium: 52 mg

❉ *Tomato Zinger* ❉

YIELD: 4 servings (1 cup each) • *PREPARATION TIME: 5 minutes*

Tomato juice is given a new personality with the addition of horseradish and Tabasco sauce.

4 cups tomato juice
2 teaspoons prepared horseradish

$1/4$ teaspoon Tabasco sauce
Lemon slices

1. Combine tomato juice, horseradish, and Tabasco sauce.
2. Pour into glasses with ice.
3. Garnish with lemon slices.

Calories Per Serving: 44
Fat: .1 g
Cholesterol: 0 mg
Protein: 1.9 g

Carbohydrates: 10 g
Dietary Fiber: 2.8 g
Sodium: 53 mg

❉ *Watermelon-Banana Shake* ❉

YIELD: 4 servings (1 cup each) • *PREPARATION TIME: 15 minutes plus overnight banana freezing time*

Ripe watermelon, frozen bananas, and apple juice are the trio featured in this shake.

2 bananas, peeled, placed in a plastic bag, and frozen overnight

2 cups seeded watermelon
1 cup apple juice

Watermelon-Banana Shake *(cont'd)*

1. Place bananas, watermelon, and apple juice in a blender or food processor and process until smooth.

Calories Per Serving: 107   Carbohydrates: 26 g
Fat: .7 g   Dietary Fiber: 1.3 g
Cholesterol: 0 mg   Sodium: 3.7 mg
Protein: 1 g

✳ *Generic Cooler* ✳

YIELD: 4 servings (1½ cups each) • PREPARATION TIME: 10 minutes plus freezing time

Use the fruit juice and fruit of your choice in this refreshing recipe.

1 cup fresh or frozen fruit   *2 cups seltzer water*
3 cups fruit juice

1. Place fruit in blender or food processor and purée.
2. Combine fruit and fruit juice. Place in freezer and freeze until the mixture just begins to become firm.
3. Combine frozen fruit mixture with mineral water and serve over ice cubes.

Calories Per Serving: 102   Carbohydrates: 24 g
Fat: .4 g   Dietary Fiber: 2 g
Cholesterol: 0 mg   Sodium: 3.2 mg
Protein: 1.6 g

✳ *Lime-Yogurt Cooler* ✳

YIELD: 4 servings (1¼ cups each) • PREPARATION TIME: 10 minutes

Since this drink is similar to a lassi, a beverage often served with Indian dishes, it works well when served with curried foods.

½ cup honey   *½ cup lime juice*
1 cup nonfat plain yogurt   *3 cups sparkling mineral water*

1. Combine honey, yogurt, and lime juice.
2. Combine yogurt mixture with mineral water.
3. Pour into blender in several batches and blend until well combined.

Calories Per Serving: 170
Fat: .1 g
Cholesterol: 1 mg
Protein: 3 g

Carbohydrates: 41 g
Dietary Fiber: .1 g
Sodium: 48 gm

✻ *Honey-Vanilla Refresher* ✻

YIELD: 2 servings (1 cup each) ▪ *PREPARATION TIME: 5 minutes*

If you have trouble getting used to the taste of skim milk, try flavoring it with honey and vanilla.

2 cups skim milk
1 teaspoon vanilla extract

2 teaspoons honey

1. Pour the skim milk into two glasses.
2. Add ½ teaspoon vanilla and 1 teaspoon of honey to each and stir well.

Calories Per Serving: 115
Fat: .4 g
Cholesterol: 4 mg
Protein: 8 g

Carbohydrates: 18 g
Dietary Fiber: 0 g
Sodium: 126 mg

✻ *Apple-Carrot Pick-Me-Up* ✻

YIELD: 2 servings ▪ *PREPARATION TIME: 10 minutes*

This juicer recipe is a blend of apples and beta carotene–rich carrots.

2 large apples, cut into chunks
3 medium carrots, trimmed and cut
  into chunks

1. Process apples and carrots in a juicer according to manufacturer's instructions.

Apple-Carrot Pick-Me-Up *(cont'd)*

Calories Per Serving: 128
Fat: .7 g
Cholesterol: 0 mg
Protein: 1.3 g

Carbohydrates: 32 g
Dietary Fiber: 2 g
Sodium: 38 mg

✳ Orange-Cantaloupe-Beet Juice ✳

YIELD: 2 servings • PREPARATION TIME: 15 minutes

This juice features a splendid combination of sunset colors.

2 navel oranges, peeled
1 cup cantaloupe chunks

1 beet, trimmed and cut into chunks

1. Process oranges, cantaloupe, and beets in a juicer according to manufacturer's instructions.

Calories Per Serving: 98
Fat: .4 g
Cholesterol: 0 mg
Protein: 2 g

Carbohydrates: 23 g
Dietary Fiber: 1.5 g
Sodium: 19 mg

✳ Garden Cocktail ✳

YIELD: 2 servings • PREPARATION TIME: 15 minutes

Six vitamin-packed vegetables are blended in this powerhouse drink.

1½ cups coarsely chopped cabbage
2 medium tomatoes, quartered
2 stalks celery, halved
1 red bell pepper, quartered and
  seeded

1 large carrot, cut into chunks
1 cucumber, cut into chunks

1. Process cabbage, tomatoes, celery, red pepper, carrot, and cucumber in a juicer according to manufacturer's instructions.

Calories Per Serving: 86
Fat: .8 g
Cholesterol: 0 mg
Protein: 3.4 g

Carbohydrates: 19 g
Dietary Fiber: 2 g
Sodium: 70 mg

✳ *Carrot Refresher* ✳

YIELD: *2 servings* ▪ PREPARATION TIME: *10 minutes*

Carrots and parsley are combined in this simple, nutritious drink.

1 bunch fresh parsley
8 carrots, trimmed and cut into large
  chunks

1. Process parsley and carrots in juicer according to manufacturer's instructions.

   Calories Per Serving: 143
   Fat: .7 g
   Cholesterol: 0 mg
   Protein: 4 g

   Carbohydrates: 33 g
   Dietary Fiber: 4 g
   Sodium: 126 mg

WARM DRINKS

::

These hot fruit and vegetable drinks are sure to provide comforting warmth on a blustery day.

✳ Hot Pineapple Spice Drink ✳

YIELD: 6 servings (1 cup each) • *PREPARATION TIME: 5 minutes* •
COOKING TIME: 20 minutes

This appealing beverage is a good nonalcoholic winter party drink.

*48 ounces unsweetened pineapple
    juice*
1 2-inch cinnamon stick

Pinch of ground nutmeg
Pinch of ground allspice
Pinch of ground cloves

1. Combine pineapple juice, cinnamon stick, nutmeg, allspice, and cloves in a nonreactive saucepan. Bring to a boil over medium heat.
2. Reduce heat and simmer for 15 minutes.
3. Strain before serving.

Calories Per Serving: 140
Fat: .2 g
Cholesterol: 0 mg
Protein: .8 g

Carbohydrates: 34 g
Dietary Fiber: .2 g
Sodium: 2 mg

✳ Grapefruit Warmer ✳

YIELD: 4 servings (1 cup each) • *PREPARATION TIME: 5 minutes* •
COOKING TIME: 5 minutes

Pink grapefruit juice is spiced here with cloves, cinnamon, and nutmeg.

4 cups pink grapefruit juice
¼ teaspoon ground cloves

½ teaspoon ground cinnamon
Pinch of ground nutmeg

1. Place grapefruit juice, cloves, cinnamon, and nutmeg in a saucepan. Warm over very low heat for 5 minutes.

Calories Per Serving: 98   Carbohydrates: 23 g
Fat: .3 g   Dietary Fiber: .5 g
Cholesterol: 0 mg   Sodium: 2.4 mg
Protein: 1.2 g

✳ *Mulled Apple Warmer* ✳

YIELD: 4 servings (³/₄ cup each) • *PREPARATION TIME: 10 minutes plus 45 minutes standing time* • *COOKING TIME: 5 minutes*

Apple juice and spices are combined with brown sugar and diced apple in this recipe.

3 cups apple juice   *1 teaspoon brown sugar, firmly*
¹/₂ teaspoon ground cloves   *packed*
¹/₂ teaspoon ground cinnamon   *¹/₂ apple, cored and diced*
¹/₄ teaspoon ground allspice

1. Combine apple juice, cloves, cinnamon, allspice, and brown sugar in a saucepan. Cook over low heat for 5 minutes. Let stand for 45 minutes.
2. Reheat until warmed through. Stir in apple immediately before serving.

Calories Per Serving: 103   Carbohydrates: 25 g
Fat: .3 g   Dietary Fiber: .7 g
Cholesterol: 0 mg   Sodium: 6.5 mg
Protein: .2 g

✳ *Spicy Cranberry Warmer* ✳

YIELD: 6 servings (1¹/₄ cups each) • *PREPARATION TIME: 10 minutes* • *COOKING TIME: 10 minutes*

Cranberry juice, apple juice, and orange juice are accented here with cinnamon and cloves.

Spicy Cranberry Warmer *(cont'd)*

2 cups cranberry juice

2 cups apple juice

1/2 cup orange juice

3 cups water

2 tablespoons sugar

1 teaspoon ground cinnamon

1 teaspoon ground cloves

1. Place cranberry juice, apple juice, orange juice, water, sugar, cinnamon, and cloves in a saucepan. Cook over low heat until warmed through.

Calories Per Serving: 114

Fat: .3 g

Cholesterol: 0 mg

Protein: .3 g

Carbohydrates: 28 g

Dietary Fiber: .3 g

Sodium: 6.7 mg

✳ *Hot Lemonade* ✳

YIELD: *4 servings (1 cup each)* • PREPARATION TIME: *10 minutes plus 15 minutes standing time* • COOKING TIME: *10 to 12 minutes*

A summer treat becomes a winter delight when lemonade is simmered with cloves, allspice, and cinnamon.

3 1/4 cups water

3/4 cup lemon juice

1/2 cup brown sugar, firmly packed

8 whole cloves

6 whole allspice

2 whole cinnamon sticks

1. Combine the water, lemon juice, brown sugar, cloves, allspice, and cinnamon sticks in a saucepan and cook over light heat until warmed through.
2. Allow to stand for 15 minutes. Remove cloves, allspice, and cinnamon.
3. Cook over low heat again until hot.

Calories Per Serving: 114

Fat: 0 g

Cholesterol: 0 mg

Protein: .2 g

Carbohydrates: 30 g

Dietary Fiber: .2 g

Sodium: 8.8 mg

✳ *Hot Tomato Cocktail* ✳

YIELD: 6 servings (1 cup each) ▪ *PREPARATION TIME: 10 minutes* ▪
COOKING TIME: 10 minutes

Serve this warming drink with meals or as a snack on a chilly evening.

6 cups tomato juice
¹/₄ cup lemon juice
¹/₂ teaspoon sugar
Pinch of cayenne pepper

¹/₄ teaspoon minced garlic or
garlic powder
¹/₄ teaspoon black pepper
¹/₂ teaspoon hot chili sauce (optional)

1. Combine tomato juice, lemon juice, sugar, cayenne pepper, garlic, black pepper, and chili sauce in saucepan. Cook, stirring, over low heat until warmed through.

Calories Per Serving: 47
Fat: .2 g
Cholesterol: 0 mg
Protein: 1.9 g

Carbohydrates: 11 g
Dietary Fiber: 2.8 g
Sodium: 30 mg

DESSERTS

Maple-Lemon-Pear Cake • Apricot Upside Down Cake • Cocoa Cake • Cranapple Cake • Orange-Strawberry Cake • Carrot Cake • Gingerbread • Angel Food Cake with Sliced Peaches and Strawberry Sauce • Guilt-Free Pumpkin Pie • Blueberry-Yogurt Pie • Blueberry-Peach Cobbler • Applesauce-Cocoa Squares • Strawberry Cheesecake with Chocolate Cookie Crust • Banana-Raisin Brownies • Applesauce-Oatmeal Cookies • Pear Burritos • Mixed Berries with Whipped Topping • Meringues with Raspberries and Frozen Yogurt • Strawberry-Banana Cream • Chocolate Pudding • Blueberry Delight • Fruit Cup with Mango Sauce • Yogurt Fruit Parfait • Amaretto Fruit Delight • Fruit Mélange in Red Wine • Grapefruit with Raspberry Sauce • Cranberry Dessert • Instant Fruit Freeze • Apple-Orangesicles • Fruit Salad with Strawberry Dressing • Orange-Pineapple Freeze • Raspberry Sherbet • Nonfat Dessert Topping I • Nonfat Dessert Topping II • Blueberry-Buttermilk Ice Cream • Maple-Blueberry Topping • Spiced Creamy Topping • Maple Whipped Dessert Topping • Frozen Berry Topping • Sweet Whipped Topping

DESSERTS

::

✳ Maple-Lemon-Pear Cake ✳

YIELD: 12 servings • PREPARATION TIME: 25 minutes •
COOKING TIME: 35 minutes

This simple cake is as much at home on the breakfast table as it is at dessert time. Serve it at snack time with Spicy Cranberry Warmer (page 335).

1½ cups cake flour
1 cup sugar
1 teaspoon baking soda
1½ teaspoons cinnamon
1 teaspoon grated lemon peel
1½ cups plain nonfat yogurt

1 tablespoon arrowroot dissolved in
   ¼ cup skim milk
1 large pear, peeled, cored, and
   chopped
1 teaspoon vanilla extract
2 teaspoons maple extract

1. Preheat oven to 350 degrees. Use a 9-by-13-inch nonstick baking pan or line a baking pan with a baking pan liner or lightly spray with vegetable cooking spray.
2. Sift flour, sugar, baking soda, and cinnamon into a large mixing bowl.
3. Stir in lemon peel, yogurt, skim milk with arrowroot, pear, vanilla, and maple extract until well combined.
4. Transfer cake batter to baking pan. Bake for 35 minutes or until a wooden pick inserted in center of the cake comes out clean. Cut into 12 pieces.

Calories Per Serving: 140
Fat: .2 g
Cholesterol: .6 mg
Protein: 2 g

Carbohydrates: 32 g
Dietary Fiber: .7 g
Sodium: 93 mg

✳ Apricot Upside Down Cake ✳

YIELD: 8 servings ▪ *PREPARATION TIME: 15 minutes* ▪
COOKING TIME: 35 minutes

This traditional cake is good for dessert and can also do an encore at the breakfast table. Serve it after a dinner of Potato-Tomato Curry (page 128).

¼ cup brown sugar, firmly packed
1 cup juice-packed apricots, drained and chopped, juice reserved
1½ cups unbleached all-purpose flour

2 tablespoons baking powder
½ cup applesauce
½ cup sugar
3 egg whites, lightly beaten

1. Preheat oven to 400 degrees. Line an 8-inch-square pan with a baking pan liner or spray lightly with vegetable cooking spray.
2. Sprinkle brown sugar on bottom of pan.
3. Top with a layer of chopped apricots.
4. Combine flour and baking powder in a mixing bowl.
5. In another bowl, combine applesauce, sugar, reserved juice from apricots, and egg whites.
6. Stir wet ingredients into dry ingredients until dry ingredients are just moist.
7. Pour cake batter over apricots. Bake for 35 minutes or until a wooden pick inserted in center of cake comes out clean.
8. Remove cake from oven and cool for 10 minutes.
9. Turn cake pan upside down and release cake over plate. Slice into 8 squares.

Calories Per Serving: 187
Fat: .2 g
Cholesterol: 0 mg
Protein: 3.9 g

Carbohydrates: 42 g
Dietary Fiber: 1.2 g
Sodium: 271 mg

✳ *Cocoa Cake* ✳

YIELD: *9 servings* • PREPARATION TIME: *20 minutes* •
COOKING TIME: *30 minutes*

Prune purée is the secret ingredient in this chocolate-flavored dessert.
Serve after a dinner of Vegetable Risotto (page 139).

²/₃ *cup pitted prunes*	³/₄ *cup sugar*
1 cup plus 3 tablespoons water	³/₄ *cup unsweetened cocoa*
3 egg whites	*1¹/₂ teaspoons baking powder*
1 teaspoon vanilla extract	¹/₄ *teaspoon baking soda*
1 teaspoon chocolate extract	¹/₄ *teaspoon salt (optional)*
1 cup plus 2 tablespoons cake flour	

1. Preheat oven to 350 degrees. Use a nonstick 9-inch-square baking pan
   or line a baking pan with a baking pan liner or lightly spray with
   vegetable cooking spray.
2. Place prunes and 3 tablespoons of the water in a blender or food
   processor and purée.
3. Place prune purée, remaining 1 cup water, egg whites, vanilla, chocolate extract, cake flour, and sugar in the bowl of an electric mixer and
   mix at medium speed until combined, scraping sides and bottom of
   bowl.
4. Add cocoa, baking powder, baking soda, and salt, if using. Complete
   mixing.
5. Transfer batter to cake pan. Bake for 30 minutes or until a wooden
   pick inserted in the center of the cake comes out clean.
6. Cool on rack. Slice into 9 squares.

Variation
- Place a paper doily on the cake and sprinkle confectioners' sugar over
  it. Lift doily off the cake, leaving a lacy design.

Calories Per Serving: 165	Carbohydrates: 34 g
Fat: .9 g	Dietary Fiber: .8 g
Cholesterol: 0 mg	Sodium: 105 mg
Protein: 4 g	

❋ *Cranapple Cake* ❋

YIELD: *10 servings* ▪ PREPARATION TIME: *25 minutes* ▪
COOKING TIME: *30 minutes*

This cake makes a great fall dessert when apples are at their best and fresh
cranberries are in season. Serve with Lentil-Vegetable Stew (page 125).

¼ cup brown sugar, firmly packed	½ cup sugar
1 cup fresh or frozen cranberries	2 teaspoons baking powder
½ cup water	2 egg whites
1 teaspoon ground cinnamon	2 tablespoons skim milk
1 cup dried apple	½ cup applesauce
1½ cups all-purpose unbleached flour	1 teaspoon grated lemon peel

1. Place brown sugar, cranberries, water, and cinnamon in a small sauce-pan. Bring to a boil over medium heat for 3 minutes until the cranberries are tender. Stir apple into cranberries. Set aside to cool.
2. Preheat oven to 400 degrees. Use a nonstick 9-inch-square baking pan or line a baking pan with a baking pan liner or spray with vegetable cooking spray.
3. Combine flour, sugar, and baking powder in a mixing bowl.
4. In a separate bowl, combine egg whites, skim milk, applesauce, and lemon peel.
5. Add egg white mixture to dry ingredients. Stir until dry ingredients are just moistened.
6. Transfer cake batter to baking pan.
7. Spoon cranberry-apple mixture over top of batter.
8. Bake for 30 minutes.
9. Cool on wire rack. Cut into 10 slices.

Calories Per Serving: 152	Carbohydrates: 35 g
Fat: .3 g	Dietary Fiber: 1 g
Cholesterol: 0 mg	Sodium: 82 mg
Protein: 2 g	

✳ *Orange-Strawberry Cake* ✳

YIELD: *8 servings* • PREPARATION TIME: *15 minutes* •
COOKING TIME: *45 minutes*

Here fresh or frozen strawberries are simmered in orange juice and used as a topping for a moist cake. Serve warm with Nonfat Dessert Topping I or II (page 367).

³/₄ cup brown sugar, firmly packed	1 cup all-purpose unbleached flour
1¹/₂ cups fresh or thawed, frozen strawberries	1¹/₂ teaspoons baking powder
2 teaspoons grated orange rind	¹/₄ teaspoon salt (optional)
1³/₄ cups orange juice	¹/₂ cup skim milk
	1 teaspoon vanilla extract

1. Preheat oven to 350 degrees. Line a 2-quart casserole with a baking pan liner or lightly spray with vegetable cooking spray.
2. Place ¹/₄ cup of the brown sugar, strawberries, orange rind, and orange juice in a saucepan. Bring to a boil. Simmer for 5 minutes.
3. Combine the remaining ¹/₂ cup brown sugar, flour, baking powder, and salt, if using, in a bowl.
4. Add milk and vanilla to sugar-flour mixture. Stir until dry ingredients are just moist.
5. Transfer batter to casserole. Pour strawberry mixture over cake batter.
6. Bake for 40 minutes or until lightly browned. Cut into 8 slices.

Calories Per Serving: 170	Carbohydrates: 39 g
Fat: .4 g	Dietary Fiber: 1 g
Cholesterol: .3 mg	Sodium: 76 mg
Protein: 2 g	

✳ *Carrot Cake* ✳

YIELD: *12 servings* • PREPARATION TIME: *20 minutes* •
COOKING TIME: *45 minutes*

Fat-free carrot cake can be made with prune purée. Serve with Steamed Vegetables with Garlic-Lemon Sauce (page 138).

Carrot Cake *(cont'd)*

1¹/₃ cups pitted prunes
6 tablespoons water
4 cups grated carrots
1 cup brown sugar, firmly packed
1 cup sugar

1 cup juice-packed crushed pineapple
4 egg whites, lightly beaten
2 cups cake flour
2 teaspoons baking soda
1 teaspoon ground cinnamon

1. Preheat oven to 375 degrees. Use a nonstick 9-by-13-inch baking pan or line a baking pan with a baking pan liner or lightly spray with vegetable cooking spray.
2. Place prunes and water in a blender or food processor and purée.
3. Combine prune purée, carrots, brown sugar, sugar, pineapple, and egg whites in a mixing bowl.
4. Combine cake flour, baking soda, and cinnamon in a separate bowl.
5. Add wet ingredients to dry ingredients and stir until well combined.
6. Transfer batter to baking pan. Bake for 45 minutes or until a wooden pick inserted in center of cake comes out clean.
7. Cool on a wire rack. Slice into 12 pieces.

Variation
▪ Mix confectioners' sugar with orange juice for a butterless frosting.

Calories Per Serving: 248
Fat: .3 g
Cholesterol: 0 mg
Protein: 3 g

Carbohydrates: 60 g
Dietary Fiber: 2.5 g
Sodium: 175

✻ *Gingerbread* ✻

YIELD: 8 servings ▪ *PREPARATION TIME: 15 minutes* ▪
COOKING TIME: 30 minutes

Serve this fragrant gingerbread warm from the oven topped with Chunky Spiced Applesauce (page 206).

1¹/₄ cups unbleached all-purpose
*   flour*
1 teaspoon baking powder
1 teaspoon ground cinnamon
1 teaspoon ground ginger

¹/₄ teaspoon ground cloves
¹/₄ teaspoon salt
¹/₄ cup prune purée (see page 23),
*   applesauce, or mashed banana*
¹/₄ cup brown sugar, firmly packed

³/₄ teaspoon baking soda
¹/₂ cup molasses
³/₄ cup boiling water

2 egg whites, lightly beaten
³/₄ cups raisins

1. Preheat oven to 325 degrees. Line the bottom of an 8-inch-square baking pan with a baking pan liner or lightly spray with vegetable cooking spray. Sprinkle with flour.
2. Sift flour, baking powder, cinnamon, ginger, cloves, and salt together in a mixing bowl.
3. Combine prune purée, applesauce, or mashed banana and sugar in a separate bowl. Stir in ¹/₂ teaspoon of the baking soda and molasses.
4. Add the remaining ¹/₄ teaspoon baking soda to the boiling water.
5. Alternate adding the prune purée mixture and the boiling water to the flour mixture, stirring to combine.
6. Add the egg whites and raisins.
7. Transfer cake batter to the baking pan. Bake for 30 minutes or until a wooden pick inserted in center of the cake comes out clean.
8. Remove from pan and cool on wire rack. Cut into 8 squares.

Calories Per Serving: 142
Fat: .2 g
Cholesterol: 0 mg
Protein: 2 gm

Carbohydrates: 32 g
Dietary Fiber: .4 g
Sodium: 92 mg

Angel Food Cake with Sliced Peaches and ❋ *Strawberry Sauce* ❋

YIELD: 12 servings • *PREPARATION TIME: 20 minutes* •
COOKING TIME: 45 minutes

Angel food cake is a heavenly surprise for anyone who is trying to cut back on fat. It's a sinfully good dessert with only a trace of fat in its vital statistics. It's made without egg yolks, oil, or shortening. You can bake angel food cake from scratch from the following recipe, make it from one of the several excellent mixes on the market, or find it commercially baked.

CAKE

12 egg whites (should be 1³/₄ cups)
1¹/₂ teaspoons cream of tartar

¹/₄ teaspoon salt
1¹/₂ cups twice-sifted superfine sugar

Angel Food Cake *(cont'd)*

1¼ cups sifted cake flour
2 teaspoons vanilla

1 teaspoon fresh lemon juice
½ teaspoon almond extract

S A U C E

2½ cups fresh or thawed, frozen
strawberries
1 teaspoon lemon juice
2 tablespoons granulated sugar

4 peaches, peeled, pitted, and sliced
or 8 juice-packed canned peach
halves, drained and sliced

1. For the cake, preheat oven to 350 degrees.
2. Place egg whites in a large mixing bowl and whip until foamy. Add cream of tartar and salt. Beat until egg whites begin to form soft peaks. They should be stiff but not dry.
3. Turn mixer to lowest speed. Add sugar 1 tablespoon at a time.
4. With mixer still at lowest speed, add flour 1 tablespoon at a time. Fold in vanilla, lemon juice, and almond extract with a rubber scraper.
5. Transfer the batter with a spatula to a 10-inch ungreased nonstick angel food cake pan. The pan should have a central tube to support the batter since it is very light. Move the spatula gently through the batter to break up air pockets.
6. Place the pan on bottom rack of oven and bake for 45 minutes or until the cake is lightly golden and the top feels dry. Test by pressing lightly in the center. If the cake springs back, it is done. If not, continue baking, checking at 5 minute intervals.
7. Remove the pan from the oven, invert it, and let it cool for 1½ hours. It should be raised from the countertop at least 1 inch. If your angel food cake pan doesn't have a high center tube for this purpose, rest the pan upside down on an inverted funnel or thin bottle neck. After cooling, remove cake from pan by loosening the sides with a spatula.
8. For the sauce, place strawberries, lemon juice, and sugar in a blender or food processor and purée.
9. To serve cake, pierce with a fork at intervals to indicate 12 portions. Pull apart with two forks to avoid mashing the cake.
10. Serve slices of angel food cake topped with peaches and strawberry sauce.

Note: It is important not to let the cake ingredients come into contact with any fat, or they will not rise.

Variations

- Delete peaches and strawberry sauce. Sift 1 teaspoon cinnamon, ½ teaspoon nutmeg, and ¼ teaspoon cloves with the flour. Glaze finished cake with an orange glaze made of 1 cup sifted confectioners' sugar, 2 tablespoons chilled orange juice, and 1 tablespoon grated orange peel, stirred until smooth.
- Delete peaches and strawberry sauce. Sift ⅓ cup unsweetened cocoa powder with the flour before adding to the batter. Glaze finished cake with a glaze made from 1 cup sifted confectioners' sugar, 2 tablespoons cold skim milk, and 1 teaspoon unsweetened cocoa powder, stirred until smooth.
- Delete peaches and strawberry sauce. Sift ⅓ cup unsweetened cocoa powder and 2 teaspoons powdered instant coffee with the flour before adding to the batter.

Calories Per Serving: 138
Fat: .2 g
Cholesterol: 0 mg
Protein: 4 g
Carbohydrates: 29 g
Dietary Fiber: 1 g
Sodium: 100 mg

✳ *Guilt-Free Pumpkin Pie* ✳

YIELD: *8 servings* • PREPARATION TIME: *25 minutes plus crust cooling time* • COOKING TIME: *1 hour and 10 minutes*

This pumpkin pie is made with evaporated skim milk, egg whites, and a graham cracker crust. Serve with Maple Whipped Dessert Topping (page 370).

1½ cups nonfat graham cracker crumbs
2 tablespoons honey
1 tablespoon applesauce, mashed banana, or prune purée (see p. 23)
2 cups canned pumpkin purée

1½ cups evaporated skim milk
½ cup brown sugar, firmly packed
1 teaspoon ground cinnamon
½ teaspoon ground ginger
¼ teaspoon ground nutmeg
Pinch of ground cloves
3 egg whites

1. Preheat oven to 350 degrees.
2. Combine graham cracker crumbs, honey, and applesauce, mashed banana, or prune purée. Pat into a 9-inch pie pan.

Guilt-Free Pumpkin Pie *(cont'd)*

3. Bake for 10 minutes. Set aside to cool.
4. When crust is cool, mix pumpkin, milk, sugar, cinnamon, ginger, nutmeg, cloves, and egg whites in a bowl.
5. Transfer pie filling to crumb crust. Bake for 1 hour at 350 degrees or until a wooden pick inserted in center of the pie comes out clean. Cut into 8 pieces.

Calories Per Serving: 157
Fat: .2 g
Cholesterol: 2 mg
Protein: 6 g

Carbohydrates: 34 g
Dietary Fiber: 0 g
Sodium: 112 mg

✳ *Blueberry-Yogurt Pie* ✳

YIELD: 10 servings • PREPARATION TIME: 25 minutes plus crust cooling time and 2 hours chilling time • COOKING TIME: 10 minutes

Blueberries and a honey-flavored yogurt topping are chilled in a graham cracker crust. Serve with Couscous and Vegetables (page 119).

1½ cups nonfat graham cracker crumbs
6 tablespoons honey
1 tablespoon applesauce, mashed banana, or prune purée (see p. 23)
1⅓ cups plain nonfat yogurt
1½ cups nonfat cottage cheese, drained

1 teaspoon vanilla extract
½ teaspoon lemon juice
1 envelope unflavored gelatin
⅓ cup cold water
3 cups fresh or thawed, frozen blueberries

1. Preheat oven to 350 degrees.
2. Combine graham cracker crumbs, 2 tablespoons of the honey, and applesauce, mashed banana, or prune purée. Pat into a 9-inch pie pan.
3. Bake for 10 minutes. Set aside to cool.
4. When crust is cool, place yogurt, cottage cheese, the remaining 4 tablespoons honey, vanilla, and lemon juice in a blender or food processor and process until smooth.
5. Place gelatin and water in a small saucepan over low heat. Cook and stir until gelatin dissolves.

6. Add dissolved gelatin to blender and blend until well combined with yogurt mixture.
7. Place blueberries in bottom of graham cracker pie crust.
8. Pour yogurt mixture over berries.
9. Refrigerate for 2 hours or until set. Slice into 10 pieces.

Calories Per Serving: 197   Carbohydrates: 50 g
Fat: .5 g   Dietary Fiber: 2.9 g
Cholesterol: .4 mg   Sodium: 59 mg
Protein: 2 g

❋ *Blueberry-Peach Cobbler* ❋

YIELD: 6 servings ▪ *PREPARATION TIME: 20 minutes* ▪
COOKING TIME: 26 minutes

Fresh or frozen blueberries are mixed with canned peaches in this warming cobbler. Try substituting other fruit of your choice. Serve with Bow Ties with Eggplant Sauce (page 143).

3 tablespoons brown sugar, firmly packed
1 tablespoon cornstarch
³/₄ cup orange juice
2 cups fresh or frozen blueberries
2 cups juice-packed canned peach halves, drained and chopped

³/₄ cup unbleached all-purpose flour
1 tablespoon sugar
1 teaspoon baking powder
¹/₃ cup skim milk

1. Preheat oven to 400 degrees. Use a nonstick 8-inch-square baking pan or line a baking pan with a baking pan liner or spray lightly with vegetable cooking spray.
2. Combine brown sugar, cornstarch, and orange juice in a saucepan. Bring to a boil and cook, stirring for 1 minute.
3. Stir in blueberries and peaches. Transfer mixture to baking dish.
4. Combine flour, sugar, and baking powder in a bowl.
5. Add milk and stir until ingredients are just moistened.
6. Drop the flour mixture on the blueberries and peaches by the tablespoonful.

Blueberry-Peach Cobbler *(cont'd)*

7. Bake for 20 minutes or until cobbler topping turns golden. Slice into 6 squares.

Calories Per Serving: 161   Carbohydrates: 37 g
Fat: .5 g   Dietary Fiber: 2 g
Cholesterol: .2 mg   Sodium: 70 mg
Protein: 3 g

✳ *Applesauce-Cocoa Squares* ✳

YIELD: 16 servings • *PREPARATION TIME: 20 minutes* •
COOKING TIME: 40 minutes

These squares are rich in chocolate flavor. Store them tightly wrapped in the refrigerator and pack them for lunch with Vegetable-Cheese Bagels (page 57).

1 cup unbleached all-purpose flour   *¼ cup applesauce*
¾ cup sugar   *1 teaspoon vanilla extract*
½ cup unsweetened cocoa   *¾ cup brown sugar, firmly packed*
2 teaspoons baking powder   *1¾ cups hot water*
½ cup skim milk

1. Preheat oven to 350 degrees. Line an 8-inch-square baking pan with a baking pan liner or spray lightly with vegetable cooking spray.
2. Combine flour, sugar, ¼ cup of the cocoa, and baking powder in a mixing bowl.
3. Combine milk, applesauce, and vanilla in a separate bowl.
4. Stir wet ingredients into dry ingredients.
5. Spoon batter into pan.
6. Combine brown sugar, remaining ¼ cup cocoa, and water.
7. Pour over batter.
8. Bake for 40 minutes.
9. Remove from oven and cool in pan.
10. Cut into 16 squares.

Calories Per Serving: 134   Carbohydrates: 28 g
Fat: .8 g   Dietary Fiber: .3 g
Cholesterol: .1 mg   Sodium: 55 mg
Protein: 3 g

Strawberry Cheesecake with Chocolate ✳ *Cookie Crust* ✳

YIELD: 10 servings • PREPARATION TIME: 25 minutes plus 24 hours yogurt draining time and 2 hours chilling time • COOKING TIME: 1 hour and 10 minutes

Yogurt, honey, and egg whites are baked in a crumb crust, then topped with strawberry preserves and fresh strawberries. Serve with Havana Beans with Rice (page 160).

8 cups nonfat plain yogurt
1½ cups nonfat chocolate cookies
1 cup honey
2 teaspoons vanilla extract
4 tablespoons arrowroot

5 egg whites
¼ cup all-fruit strawberry preserves
1 cup sliced fresh or frozen strawberries

1. Line a large strainer with coffee filters or several layers of clean, dry cheesecloth.
2. Spoon in yogurt and place over large bowl.
3. Refrigerate for 24 hours. Discard liquid in bowl.
4. Preheat oven to 300 degrees.
5. Place cookies in a blender or food processor and grind crumbs until very fine. Moisten crumbs slightly and press over the bottom of a 10-inch springform pan.
6. Beat together drained yogurt, honey, vanilla, arrowroot, and egg whites in an electric mixer until well combined.
7. Pour yogurt-honey mixture over crumbs in springform pan.
8. Bake for 1 hour and 10 minutes or until center of cake is set.
9. Remove cake from oven and let stand until it reaches room temperature. Spoon strawberry preserves on top of cake. Arrange strawberries on top of preserves.
10. Chill for 2 hours before serving. Cut into 10 pieces.

Calories Per Serving: 297
Fat: .4 g
Cholesterol: 3.2 mg
Protein: 12 g

Carbohydrates: 59 g
Dietary Fiber: .5 g
Sodium: 244 mg

✳ *Banana-Raisin Brownies* ✳

YIELD: 12 servings • *PREPARATION TIME: 25 minutes* •
COOKING TIME: 35 minutes

The fat usually found in brownies is replaced here with puréed banana.
Serve with Potato-Broccoli Chili (page 154).

1 banana	*¹/₄ cup unsweetened cocoa*
¹/₄ cup orange juice	*1 teaspoon baking powder*
1¹/₂ teaspoons vanilla extract	*¹/₄ teaspoon salt (optional)*
1 cup sugar	*4 egg whites, beaten until frothy*
¹/₂ cup cake flour	*¹/₂ cup raisins*

1. Preheat oven to 350 degrees. Use a nonstick 8-inch-square baking pan, or line baking pan with a baking pan liner or spray with vegetable cooking spray.
2. Place banana, orange juice, and vanilla extract in blender or food processor. Purée.
3. Sift sugar, flour, cocoa, baking powder, and salt, if using, into a mixing bowl.
4. Stir in banana purée, egg whites, and raisins.
5. Transfer batter to baking pan. Bake for 35 minutes.
6. Cool on wire rack. Cut into 12 squares.

Calories Per Serving: 122	Carbohydrates: 28 g
Fat: .4 g	Dietary Fiber: .6 g
Cholesterol: 0 mg	Sodium: 49 mg
Protein: 2 g	

✳ *Applesauce-Oatmeal Cookies* ✳

YIELD: 30 servings (2 cookies each) • *PREPARATION TIME: 20 minutes* •
COOKING TIME: 15 minutes

You can enjoy these oatmeal cookies and many other classic cookies by substituting applesauce for the fat in traditional recipes. Store them in the refrigerator. Serve with Spiced Tea (page 385).

1 cup old-fashioned rolled oats
2½ cups unbleached all-purpose
 flour
1 teaspoon baking soda
1 teaspoon ground cinnamon
¼ teaspoon salt (optional)

1 cup brown sugar, firmly packed
¾ cup plus 2 tablespoons applesauce
1 egg white, lightly beaten
1 tablespoon vanilla extract
1 cup raisins

1. Preheat oven to 350 degrees. Use a nonstick baking sheet or line a baking sheet with baking sheet liner or lightly spray with vegetable cooking spray.
2. Combine oats, flour, baking soda, cinnamon, and salt, if using.
3. In a separate bowl, beat together brown sugar, applesauce, egg white, and vanilla until well combined.
4. Stir wet ingredients into dry ingredients. Fold in raisins.
5. Drop cookie dough on sheet by the tablespoonful. Leave 1½ inches between cookies.
6. Bake for 15 minutes. Let cookies cool on a wire rack.

Calories Per Serving: 95
Fat: .3 g
Cholesterol: 0 mg
Protein: 1 g

Carbohydrates: 21 g
Dietary Fiber: .7 g
Sodium: 32 mg

✳ *Pear Burritos* ✳

YIELD: *6 servings* • PREPARATION TIME: *20 minutes* •
COOKING TIME: *20 minutes*

Here pears are simmered with sugar and cinnamon and then baked in burrito blankets. Serve with Cannellini–Northern Bean Chili (page 155).

4 pears, peeled, cored, and sliced
½ cup apple juice
½ cup brown sugar, firmly packed

½ teaspoon ground cinnamon
6 large nonfat tortillas
½ cup nonfat grated cheese

1. Place pears, apple juice, brown sugar, and cinnamon in a saucepan. Bring to a boil, reduce heat, and simmer until pears are crisp-tender. Drain the pears, reserving the cooking liquid.
2. Preheat oven to 350 degrees. Use a shallow nonstick baking pan, or

Pear Burritos *(cont'd)*

line a shallow baking pan with a baking pan liner or lightly spray with vegetable cooking spray.

3. Spoon ⅙ of the pears into the middle of each tortilla and sprinkle with cheese. Spread the filling evenly over the surface of the tortilla, leaving a ½-inch border all around. Starting at one end, roll up the tortilla, folding up the left and right edges as you go. Place rolled tortillas seamside down on the baking pan.
4. Spoon the reserved apple juice from the saucepan over the burritos.
5. Bake burritos for 10 minutes or until they begin to brown. Serve at once.

Calories Per Serving: 197
Fat: .5 g
Cholesterol: .4 mg
Protein: 2 g

Carbohydrates: 50 g
Dietary Fiber: 2 g
Sodium: 59 mg

❋ *Mixed Berries with Whipped Topping* ❋

YIELD: 4 servings • *PREPARATION TIME: 15 minutes plus*
1½ hours milk freezing time

This whipped topping is made with evaporated skim milk and can be used with a wide variety of other desserts.

2 cups evaporated skim milk
¾ cup fresh, sliced strawberries
¾ cup fresh blueberries

¾ cup fresh raspberries
¾ cup fresh blackberries
2 tablespoons honey

1. Pour evaporated milk into a mixing bowl. Chill in the freezer for 1½ hours or until ice crystals form around the edges of the bowl. Chill beater blades at the same time.
2. Immediately before removing milk from freezer, combine strawberries, blueberries, raspberries, blackberries, and honey.
3. Beat chilled milk on high speed for 8 minutes or until it is the consistency of whipped cream.
4. Spoon berries into four stemmed glasses and serve topped with whipped milk.

Calories Per Serving: 181
Fat: .7 g
Cholesterol: 5 mg
Protein: 10 g

Carbohydrates: 34 g
Dietary Fiber: 4 g
Sodium: 149 mg

Meringues with Raspberries and ✳ *Frozen Yogurt* ✳

YIELD: 8 servings ▪ *PREPARATION TIME: 20 minutes* ▪ *COOKING TIME: 1 hour*

Meringues are one of the great fat-free desserts. These individual meringue shells are filled with raspberries. Meringues can be stored in an airtight container for up to two weeks. Serve with Angel Hair Pasta with Steamed Vegetables and Garlic Sauce (page 144).

3 large egg whites, at room
 temperature
¹/₄ teaspoon cream of tartar
¹/₂ teaspoon vanilla extract
³/₄ cup superfine sugar

1 cup all-fruit raspberry jam
1¹/₂ cups frozen nonfat vanilla
 yogurt
3 cups fresh or thawed, frozen
 raspberries

1. Preheat oven to 275. Line a baking sheet with parchment paper, brown paper, or foil.
2. Place the egg whites in the bowl of an electric mixer. Beat at medium speed until foamy.
3. Add cream of tartar. Increase mixer speed to high.
4. Add vanilla.
5. Gradually add sugar, 1 tablespoon at a time, beating constantly for about 5 minutes or until stiff, but not dry, shiny peaks form.
6. Place 8 large spoonfuls of the mixture, evenly spaced, on a baking sheet. With the back of a spoon, form the meringue into small nestlike shapes about 3 inches in diameter.
7. Bake for 1 hour or until crisp and firm. While still warm, remove from baking sheet and cool on a rack.
8. Gently heat the all-fruit jam in a small saucepan.
9. Spoon frozen yogurt into the bottom of each meringue shell and top with raspberries. Spoon warm jam over raspberries.

Meringues with Raspberries and Frozen Yogurt *(cont'd)*

Variation

- You can substitute powdered meringue for the egg whites. Powdered meringue is available where baking supplies are sold.

Calories Per Serving: 212
Fat: .3 g
Cholesterol: 0 mg
Protein: 2 g

Carbohydrates: 50 g
Dietary Fiber: 2 g
Sodium: 40 mg

❋ *Strawberry-Banana Cream* ❋

YIELD: 4 servings • PREPARATION TIME: 15 minutes plus overnight chilling time

Frozen bananas give honey-flavored yogurt the texture of sinfully rich ice cream. Mix and match fruit layers as you please. Serve with Multicolored Shells with Broccoli, Mushrooms, Red Peppers, and Ricotta Cheese (page 145).

3 medium bananas, peeled, wrapped in a plastic bag, and frozen overnight

1/2 cup plain nonfat yogurt
2 tablespoons honey
2 cups sliced, hulled strawberries

1. When ready to serve, cut frozen bananas into 1-inch slices.
2. Place yogurt and honey in a food processor or blender. Process until combined. Add banana slices and process until smooth.
3. Spoon yogurt-banana mixture into the bottom of four parfait or other tall glasses. Spoon in a layer of strawberries. Continue alternating layers of yogurt-banana mixture and strawberries.

Calories Per Serving: 150
Fat: .7 g
Cholesterol: .5 mg
Protein: 3 g

Carbohydrates: 36 g
Dietary Fiber: 3.3 g
Sodium: 24 mg

✳ *Chocolate Pudding* ✳

YIELD: 4 servings ▪ *PREPARATION TIME: 10 minutes plus 1 hour chilling time* ▪
COOKING TIME: 10 minutes

This favorite dessert is made with skim milk and cocoa. Serve with
Nonfat Dessert Topping II (page 367).

¼ cup sugar
2 tablespoons unsweetened cocoa
3 tablespoons cornstarch

2 cups skim milk
1 teaspoon vanilla extract

1. Combine the sugar, cocoa, and cornstarch.
2. Add the milk and vanilla to cocoa mixture.
3. Transfer the pudding to a heavy saucepan.
4. Cook, stirring, for 10 minutes or until smooth and thickened.
5. Pour into four small bowls and chill for 1 hour or until pudding is set.

Calories Per Serving: 128
Fat: .6 g
Cholesterol: 2 mg
Protein: 5 g

Carbohydrates: 25 g
Dietary Fiber: 0 g
Sodium: 133 mg

✳ *Blueberry Delight* ✳

YIELD: 4 servings ▪ *PREPARATION TIME: 10 minutes* ▪
COOKING TIME: 2 minutes

Here blueberries are run under the broiler with a topping of nonfat sour
cream and yogurt, and a sprinkling of brown sugar. Serve with Zucchini
and Pattypan Casserole (page 123).

2 cups fresh or thawed, frozen
  blueberries
½ cup nonfat sour cream

½ cup plain nonfat yogurt
2 tablespoons brown sugar, firmly
  packed

1. Preheat broiler. Place blueberries in a glass pie pan.
2. Combine sour cream and yogurt.
3. Spoon sour cream and yogurt over berries.
4. Sprinkle brown sugar over sour cream and yogurt.

Blueberry Delight *(cont'd)*

5. Place pie pan under broiler for 2 minutes or until sugar has melted. Divide into 4 portions.

Calories Per Serving: 84	Carbohydrates: 19 g
Fat: .3 g	Dietary Fiber: no data
Cholesterol: .8 mg	Sodium: 31 mg
Protein: 2 g	

✳ *Fruit Cup with Mango Sauce* ✳

YIELD: *4 servings* • PREPARATION TIME: *20 minutes*

Pineapple chunks, navel orange sections, and banana are topped with a lime-mango sauce.

1 large ripe chilled mango, peeled, seeded, and cut into chunks
3 tablespoons lime juice
¼ teaspoon grated lime peel
2 cups fresh or juice-packed canned pineapple chunks

1 large banana, peeled and sliced
1 large navel orange, peeled, sliced, and sectioned

1. Place mango chunks, lime juice, and lime peel in a blender or food processor and purée.
2. Toss pineapple chunks with banana and navel orange sections.
3. Serve fruit in 4 bowls each topped with mango purée.

Calories Per Serving: 118	Carbohydrates: 30 g
Fat: .4 g	Dietary Fiber: 3.4 g
Cholesterol: 0 mg	Sodium: 2.8 mg
Protein: 1.4 g	

✳ *Yogurt Fruit Parfait* ✳

YIELD: *4 servings* • PREPARATION TIME: *15 minutes plus 4 hours chilling time*

Pineapple, orange, tangerine, kiwi, and banana are the five star players in this elegant dessert. Look for plump kiwis that are firm but not hard textured. You can also alternate cubes of angel food cake between the layers of fruit. Serve with Conchiglie with Cauliflower and Sun-Dried Tomatoes (page 144).

1 cup juice-packed canned pineapple chunks
1 navel orange, peeled, sectioned, and diced
1 tangerine, peeled, sectioned, and seeded
1 kiwi, peeled and sliced
1 banana, sliced
1/2 cup pineapple juice
1 cup plain nonfat yogurt

1. Combine pineapple chunks, orange pieces, tangerine sections, and kiwi slices in a large bowl.
2. Place banana and pineapple juice in a food processor or blender and purée.
3. Pour the banana-pineapple juice mixture over the fruit in the bowl and stir to combine.
4. Chill, covered, for 4 hours.
5. Spoon the chilled fruit into 4 parfait or other tall glasses in layers alternating with the yogurt.

Calories Per Serving: 131
Fat: .5 g
Cholesterol: 1 mg
Protein: 4 g

Carbohydrates: 29 g
Dietary Fiber: 2.8 g
Sodium: 46 mg

✳ *Amaretto Fruit Delight* ✳

YIELD: *4 servings* ▪ PREPARATION TIME: *15 minutes plus 3 hours chilling time*

Amaretto liqueur is tossed with fresh fruit in this elegant dessert that's a perfect fat-free finish to a special meal. Serve with Vermicelli with Roasted Peppers (page 146).

3 large navel oranges, peeled, sliced, and sectioned
4 tablespoons amaretto liqueur
1 cup sliced fresh or thawed, frozen strawberries

Amaretto Fruit Delight *(cont'd)*

1. Place oranges in glass bowl and toss with amaretto. Chill for at least 3 hours.
2. Toss with strawberries and serve in 4 individual fruit cups.

Calories Per Serving: 58

Fat: .3 g

Cholesterol: 0 mg

Protein: 1 g

Carbohydrates: 14 g

Dietary Fiber: 3 g

Sodium: .5 mg

✳ *Fruit Mélange in Red Wine* ✳

YIELD: 4 servings ▪ *PREPARATION TIME: 20 minutes* ▪
COOKING TIME: 25 minutes

Apricots, prunes, orange, red wine, and apple juice are simmered with spices and flavored with honey in this dish. Serve with Stuffed Eggplant (page 120).

³/₄ cup dried apricots

1 cup pitted prunes

1 navel orange, peeled and sliced

1 cup red wine

1 cup apple juice

¹/₄ teaspoon ground cloves

¹/₄ teaspoon ground nutmeg

¹/₄ teaspoon ground cinnamon

*1 apple, peeled, cored, and
    thinly sliced*

2 tablespoons honey

1. Combine apricots, prunes, orange, red wine, apple juice, cloves, nutmeg, and cinnamon in a large saucepan. Bring to a boil over medium heat, partially cover the pan, and simmer for 25 minutes.
2. Pour fruit into a bowl. Add apples and honey and toss.

Calories Per Serving: 272

Fat: .6 g

Cholesterol: 0 mg

Protein: 2 g

Carbohydrates: 60 g

Dietary Fiber: 6 g

Sodium: 44 mg

✳ *Grapefruit with Raspberry Sauce* ✳

YIELD: 4 servings ▪ *PREPARATION TIME: 15 minutes*

This simple yet elegant dish combines raspberry purée with grapefruit sections. Since grapefruit are always ripe and ready to serve when you buy them, you need to look for indications of flavor and juiciness. A grapefruit should feel heavy for its size and be firm and resilient. Serve this dessert with Fusilli with Lentil Sauce (page 150).

2 cups fresh or frozen raspberries

2 medium pink or white grapefruit, peeled, sectioned, and seeded

1. Place raspberries in a blender or food processor and purée.
2. Pour purée into the bottoms of 4 shallow bowls.
3. Top with the grapefruit sections.

Calories Per Serving: 67
Fat: .5 g
Cholesterol: 0 mg
Protein: 1 g

Carbohydrates: 16 g
Dietary Fiber: 4 g
Sodium: 0 mg

✳ *Cranberry Dessert* ✳

YIELD: 8 servings ▪ *PREPARATION TIME: 20 minutes* ▪
COOKING TIME: 15 minutes

Here fresh cranberries are simmered with pears, dried apricots, and oranges. Serve warm or cold. Serve with Great Northern Bean Soup (page 102).

1½ *cups water*
½ *cup sugar*
3 medium pears, peeled, cored, and cut into chunks

12 dried apricots, chopped
2 navel oranges, peeled, sectioned, and diced
3 cups raw cranberries

1. Place water and sugar in a large, heavy saucepan and bring to a boil.
2. Add pears and apricots, reduce heat, and simmer for 5 minutes.

Cranberry Dessert *(cont'd)*
3. Add oranges to saucepan and simmer for 5 more minutes.
4. Add cranberries and cook over medium heat for 5 minutes.

Calories Per Serving: 167
Fat: .6 g
Cholesterol: 0 mg
Protein: 1.5 g

Carbohydrates: 42 g
Dietary Fiber: 4.9 g
Sodium: 7 mg

✳ *Instant Fruit Freeze* ✳

YIELD: 4 servings • PREPARATION TIME: 10 minutes plus freezing time

Keep a few cans of peaches, pears, apricots, or other fruit in the freezer so you'll always be ready to make this super-quick dessert. Enjoy it plain or over fresh fruit.

1 16-ounce can of juice-packed fruit,
  frozen solid

1. When ready to eat, run can under hot water for 1 minute.
2. Open can and place fruit in blender or food processor.
3. Process until it is the texture of sherbet. Scoop into 4 sherbet cups.

Calories Per Serving: 28
Fat: .1 g
Cholesterol: 0 mg
Protein: .5 g

Carbohydrates: 7 g
Dietary Fiber: 1 g
Sodium: 6 mg

✳ *Apple-Orangesicles* ✳

YIELD: 6 servings • PREPARATION TIME: 15 minutes plus freezing time

Yogurt, frozen orange juice, apple juice, and lime juice are used to create these refreshing treats.

2 cups plain nonfat yogurt
1 6-ounce can frozen orange juice
  concentrate

¼ cup lime juice or lemon juice
2 cups apple juice

1. Place yogurt, orange juice concentrate, lime or lemon juice, and apple juice in a blender or food processor and process until smooth.
2. Pour into 6 fruit pop molds, or 6 paper cups with wooden sticks or plastic spoons inserted, and freeze.

Calories Per Serving: 140   Carbohydrates: 29 g
Fat: .3 g   Dietary Fiber: .5 g
Cholesterol: 1.33 mg   Sodium: 61 mg
Protein: 5 g

✳ *Fruit Salad with Strawberry Dressing* ✳

YIELD: 6 servings ▪ *PREPARATION TIME: 20 minutes*

Puréed strawberry dressing tops this salad of blueberries, navel oranges, and sliced strawberries. Serve with Tomato Linguine (page 148).

3¹/₂ cups fresh or thawed, frozen strawberries
¹/₂ teaspoon dried mint leaves
¹/₂ teaspoon honey
¹/₂ cup nonfat sour cream or plain nonfat yogurt

1¹/₂ cups fresh or thawed, frozen blueberries
1¹/₂ cups navel orange slices
Red leaf lettuce leaves

1. Slice 1 cup of the strawberries and set aside. Place remaining 2¹/₂ cups of berries in a blender or food processor with the mint, honey, and sour cream or yogurt. Purée.
2. Toss reserved sliced strawberries with blueberries and navel orange slices.
3. Line 6 salad plates with red leaf lettuce. Top with tossed fruit and drizzle with dressing.

Calories Per Serving: 84   Carbohydrates: 19 g
Fat: .6 g   Dietary Fiber: 4 g
Cholesterol: .33 mg   Sodium: 20 mg
Protein: 2 g

❋ Orange-Pineapple Freeze ❋

YIELD: 6 servings (²/₃ cup each) • *PREPARATION TIME: 10 minutes plus freezing time*

This delectable pineapple dessert makes a rich and satisfying ice cream substitute. Serve with Cavatelli with Simmered Vegetable Sauce (page 147).

2 cups skim milk
1 cup instant nonfat dry milk
1 8-ounce can frozen unsweetened
  orange juice concentrate

1 cup unsweetened crushed
  pineapple

1. Mix the skim milk and the nonfat dry milk together.
2. Stir in the orange juice concentrate and the crushed pineapple.
3. Pour into a shallow metal pan, such as an ice-cube tray without the dividers, baking tin, or other freezer-safe bowl, and freeze. Stir frequently during the freezing period to equally distribute the ice crystals until the mixture is frozen firm, but not hard.

Calories Per Serving: 139
Fat: .3 g
Cholesterol: 3.3 mg
Protein: 7 g

Carbohydrates: 26 g
Dietary Fiber: .6 g
Sodium: 106 mg

❋ Raspberry Sherbet ❋

YIELD: 4 servings • *PREPARATION TIME: 10 minutes*

This is a great dish to prepare when you need something for dessert with very little notice. Serve with Black Bean Lasagna (page 153).

3 cups frozen raspberries or
  blackberries, partially defrosted
3 tablespoons frozen orange juice
  concentrate

1 navel orange, peeled and diced

1. Place partially frozen berries and orange juice in a blender or food processor.
2. Process until the berries are the consistency of a sherbet.
3. Spoon into 4 serving dishes, sprinkle with diced oranges, and serve at once.

Calories Per Serving: 82   Carbohydrates: 19 g
Fat: .6 g   Dietary Fiber: 5 g
Cholesterol: 0 mg   Sodium: .5 mg
Protein: 1 g

✳ *Nonfat Dessert Topping I* ✳

YIELD: 8 servings (2 tablespoons each) • *PREPARATION TIME: 10 minutes plus 12 hours standing time*

Use this topping on nonfat pies and cakes or fruit recipes.

2 cups plain nonfat yogurt   *1 teaspoon vanilla extract*
¹/₄ cup honey

1. Line a large strainer with a coffee filter or several layers of clean, dry cheesecloth.
2. Spoon in yogurt and place over large bowl.
3. Refrigerate for 12 hours. Discard liquid in bowl.
4. Beat yogurt, honey, and vanilla together until smooth.

Calories Per Serving: 66   Carbohydrates: 13 g
Fat: .1 g   Dietary Fiber: 0 g
Cholesterol: 1 mg   Sodium: 44 mg
Protein: 3 g

✳ *Nonfat Dessert Topping II* ✳

YIELD: 6 servings (¹/₄ cup each) • *PREPARATION TIME: 5 minutes plus partial freezing time*

This whipped topping is made with skim milk and instant nonfat dry milk for double richness. Prepare immediately before serving.

Nonfat Dessert Topping II *(cont'd)*
        ¹/₃ cup skim milk   *2 teaspoons honey*
        ¹/₃ cup instant nonfat dry milk   *¹/₄ teaspoon vanilla extract*

1. Pour skim milk into mixing bowl.
2. Place bowl and beaters from electric mixer in freezer until the milk becomes slushy, 30 to 45 minutes.
3. Beat nonfat dry milk into skim milk in bowl for 4 minutes or until soft peaks form.
4. Add honey and vanilla and beat for 2 more minutes. Use immediately.

Calories Per Serving: 26
Fat: 0 g
Cholesterol: .9 mg
Protein: 1.8 g

Carbohydrates: 4 g
Dietary Fiber: 0 g
Sodium: 27 mg

✳ *Blueberry Buttermilk Ice Cream* ✳

YIELD: 4 servings (¹/₂ cup each) • *PREPARATION TIME: 15 minutes plus 2 hours and 30 minutes freezing time*

This creamy orange-flavored concoction is packed with blueberries. Serve with Baked Mixed Vegetable Biriyani (page 126).

    2 cups fresh or frozen blueberries   *¹/₂ cup superfine sugar*
    ³/₄ cup nonfat buttermilk   *¹/₄ cup orange juice*

1. Place blueberries, buttermilk, sugar, and orange juice in a food processor or blender. Process until smooth.
2. Pour into a square freezer-safe pan.
3. Freeze for 2 hours and 30 minutes, stirring frequently to equally distribute the ice crystals. Allow to soften slightly at room temperature before serving.

Calories Per Serving: 153
Fat: .3 g
Cholesterol: .9 mg
Protein: 2 g

Carbohydrates: 37 g
Dietary Fiber: 1.7 g
Sodium: 54mg

✳ *Maple-Blueberry Topping* ✳

Yield: 6 servings (¹/₂ cup each) • *Preparation Time: 10 minutes*

Use this sweet topping on baked desserts or on fruit salads.

1 cup fresh or frozen blueberries   *¹/₂ cup plain nonfat yogurt*
2¹/₂ tablespoons maple syrup

1. Place berries in a blender or food processor and puree.
2. Mix berries with maple syrup and yogurt.

Calories Per Serving: 49   Carbohydrates: 11 g
Fat: .1 g   Dietary Fiber: .5 g
Cholesterol: .3 mg   Sodium: 30 mg
Protein: 1 g

✳ *Spiced Creamy Topping* ✳

Yield: 4 servings (¹/₄ cup each) • *Preparation Time: 10 minutes*

This whipped topping has a cinnamon-orange flavor.

¹/₂ cup plain nonfat yogurt   *2 teaspoons orange juice*
¹/₂ cup nonfat cottage cheese   *Pinch of ground cinnamon*
¹/₄ teaspoon vanilla extract

1. Combine yogurt, cottage cheese, vanilla, orange juice, and cinnamon in a blender or food processor for 30 seconds.

Variations
- Substitute maple or almond extract for the vanilla.
- Substitute apple juice or grape juice for the orange juice.
- Substitute allspice or nutmeg for the cinnamon.

Calories Per Serving: 38   Carbohydrates: 4 g
Fat: 0 g   Dietary Fiber: 0 g
Cholesterol: 2 mg   Sodium: 147 mg
Protein: 5 g

❋ Maple Whipped Dessert Topping ❋

YIELD: 4 servings (½ cup each) ▪ *PREPARATION TIME: 10 minutes plus
2 hours freezing time*

This topping is made with evaporated skim milk. Whip immediately
before serving.

12 ounces evaporated skim milk   *2 teaspoons maple syrup*
2 egg whites

1. Place the evaporated skim milk in a bowl and freeze for 2 hours. Also
   freeze the beaters from the electric mixer.
2. Add the egg whites and maple syrup to the evaporated skim milk after
   you remove it from the freezer.
3. Whip until mixture reaches the consistency of whipped cream.

Calories Per Serving: 68   Carbohydrates: 9 g
Fat: .1 g   Dietary Fiber: 0 g
Cholesterol: 2.5 mg   Sodium: 107 mg
Protein: 6 g

❋ Frozen Berry Topping ❋

YIELD: 4 servings (6 tablespoons each) ▪ *PREPARATION TIME: 15 minutes plus
2 hours freezing time*

This berry topping is rich and creamy and works well on a wide variety
of baked desserts. Whip immediately before serving.

⅔ cup skim milk   *1 tablespoon honey*
¾ cup fresh strawberries,   *1 egg white*
   raspberries, or blueberries

1. Place skim milk in a bowl in the freezer for 2 hours. Also freeze beaters
   from electric mixer.
2. At end of freezing time, place berries and honey in a blender or food
   processor and purée.

3. Whip milk for 7 minutes or until thick.
4. Beat egg white until stiff. Fold gently into milk.
5. Stir in berry purée and serve at once.

Calories Per Serving: 43
Fat: .2 g
Cholesterol: .7 mg
Protein: 2 g

Carbohydrates: 8 g
Dietary Fiber: .7 g
Sodium: 35 mg

✳ *Sweet Whipped Topping* ✳

YIELD: 10 servings (2 tablespoons each) • *PREPARATION TIME: 5 minutes plus 45 minutes freezing time*

This topping is sweetened with sugar and accented with vanilla. If you want to make it in advance, it can be stored, covered, in the refrigerator for 1 hour.

1 cup evaporated skim milk
¼ cup confectioners' sugar

1 teaspoon vanilla extract

1. Pour milk into a mixing bowl. Chill milk and beaters from electric mixer in freezer for 45 minutes or until there are ice crystals around the top of the bowl.
2. Beat for one minute.
3. Beat for 2 more minutes as you add the sugar and vanilla. The topping should be very stiff.

Variation
• Add ½ teaspoon almond, chocolate, maple, or rum extract in Step 3.

Calories Per Serving: 31
Fat: .05 g
Cholesterol: 1 mg
Protein: 1.9 g

Carbohydrates: 5.5 g
Dietary Fiber: 0 g
Sodium: 29 mg

FOR THE
MICROWAVE

Good Morning Egg-Pita Sandwich • New Potato Bites • Eggplant–
Red Pepper Canapé Spread • Chicken Broth • Hacienda Tortilla
Chips • Fruit Dip • Vegetable Broth • Vegetable Soup • Quick
Vegetable Stock • Pumpkin Soup • Tomato–Lima Bean Soup •
Orange-Carrot Soup with Ginger • Special Cocoa • Red Pepper Soup
with Navy Beans • Cranberry-Cinnamon Warmer • Spiced Tea •
Ratatouille-Stuffed Potatoes • Pinto Bean Burritos • Black Bean Chili
with Vegetables • Cannellini Beans with Potatoes and Vegetables •
Stuffed Red Peppers • Black Bean and Vegetable–Stuffed Peppers •
Eggplant Sicilian • Stuffed Pasta Shells • Spanish Vegetable Stew •
Layered Tortilla Casserole • Long-Grain Rice • Basmati Rice •
Pineapple Rice • Wild Rice • Lemon-Dill Rice • Red Pepper–Dijon
Rice Salad • Strawberry-Blueberry Rice Salad • Polenta • Curried
Rice Pilaf with Dried Apricots • Barley with Peas and Red Peppers •
Boston Brown Bread • Lemon-Ginger Asparagus • Broccoli-Corn
Toss • Broccoli with Parsley-Pepper Sauce • Calico Cauliflower •
Cannellini Beans with Potatoes and Vegetables • Hubbard Squash
with Navy Beans • Succotash • Eggplant with Chiles • Mashed
Sweet Potatoes and Applesauce • Lemon-Dijon Lima Beans • Spicy
Jalapeños and Red Bell Peppers • Tomato Red Skins • Tropical
Stuffed Sweet Potatoes • Microwave Baked Potatoes • Fiesta Red
Potatoes • Ginger-Honey Acorn Squash • Steamed Vegetables with

374 ••• SARAH SCHLESINGER

Mustard-Dill Sauce • Strawberries and Raspberries with Blueberry-Orange Sauce • Oranges with Grape Sauce • Mango Fandango Pears • Spicy Poached Apples and Pears • Ginger-Orange Applesauce • Maple Grapefruit-Orange Delight • Apple-Nutmeg Poached Plums • Lemon Prunes • Cinnamon Poached Peaches • Dried Fruit Sauce • Maple-Raspberry-Nectarine Garnish • Lemon-Vanilla Peach Sauce • Strawberry Sauce • Zucchini Topping • Red Pepper Sauce • Ricotta Bites with Orange-Honey Sauce • Raspberry-Strawberry Jam

FOR THE
MICROWAVE

∷

✳ Good Morning Egg-Pita Sandwich ✳

YIELD: 1 serving • PREPARATION TIME: 10 minutes •
COOKING TIME: 1¹/₂ minutes

Here egg whites are microwaved and served in a pita with nonfat cheese, minced red bell pepper, and minced scallion.

2 egg whites	*2 tablespoons shredded nonfat cheese*
1 teaspoon water	*1 tablespoon minced red bell pepper*
1 whole wheat pita bread	*1 teaspoon minced scallion*

1. Beat egg whites with water.
2. Place in a 4–ounce custard cup.
3. Microwave, uncovered, on MEDIUM for 1¹/₂ minutes or until egg whites are set.
4. Cut an opening in pita bread and toast lightly.
5. Spoon in egg whites, cheese, red pepper, and scallion.

Calories Per Serving: 147	Carbohydrates: 21 g
Fat: .6 g	Dietary Fiber: .7 g
Cholesterol: .6 mg	Sodium: 362 mg
Protein: 12 g	

✳ New Potato Bites ✳

YIELD: 4 servings • PREPARATION TIME: 5 minutes •
COOKING TIME: 10 minutes plus 5 minutes standing time

Serve these tiny new potatoes with nonfat plain yogurt, Dijon mustard, salsa, or Red Pepper Sauce (page 424).

New Potato Bites *(cont'd)*
12 new potatoes, 2 inches in
  diameter

1. Pierce potatoes with a fork.
2. Place 2 layers of paper towels on the microwave floor. Arrange potatoes on paper towels.
3. Microwave on HIGH for 5 minutes. Turn potatoes over. Microwave for 5 more minutes. Let stand for 5 minutes.

Calories Per Serving: 60   Carbohydrates: 13 g
Fat: .07 g   Dietary Fiber: .2 g
Cholesterol: 0 mg   Sodium: 3 mg
Protein: 1 g

✳ *Eggplant–Red Pepper Canapé Spread* ✳

YIELD: *7 servings (¹/₄ cup each)* • PREPARATION TIME: *35 minutes plus 30 minutes draining time* • COOKING TIME: *12 minutes*

This eggplant spread is also great for snacks and sandwiches. It can be refrigerated for six to seven days. Serve spread on thin slices of Whole Wheat Baguette (page 310) or nonfat crackers.

1 medium eggplant   *¹/₂ teaspoon ground coriander*
1 large red bell pepper   *¹/₄ teaspoon black pepper*
1 garlic clove, halved
3 tablespoons nonfat plain yogurt or
  nonfat sour cream

1. Pierce skin of eggplant in four places. Place eggplant and red pepper on paper plate in microwave. Microwave on HIGH for 12 minutes or until both the eggplant and the pepper are very soft.
2. Cut the eggplant and the pepper in half and drain in a colander for 30 minutes.
3. Remove the skin and seeds from the pepper and cut flesh into chunks.
4. Scrape the eggplant pulp into a food processor or blender. Add the red pepper, garlic, yogurt or sour cream, coriander, and pepper.
5. Purée until smooth.

Variations
- Delete the coriander and replace with ¼ teaspoon cumin, a pinch of cayenne pepper, and 2 tablespoons chopped parsley.
- Instead of putting ingredients in food processor or blender in Step 4, mash with a pastry cutter.
- Delete red bell pepper and yogurt. Replace with 2 large tomatoes, chopped, and 2 teaspoons fresh green hot chile pepper.

Calories Per Serving: 18
Fat: .2 g
Cholesterol: .1 mg
Protein: .8 g

Carbohydrates: 3 g
Dietary Fiber: 1 g
Sodium: 6 mg

✳ Chicken Broth ✳

YIELD: *7 servings (1 cup each)* • PREPARATION TIME: *15 minutes plus cooling time* • COOKING TIME: *45 minutes*

This nonfat chicken broth can be used in many of the other recipes in this book and takes less time to prepare in the microwave than on top of your stove.

7 cups cold water
2 chicken breasts, skin and fat removed
1 small onion, chopped
1 large carrot, chopped
1 stalk celery, chopped

¼ cup chopped fresh parsley
1 bay leaf
½ teaspoon dried thyme leaves
Pinch of cayenne pepper
½ teaspoon black pepper

1. Place water, chicken, onion, carrot, celery, parsley, bay leaf, thyme, cayenne, and black pepper in a very large microwave-safe bowl. Cover tightly and microwave on HIGH for 45 minutes.
2. Strain broth through a fine sieve or a strainer lined with clean, dry cheesecloth. Press down on the solids gently while straining to extract as much liquid as possible. Discard solids.
3. Let broth stand at room temperature until lukewarm. Refrigerate for several hours or overnight. Skim off all fat that has risen to the surface or pour through a soup strainer.

Chicken Broth *(cont'd)*
Variation

- Microwave strained broth on HIGH uncovered for about 40 minutes until reduced to 1 cup to use as a consommé or as a glaze for making sauces.

Calories Per Serving: 25
Fat: .2 g
Cholesterol: 0 mg
Protein: .9 g

Carbohydrates: 5.7 g
Dietary Fiber: 1.6 g
Sodium: 24.8 mg

✳ *Hacienda Tortilla Chips* ✳

YIELD: *2 servings* • PREPARATION TIME: *5 minutes* • COOKING: *4 minutes*

These chips, made with fat-free tortillas, replace fat-laden fried corn chips. Serve with dips, salsas, or bean dishes. If you wish, you can sprinkle the chips with grated nonfat cheddar cheese, minced scallions, and minced jalapeño peppers, and microwave on MEDIUM until the cheese melts. Serve with Pico de Gallo Dip (page 67).

2 tortillas

1. Cut each tortilla into 8 wedges.
2. Place on a paper towel on a microwave-safe plate. Cover plate with a paper towel and microwave on HIGH for 4 minutes if using flour tortillas and for 3 minutes if using corn tortillas.

Calories Per Serving: 50
Fat: 0 g
Cholesterol: 0 mg
Protein: 1 g

Carbohydrates: 13 g
Dietary Fiber: no data
Sodium: 28 mg

✳ *Fruit Dip* ✳

YIELD: *8 servings (5 tablespoons each)* • PREPARATION TIME: *15 minutes* • COOKING TIME: *3 minutes*

This pure fruit dip can be served with slices of apple and pear dipped in lemon juice or whole strawberries.

2 pears, peeled, cored, and sliced
1 tablespoon lemon juice
1/2 cup fresh or thawed, frozen
   strawberries or blackberries

Pinch of minced gingerroot
1 kiwi, peeled and diced
1/2 cup chopped pitted cherries

1. Place the pear slices and lemon juice in a shallow microwave-safe casserole. Cover with vented plastic wrap. Microwave on HIGH for 3 minutes.
2. Place microwaved pears, berries, and ginger in a food processor or blender and process until smooth.
3. Stir in kiwi and cherries.

Calories Per Serving: 39
Fat: .3 g
Cholesterol: 0 mg
Protein: .4 g

Carbohydrates: 10 g
Dietary Fiber: 1.6 g
Sodium: 1 mg

✳ *Vegetable Broth* ✳

YIELD: 8 servings (1 cup each) • *PREPARATION TIME: 20 minutes* •
COOKING TIME: 1 hour plus 1 hour standing time

This broth has a more intense flavor than the Quick Vegetable Stock on page 381 due to its longer cooking time.

7 cups finely chopped vegetables
   (you can include carrots, onions or
   leeks, butternut squash or
   zucchini, tomatoes, celery, red
   bell pepper, and turnips or
   parsnips)

1/4 cup chopped fresh parsley
2 cloves garlic, halved
1 bay leaf
1/2-inch piece fresh gingerroot
9 cups water
1/2 teaspoon black pepper

1. Combine vegetables, parsley, garlic, bay leaf, gingerroot, water, and pepper in a 6-quart microwave-safe bowl. Cover with plastic wrap, sealing tightly.
2. Microwave on HIGH for 60 minutes.
3. Let stand for 10 minutes.
4. Remove plastic wrap carefully to avoid steam burns.
5. Cool to room temperature. Strain the liquid, pushing down on solids gently to extract as much liquid as possible. Discard solids.

Vegetable Broth *(cont'd)*

Variation

- Place unstrained soup and solids in a food processor or blender and blend until liquefied.

Calories Per Serving: 33
Fat: .2 g
Cholesterol: 0 mg
Protein: 1.3 g

Carbohydrates: 7.6 g
Dietary Fiber: 2.1 g
Sodium: 39.7 mg

✳ *Vegetable Soup* ✳

YIELD: *10 servings (1½ cups each)* • PREPARATION TIME: *25 minutes* •
COOKING TIME: *60 minutes*

Eight vegetables are combined with nonfat chicken broth and herbs in this soothing soup. Serve with Maple Grapefruit-Orange Delight (page 419).

1 carrot, finely chopped
1 stalk celery, finely chopped
1 onion, finely chopped
1 green bell pepper, seeded and
  finely chopped
3 garlic cloves, chopped
2 cups shredded cabbage
2 cups cauliflower florets

1 cup diced new potatoes
3 cups chopped fresh or low-sodium
  canned plum tomatoes
½ teaspoon dried rosemary leaves
½ teaspoon dried thyme leaves
8 cups nonfat chicken broth
¼ teaspoon black pepper

1. Place carrot, celery, onion, green pepper, garlic, cabbage, cauliflower, potatoes, tomatoes, rosemary, thyme, chicken broth, and black pepper in a large, microwave-safe bowl. Seal with a double layer of unvented plastic wrap.
2. Microwave on HIGH for 60 minutes. Remove plastic wrap very carefully to avoid steam burns.

Calories Per Serving: 49
Fat: .3 g
Cholesterol: 0 mg
Protein: 3 g

Carbohydrates: 9 g
Dietary Fiber: 2 g
Sodium: 124 mg

✳ *Quick Vegetable Stock* ✳

Yield: 3 servings ▪ *Preparation Time: 15 minutes* ▪
Cooking Time: 20 minutes

This recipe is a quick and easy way to create a supply of vegetable stock to use for fat-free cooking.

1 clove garlic, minced
½ cup chopped celery
1 medium onion, chopped
1 cup chopped zucchini

1 carrot, chopped
1 bay leaf
4 cups water

1. Place garlic, celery, onion, zucchini, carrot, bay leaf, and water in a 2½-quart microwave-safe casserole.
2. Microwave on HIGH for 20 minutes.
3. Allow soup to cool to room temperature. Strain the liquid, pushing down on solids to extract as much liquid as possible. Discard solids.

Variation
▪ Place unstrained soup and solids in a food processor or blender and blend until liquefied.

Calories Per Serving: 35
Fat: .2 g
Cholesterol: 0 mg
Protein: 1.4 g

Carbohydrates: 7.7 g
Dietary Fiber: 2.4 g
Sodium: 37.7 mg

✳ *Pumpkin Soup* ✳

Yield: 4 servings (1½ cup each) ▪ *Preparation Time: 5 minutes* ▪
Cooking Time: 10 minutes

This maple-ginger pumpkin soup is a snap to prepare in your microwave. Serve with Black Bean and Vegetable–Stuffed Peppers (page 390).

5 scallions, sliced
¼ cup water
2 cups canned pumpkin purée
¼ teaspoon ground ginger

1 cup evaporated skim milk
1 cup skim milk
2 cups hot water
1 teaspoon maple syrup

Pumpkin Soup (cont'd)

1. Place scallions and water in a large microwave-safe casserole. Microwave on HIGH for 3 minutes or until the scallions are tender.
2. Add pumpkin purée, ginger, milk, hot water, and maple syrup to casserole. Microwave on HIGH for 6 to 7 minutes or until heated through. Stir every 2 minutes.

Calories Per Serving: 120
Fat: .6 g
Cholesterol: 3.5 mg
Protein: 8 g

Carbohydrates: 22 g
Dietary Fiber: 2.5 g
Sodium: 118 mg

❋ Tomato–Lima Bean Soup ❋

YIELD: 4 servings (1½ cups each) ▪ PREPARATION TIME: 15 minutes ▪
COOKING TIME: 30 minutes

Lima beans, tomatoes, and scallions are microwaved with nonfat chicken broth or vegetable broth in this recipe. Serve with Mango Fandango Pears (page 417).

1¼ cups frozen lima beans
3 cups nonfat chicken broth or
    vegetable broth
½ teaspoon dried thyme leaves
¼ teaspoon dried marjoram leaves

2½ cups diced fresh or low-sodium
    canned tomatoes
¼ cup minced scallions
¼ teaspoon black pepper

1. Place lima beans, broth, thyme, and marjoram in a large microwave-safe bowl. Seal with a double layer of unvented plastic wrap. Microwave on HIGH for 20 minutes.
2. Remove plastic wrap with extreme care to avoid steam burns. Add tomatoes. Reseal with double layer of unvented plastic wrap.
3. Microwave on HIGH for 10 minutes. Stir in black pepper and scallions before serving.

Calories Per Serving: 93
Fat: .6 g
Cholesterol: 0 mg
Protein: 6 g

Carbohydrates: 17 g
Dietary Fiber: 3.8 g
Sodium: 149 mg

✳ *Orange-Carrot Soup with Ginger* ✳

YIELD: 6 servings (2 cups each) ▪ *PREPARATION TIME: 25 minutes* ▪
COOKING TIME: 21 minutes plus 5 minutes standing time

This spicy, sunset-colored soup can be served hot or cold. Serve with Ratatouille-Stuffed Potatoes (page 386).

1 medium onion, chopped	*3 cups vegetable broth or water*
1 clove garlic, minced	*1 cup orange juice*
6 cups sliced carrots	*1 cup skim milk*
1 cup diced white potatoes	*1 tablespoon honey*
1½ teaspoons grated fresh gingerroot	

1. Place the onion, garlic, carrots, potatoes, ginger, and 1 cup of the stock or water in a large microwave-safe casserole. Cover with vented plastic wrap and microwave on HIGH for 15 minutes or until the carrots are tender.
2. Transfer the carrot mixture along with the remaining 2 cups broth to a blender or food processor and purée. Return to casserole.
3. Add orange juice, skim milk, and honey to the casserole.
4. Recover the casserole and microwave on HIGH for 6 minutes or until the soup is thoroughly warm. Let stand for 5 minutes.

Calories Per Serving: 122	Carbohydrates: 27 g
Fat: .5 g	Dietary Fiber: 4.5 g
Cholesterol: .7 mg	Sodium: 65 mg
Protein: 3.5 g	

✳ *Special Cocoa* ✳

YIELD: 3 servings (1 cup each) ▪ *PREPARATION TIME: 10 minutes* ▪
COOKING TIME: 5 minutes

This delectable drink is an ideal warmer for a chilly winter evening. Top with a dab of Nonfat Dessert Topping II (page 367).

½ cup unsweetened cocoa	*2 tablespoons sugar*
½ cup instant nonfat dry milk	*½ teaspoon ground cinnamon*
3 cups skim milk	*1 teaspoon vanilla extract*

Special Cocoa *(cont'd)*

1. Place cocoa, dry milk, skim milk, sugar, cinnamon, and vanilla in a blender or food processor and process for 30 seconds.
2. Pour cocoa mixture into a microwave-safe bowl and cover with a double layer of plastic wrap. Microwave on HIGH for 5 minutes.
3. Uncover with care to avoid steam burns and stir.

Calories Per Serving: 173
Fat: 1 g
Cholesterol: 5.6 mg
Protein: 12.9 g

Carbohydrates: 27 g
Dietary Fiber: 0 g
Sodium: 182 mg

✳ *Red Pepper Soup with Navy Beans* ✳

YIELD: 4 servings (2 cups each) • *PREPARATION TIME: 15 minutes plus bean cooking time* • *COOKING TIME: 30 minutes*

Red bell peppers and onions are flavored here with garlic and ginger, puréed, and combined with cannellini beans.

4 cups red bell pepper chunks
1/2 cup chopped onion
1 clove garlic, chopped
1 teaspoon grated fresh gingerroot
3 cups nonfat chicken broth or
*   vegetable broth*

1/4 teaspoon black pepper
1 1/4 cups home-cooked or canned
*   navy or cannellini beans, drained*
*   and rinsed*
2 tablespoons chopped fresh parsley

1. Place red peppers, onion, garlic, and gingerroot in a microwave-safe bowl and microwave on HIGH for 15 minutes.
2. Add the broth. Cover with 2 layers of unvented plastic wrap. Microwave on HIGH for 10 minutes.
3. When cool, purée in a blender of food processor.
4. Return broth-pepper purée to microwave-safe bowl with black pepper and beans. Microwave on HIGH for 5 minutes.
5. Serve garnished with parsley.

Calories Per Serving: 102
Fat: .7 g
Cholesterol: 0 mg
Protein: 6 g

Carbohydrates: 18 g
Dietary Fiber: 4 g
Sodium: 109 mg

✳ *Cranberry-Cinnamon Warmer* ✳

YIELD: 2 servings (1 cup each) • *PREPARATION TIME: 5 minutes* •
COOKING TIME: 3 minutes

Try this combination of cranberry juice, apple juice, and cinnamon as
your wake-up beverage on a frosty morning. Serve with a slice of Banana
Quick Bread (page 314).

1¹/₂ cups cranberry juice	*1 cinnamon stick*
¹/₂ cup apple juice	*2 tablespoons finely chopped apple*

1. Place cranberry juice, apple juice, and cinnamon stick in a microwave-
   safe container. Microwave on HIGH for 3 minutes.
2. Transfer juice to cups and stir a tablespoon of apple into each cup.

Variation
• Substitute orange juice for the apple juice and 2 tablespoons of chopped
  navel orange sections for the apple.

Calories Per Serving: 144	Carbohydrates: 36 g
Fat: .2 g	Dietary Fiber: .3 g
Cholesterol: 0 mg	Sodium: 9.3 mg
Protein: .1 g	

✳ *Spiced Tea* ✳

YIELD: 4 servings (³/₄ cup each) • *PREPARATION TIME: 5 minutes* •
COOKING TIME: 9 minutes plus 3 minutes standing time

Here's a quick way to make a cup of herb tea into a special event. Serve
with Applesauce Quick Bread (page 312).

6 spiced herb tea bags (without	*¹/₄ cup honey*
staples)	*4 cinnamon sticks*
3 cups water	*4 whole cloves*

1. Place tea bags and water in a microwave-safe container. Microwave
   on HIGH for 4 minutes.

Spiced Tea *(cont'd)*
2. Let stand for 3 minutes.
3. Discard tea bags.
4. Add honey, cinnamon sticks, and cloves. Microwave on MEDIUM for 5 minutes.
5. Pour into 4 cups through a strainer.

Calories Per Serving: 65
Fat: 0 g
Cholesterol: 0 mg
Protein: 0 g

Carbohydrates: 17 g
Dietary Fiber: .1 g
Sodium: 1.2 mg

✳ *Ratatouille-Stuffed Potatoes* ✳

YIELD: 4 servings (1 potato each) • PREPARATION TIME: 15 minutes •
COOKING TIME: 25 minutes plus 15 minutes standing time

Stuffed baked potatoes are topped with a medley of vegetables and herbs. Serve with Oranges with Grape Sauce (page 416).

4 large baking potatoes
1 clove garlic, minced
1 small onion, chopped
¼ cup water
1 medium eggplant, diced
1 red bell pepper, seeded and diced
1 small zucchini, diced

2 teaspoons dried basil leaves
2 medium tomatoes, diced
¼ teaspoon black pepper
2 tablespoons chopped fresh parsley
½ cup plain nonfat yogurt
¼ cup grated nonfat mozzarella cheese (optional)

1. Pierce potatoes. Place in microwave on paper towel, leaving 1 inch between potatoes.
2. Microwave potatoes on HIGH for 6 minutes. Turn over. Microwave on HIGH for 7 minutes. Let stand for 10 minutes.
3. Combine the garlic, onion, and water in a microwave-safe casserole. Cover with vented plastic wrap and microwave on HIGH for 3 minutes.
4. Add eggplant and red pepper. Microwave on HIGH for 3 minutes. Stir. Microwave on HIGH for 2 minutes.
5. Add zucchini, basil, tomatoes, black pepper, and parsley. Cover with vented plastic wrap and microwave on HIGH for 2 minutes. Stir. Microwave on HIGH for 3 minutes. Let stand for 5 minutes.

6. Cut ¹/₂ inch off the top of each potato. Scoop out the potato pulp, leaving a ¹/₄-inch shell. Mash the potato pulp and stir in yogurt and ratatouille.
7. Fill the potato shells with the potato ratatouille mixture. Place the stuffed potatoes on a microwave-safe plate. If using cheese, sprinkle on top of potatoes. Microwave on HIGH for 10 minutes.

Calories Per Serving: 229
Fat: .7 g
Cholesterol: 3 mg
Protein: 10.7 g

Carbohydrates: 46 g
Dietary Fiber: 7.3 g
Sodium: 160 mg

✳ Pinto Bean Burritos ✳

YIELD: 4 servings (1 burrito each) • *PREPARATION TIME: 15 minutes plus bean cooking time and 2 minutes standing time* • *COOKING TIME: 3¹/₂ minutes*

These burritos are ready in a jiffy. They make a great meal on a night when you don't have much time or energy for cooking. Serve with a green salad with Creamy Buttermilk Dressing (page 277).

*2 cups home-cooked or canned pinto
  beans, drained and rinsed
¹/₄ cup chopped scallions
¹/₂ teaspoon dried oregano leaves
¹/₂ teaspoon ground cumin*

*¹/₄ cup minced red bell pepper
1 clove garlic, minced
4 nonfat flour or corn tortillas
2 tomatoes, chopped
2 tablespoons grated nonfat cheese*

1. Mash pinto beans.
2. Combine with scallions, oregano, cumin, red pepper, and garlic.
3. Divide bean mixture among the tortillas. Roll up tortillas and place seam-side down in a 9-inch glass pie plate. Top with chopped tomatoes.
4. Cover pie plate with vented plastic wrap and microwave on HIGH for 3¹/₂ minutes.
5. Remove plastic wrap, sprinkle with cheese, and let stand for 2 minutes.

Calories Per Serving: 182
Fat: .7 g
Cholesterol: .2 mg
Protein: 9.4 g

Carbohydrates: 37 g
Dietary Fiber: 7 g
Sodium: 48 mg

❋ *Black Bean Chili with Vegetables* ❋

YIELD: 8 servings (1 cup each) ▪ *PREPARATION TIME: 20 minutes plus bean
cooking time* ▪ *COOKING TIME: 1 hour and 7 minutes plus
10 minutes standing time*

This robust chili is made with black beans. Garnish with nonfat grated
cheese, chopped scallions, and nonfat sour cream. Serve with Pear Burritos (page 355).

¼ cup water	1 tablespoon dried basil leaves
4 garlic cloves, minced	1 teaspoon dried thyme leaves
1 onion, chopped	1 teaspoon ground cinnamon
2 green bell peppers, seeded and chopped	2 cups chopped fresh or low-sodium canned tomatoes
1 medium zucchini, chopped	2 cups water or vegetable broth
3 tablespoons chili powder	3 cups home-cooked or canned black beans, drained and rinsed
2 tablespoons ground cumin	¼ cup balsamic vinegar
1 tablespoon dried oregano leaves	

1. Combine water, garlic, onion, green peppers, and zucchini in a large
   microwave-safe casserole. Cover with vented plastic wrap. Microwave on HIGH for 3 minutes.
2. Add chili powder, cumin, oregano leaves, basil leaves, thyme leaves,
   and cinnamon. Microwave, uncovered, on HIGH for 4 minutes.
3. Add tomatoes, water or broth, and beans. Cover with vented plastic
   wrap and microwave on HIGH for 15 minutes or until liquid boils.
4. Remove cover and microwave on MEDIUM for 15 minutes.
5. Add vinegar. Microwave on MEDIUM for 30 minutes. Let stand for 10
   minutes.

Calories Per Serving: 124	Carbohydrates: 23 g
Fat: 1 g	Dietary Fiber: 2.5 g
Cholesterol: 0 mg	Sodium: 23 mg
Protein: 7 g	

Cannellini Beans with
✳ Potatoes and Vegetables ✳

YIELD: 4 servings • *PREPARATION TIME: 20 minutes plus bean cooking time* •
COOKING TIME: 6 minutes

Here cannellini beans are tossed with celery, yellow bell pepper, green peas, onion, and balsamic vinegar. Serve with Fiesta Red Potatoes (page 412).

1 cup cubed potatoes
2 tablespoons water, nonfat chicken broth, or vegetable broth
1/2 cup frozen green peas
1/4 cup chopped celery
1/4 cup chopped yellow or red bell pepper
1/2 cup minced onion

1 clove garlic, minced
1 1/2 cups home-cooked or canned cannellini beans, drained and rinsed
1/3 cup lemon juice
1 tablespoon balsamic vinegar
1 teaspoon dried thyme leaves

1. Place the potatoes and water or broth in a microwave-safe bowl, cover, and microwave on HIGH for 4 minutes or until the potatoes are just tender.
2. Add the peas to the potatoes, cover, and microwave on HIGH for 2 minutes more.
3. Drain peas and potatoes.
4. Toss peas and potatoes with celery, yellow or red pepper, onion, garlic, cannellini beans, lemon juice, balsamic vinegar, and thyme.

Calories Per Serving: 141
Fat: .6 g
Cholesterol: 0 mg
Protein: 7 g

Carbohydrates: 28 g
Dietary Fiber: 5 g
Sodium: 32 mg

✳ Stuffed Red Peppers ✳

YIELD: 6 servings (1 pepper each) • *PREPARATION TIME: 15 minutes plus rice cooking time* • *COOKING TIME: 10 minutes*

These stuffed red peppers are packed with brown rice, corn, red onion, and an array of spices.

Stuffed Red Peppers *(cont'd)*

6 large red bell peppers	¼ teaspoon turmeric
¾ cup cooked brown rice	½ cup nonfat grated cheddar cheese
½ cup frozen peas	(optional)
½ cup fresh, frozen, or canned corn kernels	3 medium tomatoes, cored and quartered
¾ cup shredded zucchini	2 tablespoons chopped fresh parsley
2 tablespoons chopped red onion	½ teaspoon dried basil leaves
½ teaspoon chili powder	½ teaspoon dried oregano leaves
½ teaspoon ground cumin	½ cup minced green bell pepper

1. Slice the tops off the red peppers and scoop their insides out with a spoon. Wrap each pepper in waxed paper and microwave for 4 minutes. Remove from microwave and set aside to cool.
2. Combine brown rice, peas, corn, zucchini, onion, chili powder, cumin, and turmeric.
3. Stuff cooled peppers with rice mixture. Set peppers in a microwave-safe casserole. Cover with vented plastic wrap and microwave on HIGH for 6 minutes. Uncover and sprinkle with cheese, if desired.
4. Place tomatoes, parsley, basil, oregano, and green pepper in a food processor or blender. Process until smooth.
5. Spoon tomato sauce over stuffed red peppers. Heat sauce in a small sauce pan on a conventional range top.

Calories Per Serving: 90	Carbohydrates: 18 g
Fat: .9 g	Dietary Fiber: 3.7 g
Cholesterol: .4 mg	Sodium: 48 mg
Protein: 3.9 g	

✳ Black Bean and Vegetable–Stuffed Peppers ✳

YIELD: 4 servings (½ pepper each) • *PREPARATION TIME: 15 minutes plus rice and bean cooking time* • *COOKING TIME: 15 minutes*

These green bell peppers are stuffed with black beans, corn, onion, tomato sauce, and rice. Serve with a salad of chicory, mushrooms, and Green Goddess Dressing (page 286).

1 cup fresh, frozen, or canned corn kernels	½ cup chopped onion
	2 tablespoons water

1 cup low-sodium tomato sauce
¼ teaspoon black pepper
⅔ cup cooked long-grain white or brown rice
2 cups home-cooked or canned black beans, drained and rinsed

2 large red bell peppers, cut in half lengthwise and seeded
4 tablespoons shredded nonfat cheese

1. Combine corn, onion, and water in a microwave-safe casserole. Cover with vented plastic wrap and microwave on HIGH for 3 minutes.
2. Add tomato sauce and black pepper. Cover with vented plastic wrap and microwave on HIGH for 3 minutes or until tomato sauce bubbles.
3. Remove casserole from microwave. Stir rice and beans into tomato-corn mixture. Cover and set aside.
4. Place pepper halves on a microwave-safe plate. Cover with vented plastic wrap. Microwave on HIGH for 5 minutes or until almost tender. Drain.
5. Stuff peppers with bean mixture. Cover with vented plastic wrap and microwave on HIGH for 4 minutes or until beans and rice are heated through and green pepper halves are tender.

Calories Per Serving: 224
Fat: 1 g
Cholesterol: 3 mg
Protein: 11.7 g

Carbohydrates: 44 g
Dietary Fiber: 6.8 g
Sodium: 40 mg

✳ *Eggplant Sicilian* ✳

YIELD: 4 servings ▪ *PREPARATION TIME: 15 minutes* ▪
COOKING TIME: 25 minutes

In this dish eggplant is combined with celery, red onion, garlic, tomato, red wine vinegar, and balsamic vinegar. Serve with Rosemary Potatoes (page 193).

1 medium eggplant, cut into ½-inch slices
½ cup diced celery
½ cup diced red onion
¼ cup water
1 clove garlic, minced

1 cup diced fresh tomato
1 tablespoon red wine vinegar
1 teaspoon balsamic vinegar
1 tablespoon chopped fresh parsley
¼ teaspoon black pepper

Eggplant Sicilian *(cont'd)*

1. Combine the eggplant, celery, onion, water, and garlic in a microwave-safe casserole. Microwave, uncovered, on HIGH for 5 minutes. Stir. Microwave on HIGH for 5 minutes more.
2. Add tomato. Microwave, uncovered, for 10 minutes.
3. Stir in red wine vinegar and balsamic vinegar. Microwave on HIGH uncovered, for 5 minutes. Stir in parsley and black pepper.

Calories Per Serving: 33
Fat: .3 g
Cholesterol: 0 mg
Protein: 1 g

Carbohydrates: 7.7 g
Dietary Fiber: .9 g
Sodium: 32 mg

✳ *Stuffed Pasta Shells* ✳

YIELD: 4 servings ▪ *PREPARATION TIME: 20 minutes plus pasta cooking time* ▪
COOKING TIME: 10 minutes

Here pasta shells are stuffed with a mixture of onion, garlic, bell pepper, tomatoes, and nonfat ricotta cheese. Serve with Broccoli-Corn Toss (page 403).

1 tablespoon water
1 onion, diced
2 cloves garlic, minced
1 cup seeded minced green bell
    pepper
½ cup chopped low-sodium canned
    tomatoes
1 teaspoon dried thyme leaves
Pinch of black pepper

1⅓ cups nonfat ricotta cheese
½ cup nonfat shredded mozzarella
    cheese
1 teaspoon dried basil leaves
¼ cup nonfat Parmesan cheese
¼ cup chopped fresh parsley
16 jumbo pasta shells, cooked al
    dente and well drained in a
    colander

1. Place water and onion in a microwave-safe bowl. Cover with vented plastic wrap. Microwave on HIGH for 1 minute. Add garlic. Re-cover and microwave on HIGH for 2 minutes.
2. Add green pepper. Re-cover and microwave on HIGH for 2 minutes.
3. Combine microwaved vegetables with tomatoes, thyme, and black pepper.

4. Combine ricotta cheese, mozzarella cheese, basil leaves, Parmesan cheese, and fresh parsley in a mixing bowl.
5. Spoon the cheese mixture into the pasta shells. Arrange shells on a microwave-safe dish in a single layer. Spoon the sauce over the shells. Microwave, uncovered, for 5 minutes or until hot.

Calories Per Serving: 234
Fat: .9 g
Cholesterol: 5.9 mg
Protein: 17 g

Carbohydrates: 47 g
Dietary Fiber: 0 g
Sodium: 275 mg

✳ *Spanish Vegetable Stew* ✳

YIELD: 6 servings • PREPARATION TIME: 20 minutes •
COOKING TIME: 1 hour and 25 minutes plus 10 minutes standing time

This hearty stew includes onions, garlic, bell pepper, long-grain white rice, tomatoes, celery, corn, and peas.

1/4 cup water
2 onions, thinly sliced
2 garlic cloves, minced
1 green bell pepper, seeded and chopped
2 cups uncooked long-grain white or brown rice
1/2 teaspoon ground saffron

4 1/2 cups vegetable broth or water
1 1/2 cups chopped fresh or low-sodium canned tomatoes
2 stalks celery, chopped
1 cup fresh, frozen, or canned corn kernels
1 cup thawed, frozen green peas
3 tablespoons chopped fresh parsley

1. Place water, onions, and garlic in a large microwave-safe casserole. Microwave on HIGH for 6 minutes or until onions are tender.
2. Add green pepper and rice. Microwave on HIGH for six minutes.
3. Add saffron, 3 1/2 cups of the broth or water, tomatoes, celery, and corn to casserole. Cover with vented microwave-safe plastic wrap. Microwave on HIGH for 18 minutes or until the liquid is boiling. Stir stew.
4. Recover casserole and microwave on MEDIUM for 55 minutes or until rice is tender. Add the remaining cup of broth if necessary during this cooking period.
5. Stir in peas and parsley. Cover again and let stand for 10 minutes.

Spanish Vegetable Stew *(cont'd)*

Calories Per Serving: 305	Carbohydrates: 66 g
Fat: .9 g	Dietary Fiber: 1.6 g
Cholesterol: 0 mg	Sodium: 55 mg
Protein: 8 g	

✳ *Layered Tortilla Casserole* ✳

YIELD: 4 servings • *PREPARATION TIME: 20 minutes plus bean and corn cooking time* • *COOKING TIME: 20 minutes plus 5 minutes standing time*

Corn tortillas are layered here with corn, beans, tomato sauce, and nonfat cheese. Serve with a salad of mixed greens with Quick Garlic-French Dressing (page 273).

¼ cup water, nonfat chicken broth, or vegetable broth
1 cup chopped onion
1 clove garlic, minced
1 cup chopped celery
1 tablespoon chili powder
Pinch of cayenne pepper
1 cup cooked fresh, frozen, or canned corn kernels
1 cup low-sodium tomato sauce
1 cup home-cooked or canned kidney beans, drained and rinsed
1 cup home-cooked or canned Great Northern beans, drained and rinsed
6 nonfat corn tortillas
1 cup nonfat cottage cheese or ricotta cheese
½ cup grated nonfat cheddar cheese

1. Combine the water or broth, onion, garlic, and celery in a microwave-safe casserole. Microwave, uncovered, on HIGH for 5 minutes or until onions and celery are tender.
2. Combine with chili powder, cayenne pepper, corn, beans, and tomato sauce.
3. Place 3 corn tortillas on the bottom of a 2-quart microwave-safe casserole dish.
4. Top with ½ of the tomato-bean mixture.
5. Spread ½ cup of the cottage cheese or ricotta over the tomato-bean mixture. Sprinkle with ¼ cup of the grated cheddar cheese.
6. Top with remaining 3 corn tortillas, the remaining tomato-bean mixture, the remaining ½ cup cottage cheese, and the remaining ¼ cup cheddar cheese.

7. Microwave uncovered on HIGH for 12 minutes or until cheese has melted and ingredients are warmed through. Let stand 5 minutes before serving.

Calories Per Serving: 276
Fat: 1 g
Cholesterol: 1 mg
Protein: 13 g

Carbohydrates: 58 g
Dietary Fiber: 9 g
Sodium: 150 mg

✳ *Long-Grain Rice* ✳

YIELD: 4 servings ▪ *PREPARATION TIME: 3 minutes* ▪
COOKING TIME: 17 minutes plus 5 minutes standing time

The microwave does an excellent job of turning out rice that does not stick or burn.

1³/₄ cups water, nonfat chicken broth, or vegetable broth

1 cup uncooked long-grain white rice

1. Place rice and water or broth in a 3-quart microwave-safe casserole. Cover tightly. Cook on HIGH for 4 to 7 minutes until the liquid boils. Cook on MEDIUM for 10 minutes or until all the liquid is absorbed. Let stand, covered, for 5 minutes.

Note: When reheating long-grain rice, cover and cook on HIGH for 1 to 6 minutes until heated through. Stir every minute.

Calories Per Serving: 169
Fat: .3 g
Cholesterol: 0 mg
Protein: 3.3 g

Carbohydrates: 37 g
Dietary Fiber: .4 g
Sodium: 138 mg

✳ *Basmati Rice* ✳

YIELD: 4 servings ▪ *PREPARATION TIME: 3 minutes* ▪
COOKING TIME: 20 minutes plus 5 minutes standing time

Basmati rice has a sweet aroma and is quite delicious when prepared in the microwave. Serve with curried vegetable dishes.

Basmati Rice *(cont'd)*

1 cup uncooked basmati rice, rinsed
    to remove small stones or seeds
2 cups water, nonfat chicken broth,
    or vegetable broth

1 tablespoon chopped fresh parsley
¼ teaspoon black pepper

1. Place rice and water or broth in a large microwave-safe casserole. Cover tightly. Cook on HIGH for 20 minutes.
2. Let stand, covered, for 5 minutes.
3. Stir in parsley and black pepper.

Calories Per Serving: 169
Fat: .3 g
Cholesterol: 0 mg
Protein: 3.3 g

Carbohydrates: 37 g
Dietary Fiber: .4 g
Sodium: 138 mg

✳ *Pineapple Rice* ✳

YIELD: 4 servings • *PREPARATION TIME: 15 minutes* •
COOKING TIME: 19 minutes plus 7 minutes standing time

Long-grain rice is combined with pineapple juice, ground ginger, crushed pineapple, green bell pepper, and water chestnuts in this dish. Serve with oriental vegetable dishes.

1 cup uncooked long-grain white rice
1¾ cups unsweetened pineapple
    juice
¼ teaspoon ground ginger

1 cup juice-packed crushed pineapple
½ green bell pepper, seeded and
    minced
½ cup minced water chestnuts

1. Place rice, pineapple juice, and ginger in a 3-quart microwave-safe casserole. Cover tightly. Cook on HIGH for 4 to 7 minutes until the liquid boils. Cook on MEDIUM for 10 minutes or until all the liquid is absorbed. Let stand, covered, for 5 minutes.
2. Place crushed pineapple, green pepper, water chestnuts in a microwave-safe bowl and microwave on HIGH for 2 minutes.
3. Stir pineapple mixture into rice. Microwave for 2 minutes.

Calories Per Serving: 151
Fat: .6 g
Cholesterol: 0 mg
Protein: 2 g

Carbohydrates: 36 g
Dietary Fiber: 2 g
Sodium: 273 mg

✳ Wild Rice ✳

YIELD: *6 servings* • PREPARATION TIME: *3 minutes* •
COOKING TIME: *32 minutes plus 5 minutes standing time*

The kernels of wild rice steam and the grains burst open as they cook.

²/₃ cup uncooked wild rice   *1¹/₂ cups water*

1. Place rice and water in a 3-quart microwave-safe casserole. Cover tightly and microwave on HIGH for 7 minutes or until the water begins to boil. Microwave on MEDIUM for 20 to 25 minutes. Most of the kernels should have burst open. Let stand for 5 minutes. Drain before serving.

Calories Per Serving: 36
Fat: .3 g
Cholesterol: 0 mg
Protein: .8 g

Carbohydrates: 7.5 g
Dietary Fiber: .5 g
Sodium: 4 mg

✳ Lemon-Dill Rice ✳

YIELD: *4 servings* • PREPARATION TIME: *15 minutes* •
COOKING TIME: *17 minutes plus 5 minutes standing time*

Here long-grain rice is combined with lemon juice, lemon peel, dill, parsley, and scallion. Serve with Steamed Vegetables with Mustard-Dill Sauce (page 414).

1 cup uncooked long-grain white rice
1³/₄ cups water
2 tablespoons lemon juice
1 teaspoon grated lemon peel

2 tablespoons chopped fresh parsley
1 teaspoon dried dill weed
1 scallion, minced

Lemon-Dill Rice *(cont'd)*

1. Place rice, water, lemon juice, and lemon peel in a 3-quart microwave-safe casserole. Cover tightly. Cook on HIGH for 4 to 7 minutes until the liquid boils. Cook on MEDIUM for 10 minutes or until all the liquid is absorbed. Let stand, covered, for 5 minutes.
2. Stir parsley, dill weed, and scallion into rice.

Note: When reheating long-grain rice, cover and cook on HIGH for 1 to 6 minutes until heated through. Stir every minute.

Calories Per Serving: 58   Carbohydrates: 12 g
Fat: .5 g   Dietary Fiber: .9 g
Cholesterol: 0 mg   Sodium: 136 mg
Protein: 1.4 g

✳ Red Pepper–Dijon Rice Salad ✳

YIELD: 4 servings • PREPARATION TIME: 15 minutes •
COOKING TIME: 17 minutes plus 5 minutes standing time

Long-grain rice is combined here with red bell pepper, fresh parsley, scallions, yogurt, and Dijon mustard. This dish can be served at room temperature or chilled. Serve with Greek Zucchini Casserole (page 124).

1 cup uncooked long-grain white rice   *2 scallions, chopped*
1³/₄ cups water   *¹/₄ cup nonfat plain yogurt*
1 red bell pepper, seeded and diced   *¹/₄ cup nonfat mayonnaise*
¹/₃ cup chopped fresh parsley   *¹/₂ teaspoon Dijon mustard*

1. Place rice and water in a 3-quart microwave-safe casserole. Cover tightly. Cook on HIGH for 4 to 7 minutes until the water boils. Cook on MEDIUM for 10 minutes or until all the liquid is absorbed. Let stand, covered, for 5 minutes.
2. Stir red pepper, parsley, and scallions into rice.
3. Combine yogurt, mayonnaise, and mustard. Stir into rice.

Calories Per Serving: 204   Carbohydrates: 44 g
Fat: .4 g   Dietary Fiber: 1 g
Cholesterol: .25 mg   Sodium: 303 mg
Protein: 4 g

✻ *Strawberry-Blueberry Rice Salad* ✻

YIELD: 4 servings ▪ *PREPARATION TIME: 3 minutes plus 1 hour chilling time* ▪
COOKING TIME: 17 minutes plus 5 minutes standing time

In this dish long-grain rice is combined with strawberries and blueberries and tossed with a yogurt–brown sugar dressing accented with lime juice. You can substitute 2 cups of other berries or chopped fruit in season. Serve with Lemon–Ginger Asparagus (page 403).

1 cup uncooked long-grain rice	*³/₄ cup nonfat plain yogurt*
1³/₄ cups water	*¹/₄ cup brown sugar, firmly packed*
1 cup sliced strawberries	*1 tablespoon lime juice*
1 cup blueberries	

1. Place rice and water in a 3-quart microwave-safe casserole. Cover tightly. Microwave on HIGH for 4 to 7 minutes or until the water boils. Microwave on MEDIUM for 10 minutes or until the liquid is absorbed. Let stand, covered, for 5 minutes.
2. Chill rice for 1 hour.
3. Combine rice with strawberries and blueberries.
4. Combine yogurt, sugar, and lime juice.
5. Toss rice mixture with yogurt sauce.

Variation
▪ In Step 1, substitute 1 cup brown rice and 2¹/₃ cups water, nonfat chicken broth, or vegetable broth. Microwave on HIGH for 6 to 10 minutes until liquid comes to a boil. Then microwave at MEDIUM for 25 to 30 minutes or until liquid is absorbed. Let stand, covered, for 5 minutes.

Calories Per Serving: 277	Carbohydrates: 61 g
Fat: .7 g	Dietary Fiber: 2.2 g
Cholesterol: .8 mg	Sodium: 45 mg
Protein: 6 g	

✳ *Polenta* ✳

YIELD: *4 servings* • PREPARATION TIME: *10 minutes* •
COOKING TIME: *10 minutes plus 5 minutes standing time*

Cornmeal polenta is easy to prepare in the microwave. You can serve it topped with a tomato or vegetable sauce. Serve with Spanish Vegetable Stew (page 393).

1 cup skim milk
2¹/₂ cups water
1 cup yellow cornmeal

¹/₄ teaspoon dried basil
¹/₄ cup nonfat Parmesan cheese

1. Place milk, water, cornmeal, and basil in a 3-quart microwave-safe casserole. Cover with vented plastic wrap.
2. Microwave on HIGH for 5 minutes. Stir.
3. Microwave on HIGH for 5 more minutes. Polenta should be thickened and almost all of the water should be absorbed.
4. Stir in the Parmesan cheese.
5. Cover and let stand for 5 minutes or until polenta is firm.

Calories Per Serving: 108
Fat: 1 g
Cholesterol: 1 mg
Protein: 4 g

Carbohydrates: 21 g
Dietary Fiber: 3.7 g
Sodium: 58 mg

✳ *Curried Rice Pilaf with Dried Apricots* ✳

YIELD: *4 servings* • PREPARATION TIME: *15 minutes* •
COOKING TIME: *21 minutes*

Here rice is cooked with curry powder, dried apricots, raisins, onion, and garlic. Serve with Broccoli with Parsley–Pepper Sauce (page 404).

¹/₄ cup onion, finely chopped
1 clove garlic, finely chopped
¹/₄ cup skim milk
1 cup uncooked long-grain white rice
2 cups water, nonfat chicken broth,
   or vegetable broth

¹/₄ teaspoon black pepper
2 teaspoons curry powder
2 tablespoons chopped dried apricots
2 tablespoons raisins

1. Place the onion, garlic, and milk in a large microwave-safe bowl. Cover and microwave on HIGH for 3 minutes.
2. Add the rice, water or broth, pepper, curry powder, apricots, and raisins. Cover and microwave on HIGH for 18 minutes or until all the liquid is absorbed.

Calories Per Serving: 96
Fat: .7 g
Cholesterol: .3 mg
Protein: 3 g

Carbohydrates: 20 g
Dietary Fiber: 1.9 g
Sodium: 80 mg

✳ *Barley with Peas and Red Peppers* ✳

YIELD: 4 servings ▪ *PREPARATION TIME: 10 minutes* ▪
COOKING TIME: 22 minutes plus 5 minutes standing time

Barley cooks very quickly in the microwave. In this recipe pearl barley is prepared with red bell peppers, green peas, and parsley. You'll find barley in the rice and pasta aisle of your supermarket. Serve with Eggplant with Chiles (page 407).

3 ounces medium pearl barley
1 cup water
2 cloves garlic, minced
1 cup frozen green peas

1 cup chopped red bell peppers
¼ cup nonfat chicken broth
2 tablespoons chopped fresh parsley
1 tablespoon nonfat Parmesan cheese

1. Combine barley, water, and garlic in a microwave-safe casserole. Cover with vented plastic wrap. Microwave on HIGH for 5 minutes. Stir. Microwave on HIGH for 7 more minutes. Stir. Microwave on MEDIUM for 5 minutes.
2. Add green peas, red peppers, chicken broth, parsley, and Parmesan cheese. Microwave on HIGH for 5 minutes. Let stand 5 minutes before serving.

Calories Per Serving: 99
Fat: .4 g
Cholesterol: 0 mg
Protein: 4 g

Carbohydrates: 20 g
Dietary Fiber: 4.5 g
Sodium: 55 mg

❋ *Boston Brown Bread* ❋

YIELD: 10 servings (1 slice each) ▪ *PREPARATION TIME: 15 minutes* ▪
COOKING TIME: 14 minutes plus 20 minutes standing time

Boston Brown Bread, which takes three hours in a conventional oven, can be made in just a few minutes in a microwave. Spread Boston Brown Bread slices with fruit spreads or nonfat cream cheese. Serve it with Molasses–Apple Baked Beans (page 205).

½ cup whole wheat flour
½ cup yellow cornmeal
½ cup unbleached all-purpose flour
½ teaspoon baking powder
½ teaspoon baking soda

½ cup molasses
⅔ cup nonfat buttermilk
2 egg whites
¾ cup raisins

1. Combine whole wheat flour, cornmeal, all-purpose flour, baking powder, baking soda, molasses, buttermilk, egg whites, and raisins in a mixing bowl.
2. Line the bottom of a 2-cup glass measure with a waxed paper circle. (Boston Brown Bread should be log shaped.)
3. Pour in half the batter. Cover with vented plastic wrap. Microwave on MEDIUM for 7 minutes. Test with a toothpick. Bread is done when toothpick comes out clean. Remove and let stand for 10 minutes.
4. After standing period, run a knife around the edge of the measure to release the bread. Turn out onto a serving plate.
5. Wipe out glass measure and repeat steps 2 and 3 with the remaining half of the batter.
6. To cut without crumbling, use cotton kitchen string and cut with a sawing motion. Slice each cylindrical loaf into 5 slices.

Calories Per Serving: 147
Fat: .4 g
Cholesterol: .3 mg
Protein: 3.5 g

Carbohydrates: 33 g
Dietary Fiber: 2.4 g
Sodium: 92 mg

✳ *Lemon-Ginger Asparagus* ✳

YIELD: *4 servings* • PREPARATION TIME: *10 minutes* •
COOKING TIME: *11 minutes*

Here asparagus is microwaved and then topped with a lemon-and-ginger-flavored sauce. Serve with Red Pepper–Dijon Rice Salad (page 398).

1 pound asparagus spears, ends trimmed
2 tablespoons water
½ cup skim milk
¼ cup nonfat chicken broth

1½ teaspoons arrowroot or cornstarch
¼ teaspoon grated fresh gingerroot
¼ teaspoon grated lemon peel

1. Place asparagus in a microwave-safe baking dish. Add water. Cover with vented plastic wrap.
2. Microwave on HIGH for 5 minutes. Rearrange spears. Microwave for 4 minutes more. Drain and set aside.
3. Combine milk, broth, arrowroot or cornstarch, gingerroot, and lemon peel in a glass bowl. Microwave for 1 minute and stir. Microwave for 30 seconds, stir again. Microwave for 30 more seconds.
4. Pour sauce over asparagus and serve.

Calories Per Serving: 47
Fat: .5 g
Cholesterol: .5 mg
Protein: 4 g

Carbohydrates: 8 g
Dietary Fiber: 1.3 g
Sodium: 30 mg

✳ *Broccoli-Corn Toss* ✳

YIELD: *4 servings* • PREPARATION TIME: *10 minutes plus corn cooking time* •
COOKING TIME: *9 minutes plus 3 minutes standing time*

These broccoli florets are tossed with corn, tomato, oregano, and minced scallions. Select broccoli with rich green buds (some varieties may have a dark blue or purple cast) and avoid any with yellow spots. Serve with Lemon-Dill Rice (page 397).

Broccoli-Corn Toss *(cont'd)*

1 pound broccoli florets

¼ cup plus 2 tablespoons water, nonfat chicken broth, or vegetable broth

1¼ cups cooked fresh, frozen, or canned corn kernels

½ teaspoon dried oregano leaves

2 scallions, minced

1 medium tomato, chopped

1. Place broccoli florets and ¼ cup of the water or broth in a microwave-safe casserole. Cover with vented plastic wrap. Microwave on HIGH for 5 minutes. Let stand for 3 minutes.
2. Place corn kernels in a 1½-quart microwave-safe casserole with 2 remaining tablespoons water or broth. Cover with vented plastic wrap. Microwave on HIGH for 4 minutes.
3. Toss broccoli with corn, oregano, scallions, and chopped tomato.

Calories Per Serving: 130

Fat: 1 g

Cholesterol: 0 mg

Protein: 10 g

Carbohydrates: 28 g

Dietary Fiber: 9 g

Sodium: 78 mg

✳ *Broccoli with Parsley-Pepper Sauce* ✳

YIELD: 4 servings ▪ *PREPARATION TIME: 15 minutes* ▪
COOKING TIME: 15 minutes

Here broccoli is microwaved with a flavorful sauce. Serve with Mashed Sweet Potatoes and Applesauce (page 408).

2 medium red bell peppers, seeded, cored, and cut in chunks

2 cloves garlic, minced

¼ cup lemon juice

½ teaspoon paprika

¼ teaspoon cayenne pepper

½ teaspoon black pepper

2 tablespoons chopped fresh parsley

2 cups broccoli florets

1. Place bell pepper chunks and garlic in a microwave-safe bowl. Cover with vented plastic wrap and microwave on HIGH for 7 minutes.
2. Place bell pepper and garlic, lemon juice, paprika, cayenne, black pepper, and parsley in a blender or food processor and purée.

3. Place broccoli and bell pepper purée in a microwave-safe bowl. Cover with vented plastic wrap and microwave for 8 minutes.

Variations
- Substitute 2 cups brussels sprouts, bottoms trimmed, for the broccoli.
- Substitute ½ teaspoon ground ginger for the paprika and cayenne. Substitute cauliflower for the broccoli.

Calories Per Serving: 29   Carbohydrates: 6.6 g
Fat: .4 g   Dietary Fiber: 2 g
Cholesterol: 0 mg   Sodium: 15 mg
Protein: 1.9 g

✳ *Calico Cauliflower* ✳

YIELD: 4 servings • *PREPARATION TIME: 15 minutes* •
COOKING TIME: 6 minutes plus 3 minutes standing time

These cauliflower florets are tossed with minced red and green peppers. Serve with Curried Rice Pilaf with Dried Apricots (page 400).

4 cups cauliflower florets
¼ cup water, nonfat chicken broth,
*   or vegetable broth*
1 red bell pepper, seeded and minced
1 green bell pepper, seeded and
*   minced*

¼ teaspoon black pepper
¼ teaspoon grated lemon peel
¼ teaspoon dried basil leaves
1 tablespoon chopped fresh parsley

1. Place cauliflower florets and water or broth in a microwave-safe casserole. Cover with vented plastic wrap. Microwave on HIGH for 6 minutes. Let stand for 3 minutes.
2. Toss cauliflower with minced red and green peppers, black pepper, lemon peel, basil, and parsley.

Calories Per Serving: 34   Carbohydrates: 7 g
Fat: .4 g   Dietary Fiber: 3 g
Cholesterol: 0 mg   Sodium: 17 mg
Protein: 2.3 g

Cannellini Beans with
✳ Potatoes and Vegetables ✳

YIELD: 4 servings • *PREPARATION TIME: 20 minutes plus bean cooking time* •
COOKING TIME: 6 minutes

Cannellini beans are tossed here with celery, yellow bell pepper, green
peas, potatoes, onion, and balsamic vinegar.

1 cup cubed potatoes
*2 tablespoons water, nonfat chicken
   broth, or vegetable broth*
¹/₂ cup frozen green peas
¹/₄ cup chopped celery
*¹/₄ cup chopped yellow or red bell
   pepper*
¹/₂ cup minced onion

1 clove garlic, minced
*1¹/₂ cups home-cooked or canned
   cannellini beans, drained and
   rinsed*
¹/₃ cup lemon juice
1 tablespoon balsamic vinegar
1 teaspoon dried thyme leaves

1. Place the potatoes and the water or broth in a microwave-safe bowl,
   cover, and microwave on HIGH for 4 minutes or until the potatoes are
   just tender.
2. Add the peas to the potatoes, cover with vented plastic wrap, and
   microwave on HIGH for 2 minutes more.
3. Drain peas and potatoes.
4. Toss peas and potatoes with celery, yellow pepper, onion, garlic,
   cannellini beans, lemon juice, balsamic vinegar, and thyme.

Calories Per Serving: 141
Fat: .6 g
Cholesterol: 0 mg
Protein: 7 g

Carbohydrates: 28 g
Dietary Fiber: 5 g
Sodium: 32 mg

✳ *Succotash* ✳

YIELD: *4 servings* • PREPARATION TIME: *10 minutes* •
COOKING TIME: *8 minutes plus 3 minutes standing time*

This classic vegetable dish is quick and easy to prepare in the microwave.
Serve with Tomato Red Skins (page 410) and Cauliflower-Mushroom
Salad with Balsamic Dressing (page 231).

2 tablespoons water
2 cups fresh, frozen, or canned corn
 kernels
2 cups frozen lima beans, defrosted

1 medium green or red bell pepper,
 finely chopped
¹/₄ teaspoon white pepper

1. Place water, corn, lima beans, green or red pepper, and white pepper
   in a microwave-safe casserole. Cover with vented plastic wrap.
2. Microwave on HIGH for 8 minutes.
3. Let stand, covered, for 3 minutes.

Calories Per Serving: 157
Fat: .4 g
Cholesterol: 0 mg
Protein: 7.7 g

Carbohydrates: 33 g
Dietary Fiber: 6 g
Sodium: 50 mg

✳ *Eggplant with Chiles* ✳

YIELD: *4 servings* • PREPARATION TIME: *20 minutes* •
COOKING TIME: *9 minutes plus 3 minutes standing time*

Eggplant, tomatoes, and chiles are cooked with oregano and cumin in
this dish. Serve with Microwave Baked Potatoes (page 412).

1 medium eggplant
2 tablespoons water
2 cups fresh or low-sodium canned
 chopped tomatoes
1 4-ounce can chopped green chile
 peppers, drained

¹/₂ teaspoon dried oregano leaves
¹/₄ teaspoon ground cumin
¹/₃ cup nonfat grated cheese

Eggplant with Chiles *(cont'd)*

1. Cut top off eggplant. Cut into ½-inch slices. Place in a microwave-safe baking dish with water. Cover with vented plastic wrap. Microwave on HIGH for 7 minutes. Drain.
2. Combine tomatoes, chile peppers, oregano, and cumin.
3. Pour sauce over eggplant. Microwave covered with vented plastic wrap on HIGH for 2 minutes.
4. Remove from microwave and sprinkle with cheese. Let stand for 3 minutes or until cheese melts.

Calories Per Serving: 52 Carbohydrates: 11 g
Fat: .5 g Dietary Fiber: 3 g
Cholesterol: .4 mg Sodium: 42 mg
Protein: 2.5 g

✳ *Mashed Sweet Potatoes and Applesauce* ✳

YIELD: 4 servings ▪ *PREPARATION TIME: 25 minutes (including microwaving and mashing sweet potatoes)* ▪ *COOKING TIME: 12 minutes plus 3 minutes standing time*

Cooked, mashed sweet potatoes and applesauce are puréed and seasoned with orange peel, cinnamon, and nutmeg in this dish. It is best to buy sweet potatoes loose rather than those that are prepackaged to avoid getting any damaged ones. Look for those with smooth, unbroken skin without shriveled, soft, or sunken patches. Serve with Apple-Celery Salad (page 225) and Calico Cauliflower (page 405).

4 sweet potatoes ¼ *teaspoon ground cinnamon*
1½ cups unsweetened applesauce ¼ *teaspoon ground nutmeg*
1 teaspoon grated orange peel ¼ *teaspoon black pepper*

1. Prick sweet potatoes with a fork. Place in microwave oven on a paper towel, leaving space between the potatoes. Microwave on HIGH for 6 minutes. Rearrange potatoes and turn them over. Microwave for 6 more minutes. Let potatoes stand, covered, for 3 more minutes. Peel and mash sweet potatoes.
2. Stir applesauce, orange peel, cinnamon, nutmeg, and black pepper into mashed sweet potatoes.

Calories Per Serving: 160
Fat: .2 g
Cholesterol: 0 mg
Protein: 2 g

Carbohydrates: 38 g
Dietary Fiber: 4.8 g
Sodium: 14 mg

✳ *Lemon-Dijon Lima Beans* ✳

YIELD: 4 servings • PREPARATION TIME: 20 minutes •
COOKING TIME: 16 minutes plus 3 minutes standing time

These lima beans are steamed in the microwave and seasoned with lemon juice, Dijon mustard, and chopped chives. Serve with Maple Baked Sweet Potatoes (page 181) and Turnip and Red Grape Salad (page 245).

2 pounds fresh lima beans, shelled
  (about 2 cups)
¹/₂ cup water

1 tablespoon lemon juice
1 tablespoon Dijon mustard
1 tablespoon chopped dried chives

1. Place beans and water in a 1¹/₂ quart microwave-safe casserole. Microwave on HIGH for 7 minutes, or until water boils. Stir.
2. Microwave on HIGH for 9 minutes. Check to see if beans are tender.
3. Let stand for 3 minutes. Drain and toss with lemon juice, Dijon mustard, and chives.

Variation
- Substitute 2 cups frozen lima beans. Follow package instructions for microwaving. Proceed to Step 3.

Calories Per Serving: 109
Fat: .3 g
Cholesterol: 0 mg
Protein: 5.8 g

Carbohydrates: 20 g
Dietary Fiber: 6 g
Sodium: 64 mg

✳ *Spicy Jalapeños and Red Bell Peppers* ✳

YIELD: 4 servings • PREPARATION TIME: 15 minutes plus 2 minutes standing time
and 45 minutes marinating time • COOKING TIME: 3¹/₂ minutes

These peppers are marinated in a multiflavored sauce. Serve with crisp nonfat crackers and Three-Bean Chili (page 156).

Spicy Jalapeños and Red Bell Peppers *(cont'd)*

2 jalapeño peppers, ribs and seeds
    scraped out and cut into thin strips
3 red bell peppers, seeded and sliced
    into thin strips
2 tablespoons nonfat chicken broth
3 tablespoons lemon juice

1 tablespoon balsamic vinegar
2 cloves garlic, minced
2 tablespoon minced scallions
1 teaspoon dried rosemary leaves
1 teaspoon Dijon mustard

1. Place the jalapeño peppers and the red bell peppers in a microwave-safe container. Add the chicken broth. Seal with vented plastic wrap and microwave on HIGH for 2 minutes.
2. Stir peppers. Microwave for $1^{1}/_{2}$ minutes. Let stand for 2 minutes.
3. Combine lemon juice, vinegar, garlic, scallions, rosemary, and mustard.
4. Drain the peppers and add them to the lemon juice mixture.
5. Cover and marinate in the refrigerator for at least 45 minutes.

Calories Per Serving: 23
Fat: .4 g
Cholesterol: 0 mg
Protein: . 8 g

Carbohydrates: 5 g
Dietary Fiber: .9 g
Sodium: 147 mg

✻ *Tomato Red Skins* ✻

YIELD: 4 servings • *PREPARATION TIME: 15 minutes* •
COOKING TIME: 7 minutes plus 4 minutes standing time

Red-skinned potatoes are tossed here with tomatoes, garlic, and rosemary. Serve with Marinated Carrots and Green Beans (page 230) and Broccoli in Ginger-Mustard Sauce (page 168).

1 pound red-skinned potatoes,
    chopped into 1-inch chunks
$^{1}/_{4}$ cup water, nonfat chicken broth,
    or vegetable broth

1 clove garlic, minced
1 cup chopped tomatoes
$^{1}/_{2}$ teaspoon dried rosemary leaves

1. Place potato chunks, water or broth, and garlic in a microwave-safe casserole. Microwave covered with vented plastic wrap on HIGH for 7 minutes. Let stand for 4 minutes.
2. Toss potatoes with tomatoes and rosemary leaves.

Calories Per Serving: 97
Fat: .2 g
Cholesterol: 0 mg
Protein: 2.2 g

Carbohydrates: 22 g
Dietary Fiber: 1.5 g
Sodium: 7.7 mg

❋ *Tropical Stuffed Sweet Potatoes* ❋

YIELD: *4 servings* • PREPARATION TIME: *5 minutes* •
COOKING TIME: *17 minutes*

These sweet potato shells are filled with a stuffing of crushed pineapple and mashed sweet potatoes. Serve with Creamy Baked Corn with Zucchini and Red Bell Pepper (page 174) and Asparagus with Orange Sauce (page 167).

4 medium sweet potatoes
½ cup skim milk
Pinch of black pepper

1 cup crushed juice-packed canned
pineapple, drained

1. Pierce the potato skins. Arrange on a paper towel, leaving 1 inch between the potatoes. Microwave on HIGH for 7 minutes. Turn potatoes and microwave on HIGH for 6 minutes. Check to be sure potatoes are tender.
2. Cut a slice off one of the long sides of each potato. Scoop out, placing pulp in a bowl and leaving a ¼-inch-thick shell.
3. Mash the sweet potato pulp with the milk and pepper. Stir in the crushed pineapple.
4. Refill the potato shells with the sweet potato–pineapple mixture.
5. Place the filled potato shells on a microwave-safe plate. Microwave on HIGH for 4 minutes.

Calories Per Serving: 149
Fat: .2 g
Cholesterol: .5 mg
Protein: 3.2 g

Carbohydrates: 34 g
Dietary Fiber: 3.9 g
Sodium: 29 mg

✳ Microwave Baked Potatoes ✳

*YIELD: 4 servings • PREPARATION TIME: 5 minutes •
COOKING TIME: 8 minutes plus 10 minutes standing time*

Baked potatoes cook quickly in your microwave and can become a staple food even when you're in a hurry. Serve topped with Lentils in Tomato Sauce (page 204).

*4 medium white potatoes, yams, or
    sweet potatoes*

1. Scrub potatoes and pierce with a fork to allow steam to escape.
2. Arrange in the microwave like the spokes of a wheel, at least an inch apart, with the plumpest ends toward the middle.
3. Microwave on HIGH for 4 minutes.
4. Turn potatoes over and microwave for 4 additional minutes.
5. Remove potatoes from microwave and place under an inverted bowl. Let stand for 10 minutes before eating.

Calories Per Serving: 145   Carbohydrates: 33 g
Fat: .2 g   Dietary Fiber: 3.7 g
Cholesterol: 0 mg   Sodium: 8 mg
Protein: 3 g

✳ Fiesta Red Potatoes ✳

*YIELD: 4 servings • PREPARATION TIME: 20 minutes •
COOKING TIME: 9 minutes plus 3 minutes standing time and 2 minutes broiling time*

Here red-skinned potatoes are topped with tomatoes, green pepper, Mexican spices, and nonfat cheddar cheese. Serve with Garlic Chile, Corn, and Summer Squash (page 175).

*3/4 pound red-skinned potatoes,   3 scallions, minced
    thinly sliced   1/2 teaspoon ground cumin
2 tablespoons water   1/2 teaspoon chili powder
2 medium tomatoes, chopped   1/2 teaspoon dried oregano leaves
1 medium green bell pepper, seeded   2/3 cup grated nonfat cheddar cheese
    and chopped*

1. Place potato slices and water in a shallow microwave-safe casserole. Cover with vented plastic wrap and microwave on HIGH for 6 minutes. Let stand for 3 minutes. Drain potatoes.
2. Sprinkle potatoes with tomatoes, scallions, green pepper, cumin, chili powder, oregano, and cheese. Cover with vented plastic wrap and microwave on MEDIUM for 3 minutes.
3. Remove plastic wrap and run casserole under the preheated broiler for 2 minutes or until lightly browned.

Calories Per Serving: 86
Fat: .4 g
Cholesterol: .8 mg
Protein: 3.4 g

Carbohydrates: 18 g
Dietary Fiber: 2 g
Sodium: 61 mg

✳ *Ginger-Honey Acorn Squash* ✳

YIELD: 4 servings • *PREPARATION TIME: 10 minutes* •
COOKING TIME: 8 minutes plus 5 minutes standing time

You'll want to start including winter squash in your menu plans more often when you realize how quickly it cooks in the microwave. Serve with Lima Beans with Corn and Tomatoes (page 180) and Curried Tangerine Rice (page 197).

1 pound acorn squash
2 tablespoons honey

½ teaspoon ground ginger
½ teaspoon ground cinnamon

1. Cut acorn squash in half. Scoop out seeds and stringy pulp.
2. Top each half with 1 tablespoon honey and sprinkle with ginger and cinnamon.
3. Wrap in plastic wrap and microwave on HIGH for 8 minutes. Let stand for 5 minutes before serving.

Calories Per Serving: 87
Fat: .7 g
Cholesterol: 0 mg
Protein: 2.6 g

Carbohydrates: 20 g
Dietary Fiber: 3 g
Sodium: 9.6 mg

✳ *Hubbard Squash with Navy Beans* ✳

YIELD: 8 servings • PREPARATION TIME: 20 minutes plus bean cooking time •
COOKING TIME: 16 minutes

Hubbard squash is combined with Great Northern beans in tomato sauce
in this dish. To soften the squash in your microwave before peeling and
cutting, microwave whole squash for 1 minute on HIGH. Serve with
Lemon–Thyme Vegetable Rice (page 197).

1½ cups water, nonfat chicken
  broth, or vegetable broth
¾ cup chopped onion
½ teaspoon ground cumin
1 clove garlic, minced
3 cups cubed peeled Hubbard or
  butternut squash

2½ cups cooked or canned Great
  Northern beans, drained and
  rinsed
2½ cups chopped fresh or low-
  sodium canned tomatoes

1. Place ¼ cup of the water or broth, onion, cumin, and garlic in a
   microwave-safe bowl. Cover with vented plastic wrap and microwave
   on HIGH for 3 minutes.
2. Add squash and the remaining 1¼ cups water or broth. Cover and
   microwave on HIGH for 5 minutes. Stir. Microwave on HIGH for 5
   more minutes.
3. Add beans and tomatoes. Cover and microwave on HIGH for 3
   minutes.

Calories Per Serving: 117
·Fat: .9 g
Cholesterol: 0 mg
Protein: 6.9 g

Carbohydrates: 22 g
Dietary Fiber: 5 g
Sodium: 20 mg

Steamed Vegetables with ✳ *Mustard-Dill Sauce* ✳

YIELD: 6 servings • PREPARATION TIME: 15 minutes plus 5 minutes standing time
• COOKING TIME: 15 minutes

These steamed vegetables are served with a tangy sauce.

14 spears slender asparagus,
     trimmed
6 mushrooms
1 medium yellow summer squash,
     cut into ¹/₂-inch slices
1 medium zucchini, cut into ¹/₂-inch
     slices

1 carrot, cut into ¹/₄-inch strips
1 red bell pepper, seeded and sliced
2 tablespoons water
Mustard-Dill Dressing (page 282)

1. Arrange asparagus in the center of a large microwave-safe plate.
2. Surround with mushrooms, yellow summer squash, zucchini, and carrot.
3. Arrange red bell pepper rings over the top.
4. Sprinkle water over vegetables. Cover with vented plastic wrap.
5. Microwave on HIGH for 9 minutes or until vegetables are soft. Let stand, covered, for 5 minutes.
6. Drizzle with Mustard-Dill Dressing and serve.

Calories Per Serving: 31
Fat: .3 g
Cholesterol: 0 mg
Protein: 2.3 g

Carbohydrates: 6 g
Dietary Fiber: 1 g
Sodium: 8 mg

Strawberries and Raspberries with
✳ Blueberry-Orange Sauce ✳

YIELD: 4 servings • PREPARATION TIME: 10 minutes •
COOKING TIME: 2 minutes plus 2 minutes standing time

Here fresh or frozen strawberries and raspberries are topped with a sauce of blueberries, orange juice, and honey.

1 cup fresh or frozen blueberries
2 tablespoons orange juice
¹/₄ teaspoon grated orange peel
2 tablespoons honey

2 cups fresh or thawed, frozen
     strawberries
2 cups fresh or thawed, frozen
     raspberries

1. Combine blueberries, orange juice, orange peel, and honey in a microwave-safe bowl. Cover with vented plastic wrap and microwave on HIGH for 2 minutes. Let stand for 2 minutes.

Strawberries and Raspberries with Blueberry-Orange Sauce *(cont'd)*

2. Place blueberries in a food processor or blender and process until smooth.
3. Toss strawberries with raspberries and place in 4 small bowls.
4. Top with blueberry sauce.

Calories Per Serving: 110
Fat: .8 g
Cholesterol: 0 mg
Protein: 1 g

Carbohydrates: 26 g
Dietary Fiber: 5.6 g
Sodium: 3.8 mg

✳ Oranges with Grape Sauce ✳

YIELD: 4 servings • *PREPARATION TIME: 10 minutes* •
COOKING TIME: 2 minutes plus 5 minutes standing time

These juicy navel orange sections are tossed with a creamy mixture of red grapes and yogurt. Serve with Green Pea–Spinach Soup (page 102).

1 cup seedless red grapes
1/3 cup lime juice
1/4 cup plain nonfat yogurt

1/4 teaspoon vanilla extract
4 navel oranges, sectioned

1. Place grapes and lime juice in a food processor or blender. Process until smooth.
2. Place grapes in a small microwave-safe bowl and cover with vented plastic wrap. Microwave on HIGH for 2 minutes. Let stand for 5 minutes.
3. Combine grapes with vanilla and yogurt.
4. Toss oranges with grape sauce.

Calories Per Serving: 91
Fat: .3 g
Cholesterol: .25 mg
Protein: 2 g

Carbohydrates: 22 g
Dietary Fiber: 3.5 g
Sodium: 11.5 mg

✳ *Mango Fandango Pears* ✳

YIELD: 4 servings ▪ *PREPARATION TIME: 10 minutes* ▪
COOKING TIME: 6 minutes plus 5 minutes standing time

Sliced fresh pears are served with mango sauce in this dish. Serve with
Potato-Leek Soup (page 106).

1 ripe mango	*Dash of vanilla extract*
1/3 cup lime juice	*3 pears, sliced vertically*

1. Peel mango and cut into chunks. Place mango chunks, lime juice, and
   vanilla in a food processor or blender. Process until smooth.
2. Place pears in a shallow microwave-safe casserole and cover with
   vented plastic wrap. Microwave on HIGH for 6 minutes. Let stand for
   5 minutes.
3. Place pear slices on small plates. Top with mango sauce.

Calories Per Serving: 113	Carbohydrates: 29 g
Fat: .7 g	Dietary Fiber: 4.4 g
Cholesterol: 0 mg	Sodium: 1.9 mg
Protein: .8 g	

✳ *Spicy Poached Apples and Pears* ✳

YIELD: 4 servings ▪ *PREPARATION TIME: 20 minutes* ▪
COOKING TIME: 12 minutes plus 15 minutes standing time

Here apples and pears are poached with raisins, apple juice, lemon juice,
ginger, and cloves. Serve with Broccoli-Stuffed Shells (page 140).

3 medium apples, cored and cut into 1/2-inch chunks	*1/2 cup apple juice*
	2 tablespoons honey
2 medium pears, cored and cut into 1/2-inch chunks	*1 tablespoon lemon juice*
	1/2 teaspoon fresh minced gingerroot
1 cup raisins	*1/4 teaspoon ground cloves*

1. Place the apples, pears, raisins, apple juice, honey, lemon juice, gingerroot, and cloves in a microwave-safe casserole. Cover with vented
   plastic wrap.

Spicy Poached Apples and Pears *(cont'd)*

2. Microwave on HIGH for 5 minutes. Stir. Microwave for 7 minutes or until the fruit is tender.
3. Let stand for 15 minutes.

Calories Per Serving: 269	Carbohydrates: 70 g
Fat: .9 g	Dietary Fiber: 6.4 g
Cholesterol: 0 mg	Sodium: 7.6 mg
Protein: 1.8 g	

✳ *Ginger-Orange Applesauce* ✳

YIELD: 6 servings • PREPARATION TIME: 15 minutes • COOKING TIME: 14 minutes

Here apples are microwaved with orange juice and lemon juice, puréed, and accented with ginger. Serve with Pinto Bean Chili Soup (page 106).

2 pounds cooking apples, washed and quartered	*1 tablespoon lemon juice*
¼ cup orange juice	*¼ cup sugar*
	1 teaspoon ground ginger

1. Combine apples, orange juice, and lemon juice in a 2-quart microwave-safe casserole.
2. Cover tightly and microwave on HIGH for 5 minutes.
3. Stir apples and continue microwaving on HIGH for 9 minutes.
4. Cool apples. Transfer to a food processor or blender and purée.
5. Stir sugar and ginger into apple purée.

Calories Per Serving: 100	Carbohydrates: 26 g
Fat: .4 g	Dietary Fiber: 2.5 g
Cholesterol: 0 mg	Sodium: .3 mg
Protein: .3 g	

✳ *Maple Grapefruit-Orange Delight* ✳

YIELD: *4 servings* • PREPARATION TIME: *15 minutes* •
COOKING TIME: *8 minutes plus 3 minutes standing time*

Grapefruit and oranges are seasoned with lime juice and maple syrup in this dish. Serve with Berry-Bran Pancakes (page 40).

2 pink grapefruit, sectioned
2 navel oranges, sectioned

2 tablespoons lime juice
2 tablespoons maple syrup

1. Place grapefruit sections, orange sections, lime juice, and maple syrup in a shallow microwave-safe casserole. Cover with vented plastic wrap.
2. Microwave on for 3 minutes. Stir. Microwave on HIGH for 5 more minutes. Allow to stand for 3 minutes before serving.

Calories Per Serving: 110
Fat: .2 g
Cholesterol: 0 mg
Protein: 1 g

Carbohydrates: 25 g
Dietary Fiber: 3 g
Sodium: 18 mg

✳ *Apple-Nutmeg Poached Plums* ✳

YIELD: *4 servings* • PREPARATION TIME: *5 minutes* • COOKING TIME: *4 minutes*

Plum halves are poached here with nutmeg, cinnamon, apple juice, and lemon juice. Enjoy chilled or warm, or serve over nonfat frozen yogurt. Serve with Tomato–Lima Bean Soup (page 382).

1¹/₂ pounds plums, halved and pitted
¹/₄ cup apple juice
¹/₂ teaspoon ground cinnamon
¹/₄ teaspoon ground nutmeg

2 tablespoons brown sugar, firmly
    packed
1 teaspoon lemon juice

1. Place the plum halves in a microwave-safe casserole.
2. Combine the apple juice, cinnamon, nutmeg, brown sugar, and lemon juice. Pour over the plums.
3. Cover tightly and microwave on HIGH for 2 to 4 minutes.

Apple-Nutmeg Poached Plums *(cont'd)*

Calories Per Serving: 116
Fat: 1 g
Cholesterol: 0 mg
Protein: 1 g

Carbohydrates: 28 g
Dietary Fiber: 3 g
Sodium: 2.6 mg

❋ *Lemon Prunes* ❋

YIELD: *8 servings* ▪ PREPARATION TIME: *10 minutes* ▪
COOKING TIME: *10 minutes*

These prunes are cooked in the microwave with lemon slices. Keep a jar of these on hand for snack time and breakfast time. Serve with Baked French Toast (page 46).

1½ pounds pitted prunes
1 lemon, thinly sliced

3 cups water
½ cup sugar

1. Place prunes, lemon slices, water, and sugar in a microwave-safe dish. Cover with vented plastic wrap.
2. Microwave on HIGH for 10 minutes.

Calories Per Serving: 195
Fat: .3 g
Cholesterol: 0 mg
Protein: 1.5 g

Carbohydrates: 52 g
Dietary Fiber: 3.9 g
Sodium: 2.5 mg

❋ *Cinnamon Poached Peaches* ❋

YIELD: *4 servings* ▪ PREPARATION TIME: *5 minutes* ▪ COOKING TIME: *5 minutes*

Here ripe peach halves are poached with cinnamon, white wine, and lemon juice. Serve cooled poached peaches with a topping of nonfat plain yogurt and fresh raspberries.

4 ripe peaches, peeled, halved, and
pitted
¼ cup dry white wine
¼ teaspoon ground cinnamon

2 tablespoons brown sugar, firmly
packed
1 teaspoon lemon juice

1. Place the peach halves in a microwave-safe casserole.
2. Combine the white wine, cinnamon, brown sugar, and lemon juice. Pour over the peaches.
3. Cover tightly and microwave on HIGH for 2 minutes.
4. Turn the peaches over, cover the casserole, and microwave on HIGH for 3 minutes.

Calories Per Serving: 73
Fat: 0 g
Cholesterol: 0 mg
Protein: .6 g

Carbohydrates: 16 g
Dietary Fiber: 1.3 g
Sodium: 11 mg

✳ Dried Fruit Sauce ✳

YIELD: 10 servings (½ cup each) ▪ *PREPARATION TIME: 10 minutes* ▪
COOKING TIME: 15 minutes plus 5 minutes standing time

This flavored mélange of dried pears, apricots, peaches, and prunes can be used as a topping for angel food cake, vanilla nonfat frozen yogurt, or hot cereal. Other dried fruits can be substituted for variety.

2 cups water, apple juice, or white wine
½ cup brown sugar, firmly packed
½ teaspoon lemon juice
¼ teaspoon ground ginger
¼ teaspoon ground cinnamon
4 ounces dried pears
4 ounces dried peaches
4 ounces dried apricots
4 ounces dried pitted prunes

1. Combine the water, apple juice, or wine, brown sugar, lemon juice, ginger, cinnamon, pears, peaches, apricots, and prunes in a microwave-safe casserole.
2. Cover tightly and microwave on HIGH for 7 minutes. Stir. Microwave for 8 additional minutes.
3. Let stand for 5 minutes.

Calories Per Serving: 114
Fat: .2 g
Cholesterol: 0
Protein: 1 g

Carbohydrates: 29 g
Dietary Fiber: 2.4 g
Sodium: 7 mg

✳ Maple-Raspberry-Nectarine Garnish ✳

YIELD: 4 servings (¹/₂ cup each) • PREPARATION TIME: 10 minutes •
COOKING TIME: 4 minutes plus 3 minutes standing time

This topping is an ideal partner for a bowl of fresh berries. If nectarines aren't in season, drained juice-packed canned peach halves or other fruits can be substituted.

1 tablespoon maple syrup
2 tablespoons all-fruit raspberry jam
1 tablespoon lemon juice

4 nectarines, peeled, pitted, and
  halved

1. Combine maple syrup, jam, and lemon juice in a small microwave-safe container. Cover with vented plastic wrap. Microwave on HIGH for 45 seconds.
2. Place nectarines in a microwave-safe casserole and top with jam mixture. Cover with vented plastic wrap. Microwave on HIGH for 3 minutes. Let stand for 3 minutes.

Calories Per Serving: 87
Fat: .6 g
Cholesterol: 0 mg
Protein: 1.3 g

Carbohydrates: 21 g
Dietary Fiber: 2 g
Sodium: 12 mg

✳ Lemon-Vanilla Peach Sauce ✳

YIELD: 4 servings (¹/₃ cup each) • PREPARATION TIME: 10 minutes •
COOKING TIME: 4 minutes

This sauce is a great topping for peach or vanilla nonfat frozen yogurt.

¹/₄ cup water
¹/₄ cup brown sugar, firmly packed
1 tablespoon lemon juice

¹/₄ teaspoon vanilla extract
3 fresh peaches, peeled, pitted, and
  sliced

1. Combine the water, brown sugar, lemon juice, and vanilla in a microwave-safe casserole. Microwave on HIGH for 4 minutes or until the liquid boils.

2. Remove the casserole from microwave and stir in peaches. Chill before serving.

Calories Per Serving: 82
Fat: .1 g
Cholesterol: 0 mg
Protein: .5 g

Carbohydrates: 21 g
Dietary Fiber: 1 g
Sodium: 5 mg

✳ *Strawberry Sauce* ✳

YIELD: *4 servings (¹/₃ cup each)* • PREPARATION TIME: *3 minutes* •
COOKING TIME: *10 minutes*

This sauce is delicious served warm or chilled over Angel Food Cake (page 347) or a bowl of fresh raspberries.

2 cups fresh or frozen strawberries   *2 tablespoons lemon juice*
¹/₃ cup sugar

1. Place berries, sugar, and lemon juice in a microwave-safe casserole. Cover with vented plastic wrap and microwave on HIGH for 5 minutes.
2. Remove cover and microwave on HIGH for 5 more minutes or until sauce is slightly thick.

Calories Per Serving: 84
Fat: .3 g
Cholesterol: 0 mg
Protein: .5 g

Carbohydrates: 22 g
Dietary Fiber: 1.9 g
Sodium: 1 mg

✳ *Zucchini Topping* ✳

YIELD: *8 servings (6 tablespoons each)* • PREPARATION TIME: *20 minutes* •
COOKING TIME: *23 minutes plus 3 minutes standing time*

This zucchini spread can be used on baked goods and as a breakfast topping for waffles. It can be refrigerated for 3 weeks in an airtight clean jar.

Zucchini Topping *(cont'd)*

2 cups peeled, chopped zucchini
1 apple, peeled, cored, and chopped
2 tablespoons lemon juice
2 tablespoons maple syrup

1 tablespoon brown sugar, firmly
 packed
2 teaspoons ground cinnamon

1. Place zucchini, apple, and lemon juice in a microwave-safe bowl. Cover with vented plastic wrap and microwave on HIGH for 10 minutes. Let stand for 3 minutes.
2. Place zucchini mixture in a blender or food processor and purée.
3. Place zucchini purée, maple syrup, brown sugar, and cinnamon in a microwave-safe bowl. Stir until well combined.
4. Microwave on HIGH for 5 minutes. Stir.
5. Microwave for 10 more minutes or until the mixture has thickened.

Calories Per Serving: 39
Fat: .1 g
Cholesterol: 0 mg
Protein: .4 g

Carbohydrates: 9.7 g
Dietary Fiber: no data
Sodium: 10 mg

❈ *Red Pepper Sauce* ❈

YIELD: 8 servings (6 tablespoons each) • *PREPARATION TIME: 25 minutes* •
COOKING TIME: 7 minutes

This sauce works well over vegetables or pasta.

3 cups chopped red bell peppers
1 tablespoon chopped onion
1 clove garlic, minced
½ cup nonfat chicken broth

1 tablespoon low-sodium tomato
 purée or tomato paste
1 teaspoon dried basil leaves

1. Place red peppers, onion, and garlic in a microwave-safe bowl. Cover with vented plastic wrap. Microwave on HIGH for 4 minutes or until peppers are tender.
2. Add chicken broth, tomato purée, and basil leaves. Microwave with cover on HIGH for 2 minutes.
3. Transfer to a food processor or blender and purée.

Calories Per Serving: 7.5	Carbohydrates: 1.5 g
Fat: .1 g	Dietary Fiber: .3 g
Cholesterol: 0	Sodium: 10 mg
Protein: .4 g	

✳ *Ricotta Bites with Orange-Honey Sauce* ✳

YIELD: 6 servings ▪ *PREPARATION TIME: 15 minutes* ▪
COOKING TIME: 3 minutes plus 10 minutes standing time

These individual cheesecakes are made in a microwave muffin tin.

6 tablespoons nonfat graham cracker crumbs	*3 tablespoons flour*
1¼ cups nonfat ricotta cheese	*Pinch of baking powder*
3 tablespoons sugar	*¼ teaspoon vanilla extract*
	Orange-Honey Sauce (page 294)

1. Lightly spray a microwave muffin pan with vegetable cooking spray. Place 1 tablespoon of graham cracker crumbs in the bottom of each of 6 microwave-safe muffin cups. Shake muffin tin so that bottoms and sides of cups are coated with crumbs.
2. Combine ricotta cheese, sugar, flour, baking powder, and vanilla. Spoon the cheese mixture into the crumb-lined muffin cups.
3. Microwave on HIGH for 3 minutes. Remove from microwave and let stand for 10 minutes.
4. Turn pan upside down and gently tap each muffin cup to release Ricotta Bites. Cool on wire rack.
5. Serve with Orange-Honey Sauce spooned over the top of the Ricotta Bites.

Variation
- Top with 1½ cups juice-packed crushed pineapple.

Calories Per Serving: 157	Carbohydrates: 31 g
Fat: .09 g	Dietary Fiber: .6 g
Cholesterol: 3.3 mg	Sodium: 74 mg
Protein: 8 g	

✳ *Raspberry–Strawberry Jam* ✳

YIELD: 16 servings (2 tablespoons each) • *PREPARATION TIME: 10 minutes* • *COOKING TIME: 6 minutes*

This scrumptious jam is easy to prepare in your microwave and it will keep in the refrigerator for a month. Serve with Corn Bread Muffins (page 45).

2 cups fresh or thawed, frozen
   raspberries
2 cups fresh or thawed, frozen
   strawberries

¹/₃ cup apple juice
¹/₃ cup orange juice
¹/₄ cup lemon juice
¹/₄ cup honey

1. Place the raspberries, strawberries, apple juice, orange juice, lemon juice, and honey in a food processor or blender. Purée.
2. Place the jam mixture in a microwave-safe dish. Microwave on HIGH for 6 minutes or until mixture is thick.
3. Allow to cool, then pack in clean jars.

Calories Per Serving: 35
Fat: .2 g
Cholesterol: 0 mg
Protein: .3 g

Carbohydrates: 8.8 g
Dietary Fiber: 7.4 g
Sodium: .7 mg

INDEX

::

ABOUT THE AUTHOR

SARAH SCHLESINGER began researching and writing about healthful cooking in response to her husband's ongoing battle against coronary-artery disease. She is the author of *The Garden Variety Cookbook* and the coauthor of *The Low-Cholesterol Oat Plan* and *The Low-Cholesterol Olive Oil Cookbook*. She also wrote *The Pointe Book,* which focuses on health issues for dancers. She is the author of a monthly food column in *Maryland Family Magazine*. Ms. Schlesinger is on the faculty of the Graduate Musical Theatre Writing Program at the Tisch School of the Arts, New York University.